SCHOOL OF ADVANCED STUDY UNIVERSITY OF LONDON

Institute of Germanic & Romance Studies

Writing and Muslim Identity
Representations of Islam in German and English Transcultural Literature, 1990–2006

igrs books

Established by the Institute of Germanic & Romance Studies, this series aims to bring to the public monographs and collections of essays in the field of modern foreign languages. Proposals for publication are selected by the Institute's editorial board, which is advised by a peer review committee of thirty-six senior academics in the field. To make titles as accessible as possible to an English-speaking and multi-lingual readership, volumes are written in English and quotations given in English translation.

For further details on the annual competition, visit:
http://igrs.sas.ac.uk/publications/IGRS_books_2011.php

igrs books **Volume 6**

Volume Editor
Dr Godela Weiss-Sussex

Writing and Muslim Identity
Representations of Islam in German and English Transcultural Literature, 1990–2006

Frauke Matthes

SCHOOL OF ADVANCED STUDY UNIVERSITY OF LONDON

Institute of Germanic & Romance Studies

2011

Published by the

Institute of Germanic & Romance Studies
School of Advanced Study, University of London
Senate House, Malet Street, London WC1E 7HU
http://igrs.sas.ac.uk

Cover image

Cover image by Paul Melo e Castro, by kind permission of the photographer.

First published 2011

ISBN 978 0 85457 231 1

Contents

Acknowledgements

My thanks are due to all those have helped me to see this project to fruition. My principal debt is to Sarah Colvin who has been an encouraging, challenging and kind supervisor, and from whose recommendations and suggestions I have benefited greatly. My assistant supervisors, Carole Hillenbrand, Aedín Ní Loingsigh, Elisabeth Kendall and Mary Cosgrove gave valuable feedback and have been helpful throughout. I am grateful to all those at the University of Edinburgh who have helped me in my work, above all the German Section and the Department of Islamic and Middle Eastern Studies in whose friendly and warm atmospheres I have always felt supported and encouraged. I am also indebted to my examiners Jim Jordan and Kamran Rastegar for their thorough reading of my thesis and helpful comments, which encouraged me to publish this study.

I would like to acknowledge my gratitude for the Arts and Humanities Research Council for their support. The Leverhulme Trust gave me the space with an Early Career Fellowship to complete the book. The Association for German Studies in Great Britain and Ireland (formerly the Conference of University Teachers of German in Great Britain and Ireland) and Women in German Studies provided travelling grants that enabled me to present work at conferences.

I would also like to thank the readers, Naomi Segal, and especially my editor, Godela Weiss-Sussex, for their insightful reading of and comments on the manuscript; it is through their help and commitment that the book came into existence as it is now.

Furthermore, I found the conferences 'Betwixt and Between: Place and Cultural Translation' (Queen's University, Belfast; April 2005) and 'German Encounters with Islam' (NUI, Maynooth; March 2007) particularly inspiring for my work.

The list of colleagues and friends who read, or listened to, parts of this book can only be incomplete. I would therefore like to thank all those in Edinburgh, Leipzig and various other places whose comments influenced my work and with whom I had fruitful discussions. I thank you for your friendship which made much of my research enjoyable. I should, nevertheless, mention with gratitude Bridget Schreiner for her continuous help with translations and for her consistent interest right from the beginning of this project.

Special thanks go to Ilija Trojanow, who kindly met me in Glasgow for an interview and gave me permission to quote some of his comments in this book. Speaking to him made this project more real.

Paul Melo e Castro I thank for his kind permission to use his photograph as the cover image, and for the time he spared to allow us to take it. I would also like to thank the University of Edinburgh's Department of Islamic and Middle Eastern Studies, especially Rhona Cullen, for letting us use their library for this purpose.

Above all, I thank my parents who have always believed in me and encouraged me to fulfil my potential. Thank you for all your love and unfailing support.

Although this book was written as a coherent whole, parts of the various chapters were published as separate articles elsewhere. They have been revised for this book. They are:

- parts of my discussion of translation and migration in Chapter 1, in 'Defining "Home": Cultural Translation as Self-Exploration in Emine Sevgi Özdamar's *Das Leben ist eine Karawanserei*', in *Betwixt and Between: Place and Cultural Translation*, ed. Stephen Kelly and David Johnston (Newcastle: Cambridge Scholars Publishing, 2007), 158–69;
- sections on Emine Sevgi Özdamar's *MutterZunge* and *Das Leben ist eine Karawanserei* in relation to language in Chapters 1 and 4, in '"Migrating Words": Emine Sevgi Özdamar's Approach to Gaining and Owning Language', in *When 'Abroad' Becomes 'Home': The Cultural Consequences of Migration*, Proceedings to the 10th Annual International Ege University Cultural Studies Symposium, ed. Günseli Sönmez İşçi, Dilek Direnç and Gülden Hatipoğlu (Bornova-İzmir: Ege University Press, 2007), 273–84;
- sections on V. S. Naipaul's perception of Islam in non-Arab Muslim countries in Chapter 2, in 'Inauthentic Islam? V. S. Naipaul's *Among the Believers* and *Beyond Belief*', *Islam in Südasien*, Themenschwerpunkt des Südasien-Informationsnetz e.V.: *suedasion.info*, ed. Nadja-Christina

Schneider, Maria Framke and Christoph Sprung (2006), www.suedasien.info/analysen/1462 [accessed 28 June 2010] (29 para.);

- parts of my analysis of Ilija Trojanow's hajj account in Chapter 2, in 'Encountering Islam at its Roots: Ilija Trojanow's *Zu den Heiligen Quellen des Islam*', in *Encounters with Islam in German Literature and Culture*, ed. James Hodkinson and Jeff Morrison (Rochester, NY: Camden House, 2009), 236–46;
- parts of my discussion of Feridun Zaimoğlu's *Kanak Sprak* and *Koppfstoff* in relation to cultural, national and gender identity in Chapters 3 and 4, in '"Was deutsch ist, bestimmen wir": Definitions of (Turkish-)Germanness in Feridun Zaimoğlu's *Kanak Sprak* and *Koppstoff*', *Focus on German Studies*, 14 (2007), 19–35;
- and parts of my analysis of the connection between religion and sexuality in *Kanak Sprak* in Chapter 3, as well as some of my descriptions of the current position of Muslims, Muslim writers and Zaimoğlu in the Conclusion, in 'Of *Kanaken* and *Gottes Krieger*: Religion and Sexuality among Feridun Zaimoğlu's Young Muslim Men', in *Edinburgh German Yearbook*, 2: *Masculinities in German Culture*, ed. Sarah Colvin and Peter Davies (Rochester, NY: Camden House, 2008), 250–61.
- An abbreviated version of the unpublished interview with Ilija Trojanow conducted prior to his reading at the Goethe Institute Glasgow on 14 November 2006 was published as 'Die Fremde muss wie ein Stein sein', *Kreuzer*, 1/2007, 57.

I thank all editors and publishers for permission to reproduce this material.

Abbreviations and Textual Notes

Throughout this book all translations into English, unless otherwise attributed, are my own and reference is given to the original text. All titles of primary, though not secondary texts, not originally published in English are translated.

Further references to a cited text will appear after quotations; passages without page reference are from the last-cited page and page-numbers without specified text are similarly from the last one named. Unless otherwise stated, all italics are my own.

Expressions such as 'the West', 'the Orient' or 'the Other' appear without scare-quotes, to ensure the readability of the text. However, I am aware of the problem of such concepts, and wish to distance myself from the dichotomies these terms can imply, such as 'West' – 'Other'.

All foreign-language words not commonly used in English are italicized. For Arabic words, I use the transliteration system suggested by the *International Journal of Middle East Studies,* but preserve the original transliteration in quotations. In quotations, I follow the original, that is, mainly Germanized or Anglicized spelling of Turkish names. In my own writing, however, I use the original Turkish spelling.

Abbreviated titles used for texts cited in this book are given below in alphabetical order of abbreviation; full details can be found in the Bibliography.

ABL Monica Ali, *Brick Lane*

AMi Leila Aboulela, *Minaret*

ATr Leila Aboulela, *The Translator*

KBA Hanif Kureishi, *The Black Album*

KMS Hanif Kureishi, 'My Son the Fanatic'

NAB V. S. Naipaul, *Among the Believers: An Islamic Journey*

NBB V. S. Naipaul, *Beyond Belief: Islamic Excursions Among the Converted Peoples*

ÖLC Emine Sevgi Özdamar, *Life Is a Caravanserai Has Two Doors I Came In One I Went Out the Other*, trans. Luise von Flotow

ÖLK Emine Sevgi Özdamar, *Das Leben ist eine Karawanserei hat zwei Türen aus einer kam ich rein aus der anderen ging ich raus*

ÖMT Emine Sevgi Özdamar, *Mother Tongue*, trans. Craig Thomas

ÖMZ Emine Sevgi Özdamar, *MutterZunge*

TMM Ilija Trojanow, *Mumbai to Mecca*, trans. Rebecca Morrison

TZH Ilija Trojanow, *Zu den heiligen Quellen des Islam: Als Pilger nach Mekka und Medina*

ZKS Feridun Zaimoğlu, *Kanak Sprak: 24 Mißtöne vom Rande der Gesellschaft*

ZKSt Feridun Zaimoğlu, *Koppstoff: Kanaka Sprak vom Rande der Gesellschaft*

Language may be one of many elements that allow us to make sense of things, of ourselves [...] [, and] making sense of ourselves is what produces identity.

Gayatri Chakravorty Spivak, 'The Politics of Translation'

Introduction: Islam and Transcultural Literature

Encounters between cultures are regarded as part of the 'human condition' in the twentieth and twenty-first centuries: the interaction – sometimes referred to as 'the clash' [of civilizations][1] – of diverse cultural heritages and current cultural trends, languages and religions have shaped (and continue to shape) people's perceptions of themselves and the Other. Graham Huggan suggests that we live in an 'age of fragmentation' and that cosmopolitanism today is a widespread experience.[2] This development is reflected in travel and migratory movements. In this book I shall call the continuing acts of making sense of what happens on those journeys between known and unfamiliar places 'translation processes'.

Islam has been allocated a 'special' role in the discourses of cultural encounters: this religion and its extremist forms have become a widely debated topic over the last years, increasingly since the Islamic fundamentalist motivated suicide attacks on the World Trade Centre in New York City and the Pentagon in Arlington, Virginia, on 11 September 2001 (9/11). The youngest of the monotheistic religions seems to have been demonized as an object of counter-identification for the West. This has a long history: tensions between East and West have coloured Western thought since the rise of the Ottoman and Holy Roman Empires, and the Crusades. The East-West encounter enables cultural identification, and there is a growing focus on Islamic fundamentalism.[3] As an Other, a worldwide

1 S. Huntington, *The Clash of Civilizations and the Remaking of the World Order* (London: Touchstone, 1998).

2 G. Huggan, *The Postcolonial Exotic: Marketing the Margins* (London: Routledge, 2001), 9–10.

3 John L. Esposito dismisses the term 'fundamentalism'. He regards '"fundamentalism" as too laden with Christian presuppositions and Western stereotypes, as well as implying a monolithic threat that does not exist; more

'threat to Western civilization',[4] this is understood to be something whose extreme forms, which are often personified by young radical Muslims, must be fought. It has been discussed extensively in the media in connection with Western social and political concerns. The West's — or, more specifically in the context of this book, the UK's and Germany's — crucial role in constructing a negative perception of Islam as a violent religion is often ignored. These countries' histories (British colonialism and its subsequent migration processes, and the history of German *Gastarbeiter*) have significantly contributed to the tensions between Muslims and non-Muslims.[5] The debates in the UK and Germany focus primarily on the domestic results of historical developments such as multiculturalism, and on immigration and its 'problems' regarding, for instance, citizenship, education and knowledge of the language of the migrants' new country of abode. However, on the Muslim side, there is an increasing awareness of the political dimension of being 'different'.[6] This is reflected, for example, in a growing (literary) outspokenness. Many Muslims have developed a 'refusal to remain invisible'[7] — and writing is part of that refusal.

fitting general terms are "Islamic revivalism" or "Islamic activism", which are less value-laden and have roots within the Islamic tradition. In recent years, the terms "political Islam" and "Islamism" have become more common usage. Islam possesses a long tradition of revival (*tajdid*) and reform (*islah*) which includes notions of political and social activism dating from the early Islamic centuries to the present day. Thus I prefer to speak of Islamic revivalism and Islamic activism rather than of Islamic fundamentalism', J. L. Esposito, *The Islamic Threat: Myth or Reality?*, 3rd edn (New York: Oxford University Press, 1999 [1992]), 6.

4 E. W. Said, *Covering Islam: How the Media and the Experts Determine How We See the Rest of the World*, fully rev. edn with a new Introduction (London: Vintage, 1997 [1981]), 144. Said wrote this in 1981, shortly after the Iranian Revolution, when Islam had become a largely negative news item.

5 *Gastarbeiter* [guest workers] (primarily male) were recruited by the German state from Southern Europe and Turkey in the 1960s to solve the shortages on the labour market after the construction of the Berlin Wall, when East German workers could no longer work in West Germany. They were meant to stay for a short time only (hence the prefix *Gast* [guest]). With increasing unemployment as a result of European recession, the then German chancellor Willy Brandt issued the *Anwerbestopp* [halting of recruitment] to end the influx of foreign labour. However, many *Gastarbeiter* stayed on and even brought their families to Germany for an economically better future. See J. Helicke, 'Turks in Germany: Muslim Identity "Between" States', in *Muslim Minorities in the West: Visible and Invisible*, ed. Y. Yazbeck Haddad and J. I. Smith (Walnut Creek, CL: AltaMira, 2002), 179–80.

6 R. Ranasinha, *Hanif Kureishi* (Tavistock: Northcote House in association with the British Council, 2002), 2.

7 P. Lewis, *Islamic Britain: Religion, Politics and Identity Among British Muslims: Bradford in the 1990s* (London: I. B. Tauris, 1994), 24.

It took a long time until Muslims could overcome their invisibility, even though Islam has been part of Western thought, literature and culture since its beginnings. Islam is the youngest of the 'three religions of the book', and Christians soon regarded it as an opposition, even a threat, to their religion. According to Rana Kabbani, 'Islam was seen as a negation of Christianity; Muhammad as an imposter, an evil sensualist, an Antichrist in alliance with the Devil. The Islamic world was seen as Anti-Europe [...], and was held in suspicion as such'.[8] This suspicion was fostered by comparisons between Christianity and Islam and their respective values, which still today are the basis for fundamental misunderstandings. Ziauddin Sardar connects them to the Reformation as the origin of secularization in the West.[9] Secularism, he arguably opines, 'was also a form of religion' (255). Christianity often ignores the fact that 'Islam, while a source of self-definition, is more of an ethnocultural qualification than a theological weltanschauung'.[10] In this book, the religion of Islam is understood as both belief and culture, depending on the writers' (and their characters') interpretation. Yasemin Karakasoglu points out that within a Turkish context '[t]he term "Muslim" is primarily a cultural attribution that is by no means synonymous with actual religious practices'.[11] Turkey serves as an excellent example for the wide spectrum of interpretations of Islam: it can reach from conscious, public demonstrations of belief, via conservative or even fundamentalist perceptions of Islam, to atheist attitudes influenced by Mustafa Kemal Atatürk's secularization politics. Karakasoglu continues: 'If nothing else, [...] Islam will have played a key role in most people's upbringing [in Turkey]'. This also holds true for the writers in this study, whose Islam originates in various countries (Turkey, Bangladesh, Pakistan, Sudan and Bulgaria) and has been influenced by their diverse cultural and social practices; the religion of Islam — in whatever form, whether as a belief system, cultural or political expression — is a significant subject matter in their work.

It is for that reason that I broadly follow Amin Malak's differentiation between 'Muslim' and 'Islamic':

8 R. Kabbani, *Imperial Fictions: Europe's Myth of Orient*, rev. and expanded edn (London: Pandora, 1994 [1986]), 5.

9 Z. Sardar, *Desperately Seeking Paradise: Journeys of a Sceptical Muslim* (London: Granta, 2004 [2005 printing]), 250.

10 A. Malak, *Muslim Narratives and the Discourse of English* (Albany: State University of New York Press, 2005), 68.

11 Y. Karakasoglu, 'Turkish Cultural Orientations in Germany and the Role of Islam', in *Turkish Culture in German Society Today*, ed. D. Horrocks and E. Kolinsky (Providence, RI: Berghahn, 1996), 158.

> *Muslim* is derived from the Arabic word that denotes the *person* who espouses the religion of Islam or is shaped by its cultural impact, irrespective of being secular, agnostic or practising believer. The term *Islamic* emphasizes the *faith* of Islam. It denotes thoughts, rituals, activities, and institutions specifically proclaimed and sanctioned by Islam or directly associated with its theological traditions. (5, italics Malak's)

In that respect I also use the adjective 'Islamic' for a devout believer.

However Muslims define 'their' Islam, the assumption is made in the West that Islam is fundamentally different and barely understandable. As an Other, Islam soon turned into the idea of Islam with a focus on its negative aspects. The West often does not acknowledge it as a multifaceted religion which has been influenced by the various cultures of the countries where it can be found.[12]

This reduction has been part of the knowledge-power-control mechanism which was strongly linked to Western colonial interests in Muslim areas such as the Middle East and North Africa. Getting to know the Orient was a political concern: the colonizers could then dominate and control it, and keep it weak. This contributed to the creation of an Orient that existed entirely in the colonialists' mind. As Edward Said explains: 'Knowledge of the Orient, because generated out of strength, in a sense *creates* the Orient, the Oriental, and his world' (40, 41, italics Said's). Whilst conquering forces were at work in the colonies, Orientalist scholarship 'at home', such as the learning of languages and scholarship in history and politics, was simultaneously fostered. Gathering knowledge about the Orient was to contribute to the colonial mission.

Similarly, Islam has been part of an ongoing European literary interest: the Orient (by which I mean not exclusively Muslim countries) has always triggered desires and fascination in artists and writers. In the shape of the Holy Land, the Orient also became a place of Christian pilgrimage, which was textualized in, for example, John Bunyan's *The Pilgrim's Progress* (1678).[13] Later, a more specific interest in Islam came to the fore: for example, Gotthold Ephraim Lessing's play *Nathan der Weise* [*Nathan the Wise*] (1779) is a plea for religious tolerance between the three 'religions of the book', Judaism, Christianity and Islam, expressed mainly in the play's 'Ringparabel'

12 Cf. E. W. Said, *Orientalism: Western Conceptions of the Orient*, repr. with a new Afterword (London: Penguin, 1995 [1978]), 5.

13 J. Bunyan, *The Pilgrim's Progress*, Nelson's Royal Classics (Nashville: Nelson, 1999; originally publ. as *The Pilgrim's Progress from This World, to That Which Is to Come: Delivered Under the Similitude of a Dream*, 1678).

[ring parable].[14] Johann Wolfgang von Goethe showed the influence of the Persian poet Hafiz on some of his lyric poems collected in the *West-östlicher Divan* [*West-Eastern Divan*] (1819). In his book, Goethe also developed his theory of translation: '[D]er Übersetzer, der sich fest an sein Original anschließt, gibt mehr oder weniger die Originalität seiner Nation auf, und so entsteht ein Drittes, wozu der Geschmack der Menge sich erst heranbilden muß' [The translator who follows an original closely more or less gives up the originality of his nation, and thus a third thing is created for which the crowd still have to develop a taste].[15] Critics therefore often regard the *West-östlicher Divan* as one of the first literary works that addresses notions of intercultural understanding.[16]

Todd Kontje points out that 'the very lack of a unified nation-state and the absence of empire contributed to the development of a peculiarly German Orientalism. German writers oscillated between identifying their country with the rest of Europe against the Orient and allying themselves with selected parts of the East against the West'.[17] In contrast to British and other European colonizers, German Orientalists had a primarily intellectual interest in the Orient which was also meant to signify that Germany 'belonged to modern European civilization' (5). In this context, a number of Romantics openly displayed their admiration for India. For Friedrich Schlegel, for instance, the Orient was — as Said phrases it in *Orientalism* — 'the purest form of Romanticism' (137), which he outlined in *Über die Sprache und Weisheit der Indier* [*On the Language and Wisdom of the Indians*] (1808).[18] Others, especially Edgar Quinet in his *Le Génie des*

14 G. E. Lessing, *Nathan der Weise: Ein dramatisches Gedicht, in fünf Aufzügen*, in *Werke und Briefe in zwölf Bänden*, ed. W. Barner *et al.* (Frankfurt a.M.: Deutscher Klassiker Verlag, 1993), IX: *Werke 1778–1780*, ed. K. Bohnen and A. Schilson, Bibliothek Deutscher Klassiker, 94, 483–666.

15 J. W. von Goethe, *Sämtliche Werke nach Epochen seines Schaffens*, Münchner Ausgabe, ed. K. Richter *et al.* (Munich: Hanser, 1998), XI.I.II: *West-östlicher Divan*, ed. K. Richter with the assistance of K. Mommsen and P. Ludwig, in sec. 'Besserem Verständniss', 264.

16 For example, M. Hofmann, *Interkulturelle Literaturwissenschaft: Eine Einführung* (Paderborn: Fink, 2006), 79–81.

17 T. Kontje, *German Orientalisms* (Ann Arbor: The University of Michigan Press, 2004), 2–3.

18 F. Schlegel, *Über die Sprache und Weisheit der Indier: Ein Beitrag zur Begründung der Altertumskunde von Friedrich Schlegel: Nebst metrischen Uebersetzungen indischer Gedichte* (Heidelberg: Mohr und Zimmer, 1808; repr. in *History of Linguistics: 18th and 19th Century German Linguistics*, 8 vols, with a new Introduction by C. Hutton (London: Routledge and Thoemmes, 1995)).

religions [*The Genius of Religions*] (1842),[19] 'placed the Orient and the West in a functional relationship with each other' (Said, *Orientalism*, 137), which resulted in the confirmation of both identities in the encounter.

Said also points out that the Orient was a place for (sexual) pleasure, a place associated with lascivious sensuality (182). Gustave Flaubert's and Gérard de Nerval's accounts of their experiences in Egypt (in Flaubert's *Lettres d'Orient* [*Letters from the Orient*] (1849–1851) and Nerval's *Voyage en Orient* [*Journey to the Orient*] (1851)) can be seen in this light.[20]

However the Orient was perceived, it 'remained fixed in time and place for the West' (Said, *Orientalism*, 108). Stereotypes served thereby as a means of dominating and holding the Other in place.[21] The practice of limiting the Other to a readily comprehensible number of characteristics has been persistent in literature until now; yet the intention to convey the dominance of the West over the Orient as many imperial travel accounts would have done (Said, *Orientalism*, 196) has lost its appeal: towards the end of the twentieth century, a growing Western readership has developed a general interest in getting to know Islam, which is also reflected on the literary market. Its greatest expression is found in travel writing (93, 127). Towards the end of the twentieth century, thoughtful travel writing about the Middle East has started to be published, for example Jonathan Raban's *Arabia Through the Looking Glass* (1979).[22]

Although Said's *Orientalism* questioned Western perceptions of 'the Orient' in a groundbreaking way, its author has often been accused of doing exactly what he criticizes: pursuing the oppositional thinking between 'Occident' and 'Orient'. Said is said to focus too much on the Western canon and Western thinking,[23] thereby 'appropriat[ing] the idea of human from within the Western

19 E. Quinet, *Le Génie des religions* (Paris: [?], 1842).

20 G. Flaubert, *Lettres d'Orient*, Foreword P. Bergouioux, Collection 'de mémoire' (Bordeaux: L'Horizon chimérique, 1990; first publ. in *Correspondance*, I, Bibliothèque de la Pléïade (Paris: Gallimard, 1973)); G. de Nerval, *Voyage en Orient*, 2 vols, ed. M. Jeanneret (Paris: Ganier-Flammarion, 1980; first publ. Paris: Carpentier, 1851).

21 See H. K. Bhabha, 'The Other Question: Stereotype, Discrimination and the Discourse of Colonialism', in Bhabha, *The Location of Culture* (London: Routledge, 1994), 66–84.

22 J. Raban, *Arabia Through the Looking Glass* (London: Fontana/Collins, 1980 [1979]).

23 A. Ahmad, *In Theory: Classes, Nations, Literatures* (London: Verso, 1994 [1992]), 163–64.

humanist tradition in order to oppose the Occidental representation of the Orient'.[24] This practice implies a danger of coming 'close to an Orientalist position' (Ashcroft and Ahluwalia, 80, referring to Young, 130). Above all, Said is criticized for making assumptions about Islam, not examining them 'because they enter into language itself' (Ashcroft and Ahluwalia, 9–11): Said's study seems to imply that there is a real Orient.[25] The author does not therefore offer any alternatives to Orientalism (Ashcroft and Ahluwalia, 80; Clifford, *The Predicament of Culture*, 261; Young, 127). (In 'Orientalism Reconsidered', Said comments on, though does not agree with, these claims.[26]) This is also due to the fact that Said rarely discusses postcolonial thinkers (Ashcroft and Ahluwalia, 18) or 'voices of resistance and opposition' (29). 'Counter-hegemony', indeed alternatives within the discourse of Orientalism seem impossible (77, commenting on Porter), because, as Dennis Porter points out, there are methodological problems: for Porter, citing Michel Foucault and Antonio Gramsci, discourse theory and hegemony theory are incomparable (151). Furthermore, Said fails to see hegemony as a process, he 'claim[s] a continuity of representation' (152) instead. For critics such as Porter, this practice puts Said in danger of regarding whatever is linked to the Orient as positive and Western perceptions of the Orient as negative (see my comments on Occidentalism below). Said is seen in my study as an important postcolonial thinker for the analysis of perceptions of Islam; however, my book aims to show alternative ways of representing Islam by letting 'voices of resistance and opposition' speak, voices from the 'centre' as well as the 'margin', voices that may or may not be rooted in Islam. All of them show that there is no single 'Islam', but many 'Islams'.

Although the Marxist critic Aijaz Ahmad 'is disturbed about [...] the privileged locations within the West that figures such as Said,

24 B. Ashcroft and P. Ahluwalia, *Edward Said: The Paradox of Identity* (London: Routledge, 1999), 80. The authors are referring to R. Young, *White Mythologies: Writing History and the West* (London: Routledge, 1990), 131–33, here. They also include J. Clifford, *The Predicament of Culture: Twentieth-Century Ethnography, Literature, and Art* (Cambridge, MA: Harvard University Press, 1988), 261, 263, 276, in their discussion of Said's 'Western thinking'.

25 For example, D. Porter, '*Orientalism* and its Problems', in *Colonial Discourse and Post-colonial Theory: A Reader*, ed. P. Williams and L. Chrisman (New York: Columbia University Press, 1993), 151 (originally publ. in *The Politics of Theory*, ed. F. Barker *et al.*, Proceedings of the Essex Sociology of Literature Conference, University of Colchester, 1983, 179–93).

26 E. W. Said, 'Orientalism Reconsidered', *Cultural Critique*, 1 (Autumn 1985), 89–107.

Spivak and Rushdie occupy, and the manner in which they use these locations to theorise their diasporic marginality' (Ashcroft and Ahluwalia, 80), 'privileged' postcolonial voices can offer both 'inside' and 'outside' views on Islam. It is due to increasing Muslim migration to Europe that we have gained access to a number of texts reflecting on Islam from a contemporary Muslim point of view. Salman Rushdie's *The Satanic Verses* (1988) is a prime example.[27] My study will look into representations of Islam in German- and English-language writing of the 1990s and the beginning of the twenty-first century. I have chosen texts by authors of diverse backgrounds, both Muslim and non-Muslim, in order to give a differentiated view on this religion. These 'inside views' do not stem from less privileged, but rather successful writers, yet they often address issues of social, political, cultural or religious discrimination in their texts through less privileged characters. These views, alongside 'outside views', give access to a diverse picture of Islam as it is lived in Europe.

In the post-colonial era of the 1950s and 1960s, which began with the independence of a number of former British colonies such as India after the Second World War, many Muslims became migrants to their former colonizing countries to work and establish an economically better life. This had implications for the development of Islam as a belief system and culture: Islam moved to Europe, and could not be ignored. German and British (and other European) Muslim identities have since been established (Lewis, 7). This raises questions regarding how Islam is lived in a 'foreign' environment where on the one hand religion tends to be practised in the private domain, yet where on the other it plays an increasingly important role.[28] Although we can still speak of Germany and the UK as secular societies in which religion (predominantly Christianity with its various denominations) is largely perceived as a private matter, Jürgen Habermas points out that religion has become 'eine wichtige moralische Ressource' [an important moral resource], especially since 9/11 (15). For Habermas, the term 'postsecular' 'bringt dabei zum Ausdruck, daß sich auch die modernen Gesellschaften auf den Fortbestand der Religionen einstellen und den konstruktiven Dialog mit diesen suchen sollten' (16) [shows that even modern societies should brace themselves for the continuous existence of religions and seek constructive dialogues

27 S. Rushdie, *The Satanic Verses* (London: Vintage, 1998 [1988]).

28 M. Reder and J. Schmidt SJ, 'Habermas und die Religion', in *Ein Bewußtsein von dem, was fehlt: Eine Diskussion mit Jürgen Habermas*, ed. M. Reder and J. Schmidt (Frankfurt a.M.: Suhrkamp, 2008), 9.

with them].[29] This book will point to the tensions arising from the supposed division between secularism and religiosity as well as question the viability of this dichotomy.

Islam is also specifically 'a social event',[30] an experience of the *umma*. This also partly holds true for other religions such as Judaism where believers seek a supra-national (diasporic) sense of community, a common culture, history and heritage to assert their faith. In this sense, religion has always been noticeable in Western societies and has played a significant role, even in secular processes.[31] As Geoffrey Brahm Levey notes, 'religion is integral to the history of liberalism'.[32]

In non-Islamic societies in which religion is not meant to have an effect on public life, but in which it is part and parcel of history and cultural or national identity, the question of how Islam can be identified — as a belief, a culture or a way of living — determines the interaction between Muslims and non-Muslims, and Islam's further development. Brahm Levey has observed that 'the view is increasingly put that the Muslim presence challenges the liberal secular state *and* condemns the liberal multicultural state' (3; italics Brahm Levey's). It is for such perceptions of Islam that Tariq Modood calls for a 'moderate secularism as an implication of multicultural equality' by which he means 'the relative autonomy of politics so that political authority, public reasoning and citizenship does [*sic*] not depend upon shared religious conviction and motivation'.[33] It remains to be seen what position Islam may acquire in today's 'multicultural' West.

In recent years, there has been an Islamic revival both in the West and in Muslim countries such as Turkey. There is a desire to return to religious roots which particularly concerns the younger generations, children of former migrants. Ron Geaves reads this 'as a response to colonial and post-colonial discourse and conditions', and as a way of participating in Western society.[34] Islamic revivalism is also partly a

29 See J. Habermas, 'Ein Bewußtsein von dem, was fehlt', in *Ein Bewußtsein von dem, was fehlt*, ed. M. Reder and J. Schmidt, 31–33.

30 See E. Beck-Gernsheim, *Wir und die Anderen* (Frankfurt a.M.: Suhrkamp, 2004), 30.

31 M. Reder, 'Wie weit können Glaube und Vernunft unterschieden werden?', in *Ein Bewußtsein von dem, was fehlt*, ed. M. Reder and J. Schmidt, 53.

32 G. Brahm Levey, 'Secularism and Religion in a Multicultural Age', in *Secularism, Religion and Multicultural Citizenship*, ed. G. Brahm Levey and T. Modood (Cambridge: Cambridge University Press, 2009), 4.

33 Tariq Modood, *Multiculturalism: A Civic Idea* (Cambridge: Polity, 2007), 78, 73.

34 R. Geaves, 'Who Defines Moderate Islam "Post"-September 11?', in *Islam and the West Post 9/11*, ed. R. Geaves *et al.* (Aldershot: Ashgate, 2004), 71.

response to what Muslims have to face in the non-Muslim world: for instance, prejudices against Islam as a 'fundamentalist', patriarchal and sexist religion, which are part and parcel of the Western image of Muslims and Muslim societies, or violent outbreaks such as 'Paki-bashing' as a reaction against 'Islam as threat' (as triggered by, for example, the 'Rushdie affair', the worldwide reactions to the *fatwa* [religious edict], which called for his death, issued by Iran's Supreme Leader Grand Ayatollah Ruhollah Khomeini after the publication of *The Satanic Verses*). All this is bound to undermine successful communication between Muslims and non-Muslims.[35] The question is whether there is any genuine cultural exchange between Islam and the West. Muslims have been living in Western cities for decades. They have brought their religion, cultures and languages with them, and have influenced British and German society. Malak points out that 'Islam, both as a faith and a civilization, has, in aggregate, acquired a global, cross-cultural reach that embraces diversities of languages, races, ethnicities and regions' (5). Today, this also holds true in the Western world. All these issues are addressed in contemporary fictional and semi-fictional writing by German- and English-language authors, Muslim and non-Muslim.

The writers selected for this study also engage with Muslims' perceptions of the West. In the context of this book, Occidentalism refers to the prejudice of the non-Western minority with regards to the Western majority resulting from a feeling of being dominated by Western concepts and values. Couze Venn defines Occidentalism as follows:

> Occidentalism [...] is the conceptual and historical space in which a particular narrative of the subject and a particular narrative of history have been constituted; these have become hegemonic with modernization, having effects throughout the world because of the universal scope of the project of modernity and the global reach of European colonization.[36]

In conservative and traditional Muslim eyes, the West and its association with modernity and privilege can be seen as a potential threat that damages Islam. Thus we can find among some Muslim immigrants hostility against 'the sinful City, 'the reasoned mind of the

35 For an analysis of the political dimension of Islam, which is at the centre of the attention of Western media, see B. Tibi, *Islam Between Culture and Politics*, 2nd edn (Basingstoke: Palgrave Macmillan in association with The Weatherhead Center for International Affairs, Harvard University, 2005 [2001]).

36 C. Venn, *Occidentalism: Modernity and Subjectivity* (London: Sage, 2000), 2.

West' and 'the settled bourgeoist and the infidel'.[37] Ian Buruma and Avishai Margalit point out that Occidentalism is 'at least as reductive [as Orientalism]; its bigotry simply turns the Orientalist view upside down' (10); there is the likelihood that Occidentalism is on the same continuum of subtle-to-crass as Orientalism. This study will also look into forms of resistance to the West: these can extend from subtle ways of showing solidarity with Islam by deciding consciously to wear the hijab or openly expressing anger about the treatment of Muslims in Germany and the UK, to more radical actions such as burning 'anti-Islamic' books like *The Satanic Verses*. The question will be what kinds of Islam are evoked by such 'anti-Western' actions and what influence they have on the perception of Islam both within and outside of Muslim communities in non-Muslim countries such as Germany and the UK.

A comparison between Germany and the UK will give access to a differentiated understanding of perceptions of Islam in Europe. Firstly, the different conditions for Muslim migration suggest different attitudes towards Muslims in these two countries: in the UK, Muslim migration was primarily the result of colonialism, whereas in Germany, which never had colonies in the Muslim world, Muslim migration took place for entirely economic reasons (the *Gastarbeiter*-movement). For this reason, Islam has been in the public eye for longer in the UK than in Germany. The differences in Muslim immigration as well as the cultural and historical distinctions which differentiate on the one hand a largely rural Turkish immigrant population in Germany and on the other an immigrant population of mainly Punjabi and Bengali derivation alongside, for instance, Afro-Caribbeans, Hindus and Jews in the UK may have had an effect on the literary representations of Islam in these countries.

Secondly, these migration processes and the visibility or invisibility of Muslims have had effects on the politics of the literary market.[38] Germany seems to produce migrant or what I call 'transcultural literature' which, at least until recently, has mainly found critical attention in academia. With their largely innovative, 'postmodern' styles and language, German works of transcultural literature often receive literary prizes; they have been less accessible to the wider reading public than, for example, more broadly disseminated

37 I. Buruma and A. Margalit, *Occidentalism: A Short History of Anti-Westernism* (London: Atlantic Books, 2004), 11.

38 I am indebted to Professor Peter Davies (University of Edinburgh) for advising me to think about the politics of the literary market in relation to the comparison between German and English transcultural writing.

films with multicultural subject matter. Yet the latter's commercial success has also resulted in greater attention to German transcultural literature. In the UK, transcultural writing has been hugely popular (as have its translations in Germany).[39] Multiculturalism has been visible longer in the UK than in Germany. A popular interest in the Other stems in large part from economic success and the resulting tourism from Western countries to the Muslim world, but also from the longer visibility and thus awareness of the Other within the UK than within Germany. Of course, Germany has always had its Others such as Jews, but post-war German society has largely constructed itself as homogeneous.[40] This is highlighted by the fact that it was only in the early 2000s, after a number of legislative changes in German nationality law, that Germany began to perceive itself as a country of immigration. Furthermore, the style of English transcultural writing tends to be less innovative than that of German transcultural writing, which ensures the former's accessibility to the mainstream reading public. These differences in the literary systems, which also often influence the writers' choice of genre (mainly fiction in the UK and more semi- or non-fictional writing in Germany), have had a great impact on the popularity of this literature and material in other media such as television and film. By examining possible German and British ways of dealing with Islam in transcultural writing and by concluding with the question whether they might have an influence on its reception in the two countries, we will learn more about European understandings of Islam which are based on different historical developments and textual realizations.

In order to reach this differentiated understanding of Islam, this book focuses on movement (travel and migration) as a mode of cultural encounter. As a vital learning process, travel is highly significant in Islam.[41] It has its roots in the *hijra*, the 'migration', that is, the forced

39 Other European transcultural writing in German translation, for example from France, has not been as successful as English transcultural writing. In the UK, German transcultural writing in translation (such as Emine Sevgi Özdamar's *Life Is a Caravanserai*) has not received major public attention. I received this information from the editor of the Middlesex University World Literature Series, Peter Bush, during a conversation at the conference 'Betwixt and Between: Place and Cultural Translation' at Queen's University, Belfast (April 2005).

40 See M. Biller, 'Die dritte Ethnie', in F. Akin, *Gegen die Wand: Das Buch zum Film: Drehbuch, Materialien, Interviews und Pressestimmen* (Cologne: Kiepenheuer & Witsch, 2004), 267–68 (originally publ. in *FAZ Sonntagszeitung*, 22 June 2003).

41 D. F. Eickelman and J. Piscatori, 'Preface', in *Muslim Travellers: Pilgrimage, Migration, and the Religious Imagination*, ed. D. F. Eickelman and

journey into exile, which marks the beginning of Islamic history.[42] Since then Muslims have travelled as well as migrated to destinations far beyond the Muslim world. Although (in contrast to travel as a privileged form of movement) migration is not voluntary when it is caused by economic or political necessity, it too always involves a learning process – about oneself as well as the new country. I read both travel and migration as translation processes within and between cultures. Both involve movement, literally between places, and also metaphorically between cultures, languages and religions. According to Iain Chambers, the main difference between travel and migration is that the former 'implies movement between fixed positions, a site of departure, a point of arrival, the knowledge of an identity',[43] whereas the latter 'involves a movement in which neither the points of departure nor those of arrival are immutable or certain. It calls for [...] identities that are constantly subject to mutation'. Migration, more than travel, therefore enforces a mirroring of the self in the Other.[44] If, like Said, one regards movement as a form of creative placelessness, then ideally one will experience what he terms 'worldliness'.[45] For Said, worldliness is the positively connoted 'hybridisation of postcolonial metropolitan culture', where 'intellectual and scholarly work from the peripheries' is acknowledged. Huggan points out, however, that worldliness is not necessarily a positive concept as 'Said appears to exclude those who have no access [...] to the world's metropolitan cultures', thus displaying a certain degree of ethnocentrism. The latter is also associated with cosmopolitanism,[46] especially if one relates this concept to the idea of the 'citizen of the world'. Yet, as Sheldon Pollock *et al.* point out, cosmopolitanism from a post-Cold War perspective captures the

J. Piscatori (London: Routledge, 1990), xii-xxii, and 'Social Theory in the Study of Muslim Societies', in *Muslim Travellers*, ed. D. F. Eickelman and J. Piscatori, 3–25.

42 B. Melman, 'The Middle East/Arabia: "The Cradle of Islam"', in *The Cambridge Companion to Travel Writing*, ed. P. Hulme and T. Youngs (Cambridge: Cambridge University Press, 2002), 110–12, 116–19.

43 I. Chambers, *Migrancy, Culture, Identity* (London: Routledge, 1994), 5.

44 As explored in G. C. Spivak, 'The Rani of Simur: An Essay in Reading the Archives', *History and Theory*, 24.3 (1985), 247–72 (repr. in *Europe and its Others*, I: *Proceedings of the Essex Conference on the Sociology of Literature 1984, University of Essex*, ed. F. Barker *et al.* (Colchester: University of Essex, 1985), 128–51).

45 Said cited in Huggan, *The Postcolonial Exotic*, 9. Huggan refers to Said's article 'Third World Intellectuals and Metropolitan Culture', *Raritan*, 9.3 (1990), 30, where Said explores the two positions of 'worldliness' and 'cosmopolitanism'.

46 See B. Robbins, *Secular Vocations: Intellectuals, Protestantism, Culture* (New York: Verso, 1993). See also T. Brennan, *At Home in the World: Cosmopolitanism Now* (Cambridge, MA: Harvard University Press, 1997), 27.

'experience of cultural and political displacement',[47] 'of historic and cultural transition' (4). For them, '[c]osmopolitans today are often the victims of modernity, failed by capitalism's upward mobility, and bereft of those comforts and customs of national belonging. [...] Cultural pluralism recognizes difference so long as the general category of the people is still fundamentally understood within the national frame' (6). Cosmopolitanism does not therefore equate an idealistic, unquestioning and at times unrealistic multiculturalism, something which also comes to the fore in the texts selected for this study. Although largely privileged, the writers are aware of their privileged positions as well as their (and their characters') difference from mainstream German and British people. They recognize the changing circumstances many (post-)migrants have undergone and the conflicts associated with cosmopolitanism. But some of the writers also acknowledge their transcultural experience as something positive, and this is in accordance with Said's worldliness.

These writers highlight the fact that Islam has been a cosmopolitan religion and has influenced the West's urban culture. Yet the complexity of the mixed nature of its environment needs to be considered. For example, some Muslims live in an environment that almost entirely consists of co-religionists who have arrived more or less recently from the same place; it might be a mixed one of a variety of cultures and religions; one can also come across 'ghettos', societies within societies which may or may not have been established voluntarily; some Muslims, especially those who were not *Gastarbeiter* and did not come from Anatolia such as Iranian immigrants, live with largely ethnically German neighbours. These different environments have an influence on how Islam can be, indeed is, lived in Germany and the UK, and are another indicator of its diversity.

The second focus of this study is cultural translation as a means of communicating between the place the traveller is from and the place they are going or currently living, and who they are interacting with (Muslims of different cultural backgrounds or with different attitudes towards their backgrounds as well as non-Muslims). I appropriate the concept of linguistic translation and apply it to the translation between known and unknown cultures as a process of making sense of the unfamiliar. In 'Die Aufgabe des Übersetzers' [The Task of the Translator], Walter Benjamin argues that the interrelations between languages are made visible through translation processes, but that a

47 S. Pollock *et al.*, 'Cosmopolitanisms', in *Cosmopolitanism*, ed. C. A. Breckenridge *et al.* (Durham, NC: Duke University Press, 2002), 2.

certain degree of 'Fremdheit' [foreignness/otherness] remains.[48] This also holds true for cultures: as cultures cannot be fixed, a one-to-one relationship between cultures in translation processes does not exist. Translation is the negotiation of meanings; it does not assume that one culture is stable and can easily be transferred into another culture. Instead, translation (as travel) provides the basis for the creation of something new. The translator, the migrant, chooses their translation 'materials' and lets them interact to describe their situation. They may make use of the 'gaps' and 'impurities' (Chambers, 75), something that cannot be translated accurately. This marginal position is the space where migrants can negotiate multiple identities and re-create cultures. Homi Bhabha regards culture as the 'locus [rather than the object] of translation'.[49] Similarly, Michael Cronin points out that '[m]inority-language cultures are translation cultures *par excellence*'.[50] Migration is a condition which is also expressed in terms of language. Language appears as a dislocated item of a migrant's cultural baggage which is removed from its original context and land and which now influences the language of the majority in the new country of abode. In defining a new language in a new country, the language of the migrant denotes their physical displacement. However, some migrant writers deliberately try to conform to the standards of the language in which they are writing, and therefore do not reflect on their migratory experiences in linguistic terms in their texts. It will also be explored what this says about their self-perception as writer and their perceived task as a literary figure in a wider cultural context.

A further linguistic aspect to consider is the role of Arabic and its influence on the perception of Islam. Apart from one writer, none of

48 W. Benjamin, 'Charles Baudelaire, Tableaux parisiens. Deutsche Übertragung mit einem Vorwort über die Aufgabe des Übersetzers', in *Gesammelte Schriften*, with the assistance of T. W. Adorno and G. Scholem, ed. R. Tiedemann and H. Schweppenhäuser (Frankfurt a.M.: Suhrkamp, 1972), IV.I.: *Gesammelte Schriften*, ed. T. Rexroth, 14 (originally publ. in C. Baudelaire, *'Tableaux parisiens': Deutsche Übertragung mit einem Vorwort über die Aufgabe des Übersetzers, von Walter Benjamin* (Heidelberg: Weißbach, 1923)).

49 Bhabha referred to in M. Wolf, 'Culture as Translation — and Beyond: Ethnographic Models of Representation in Translation Studies', in *Crosscultural Transgressions: Research Models in Translation Studies II: Historical and Ideological Issues*, ed. T. Hermans (Manchester: St. Jerome, 2002), 189.

50 M. Cronin, 'The Cracked Looking Glass of Servants: Translation and Minority Languages in a Global Age', in *Translation and Minority*, ed. L. Venuti (= Special Issue, *The Translator*, 4.2 (1998)), 147. See also his *Across the Lines: Travel, Language, Translation* (Cork: Cork University Press, 2000), 26–32, 95.

the writers selected for this study are native speakers of Arabic. 'The language of Islam' is therefore often an abstract object, but through its use in prayers or everyday expressions it is also familiar. Thus Arabic and the conscious reflection on this language by its translation into other languages spoken by Muslims offer creative ways into understanding Islam.

In translation processes, gender is often the site of struggle, cultural concerns and the search for one's identity. My third focus is, therefore, the question of how male and female migrants come to terms with their need to settle in. Stereotypes relating to gender seem particularly prominent: many people of Western origin associate male dominance over women with Islamic culture. This perception swings, however, between criticism and idealization (see Malak, 119–20): there are people in the West who, on the one hand, genuinely want to help overcome the negative implications of patriarchy as it is — and they often forget this — also lived out in many non-Muslim cultures; on the other, they need the patriarchal system of Islam as a counter-culture to underline their own supposedly gender-equal culture. I am interested in the negotiation of gender and its roles from a Muslim point of view in order to understand Muslim (post-)migration, and men's and women's different approaches to their migratory experiences. Judith Butler's notion of gender performativity 'not [as] a conscious act, but [as] the effect of gender discourse that comes across as the non-intentional repetition or re-staging of norms' provides the path to a consideration of these aspects.[51] It helps us understand the idea that a Muslim's gender identity (like any other form of identity) can be both unconsciously repeated due to established conventions in Butler's sense, but also, and this is where my understanding of performing one's gender identity diverges from Butler's definition of performativity, constantly and above all consciously re-valued in non-Muslim environments.[52] It is here that non-Muslims repeatedly challenge Muslim identity and Muslims often feel the need to defend who they are. The authors studied in this book engage primarily with the construction of their and their characters' Muslim identities in the latter sense. In this context, some feminist critics have taken a closer look at language, especially in connection with power relations

51 J. Culler, 'Philosophy and Literature: The Fortunes of the Performative', *Poetics Today*, 21.3 (Fall 2000), 514.

52 Butler changes her perception of performativity in her later work to something more in line with my understanding of performativity as something which can also be based on the conscious re-valuation and repetition of acts that constitute a person's identity.

between male and female migrants, as many Muslim women increasingly reclaim their voices and liberate their language from patriarchal uses.[53] Travel, translation and gender pave the way for this book's approach to the transcultural texts selected. The issues connected with these three notions — immigration, transculturality, gender roles, differences in generations in relation to language or religious observance, or religious and cultural confusions — focus on Islam in this study. My exploration of them should be read with an awareness for the fact that they are, of course, universal across time and also affect other religious groups such as Jews or Catholics.

***

This book explores and compares German and English 'transcultural writing'. This term is not unproblematic, because — as Huggan points out — it 'is being used to conjure up a far more positive picture of the world than a more historically informed and, particularly, a more economically driven argument would allow'.[54] However, other terms that try to grasp processes of cultural interaction are counterproductive for my reading of the selected texts.[55] The term 'intercultural', which is employed in *Interkulturelle Germanistik* (Intercultural German Studies), is not a suitable one to describe my texts comprehensively for it does not adequately capture the idea of movement. The term implies that any given traditions are to be considered in isolation rather than in interaction;[56] it traditionally understands culture as something separate,

53 See M. Badran, 'Islamic Feminism Revisited', *Al-Ahram Weekly Online*, no. 781, 9–15 February 2006, http://weekly.ahram.org.eg/2006/781/cu4.htm [accessed 28 June 2010] (30 para.).

54 G. Huggan, 'Derailing the "Trans"? Postcolonial Studies and the Negative Effects of Speed', in *Inter- und Transkulturelle Studien: Theoretische Grundlagen und interdisziplinäre Praxis*, ed. H. Antor (Universitätsverlag Winter: Heidelberg, 2006), 59.

55 I am aware that Norbert Mecklenburg, in his *Das Mädchen aus der Fremde: Germanistik als interkulturelle Literaturwissenschaft* (Munich: Iudicium, 2008), differentiates between the terms 'intercultural' and 'transcultural', and has reservations about the frequent use of 'transcultural'. He also discusses postcolonial theories and such postcolonial terms as hybridity, including their inherent contradictions and usefulness for German literature (see C. Cerri's review in *Zeitschrift für Interkulturellen Fremdsprachenunterricht*, 15.1 (April 2010), 125-28, http://zif.spz.tu-darmstadt.de/jg-15-1/docs/Mecklenburg.pdf [accessed 18 June 2011] (15 para.)). However, due to its publication schedule, I have not been able to consult the book myself.

56 L. A. Adelson, 'Against Between: A Manifesto', in *Zafer Şenocak*, ed. T. Cheesman and K. E. Yeşilada (Cardiff: University of Wales Press, 2003), 23.

thus stressing difference.[57] This goes back to Johann Gottfried Herder's concept of the homogeneous 'Volkskultur' [folk culture] distant from the Other which Herder developed in his *Ideen zur Philosophie der Geschichte der Menschheit* [*Outlines of a Philosophy of the History of Man*] (1782–1791).[58] Such a conception of culture nourishes the danger of a clash of cultures (Welsch, 'Transculturality', 196; cf. Huntington).

Huggan has another interesting point to make. He identifies the 'exoticization' of other cultures within supposedly homogeneous societies:

> While interculturalism has the definite virtue of drawing attention to the political as well as aesthetic demands of cultural difference and diversity, it tends ironically to founder on precisely the hypostatised, even fetishised, appreciation of 'other' cultures [...] to which its purportedly dynamic understanding of cultural exchange and interaction is designed to show the door. ('Derailing the "Trans"?', 58)

In this sense, 'intercultural' as well as the term 'multicultural', which refers to cultures *within* the same community (Welsch, 'Transculturality', 196), supports the concept of the *in-between*, and thus suggests 'clear and absolute boundaries' (Adelson, 'Against Between', 4) *between* cultures. It posits possible hierarchies among cultures which many transcultural writers aim to overcome. Furthermore, 'multicultural' 'seeks opportunities for tolerance and understanding' (Welsch, 'Transculturality', 196) which implies the danger of ghettoization or cultural fundamentalism (197). Neither 'intercultural' nor 'multicultural' can capture the experiences of those (post-)migrants who have moved beyond Bhabha's *Third Space* of the *in-between* to a space where the *in-between* is no longer a question but where migrants and migrant writers can draw on the movements that determine their lives and explore individual and alternative forms of identity, while acknowledging that this is not necessarily a smooth process.[59] According to Leslie A. Adelson the *in-between* 'is effectively incapable of accounting for cultures of migration *as historical formations*' ('Against Between', 3, italics Adelson's).

57 W. Welsch, 'Transculturality: The Puzzling Form of Cultures Today', in *Spaces of Culture: City — Nation — World*, ed. M. Featherstone and S. Lash (London: Sage, 1999), 194–97.

58 J. G. Herder, *Ideen zur Philosophie der Geschichte der Menschheit*, in *Werke*, ed. M. Bollacher *et al.* (Frankfurt a.M.: Deutscher Klassiker Verlag, 1989), VI, ed. M. Bollacher, Bibliothek Deutscher Klassiker, 41.

59 H. K. Bhabha, 'The Commitment to Theory', in Bhabha, *The Location of Culture*, 36–39. For a more detailed discussion of Bhabha's *Third Space* of the *in-between*, see Chapter 1, 48–49.

Adelson's comment goes hand-in-hand with my understanding of 'hyphenated identities'. Originating from the US-American history of immigration and now widely appropriated for postcolonial contexts, the hyphen on the one hand pays tribute to the dual ethnic origins of particular Americans, but on the other it opens up questions of belonging and cultural and ethnic loyalty. Although the hyphen can denote pride in one's roots and in an at least dual identity which is common in the twentieth and twenty-first centuries when migration has been experienced by many people, it can also express shame for having to choose one identity over another, for being torn between them or even for being expected to feel 'in-between' cultures.[60] The hyphen is associated increasingly with the latter. I am aware of the tensions and conflicts arising from migratory experiences and I do not wish to propose a naïve understanding of transculturality. Yet because of its potential interpretation as a symbol of separation,[61] I have decided to drop the hyphen when referring to writers or characters who combine more than one ethnic and cultural background in their identities. They are, for example, not German-Turkish, but German Turkish. This practice is consistent with my rejecting of 'interculturality', its implicit hierarchy of cultures and my being 'against the *in-between*' as argued by Adelson.

The same holds true for other metaphors such as 'bridges',[62] 'crossings' and 'thresholds'.[63] These terms are meant to acknowledge the writer's role as translator between languages and cultures. Most of the terms for transcultural writing imply what Jim Jordan calls a 'two worlds paradigm',[64] the irreconcilable clashing of cultures, religions and languages, and not a creative movement among them.

60 L. A. Strasheim, 'We're all Ethnics: "Hyphenated" Americans, "Professional" Ethnics, and Ethnics "By Attraction"', *The Modern Language Journal*, 59.5/6 (1975), 244.

61 See J. Lahiri, 'My Two Lives', *Newsweek*, 6 March 2006, www.newsweek.com/2006/03/05/my-two-lives.html [accessed 26 July 2010] (7 para.).

62 For a detailed analysis of the image of the bridge in German Turkish writing, see M. McGowan, 'Brücken und Brücken-Köpfe: Wandlungen einer Metapher in der türkisch-deutschen Literatur', in *Die andere deutsche Literatur: Istanbuler Vorträge*, ed. M. Durzak and N. Kuruyazıcı with the assistance of C. Şenöz Ayata (Würzburg: Königshausen & Neumann, 2004, 31–40).

63 See C. Begemann, '"Kanakensprache": Schwellenphänomene in der deutschsprachigen Literatur ausländischer AutorInnen der Gegenwart', in *Schwellen: Germanistische Erkundungen einer Metapher*, ed. N. Saul *et al.* (Würzburg: Königshausen & Neumann, 1999), 209–20.

64 J. Jordan, 'More than a Metaphor: The Passing of the Two Worlds Paradigm in German-Language Diasporic Literature', in *Crossing Boundaries*, ed. J. Jordan (= Special Number, *German Life and Letters*, 59.4 (2006)), 488–99.

It seems to be the writers' task to bridge these worlds, partly because the audience expects them to do so. However, in Jordan's words, 'authors no longer conceive of themselves as between cultures' (491), or stuck in what Azade Seyhan refers to as 'borderlands'.[65] As a result, some writers apply metaphors themselves to their work: Özdamar, for example, chooses the word 'caravanserai' as part of the title of one of her novels in order to characterize her protagonist's life as a migrant. Trains feature in her work prominently as a metaphor for a life which is constantly on the move, which one passes through and from which a migrant's identity springs.[66] Another clear example is the early work of Feridun Zaimoğlu: he focuses on the second and third generations of migrants who, in opposition to their parents' generation, no longer see themselves as 'victims' of a 'cold' Germany. Instead, they have carved out their own creative spaces beyond definitions and expectations of being placed in the *in-between*,[67] spaces that challenge 'anxieties about worlds, nations, and cultures in flux' (Adelson, 'Against Between', 5).

Thus the term 'transcultural' suggests that writers critically, actively and creatively engage with the cultures, languages and histories available to them; it points out that they constantly move among them.[68] Although established in a different context and with different intentions, Fernando Ortiz's concept of *transculturation* is a useful point of departure when engaging with 'cultures on the move'. Ortiz's *transculturation* is 'a process in which all the new elements

65 A. Seyhan, 'Geographies of Memory: Protocols of Writing in the Borderlands', in *Multiculturalism in Transit: A German-American Exchange*, ed. K. J. Millich and J. M. Peck, International Political Currents, 3 (New York: Berghahn, 1998), 193–212.

66 For example, at the end of *Das Leben ist eine Karawanserei*, the narrator leaves Turkey by train to go to Germany. In an interview with Annette Wierschke, Özdamar compares being at home with being on a train (in A. Wierschke, *Schreiben als Selbstbehauptung: Kulturkonflikt und Identität in den Werken von Aysel Özakin, Alev Tekinay und Emine Sevgi Özdamar; mit Interviews* (Frankfurt a.M.: IKO, 1994) (= doctoral thesis, University of Minnesota, 1994), 259).

67 See, for example, F. Zaimoğlu, 'Gastarbeiterliteratur: Ali macht Männchen', in *Globalkolorit: Multikulturalismus und Populärkultur*, ed. R. Mayer and M. Terkessidis (St Ändra-Wördern: Hannibal, 1998), 91.

68 See, for example, W. Welsch, 'Transkulturalität: Zwischen Globalisierung und Partikularisierung', *Jahrbuch DaF*, 26 (2000), 327–51. He specifically dismisses Alois Wierlacher's concept of the *intercultural* which the latter researched at the Department of German as a Foreign Language at the Ludwig-Maximilians-University in Munich in the 1980s (A. Wierlacher, *Das Fremde und das Eigene: Prolegomena zu einer interkulturellen Germanistik*, Publikationen der Gesellschaft für Interkulturelle Germanistik, 1 (Munich: Iudicium, 1985).

[of cultures] are fused, adopting forms that are already established while at the same time introducing exotic touches of their own and generating new ferments'.[69] Transcultural literature engages explicitly with movement between languages, cultures and religions, but it no longer needs to be defined via migration alone.[70] Wolfgang Welsch even goes as far as saying that we are all 'cultural hybrids', that 'there is no longer anything absolutely foreign' and 'no longer anything exclusively "own" either' ('Transculturality', 198). Such an approach would, however, weaken the idea of transculturality, as it seems to deny experience as something relative. In this study, transculturality is understood as something that reclaims the individuality that 'the migrant population' or, by extension, writers with a migrant background are often denied. The focus is on Islam, and Muslim migrants and post-migrants. These are people with a Muslim background – religiously, culturally, historically, geographically or linguistically – and with the experience of migration, which may have taken place a generation before them but which, as post-migrants, they have 'inherited' from their migrant parents. Transcultural literature examines differences and similarities between cultures, investigates what these tensions may say about contemporary German and British culture and explores the possibilities of undergoing transitions. The transcultural texts selected comprise an element of 'writing at the margins', which Huggan describes as an 'oppositional discursive strategy' (*The Postcolonial Exotic*, 5, 20), a form of counter-writing that consciously unsettles the fallacious notion of a homogeneous German or British culture.

Tom Cheesman employs the term 'axial writing' for German Turkish writing to describe a literature 'that thematis[es] migrant experience'.[71] For him, axial writers carry the 'burden of representation [of migrants or a minority of which these writers might not see themselves as being part] [...] which is imposed on

69 F. Ortiz, *Cuban Counterpoint: Tobacco and Sugar,* trans. H. de Onís, intro. B. Malinowski (New York: Alfred A. Knopf, 1947), xii.

70 H. Schmitz, 'Einleitung: Von der nationalen zur internationalen Literatur', in *Von der nationalen zur internationalen Literatur: Transkulturelle deutschsprachige Literatur und Kultur im Zeitalter globaler Migration,* ed. H. Schmitz, Amsterdamer Beiträger zur neueren Germanistik, 69/2009 (Amsterdam: Rodopi, 2009), 9. Huggan has identified a 'transcultural turn' in postcolonial studies which increasinly engage with topics related to transculturality as well as issues of globalization ('Derailing the "Trans"?', 56–57).

71 T. Cheesman, 'Juggling Burdens of Representation: Black, Red, Yellow and Turquoise', in *Crossing Boundaries,* ed. J. Jordan (= Special Number, *German Life and Letters,* 59.4 (2006)), 471.

them by the public'. He challenges the generational categorization of German Turkish writing which argues that migrant writing started as *Opferliteratur* [literature of victims], then became 'ethnic' writing and later turned into 'diasporic' writing, which

> explores or forges connections between a given minority and other minorities, past and present, in Germany and other countries, drawing on postcolonial thinking in order to deconstruct the stereotypes of 'self' and 'other' which erect boundaries and damage communication between minorities and majorities generally. (473–74)[72]

The longer established Anglophone postcolonial literatures have set the standards for communicating (post-)migrant experiences which have been taken up in contemporary German transcultural writing.[73]

Salman Rushdie's notion of 'imaginary homelands' and Benedict Anderson's idea of 'imagined communities' that are created in diasporas come into play here.[74] They refer to the artificiality of being removed from home and the consequent necessity to retain something of that old home in a new place, to create a 'home of the mind' (Rushdie, 'Imaginary Homelands', 10), something that belongs only to that community. These ideas are also explored in transcultural writing which, however, takes them further: it looks into the consequences of these 'imagined homelands' or 'communities' for today's post-migrants. Thus transcultural literature as it is discussed here outlines places 'outside the nation' and outside specific cultures

72 Cheesman also points to 'four basic strategies, four ways in which writers deal with the burden of representation and thereby explore [...] the meaning of integration': they are 'axialism' ('the kind of writing that fulfils public expectations of "minority" writers'), 'refusal', 'parodic ethnicisation' and 'glocalism' (477–87). These strategies represent the grouping of German Turkish writing according to generations. See also T. Cheesman, *Novels of Turkish German Settlement: Cosmopolite Fictions* (Rochester, NY: Camden House, 2007), 3, 82–97, for a history of the Turkish German novel.

73 Throughout this book, the term 'postcolonial' applies to the transcultural practice of producing literature which, above all, considers the interaction of various cultures and languages, notions of power and hierarchy, self and Other, and the questioning of canons and the distinction between 'centre' and 'margin'. 'Postcoloniality' is often (but not necessarily, as in Germany) the result of 'post-coloniality' which is to mean literally 'after colonialism' and which often entails migratory movements. On this basis, I differentiate between 'postcolonial' and 'post-colonial'.

74 S. Rushdie, 'Imaginary Homelands' (1982), in *Imaginary Homelands: Essays and Criticism 1981–91* (London: Granta in association with Penguin, 1991 [1992 printing]), 9–21, and B. Anderson, *Imagined Communities: Reflections on the Origin and Spread of Nationalism*, rev. and extended edn (London: Verso, 1991 [1983]).

where translation processes take place and where its writers' creativity lies:[75] translations as such imply creative movements among languages and their associated cultures, not least because they are based on the experience of physical movements. I therefore regard the term 'transcultural' as the closest definition of what the writers represent and depict in their writing: they live among as well as beyond various cultures due to movement (whether experienced or 'inherited'), and write about cultural encounters and their challenges for the transcultural migrant and writer.

***

This book is concerned with post-*Gastarbeiter* and post-first generation literature,[76] and how literature reflects the development from passive *Gastarbeiter* or migrants to self-aware German and British Muslims. First-generation migrant writing has long been the subject of literary critics. This book, however, will address the aftermath of migration as it is represented in transcultural literature of the late 1990s and early 2000s. Examining this kind of literature – rather than earlier migrant writing – will point out the significance of current political trends in the West and the cultural implications of the West's interaction with Islam. Furthermore, this study's transcultural writers have chosen various and often more challenging genres than their predecessors to capture their or their protagonists' migratory experiences (ranging from the fictional novel to the supposedly authentic travel account).[77] These genres reveal the writers' agendas, which may be religiously,

75 See A. Seyhan, *Writing Outside the Nation*, Translation, Transnation (Princeton: Princeton University Press, 2001). Seyhan has developed this idea further, by which it coincides with the increasing perception of writers as 'non-in-between' writers, in 'From Minor Literature, Across Border Culture, to Hyphenated Criticism', in *Reading the Shape of the World: Toward an International Cultural Studies*, ed. H. Schwarz and R. Dienst, Politics and Culture, 4 (Oxford: Westview Press, 1996), 15–29.

76 Throughout this book, I refer to generations of writers primarily in relation to when they came to Germany or the UK, or when they were born there. Although this might also have an effect on their writing styles or choice of subject-matter, my generational typology does not foreground these aspects.

77 Moray McGowan points out that, by contrast to the 'unsophisticated literature of labour migration', contemporary German Turkish writing is 'thematically and aesthetically at least as diverse and irreducible to ethnic generalisations as the Turkish-German population at large' ('Turkish-German Fiction since the mid 1990s', in *Contemporary German Fiction: Writing in the Berlin Republic*, ed. S. Taberner (Cambridge: Cambridge University Press, 2007), 196).

politically or personally motivated and are frequently a reaction to current cultural and political interests.

The writers are a selection of people from diverse non-German and non-British backgrounds who write in German and English. They position themselves variously within German and English literature: some of them perceive themselves as part of the canon (Naipaul); others see themselves as part of their 'original' culture (Özdamar); yet others are not concerned with these classifications and have their own, clearly vocalized agenda (Aboulela); and for some writers it took a long time for them to admit that they have established themselves within the mainstream and rather consciously shed their role of marginal writer (Zaimoğlu). However, they are all transcultural: their writing is based on movement as they either went through migration themselves or 'inherited' an experience of migration which they now relate to on the level of the content and/or the style of their writing;[78] they write from a space beyond the *in-between*, beyond fixed notions of cultures and nations, but within what Adelson calls 'touching tales' that tell of the 'cultural effects of migration' on 'host' countries and of 'approximating postnational intimacy' ('Against Between', 20, 22, 23).[79] The authors explore Islam as part of their transcultural experience. Apart from V. S. Naipaul, who has an explicit intellectual interest in Islam, they are all Muslim writers, one of them an Islamic writer, someone who accentuates the significance of her religious belief in her writing (Aboulela). The writers do not necessarily call themselves Muslim; however, they all deal with their Muslim or Islamic background in their writing, both overtly and subtly.

Chapter 1, 'Moving with Islam', deals with the migration and arrival processes of the first generation. The selected texts go beyond notions of what in Germany is known as *Opferliteratur* [literature of victims] or *Literatur der Betroffenheit* [literature of dismay]: literature written by former *Gastarbeiter* who regarded Germany as a cold and hostile place; it is often written in the writers' mother tongue. One

78 This is also the reason for calling this literature 'migrant writing'. I shall also use this term in this book. See, for example, J. Jordan, 'Migrant Writing in Germany and the Politics of the Multicultural Society: Three Case Studies', in *Migrants in German-Speaking Countries: Aspects of Social and Cultural Experience*, ed. J. Jordan and P. Barker, Modern German Studies, 2 (London: CILT Publications, 2000), 97–113.

79 Adelson specifically examines the 'cultural effects of Turkish migration' (22) on Germany, but her idea can be extended to the other cultures and nations discussed in this study. See also her monograph *The Turkish Turn in Contemporary German Literature: Toward a New Critical Grammar of Migration* (New York: Palgrave Macmillan, 2005) for extensive analyses of this issue.

of the currently most prominent German Turkish writers, Emine Sevgi Özdamar, came to Germany as a *Gastarbeiterin*. She has left the *Opferliteratur* of the first generation of migrant writers behind; instead, she shows the consciously innovative side of the German Turkish migrant writer who feels and uses the advantage of being able to draw upon various languages and cultures for her writing. Her novel *Das Leben ist eine Karawanserei hat zwei Türen aus einer kam ich rein aus der anderen ging ich raus* [*Life Is a Caravanserai Has Two Doors I came in One I Went Out the Other*] (1992) explores the pre-story of migrants and builds on the hybridity in the protagonist's life and on Turkey's heterogeneity in terms of culture and religion. It thematizes the creation of a home on the move, an experience that the protagonist takes further, to Germany. There she reflects on her transcultural experiences in Turkey in the German language, which is an expression of her ultimate transculturality. Despite engaging with migration within Turkey, rather than with a new country of abode, this text can effectively be compared with Monica Ali's popular and stylistically less challenging novel, *Brick Lane* (2003). In the latter, a different notion of home as a fixed place that secures stability is central. This idea of home is linked to the migration experiences of the first generation of British Muslims. This chapter therefore also explores what happens to Islam when it travels, what role(s) Islam can occupy and whether there are differences between the perceptions of migration between the generations and sexes. The focus is on where and how cultural translation processes take place, both as interactions between cultures, religions and languages and between the characters' past/heritage and their present. A comparative analysis of Özdamar's and Ali's texts reveals contrary notions of home (movement in the German text and stability in the English text) and transculturality, which are based on different pre-histories and histories of migration.

Chapter 2, 'Travelling to Islam', continues with an exploration of travel and the writers' contrasting approaches to and views of some parts of the Muslim world. Travel is a different movement from migration, and travel writing offers new perspectives on the significance of experiences of Islam, the interaction of Islam with other cultures and the diversity of different Islams. Here, the need to find a home is not the focus; countries are only visited, even if travel also means a return to a Muslim's religious 'home' as with the hajj. Ilija Trojanow's account of his journey to the sources of Islam (Mecca and Medina), his hajj, *Zu den Heiligen Quellen des Islam: Als Pilger nach Mekka und Medina* [*Mumbai to Mecca*; literally *To the Holy*

Sources of Islam: As Pilgrim to Mecca and Medina] (2003), describes the significance of the traditional pilgrimage for every Muslim and stresses the diversity, indeed transculturality, of Islam. The book was not widely read in Germany and found resonance only among people with an intellectual interest in Islam. V. S. Naipaul's travel books about his journeys to the 'peripheries' of Islam (non-Arab Muslim countries), *Among the Believers: An Islamic Journey* (1981) and *Beyond Belief: Islamic Excursions Among the Converted Peoples* (1998), were broadly acknowledged at the time of their publication, in both the West and the Muslim world, including South Asia. From a Western point of view, they give a curious outsider's (a secular Hindu's) perspective on the outside (Islam). Trojanow's travel account declares itself a specifically anti-Naipaul project; a comparison of these two writers' texts – a traditional and a metaphorical pilgrimage – and their different perceptions of Islam therefore sheds a valuable light on Western travel writing about Islam, especially considering that these two writers were themselves migrants. This leads to the question of how their 'ideas' of Islam correspond to their personal transcultural experiences.

The subsequent chapters look into the second generation's notions of 'having arrived', the atmosphere among young Muslims in the late 1980s and early 1990s and changes in perceptions of Muslim culture and religion between the generations. They also deal with notions of gender. Chapter 3, 'Islam, "Difference" and Masculinity', focuses on the portrayal of young male Muslims. Feridun Zaimoğlu is a prominent representative of the concerns and life styles of young German Turkish people in Germany of the 1990s. His *Kanak Sprak: 24 Mißtöne vom Rande der Gesellschaft* [*Kanak Speak: 24 Dissonances from the Margins of Society*] (1995) established his reputation as an innovative, radical writer. This collection of texts is based on allegedly authentic interviews and can therefore be regarded as documentary fiction, a genre which seems to convey the concerns of young German Turks and their primarily cultural and social experience of Islam of the time most effectively. Hanif Kureishi portrays more religious experiences among young British Muslims in his fictional novel *The Black Album* (1995). His focus is on radicalism among young British Muslim men in the late 1980s. A comparison with Zaimoğlu's portrayal of young German Turkish men – particularly in terms of the young men's gender performativity, but also in terms of the genre in which the writers choose to illustrate their views on Muslim masculinity in Germany and the UK – points up diverse appropriations of Islam as a definer for masculinity, especially since radical Islam is widely associated with young male Muslims. It highlights the similarities and differences in the transcultural experiences of the writers' characters, most notably in their relation to the German and British mainstream; to language; and to the understanding of the 'authenticity' of culture and religion and their subversions.

An exploration of masculinity leads to the examination of female experiences of Islam in Germany and the UK in Chapter 4, 'Islam, Writing and Femininity'. In Zaimoğlu's female pendant to *Kanak Sprak*, *Koppstoff: Kanaka Sprak vom Rande der Gesellschaft* [*Headstuff: Kanaka Speak from the Margins of Society*] (1998), he addresses the concerns of young female Muslims in Germany after the increased xenophobic attacks of the mid-1990s. This text is documentary fiction in line with Özdamar's semi-autobiographical text *MutterZunge* [*Mother Tongue*] (1990). These German-language texts are compared with Leila Aboulela's novels *The Translator* (1999) and *Minaret* (2005). Aboulela, who has not yet received broad academic attention, writes from between generations: strictly speaking, she is a first-generation migrant (Aboulela is not the child of immigrants: her wealthy family bought a flat in London in 1982), yet she mainly portrays the post-migratory experiences of the second generation. Female (post-) migrant experiences are significant for understanding contemporary transcultural writing, which is broadly written for an audience that is interested in Islam and Muslim women's issues. These appear most clearly when examining how the writers either use or create language to carve out representations of Muslim femininity. This also highlights the writers' agendas: Özdamar wishes to uncover the interaction between Turkish and Arabic in order to become a German Turkish migrant writer; Zaimoğlu pursues his self-portrayal through textualizing interviews with young German Turkish women; and Aboulela aims to show the power of Islam for a Muslim woman's identification in a non-Muslim environment. The appropriation and transformation of Islam in transcultural literature is most explicit when it focuses on women, as they are generally portrayed as more adaptable migrants than men.

There is extensive scholarship on the writers covered in this book, yet hardly any of it has a focus on their characters' perceptions of Islam. The criticism usually emphasizes language questions, cultural exchange or multiculturalism, migration or sub- and youth culture, but Islam is a side-issue rather than the main point of discussion.[80]

80 This is changing slowly. See, for example, a number of articles on German migrant writing in relation to Islam in *Encounters with Islam in German Literature and Culture*, ed. J. Hodkinson and J. Morrison (Rochester, NY: Camden House,

Furthermore, critics tend to focus on writers of one language rather than on comparisons between writing in German and English (or any other language).[81]

However, a comparison between German and English transcultural writing exposes the limitations of some assumptions of postcolonial theory:[82] Germany never felt the urge to 'write back' in the same way as the British (or other European) Empire(s) did in the second half of the twentieth century. Germany's 'migrant' writers (or their parents) did not come from former colonies and therefore did not have a 'colonial' relationship with Germany. Such a relationship often came to the fore through education and the need to learn the language of the colonizers, which could give colonized subjects a somewhat privileged position in terms of intellectual, economic and cultural exchange between the colonies and the so-called mother country. Responding to the experience of colonialism and its aftermath via literature, culture and art was not a pressing issue for the first generation of migrant workers to Germany who often did not speak German. Written accounts by *Gastarbeiter* are few and far between, and it is their children or grandchildren who started to respond to their (post-)migratory experiences. Their literary accounts opened the eyes of the German public to the concerns of those living at the margins of society. For this reason Helmut Schmitz points out that 'die spezifisch deutsche Situation darin besteht, dass die gesellschaftliche Entwicklung der der Literatur hinterherhinkt' (Schmitz, 9) [the specifically German situation is that the social developments lag behind those of literature]. Postcolonial theory sprang from a colonial context but, though one of the consequences of colonialism, migration is not limited to colonial experiences and therefore to the study of writers from formerly colonized societies. This is in line with the thinking of Dirk Göttsche, who claims that postcolonial studies currently regard literature as

2009). Cheesman in his *Novels of Turkish German Settlement* also includes notions of Islam in his discussion of some texts, for example Zaimoğlu's post-*Kanak Sprak* writing (74–81).

81 There are exceptions such as S. Milz, 'Ethnicity and/or Nationality Writing in Contemporary Canada and Germany: A Comparative Study of Marlene Nourbese Philip's and Emine Sevgi Özdamar's Writing of Hybridity and its Public and Critical Reception', *Zeitschrift für Anglistik und Amerikanistik*, 48.3 (2000), 254–68.

82 I am indebted to Professor Peter Davies (University of Edinburgh) for a fruitful discussion of my comparative strategy in relation to postcolonial theory.

> kulturelle Praxis mit entschiedener sozialer Funktion und konzentrieren sich auf Phänomene wie kulturelle Differenz, Mimikry, Hybridität, Kreolisierung und soziale Performanz.[83]

> [cultural practice with a significant social function and focus on phenomena such as cultural difference, mimicry, hybridity, creolization and social performance].

Thus I apply postcolonial terms when analysing German-language writing due to the similarities between German and British migration and post-migration experiences, regardless of the cause of the move to the new country of abode.

English literature often serves as the basis for comparisons with other literatures; it is the dominant component of such comparisons and thereby implies that the 'other' literature is only a tool to analyse English literature. However, German transcultural literature has gained a distinctly self-aware position within European literature. Over the past thirty years, German transcultural writers have developed the self-confidence of being different whilst being part of German literature. This holds true even if the current trend, which will be analysed briefly in the Conclusion, suggests stylistic assimilation to German mainstream writing and thus a decreasing awareness of being 'different', and renewed stylistic innovations in English transcultural writing and an increasing positive acknowledgement of 'difference'.

A comparative analysis of the treatment of language (both within the texts and on a meta-level), the exploration of the relationship between home and movement, and gender and its performativity in a post-migrant context will offer a more differentiated understanding of postcolonial notions of 're-placing language' and 're-placing the text' than could be obtained through a non-comparative analysis of traditional post-colonial literatures.[84] It will challenge methods of understanding postcolonial writing by looking from its German 'margins'. This study aims to show that German transcultural literature has as rightful a place in postcolonial criticism as English

83 D. Göttsche, 'Emine Sevgi Özdamars Erzählung *Der Hof im Spiegel*: Spielräume einer postkolonialen Lektüre deutsch-türkischer Literatur', in *Crossing Boundaries*, ed. J. Jordan (= Special Number, *German Life and Letters*, 59.4 (October 2006)), 517–18.

84 B. Ashcroft *et al.*, *The Empire Writes Back: Theory and Practice in Post-Colonial Literatures* (London: Routledge, 1989 [2001 printing]), Chapter 2, 'Re-placing Language: Textual Strategies in Post-colonial Writing', 38–77, and Chapter 3, 'Re-placing the Text: The Liberation of Post-colonial Writing', 78–115.

transcultural writing. Furthermore, a comparative reading of those literatures with their different approaches to Islam will contribute to a trans-European understanding of Islam as a belief and culture with a variety of meanings and potential interpretations.

Spivak formulates the relationship between comparative literature and Islam as follows:

> The range and diversity of the Islamic diaspora is immense. It is altogether appropriate that Comparative Literature should undo the politically monolithized view of Islam that rules the globe today, without compromising the strong unifying ideology potentially alive in that particular cultural formation.[85]

This correlates with my intention to discuss Islam in the context of movement (travel and migration) as a determinant factor of Muslim identity. I ask what kinds of Islam are evoked under transcultural conditions; what roles does Islam take on when it travels to non-Muslim countries or is visited, for men and women and for different generations? Recently, Islam has acquired a primarily negative image in the Western world. The question is therefore also what it means to live as a Muslim in a non-Muslim environment. This seems to be something which is also of concern to Westerners who are confronted with having to identify themselves in relation to Islam. This may be one of the reasons why Islam has become a popular theme in literature; the sheer volume of publications in Europe and the USA speaks for itself.[86] This study will therefore finally ask what the textualizations of Islam say about contemporary German and British societies. Malak has observed that in postcolonialism there is a 'resistance to engage with religion as a key category pertinent to the debate about contemporary neo-colonial reality' (17). This book works against this resistance and makes explicit that Islam *is* part of Europe and its literatures.

85 G. C. Spivak, *Death of a Discipline,* The Wellek Library Lectures in Critical Theory (New York: Columbia University Press, 2003), 87.

86 The Conclusion will point forward to more current publications to demonstrate the ongoing interest in Muslim transcultural writing.

1. Moving with Islam
Islam, Migration and Home: Emine Sevgi Özdamar's *Das Leben ist eine Karawanserei* and Monica Ali's *Brick Lane*

Novels such as Emine Sevgi Özdamar's *Das Leben ist eine Karawanserei hat zwei Türen aus einer kam ich rein aus der anderen ging ich raus* (1992) and Monica Ali's *Brick Lane* (2003) can be categorized as transcultural literature of migration, a literature whose protagonists move between countries, cultures and languages.[1] In their texts, migrant writers discuss a diversity of processes that negotiate identities between the places where migrants come from and the places they go to — or currently live — and related notions such as 'home'. These processes take place in transitional spaces where the migrant translates and interprets cultures. I define migration as the movement of gradual arrival, that is, the process of settling into and the familiarization with a country. It does not lead back to the place of departure. Finding a new place to live depends on processes of coming to terms with unfamiliar phenomena that concern the new place of abode as well as the migrants themselves.

Processes of negotiation and translation play a significant role in Özdamar's and Ali's works. The writers have different backgrounds: Özdamar was born in Turkey where she frequently moved around, but has lived in Germany for almost forty years, first as a *Gastarbeiterin* then as an actor, theatre director and writer, whereas Ali was brought up in the UK. The two writers respectively address the notion of

1 E. S. Özdamar, *Das Leben ist eine Karawanserei hat zwei Türen aus einer kam ich rein aus der anderen ging ich raus: Roman*, 5th edn (Cologne: Kiepenheuer & Witsch, 2003 [1992]). Translations taken from E. S. Özdamar, *Life Is a Caravanserai Has Two Doors I Came In One I Went Out the Other*, trans. L. v. Flotow (London: Middlesex University Press, 2000); M. Ali, *Brick Lane* (London: Black Swan, 2004 [2003]).

finding and defining a home and an identity in new environments within Turkey and then Germany, and in the UK.

Cultural translation plays a vital role in processes of arriving. In this context, cultural translation does not consist of coming to terms with the foreign or unknown by simply applying familiar knowledge systems and thus being able to 'capture' the unknown. This is what ethnographers or travel writers such as V. S. Naipaul in his travel accounts of non-Arab Muslim countries have done. Cultural translation is a learning process by which the migrant characters in the novels translate the unknown or unfamiliar into something understandable. I appropriate the concept of linguistic translation to the translation between cultures, and borrow the idea from Walter Benjamin that in translations 'ergänzt sich [...] die Art des Meinens zum Gemeinten' (14) [the manner of meaning and what is meant complement each other]. Translation transfers not only signifiers of a language but also whole cultural concepts. Furthermore, according to Benjamin, translation is a continuation of the original and transforms it retrospectively (12). As the analysis of the novels will show, migration and subsequent cultural translation influence both the migrant's culture and the 'host' culture, unsettling myths of origins and cultural distinctiveness. It is a mutual transformation process.

I regard translation as — in Gayatri Chakravorty Spivak's words — 'the most intimate act of reading'.[2] The prerequisite of this 'reading' of cultures, then, must be an openness to the Other as well as an openness to permitting change in the self. Yet migrants often employ their 'original' culture, including religion, as a separating device. This idea hints at translation as a way of establishing difference as a means of defining identity. As in linguistic translations, cultural translation processes are based on choices and decisions on what is to be translated and how, which can establish similarities as well as differences. This observation holds true especially for religion. As Spivak points out, '[w]estern feminists have not so far been aware of religion as a cultural instrument rather than a mark of cultural difference' (194). Yet religion is a major component in the transformation process of the identities of many Muslim migrants, and women in particular, which will become apparent in the analysis of the novels.

The migrant's identity is at the centre of translation processes. Identity is not an essential or fixed entity that is defined and natural.

2 G. C. Spivak, 'The Politics of Translation', in *Destabilizing Theory: Contemporary Feminist Debates*, ed. M. Barrett and A. Phillips (Cambridge: Polity, 1992), 181.

In fact, migration and the translation processes it entails emphasize the performative side of identity and the construction of the self in relation to an Other,[3] and thus also bring the historical, constructed nature of identity to the fore. A migrant's identity is largely constructed through their interaction with new discourses (such as languages, cultures, customs) and surroundings. In the context of the novels discussed here, the migrants' identities are a mixture of their constant personal development and choice: Özdamar's and Ali's migrants face frequently changing circumstances (in *Das Leben ist eine Karawanserei*) and new, supposedly fixed circumstances (in *Brick Lane*). Their protagonists must challenge established aspects of their identities and let new cultures influence them. This transformation depends, however, on what they choose to incorporate into their ever-changing identity. Expectations from the migrants' 'home' cultures and roles, including gender roles, also contribute to the establishing of their identity and might limit their openness to the new environment. Furthermore, identity is constructed in the face of the Other, which, for a number of characters in the novels, is represented by the West. The Other is used to create and maintain difference. In whatever way the novels' characters perceive themselves, their identity is an 'identity in transformation' (Chambers, 24), an ongoing identification that is taking place in movement.[4] This concept of identity is not limited to migrants, yet their physical movements make identity transformation processes particularly clear.

Critics often perceive the notion of cultural translation as controversial. As Michaela Wolf points out,

> this claim [that cultures can be 'translated'] is problematic not only because it presupposes the existence of stable cultural units which can be transferred between an 'original' and a 'target' culture, but also because in the final analysis such a translation turns out to be an ethnographic operation. (182)

3 See Judith Butler's analysis of performativity as a major factor in the construction of identity in, for example, *Gender Trouble: Feminism and the Subversion of Identity*, 10th anniversary edn (New York: Routledge, 1999 [1990]), and *Bodies That Matter: On the Discursive Limits of 'Sex'* (New York: Routledge, 1993); see Jaques Lacan on the self-Other relation, as discussed in his *Écrits* (Paris: Éditions du Seuil, 1966).

4 Cf. Bhabha, in J. Rutherford, 'The Third Space: Interview with Homi Bhabha', in, *Identity: Community, Culture, Difference*, ed. J. Rutherford (London: Lawrence & Wishart, 1990), 211.

I interpret the coming to terms of a migrant with their new surroundings as an 'ethnographic operation', but one which is different from that of a travel writer who visits and then leaves a country. Özdamar and Ali create 'alternative ethnographers': their protagonists are watching and examining their surroundings intensively, yet without occupying the privileged position of being able to return to a comfortable home. Migrants might perceive the unfamiliar with astonished eyes but, unlike 'travellers of leisure', they are forced to accept and incorporate it into their new version of home, or else they will feel excluded. However, their translations are initially a one-way operation: at the beginning, they only know the 'language' they have brought with them. They have to base their translation process, the making sense of the new, on guessing and finding a meaning while simultaneously learning the signifiers of the new 'language'. Wolf assumes that 'meanings are no longer perceived as being roughly the same across different cultures, but as something to be represented in codes and symbols linked to the translator's and the ethnographer's subjectivity and background' (185). This also applies to the novels' characters who are constantly deciphering everything new by initially trying to read it with their familiar codes. They soon have to learn that 'other' codes need to be considered as well, which then opens the space for genuine interaction with the new environment and thus a transcultural experience.

According to Wolf, 'translation [is] also a place where cultures merge and create new spaces' (189). This reminds us of what Homi Bhabha refers to as *Third Spaces* where migrants raise other, non-conventional voices and express linguistic and cultural diversity, heteroglossia and hybridity. Although Bhabha acknowledges the fact that hybridity 'is not a third term that resolves the tension between two cultures [...] in a dialectical play of "recognition"',[5] his perception of hybridity suggests that cultures are easily separable. He therefore reaches the conclusion that 'it is the "inter" — the cutting edge of translation and negotiation, the *in-between* space — that carries the burden of the meaning of culture' ('The Commitment to Theory', 38, italics Bhabha's). The 'inter' also 'uncovers relations of power inherent in any process of translation' (Wolf, 187). According to this understanding of cultural interaction, the 'host' culture dominates the translation process for migrants, as this is the public culture they have to settle in; in their private lives, their own culture will

5 H. K. Bhabha, 'Signs Taken for Wonders: Questions of Ambivalence and Authority Under a Tree Outside Delhi, May 1817', in Bhabha, *The Location of Culture*, 113–14.

probably play a more significant role. This power dynamics between cultures is changing, most obviously among the generations and sexes. The *in-between* is a temporal construction, in which cultures are constantly subject to new interpretations and negotiations.[6] However, the concept of the 'inter' appears useful for translation processes, as Doris Bachmann-Medick points out, 'cultures themselves do not appear as "original lifeworks" but as translations in the sense that they are already the results of translation activities'.[7] In this sense, cultures are translatable:[8] as Wolf rightly asserts, cultures are not absolute; they cannot construct an 'inter', an *in-between* space; they are by definition transcultural.

Transcultural concerns are at the centre of both *Das Leben ist eine Karawanserei* and *Brick Lane*. Emine Sevgi Özdamar undermines the idea of a homogeneous German culture by building on the ambiguities caused by cultural translation. Not only does this relate to the content of her texts but also to her style and specifically her peculiar German.[9] By questioning set definitions of what it means to be from a particular place, she explores her linguistic and cultural roots and 'routes',[10] and creates transitional spaces where she lets the various voices that have made her a transcultural writer come to the fore. Her adult-first-person-narrator remembers her younger self's migration within Turkey from where she moved on: to Germany. And it is the German language that enables her to capture her Turkish past in words. This migration on a further, linguistic level suggests a linguistic detachment from the events narrated and points to the protagonist's migration to her German Turkish self.

Monica Ali addresses the question of multiculturalism centrally in her writing. Her background is different from Özdamar's: Ali was born in Bangladesh but grew up in the UK. She felt the impact of cultural outsiderhood at a younger age than Özdamar, who first

6 H. K. Bhabha, 'DissemiNation: Time, Narrative and the Margins of the Modern Nation', in Bhabha, *The Location of Culture*, 148.

7 D. Bachmann-Medick, 'Einleitung: Übersetzung als Repräsentation fremder Kulturen', in *Übersetzung als Repräsentation fremder Kulturen*, ed. D. Bachmann-Medick (Berlin: Schmidt, 1997), 14, qtd in Wolf, 186; Wolf's translation.

8 By contrast, Bhabha argues that 'the migrant culture of the "in-between", the minority position, dramatizes the activity of culture's untranslatability' (H. K. Bhabha, 'How Newness Enters the World: Postmodern Space, Postcolonial Times and the Trials of Cultural Translation', in Bhabha, *The Location of Culture*, 224). I do not agree with Bhabha.

9 This aspect will be discussed in Chapter 4.

10 S. Hall, 'Introduction: Who Needs "Identity"?', in *Questions of Cultural Identity*, ed. S. Hall and P. du Gay (London: Sage, 1996), 4.

came to Germany when she was nineteen. Her experience as someone with a 'different' background might suggest a more conscious way of dealing with the foreign. In her novel, Ali examines alternative ways of being British. Migration becomes one of the major factors of the identity formation of her characters, the secluded Bangladeshi community in Tower Hamlets in East London.

***

As Annette Wierschke puts it in a question directed to Özdamar, 'zu Hause ist für Sie im Zug oder auf dem Weg' (*Schreiben als Selbstbehauptung,* 259) [for you being at home means being on a train or en route]. Özdamar's novel *Das Leben ist eine Karawanserei* depicts such a life 'on a train'. The caravanserai, a motel-type inn for travellers in desert regions of Asia and North Africa which traditionally has no doors, serves as a metaphor here.[11] Not only does the book open and end with the protagonist literally being-on-a-train, it also describes the metaphorical journey of a girl who finds herself between 'languages and cultures, Arabic Islam and Western-oriented Turkey',[12] and social constructions of gender. On the one hand, the novel is an unusual form of *Bildungsroman* which draws the picture of a heterogeneous and culturally diverse Turkey through the eyes of its protagonist who is a child; on the other, it is told retrospectively by a first-person narrator, a German-language Turkish migrant in Germany. According to David Horrocks, Özdamar's

> young narrator's initiation into a particular culture and community consists to a large extent of [...] [a] linguistic education. [...] By virtue of its being written in German, and thus primarily for a German readership, it also — whether the author consciously intended it or not — functions as a novel of education and initiation in a second sense. [...] It takes the reader into an unfamiliar world and affords him or her the vicarious experience of learning something of its language,

11 See Seyhan, *Writing Outside the Nation,* 142: 'The title of the book is a Turkish proverb. Caravansaries were large inns built around courtyards to accommodate caravans travelling on the long commerce routes through the Middle East and Asia. The proverb defines an individual life both as a brief sojourn on earth and a station of an infinite journey. It suggests parallels both with Özdamar's life and the history she narrates'.

12 S. Fischer and M. McGowan, 'From *Pappkoffer* to Pluralism: On the Development of Migrant Writing in the German Federal Republic', in *Turkish Culture in German Society Today,* ed. D. Horrocks and E. Kolinsky, 17.

its customs and its values just as the young central character herself learns them.[13]

In her culturally and linguistically diverse environment as found in the novel with its transcultural subject matter and its German narrative voice and as associated with the multilingual author Özdamar, who has experienced migration and, thereby, transculturality herself, the child heroine is trying to find a place and space where she can grow up. This theme, the girl's 'Binnenmigration' [inner migration] between various places within Turkey,[14] is already introduced by herself speaking from inside her sixteen-year-old mother's womb. They are on their way from Istanbul to Malatya in Anatolia, the place of her birth. Due to the father's constant unemployment and debts, the family — consisting of grandmother Ayşe, father Mustafa, mother Fatma, elder brother Ali, the heroine, whose name the reader never learns, younger brother Orhan and little sister Schwarze Rose [Black Rose] — are forced to move around Turkey. They stop in Istanbul, Yenişehir (where the heroine starts school), Bursa (where she enters puberty), Ankara and the outskirts of Ankara close to the steppe, and finally again Istanbul, from where she takes a train to Germany to start a new life as a *Gastarbeiterin*. Home as a form of stability is only provided by the family and their — partly Muslim and partly Western — customs and traditions (see Wierschke, *Schreiben als Selbstbehauptung*, 183). Özdamar shows the closeness of the family within their peripatetic lifestyle already at the beginning of the novel:

> Dem Tod gestohlen in Anatolien von einer himmelaugigen Frau namens Ayşe, saß ich vor einem Photographen, mit meinem Vater, meiner Mutter, meinem zwei Jahre älteren Bruder auf den Knien dieser himmelaugigen Frau, meiner Großmutter, Mutter meines Vaters aus Kapadokia, am Meer in Ĭstanbul, ließ mich photographieren [...] (ÖLK 15).[15]

> [Stolen away from death in Anatolia by a sky-eyed women named Ayşe, I sat facing a photographer with my father, my mother and

13 D. Horrocks, 'In Search of a Lost Past: A Reading of Emine Sevgi Özdamar's Novel *Das Leben ist eine Karawanserei, hat zwei Türen, aus einer kam ich rein, aus der anderen ging ich raus*', in *Turkish Culture in German Society Today*, ed. D. Horrocks and E. Kolinsky, 27.

14 M. E. Brunner, 'Die Türkei, ein Mutterland — Deutschland, ein Bitterland? Emine Sevgi Özdamars Buch "Das Leben ist eine Karawanserei"', *Info DaF*, 26.6 (December 1999), 562.

15 Throughout *Das Leben ist eine Karawanserei* and *Life Is a Caravanserai* 'Istanbul' is spelled 'Ĭstanbul'; the original Turkish spelling is 'İstanbul'.

> my two year older brother on the lap of this sky-eyed women, my grandmother, the mother of my father from Kapadokia, at the sea in İstanbul, letting myself be photographed [...]. (ÖLC 6)]

This first impression here is that of a traditional extended Muslim family whose bonds are extremely strong. However, there are other, more prominent factors than religion that define their kinship. Their migrations within Turkey make them more aware of their closeness. They perceive customs and traditions derived from their country's heritage as by-products rather than as determining factors. Turkey officially has a different attitude towards Islam from other Muslim countries. With his westernizing reforms in the 1920s, Mustafa Kemal Atatürk, the founder of modern Turkey and the first president of the Turkish Republic, forced upon his people a more liberal attitude towards religion and its outward symbols such as headscarves. On her family's journeys, what the heroine discovers is not a stable concept, but alternative ways of living based on her transcultural experiences.

Özdamar portrays Turkey as a heterogeneous place and, according to Wierschke, explores differences between eastern and western Turkey, and between urban and rural life (184). Wierschke continues:

> Istanbul definiert sich in Abgrenzung zur ländlichen anatolischen Provinz. Istanbuler Werte fungieren als Standard, an denen Anatolien, seine Bevölkerung und Sprache gemessen wird. Als Negativ ist Anatolien genau das Gegenstück, genau 'das Andere': das, was Istanbul nicht ist und nicht sein will.
>
> [Istanbul defines itself in opposition to the rural Anatolian countryside. The values of Istanbul function as the standard against which Anatolia, its population and language are measured. Anatolia as negative is precisely the counterpart, 'the Other' which Istanbul is not and does not wish to be].

In this context, Anatolia is often associated with a more traditional lifestyle. (Interestingly, the majority of guest workers who moved to Germany came from the countryside rather than cities.) The heroine experiences this dichotomy when she starts school in Istanbul. As a child who was born in rural Anatolia and thus an outsider she suffers discrimination and has to face prejudices that are based on her origin.

> Ich ging in die Schule. Die Lehrerin fragte alle nach ihrem Namen und danach, wo sie geboren waren. Ich sagte: 'Ich bin in Anatolien in Malatya geboren'. Die Lehrerin sagte: 'Dann bist du Kurdin, du hast einen Schwanz an deinem Arsch'. Dann lachte sie, alle anderen

lachten auch und nannten mich: 'Kurdin mit Schwanz'. Ab dann saß ich ganz hinten. (ÖLK 37)

[I started school. The teacher asked everyone for their name and where they were born. I said, 'I was born in Anatolia, in Malatya'. The teacher said, 'Then you're a Kurd, you have a tail growing on your ass. She laughed, all the others laughed too, and called me 'Kurd with a tail'. From then on I sat at the back. (ÖLC 23)]

Not only is the girl made to feel different and laughed at, but she is also spatially divided from the other children who have learned to share the teacher's (and society's) prejudices (and who do not have the migratory experiences the heroine has). As the adult-narrator reflects on this incident in German, she can be more critical about the political situation in Turkey in the 1950s and she can therefore retrospectively admit that this kind of education has a major influence on her. The heroine begins to internalize this discrimination by increasingly perceiving her birth place Malatya as an 'alien' place: 'Die Stadt war ein anderer Planet. Sie stand viel näher an der Sonne als İstanbul' (ÖLK 48) ['The city was another planet. It was much closer to the sun than İstanbul' (ÖLC 32)]. As part of this changing attitude towards her origin, she, taking a leaf of her mother's book, yearns for acceptance in Istanbul, the modern metropolis, an aspiration reflected in the wish to speak 'pure' Turkish. The influence of her background seems to be stronger than she had imagined. An example of this inner dialectics is the change in the girl's speech which triggers a change in her identity. After a holiday with her grandfather in Malatya she returns to Istanbul speaking an 'impure' Turkish exemplified by the different pronunciation of the significant word 'mother':

Ich öffnete meine Arme und schrie: 'Mutter!' […] Meine Mutter stand mir gegenüber, aber ich konnte sie nicht umarmen. Zwischen uns stand eine Mauer aus dem fremden Dialekt, den ich aus dieser anatolischen Stadt unter meiner Zunge mitgebracht hatte. Meine Mutter sagte: 'Sprich nicht so, du mußt wieder istanbultürkisch, sauberes Türkisch sprechen, verstehst du, in zwei Tagen fängt die Schule wieder an. Wenn du so anatolisch sprichst, werden alle zu dir Bauer sagen, verstehst du. So sprich doch istanbulisch'. Ich machte wieder meine Arme auf, sagte: 'Mutter-Anacuğum'. Meine Mutter sagte: 'Sag: Anneciğim! Nicht Anacuğum'. Ich sagte: 'Anacuğum'. […] Die beiden Wörter fochten in der Mitte des Zimmers […]. Meine Großmutter kam, sah dieses Fechten zwischen 'Anacuğum' und 'Anneciğim', sagte: 'İstanbuler Wörter lassen keinen süßen Geschmack auf der Zunge, die Wörter sind wie kranke Äste, sie zerbrechen hintereinander'. […] Großmutter sagte: 'Ja, sie sagt Anagı', was auch

> in ihrem Dorfdialekt in Kapadokia 'Mutter' heißt. Ihre Anagı, meine Anacuğum standen nebeneinander gegenüber İstanbuler Anneciğim. [...] So mußte ich [...] Strafe zahlen. Für meine Wörter, die ich aus der Stadt, wo meine Mutter und ich geboren wurden, mitgebracht hatte. So schnitten mir İstanbuler Messer mein Anacuğum rasch zu Anneciğim. (ÖLK 53–54)
>
> [I opened my arms and yelled, 'Mother!' [...] My mother stood facing me, but I couldn't put my arms around her. Between us stood a wall made of the strange dialect I had brought back under my tongue from the Anatolian city. My mother said, 'Don't talk like that, you have to speak İstanbul Turkish, clean Turkish, again, understand, school starts in two days. If you use that Anatolian dialect, they'll all call you peasant, understand? So speak İstanbul Turkish'. I opened my arms again, said, 'Mother-Anacuğum'. My mother said, 'Say Anneciğim! Not Anacuğum'. I said, 'Anacuğum'. [...] The two words were locked in battle in the middle of the room [...]. My grandmother came, saw the sparring between 'Anacuğum' and 'Anneciğim', said, 'İstanbul words don't leave a sweet taste on the tongue, the words are like diseased branches, they break one after the other'. [...] Grandmother said, 'Yes, she's saying Anagı,' which in her Kapadokia village dialect also meant mother. Her Anagı and my Anacuğum stood side by side across from the İstanbul Anneciğim. [...] By evening I'd paid three lira [...] in fines. For the words I brought back from the city where my mother and I were born. That's how İstanbul knives quickly trimmed my Anacuğum to Anneciğim. (ÖLC 35–36)]

The differences in the pronunciation of the word 'mother' signal a distancing from her familial background, personified by her mother, though not from her origin, symbolized by the Anatolian dialect she has adopted. This 'linguistic gulf' triggers the heroine's search for something else that is more in tune with herself (Horrocks, 28). Her longing results in her ultimate departure from Turkey at the end of the novel. In Germany, she will add another dimension to her identity: the German language. This gulf between what the adult-narrator remembers (her Turkish migrations and upbringing) and how she can talk about it (in German) reflects the protagonist's multifaceted, indeed complicated identity. Back in Turkey, the search for her identity is infused with confusion regarding other people's perceptions of the heroine's origin. In Yenişehir, for instance, she is seen as the clever girl from Istanbul. She experiences how perceptions along with people change as she grows up among several different 'Turkeys'; this lifestyle turns her into an adaptable migrant. The narrator lets the heroine personify 'home' as a concept that comprises a variety of cultural, linguistic and religious influences, and is constantly re-created: she is able to mix the different versions of Turkey, which she gets to know on her journeys, according to her desires and needs. This is the Turkey that she will take to Germany. The girl's transcultural experience in Turkey takes her beyond national borders and paves the way for the young woman's migration to Germany, which then allows the narrator to tell the heroine's story from a geographical, emotional and thus critical distance in German.

Özdamar's narrator demonstrates that Turkey is as diverse as its people are. The family serves as a comfort zone among the different 'Turkeys' they encounter when travelling around. Their bonds are, on the one hand, based on the 'Möglichkeit multipler Identitäten' (Wierschke, *Schreiben als Selbstbehauptung*, 186) [possibility of [having] multiple identities], yet, on the other, these possibilities also contribute to the heroine's separation from her familial origin. She creates a home for and within herself, a home which seems to be dependent simply on her choice of items of Turkish cultures that shall contribute to her identity, which she will continue to shape in Germany.

In *Brick Lane*, Ali portrays an immigrant family's life that, at first sight, does not seem to be based on transcultural experiences but rather on a longing for a home that is spatially situated elsewhere and belongs to the past. Out of this feeling of having lost their home, the majority of the novel's characters re-create a home, a Bangladeshi diaspora, in East London. According to Douglas Robinson,

> 'Diaspora' is a way of imagining border culture on a global scale, groups and individuals dealing with cultural differences on a daily basis, in the communities where they live and work, intermarrying, mixing cultures and races, growing up bilingual and trilingual and resisting (or succumbing to) pressures to become (or to pretend to become) monolingual. A diasporic culture is a global culture that is forever displaced, in exile, living among strangers that become the familiar characters of our homes and places of work.[16]

The characters in *Brick Lane* predominantly live a displaced life and perceive the UK, or rather Tower Hamlets, as an alien place. However, as they are constantly being made aware of their cultural differences, they start to reinvent this new home, London, according to their old home imported from Bangladesh. As a vast number of the population in Tower Hamlets is monolingual, yet in a different sense from the one Robinson describes — the women in particular tend

16 D. Robinson, *Translation and Empire: Postcolonial Theories Explained*, Translation Theories Explained, 4 (Manchester: St. Jerome, 1997), 29.

to remain monocultural based on their Bangladeshi heritage — their existence is determined by the 'going home syndrome' that reinforces their dislocation and sense of belonging elsewhere.

> 'This is another disease that afflicts us,' said the doctor. 'I call it the Going Home Syndrome. Do you know what that means?' He addressed himself to Nazneen.
>
> She felt a heat on the back of her neck and formed words that did not leave her mouth.
>
> 'It is natural,' said Chanu. 'These people are basically peasants and they miss the land. The pull of the land is stronger even than the pull of blood'.
>
> 'And when they have saved enough they will get on an aeroplane and go?'
>
> 'They don't ever really leave home. Their bodies are here but their hearts are back there. And anyway, look how they live: just recreating the villages here'. (ABL 32)

Not only does the belief in eventually returning to Bangladesh and the allegedly temporary re-creation of the migrants' old lives in new surroundings contribute to their separation from other communities, they also open up a gap between 'inside', the tower blocks as home, and 'outside', Brick Lane as part of the 'larger outside' London. This gap is reinforced by the gender construction of the Muslim woman who is stereotypically confined to her home and does not venture to leave it. However, Ali challenges this stereotype by letting Nazneen, partly accidentally, partly intentionally, leave her familiar space.

> Nazneen pulled the end of her sari over her head. [...] She walked until she reached the big crossroads and waited at the end of the kerb while the traffic roared from one direction and then the next. Twice she stepped into the road and drew back again. To get to the other side of the street without being hit by a car was like walking out in the monsoon and hoping to dodge the raindrops. A space opened before her. God is great, said Nazneen under her breath. She ran. (ABL 54)

Nazneen's initially timid, then more courageous, crossing of the literal boundaries between inside and outside opens up a number of possibilities for her. She learns that 'home' does not need to be reduced to her flat and a longing for Bangledesh — even though she associates the crossing of the road with the monsoon, with which she is familiar from her country of origin —, but that there is a world outside the housing estate. This adventure also enables the writer Ali to question ideas related to a 'good', traditional (Muslim) way of life, and a 'bad', Western (non-religious) way of life. Still greatly attached to her religious identity – Nazneen interprets the opening of the space before her as God's help and uses the expression of a religious Muslim to thank God – she nonetheless experiences fragments of a life that is unlike her previous experiences and will contribute to a new, transcultural understanding of 'home'.

This tension between Muslim and non-Muslim increasingly destabilizes the notion of any clear space that can be referred to as 'home'. With the appearance of Karim, a young neighbour with whom she falls in love, Nazneen is confused as to what 'right' behaviour is. This confusion is intensified by the fact that Karim gradually turns into an 'Islamic fundamentalist'. Being a responsible wife and mother, Nazneen feels torn not only between her family and her lover, but also between what is right in God's eyes and what is to be rejected.

> She was back on the tightrope that stretched between her husband and children, and this time the wind was high and tormenting.
>
> And there was Karim.
>
> The horror came to her now. [...]
>
> 'God sees everything. He knows every hair on your head'. Amma squatted on her haunches in the corner. (ABL 321–22)

For Nazneen, God is always present as an omniscient authority. This knowledge is based on how she was brought up, which is intensified by her mother's omnipresence in her life. Though not in London, she is almost haunting her. Thus, the place where they live, their home, is determined by what the family brought with them from Bangladesh – in terms of culture and religious upbringing. Religion is an entity that provides stability in this, especially for Nazneen, confusing world.

> She picked up the Holy Qur'an from the high shelf that Chanu, under duress, had especially built. She made her intention as fervently as possible, seeking refuge from Satan with fists clenched and fingernails digging into her palms. Then she selected a page at random and began to read.
>
> *To God belongs all that the heavens and the earth contain. We exhort you [...] to fear God. [...] God is self-sufficient and worthy of praise.*
>
> The words calmed her stomach and she was pleased. [...] She was composed. Nothing could bother her. Only God, if he chose to. [...] How would it sound in Arabic? More lovely even than in Bengali, she supposed, for those were the actual words of God. (ABL 19–20, italics Ali's)

Islam serves as a calming device for Nazneen, who frequently takes refuge in reading the Qur'an. Chanu does not seem to feel the need for religion. Although he built a shelf especially for the Holy Book, he built it 'under duress'. The reader cannot be sure, but the novel seems to suggest that Nazneen, who does not have a life beyond the immediate surroundings of her flat, made Chanu built the shelf in order to have a home in the form of religion. By contrast religion is a predominantly unconscious part of Chanu's everyday life, which also takes place outside the flat, and does not have the same calming effect for him as it has for his wife. Asking Chanu to build a shelf for the Qur'an is one of the few occasions when Nazneen is the more active one of the couple, especially at the beginning of their marriage. As she longs for comfort, she turns the Qur'an, which is placed on the shelf, into a touchable home. Yet 'home' is also defined on another, indirect level: Arabic, the original language of the Qur'an, is comforting, maybe precisely because Nazneen is familiar with it yet does not understand it. Ali therefore portrays 'home' as something that does not need to be fully grasped; it is created by 'sounds without meaning':[17] unfamiliar elements, such as the Arabic language, of an otherwise familiar terrain, such as Islam, can also leave gaps of understanding that nevertheless contribute to a calming idea of 'home'.

Both Özdamar and Ali show that migration challenges established perceptions of 'home': with the arrival in a new country, imported cultural and religious values are challenged by new cultures and their interpretations of religion. Migrants are forced to re-examine their perceptions which contributes to a new, transcultural understanding of 'home'. Since the story of Özdamar's heroine is narrated in German, the establishing of a 'home' in Turkey is even more critically commented on than in Ali's novel. Questions of language can also reveal the close link between transcultural and religious experiences.

***

For a migrant, language is one of the dominant factors for negotiating an identity. Their mother tongue can become an object of, on the one hand, deliberate differentiation from the Other (the country migrated to) and, on the other, a comforting inclusion of people from

17 J. Kristeva, *Desire in Language: A Semiotic Approach to Literature and Art*, ed. L. S. Roudiez, trans. T. Gora *et al.* (New York: Columbia University Press, 1980), 133 (originally publ. as *Σημειωτιχή: Recherches pur une sémanalyse* (Paris: Éditions du Seuil, 1969) and *Polylogue* (Paris: Éditions du Seuil, 1977).

the same country in the foreign environment. For Muslim migrants, Arabic plays an additionally significant role: this language may be the mother tongue for some (though not for the protagonists in the two novels under consideration here), but gives access for all to their religion and other parts of the Muslim world, and contributes to a culturally familiar home.

Özdamar's protagonist pays particular attention to Arabic as part of her Islamic heritage, but views it primarily as a means of self-exploration and not differentiation. As Wierschke points out, 'Sprache [ist] gleichzeitig Ausdruck von Fremdheit und Mittel zur Identitätsfindung' (*Schreiben als Selbstbehauptung*, 163) [language [is] expression of the 'foreign' as well as means of finding one's identity]. Özdamar's narrator expresses the foreign nature of Arabic primarily in relation to religion. Living in an officially secular country (Turkey), the heroine encounters Islam above all through her grandparents yet also through formal instruction. Although she has contact with texts and rituals that are based on Arabic, they remain unconsciously internalized until much later in her life. She thus finds herself caught in two dichotomies from an early age: firstly, she becomes familiar with Arabic to some extent, yet does not actually understand the language, and, secondly, she experiences both her grandparents' religiosity and her parents' secularism. Her mother, who grew up under the direct influence of Atatürk's reforms and also supports the Republicans, sends her children to Qur'an lessons nonetheless.

> Meine Mutter schickte mich und meinen Bruder Ali zur Moschee zum Koranunterricht. Sie sagte, arabische Schrift muß man lernen, um Allahs Gedanken aus dem Koran zu lesen. Meine Mutter selbst konnte nicht die arabische Schrift lesen und schreiben. [...] Ich kannte auch nur lateinische Buchstaben, aber mein Großvater konnte nicht mit lateinischen Buchstaben schreiben. Er konnte in arabischer Schrift schreiben. Wenn meine Großmutter schreiben und lesen gelernt hätte, könnte sie auch nur in arabischer Schrift schreiben. Ich dachte, wenn also mein Großvater Ahmet und meine Großmutter Ayşe stumme und taube Menschen wären und uns nur mit Schrift etwas erzählen könnten, hätte ich sie nie gekannt. So hätte ich heute keine Großmutter, Großvater. (ÖLK 69)

> [My mother sent me and my brother Ali to the mosque for instruction in the Koran. She said you have to learn Arabic script to read Allah's thoughts in the Koran. My mother couldn't read or write Arabic script herself. [...] I only knew Latin letters of the alphabet but my grandfather could not write with Latin letters. He knew how to write in Arabic. If my grandmother had learnt how to read and write, she would only have known Arabic too. I thought, if Grandfather Ahmet

> and Grandmother Ayşe were deaf and dumb and could only talk to us in writing, I would never have known either of them. And I wouldn't have a grandmother or a grandfather today. (ÖLC 49)]

In this example, the girl clearly connects the Arabic script with Turkey's past and with her grandparents, who lead a more traditional, religious life, as representatives of it. On this personal level, the text also criticizes Atatürk's westernizing reforms that denied Turkey's heterogeneity: the protagonist would not have a personal history if her grandparents were not able to communicate it to her orally. This should be read with the knowledge that until the mid-1920s Turkish was written in Arabic script. Since Atatürk's westernizing reforms Turkish has been written in Latin script, which meant a break with the literary and cultural history recorded in Arabic script.

Interestingly, her mother gives religious reasons for her decision to send her children to the Qur'an lessons: she wants them to be able to 'read Allah's thoughts'. However, in the light of the whole novel, which reveals the protagonist's parents as supporters of the Republicans, the mother's explanation comes across as a way of avoiding giving children a complicated reason based on complex ideas of a country's past and loss. The child sees through her mother's explanation and comments on Turkey's change of alphabet and its influence on her relationship with her grandparents. The text does not state clearly whether the mother is simply conforming to pressure to instruct her children in religion: at this point, the family lives in one of Turkey's religious centres, the city of Yenişehir, and the desire to send the children to the Qur'an lessons dwindles when they move to bigger and more secular cities. Outside pressure often makes religion part of everyday life, a ritual rather than a spiritual experience. Yet the mother's decision to expose her children to Arabic (even if this is only done to a limited extent) gives the impression that she feels the same rupture with her country's past as her daughter — she was not allowed to learn Arabic as a child, after all — and she wants her children at least to understand part of Turkey's cultural and religious history. The protagonist's parents' generation is excluded from any knowledge of Arabic. At least their children have limited access to this heritage, which is the result partly of a more tolerant attitude towards Islam in the Turkey of the 1950s,[18] and partly of the older generations' wish to make their (grand-)children aware of their

18 D. Shankland, *Islam and Society in Turkey* (Huntington: Eothen, 1999), 36–40. Although the Democratic Party (DP) did not lessen the significance of Atatürk and his secularist reforms for Turkey, their victory in the 1950 election introduced a

cultural and religious roots. From this perspective, the protagonist feels closer to her grandparents than to her parents, as the former provide access to a part of the Turkish child's identity that her parents will never be able to provide.

For the child, learning Arabic is a worldly rather than a spiritual experience. Trying to encourage her granddaughter to pronounce the Arabic words, the grandmother explains how Muhammad delivered God's first messages with the help of the angel Gabriel. After his first revelations Muhammad did not deliver new Qur'an verses for three years,[19] but the girl does not appear to know that this interval was a time of testing for Muhammad. She links this break with his lack of knowledge of the Arabic language and does not seem to realize that Arabic was in fact Muhammad's mother tongue and that there might have been other, spiritually-related reasons that brought the delivery of God's messages to a temporary halt. Instead, the girl compares herself with Muhammad: according to her childlike perception of learning a language, they share the experience of learning Arabic as a process that drains their strength.

As knowledge of the country's history slips away and only survives in the older generation (by storytelling, teaching their grandchildren Arabic and telling them about Turkey's history), the girl must use a lot of strength to preserve it by learning Arabic. Although formal instruction in the Arabic language and the reading of the Qur'an, which is also associated with religious education, contributes to the younger generation's understanding of Islam, this part of their heritage is hard to grasp as it is barely consciously present for the novel's younger characters, even when they are living in a more religious environment such as in Yenişehir. The girl observes: 'Es war das arabische Alphabetbuch, ein dünnes Heft, aus sehr armem Papier' (ÖLK 73) ['It was the book with the Arabic alphabet, a thin booklet of very poor paper' (ÖLC 52)]. It is only with the help of her grandparents, and her grandmother in particular, that traditions based on Turkey's Arab Islamic heritage are handed down to a generation that is not automatically opposed to them as the middle generation under Atatürk's direct influence still seems to be.

As this generational split is common in many societies, it is not surprising that the girl's upbringing in relation to Arabic is largely influenced by her grandmother. The role of Arabic in the heroine's

more open and tolerant attitude towards Islam. This pro-Islamic party successfully 'forg[ed] an alliance between Islam, business and secularism' (40).

19 R. Waris Maqsood, *Islam*, new edn (London: Hodder Education, 2003 [1994]), 7.

life comes to the fore particularly in its everyday use. Expressions such as *Maşallah* [whatever God wishes] and *İnşallah* [God willing] are customary rather than fully comprehended. Hardly any of the characters know what these phrases actually mean, and the girl needs to look them up. For example, the monotonous repetition of the phrase *Bismillâhirahmanirrahim* [In the name of God, the Compassionate, the Merciful], which opens every sura of the Qur'an, symbolizes this abstract familiarity with her heritage. It is uttered as part of the daily routine or even functions as a talisman later in the protagonist's life when the articulation of this word prevents a God-fearing man from raping her:[20]

> Großmutter sprach diese arabischen Wörter, die wie eine Kamelkarawane hintereinander liefen, in meine Augen guckend, in ihrem Kapadokia-Dorfdialekt. Die Kamelkarawane sammelte sich in meinem Mund, ich sprach die Gebete mit Großmutter, so hatten wir zwei Kamelkarawanen, ihre Kamele, die größer waren als meine, nahmen meine vor ihre Beine und brachten meinen Kamelen das Laufen bei. Beim Sitzen wackelten wir auch wie Kamele, und ich sprach:
>
> *'Bismillâhirahmanirrahim*
>
> [...]
>
> *Amin'*.
>
> Ich wußte nicht, was diese Wörter sagten, vielleicht Großmutter Ayşe auch nicht. Das Wort Bismillâhirahmanirrahim kam aus den Mündern von vielen Menschen. (ÖLK 55-56, italics Özdamar's)
>
> [Looking into my eyes and speaking her Kapadokia village dialect, Grandmother spoke Arabic words that followed each other like a caravan of camels. The caravan of camels collected in my mouth, I spoke the prayers with Grandmother, and so we had two caravans of camels, her camels which were larger than mine, placed them in front, and taught my camels to walk. Sitting there, we swayed like camels too, and I said,
>
> 'Bismillâhirahmanirrahim
>
> [...]

20 This incident happens in Özdamar's subsequent novel *Die Brücke vom Goldenen Horn* (Cologne: Kiepenheuer & Witsch, 2002 [1998]), translated as *The Bridge of the Golden Horn*, trans. M. Chalmers (London: Serpent's Tail, 2007). The three novels *Das Leben ist eine Karawanserei, Die Brücke vom Goldenen Horn* and *Seltsame Sterne starren zur Erde* [*Strange Stars Stare towards Earth*]: *Wedding – Pankow 1976/77* (Cologne: Kiepenheuer & Witsch, 2004 [2003]) constitute a trilogy. The protagonists of the three novels can be regarded as one person as the novels outline the life and development of a Turkish girl, then young woman in Turkey and Germany.

> Amin'.
> I didn't know what these words meant, maybe grandmother Ayşe didn't know either. But the word bismillâhirahmanirrahim came from the mouths of many people. (ÖLC 37–38)]

From her naïve point of view, the girl translates the Arabic words into pictures, a caravan of camels. Her translations bear a resemblance to the Arabic calligraphy that she is probably familiar with from visits to the mosque or illustrations in books. Her grandmother serves as a teacher: her bigger camels (her spoken Arabic words) teach her granddaughter's camels how to walk (how to pronounce the Arabic words). As this process takes place, the bond between grandmother and granddaughter grows stronger, in a similar way as Arabic expressions 'serv[e] in a quasi-ritualistic fashion to bind a community together' (Horrocks, 26). Furthermore, these expressions retain 'something of that submission to God's will that is central to the whole notion of Islam' (26). Although Islam does not play a central role any more in a 'modern' family like the protagonist's, it is still always present, if not fully comprehended, in language, which signifies an unconscious rather than a conscious perception of Islam, something which holds true of many cultures and religions in the same way.

The repeated pronunciation of Arabic words as part of a religious ritual draws attention to the protagonist's 'emphasis on sound rather than meaning'.[21] The association of those sounds and events with memories connected with the praying with her grandmother are more important than the actual meaning of the Arabic words. This perception of Arabic will change as the girl grows older and wishes to attach meaning to the abstractly familiar Arabic words. In *Das Leben ist eine Karawanserei*, the girl connotes the Arabic language with familiarity, even an emotional home represented by her grandmother, rather than with religious significance, which will never play a major part in the protagonist's life. As this emotional security is captured in German, the narrator provides a 'translated view' on the girl's relation to her grandmother. German is her means of reflection and memory, and helps create the protagonist's emotional home in the first place. It seems that with linguistic distance the narrator can express both criticism on the Turkey she grew up in, its politics and treatment of heritage and otherness, and emotional attachment to the people who played a positive part in the protagonist's upbringing.

21 S. Bird, *Women Writers and National Identity: Bachmann, Duden, Özdamar* (Cambridge: Cambridge University Press, 2003), 188.

Overall, rituals carried out in Arabic automatically imply a religious meaning for the oldest generation but, due to the state's increased secular influence particularly in the early days of the Turkish Republic, hardly any meaning for the youngest (or middle) generations. The novel's youngest generation, exemplified by the heroine, serves as a linking factor, a translator between the generations older than them and thus between Turkey's lost past and more recent past, culminating in its predominantly secular present: the girl approaches a more conscious dealing with her customs in the form of prayers that her grandmother teaches her. Yet she continues to perceive the Arabic words of prayer as a sensual experience rather than as expressions that carry religious meaning. Thus, Özdamar critically examines the 'unbridgeable gap in cultural continuity' left behind by Atatürk's attempts to secularize Turkey linguistically.[22]

Turkish expressions also hold an integral position in the everyday life of the heroine. It is chiefly the 'idiom used when one person suggests something and another responds in the affirmative' (Horrocks, 27), 'Tamam mı' [OK?] — 'Tamam' [OK!], that plays a vital role in communication, especially between the heroine and her brother Ali: 'Wenn Ali Tamam mı sagte, sagte ich immer Tamam' (ÖLK 185) ['When Ali said tamam mı, I said tamam' (ÖLC 141-42)]. She employs this idiom even more unconsciously than Arabic words of prayer: when the girl prays she knows that she pronounces Arabic words she does not understand, but — probably like most Turkish native speakers — she is not aware of the fact that the supposedly Turkish expression 'Tamam' is of Arabic origin.[23] Turkish speakers have completely appropriated it as a Turkish word, which implies a sense of linguistic completeness: if Arabic words have remained in the Turkish language after its reform, then their origin is often not recognized. Yet one also needs to point out the sociolinguistic dimension of the relationship between Turkish and Arabic, secular Islam and religious Islam. Arabic words (such as those of prayer) become part of ritual reiteration and social action rather than conscious reflection. This also includes loan words from other languages such as English, French and Farsi which have been incorporated into Turkish. 'Tamam' plays a vital, ritualistic role in the girl's everyday life. Although she fully understands these Turkish words on a

22 A. Seyhan, 'Lost in Translation: Re-Membering the Mother Tongue in Emine Sevgi Özdamar's *Das Leben ist eine Karawanserei*', *German Quarterly*, 69.4 (Fall 1996), 423.

23 I am indebted to Dr Elisabeth Kendall (University of Oxford) for this comment.

linguistic level, this particular expression is used in a similar way to the Arabic words of prayer. They are part of a routine rather than a conscious decision regarding what to say next. In this sense, neither literally linguistic nor cultural translation processes take place.

Özdamar demonstrates the interactive use of Turkish, the language that the protagonist is familiar with, and Arabic, the language that is part of her cultural and religious life, and thereby draws attention to her fluid movements between languages and cultures. She adds a further dimension to her protagonist's linguistic and cultural fluidity as the novel with its predominantly Turkish setting and subject matter is narrated in German. The protagonist does not have a fixed linguistic home, but moves between languages and their associated cultures to create her own version of home. This home is based on her Arab Islamic heritage which she primarily gets to know through the language of Islam, Arabic, and the everyday use of her Turkish. However, the heroine needs to migrate further, to Germany, to grow into a critical person who deliberately searches for the connection between Turkish and Arabic, present and past. Germany, which will initiate her conscious linguistic migration from Turkish to German, thus becomes the place where she can go on the linguistic journey of discovering part of the origin of her mother tongue.[24]

In *Brick Lane*, Ali also addresses the question of having a linguistic home. Here, it is mainly the men and children who speak English while the women, as pointed out in the previous section, live their lives in the family home where Bengali is spoken. Chanu, who has studied English literature, regards his knowledge of this language as extremely important, and he demonstrates this by frequently reciting *the* classic English writer, William Shakespeare. He has the advantage of the '*double* vision' of the formerly colonized.[25] Nazneen, however, is linguistically and thus culturally limited, and her linguistic heritage, Bengali and the cultural meanings attached to it, is the only source of communication she can fall back on. This limitation in her everyday communication causes her feeling of alienation and prevents her from experiencing transculturality directly: she does not interact with cultures and their languages in the same way as her husband. It also restricts her when meeting people since, at least at the beginning of the novel, she does not have any knowledge of English.

24 Özdamar explores this linguistic journey in *MutterZunge*, which will be discussed in Chapter 4.

25 H. K. Bhabha, 'Of Mimicry and Man: The Ambivalence of Colonial Discourse', in Bhabha, *The Location of Culture*, 88, italics Bhabha's.

> [Nazneen:] 'Razia is going to college to study English'.
> [Chanu:] 'Ah, good'.
> 'Perhaps I could go with her'.
> [...]
> 'What for?'
> 'For the English lessons'.
> 'You're going to be a mother'. (ABL 76–77)

The gender roles in this family are also defined in linguistic terms. It is the men's privilege to speak English since they are in touch with a world outside their four walls. Chanu deliberately prevents Nazneen from learning English in order to keep her weak and dependent on him. Like patriarchs in many cultures, he acts almost like a colonizer who wants to control his subjects. However, for the second generation, speaking English is as natural as growing up in the UK. Yet the fact that Nazneen is not able to speak the same language as her children seems to compromise her traditional role as 'good' mother. Immigration does not open the same spaces for women as it does for their husbands. It would be wrong, however, to identify this as only a feature of Muslim communities or one only related to Muslim migrants. One can view learning English as one part of the process of learning about and translating other cultures. This is a process which especially Nazneen's children, who have encountered British culture from an early age, are going though. Their heritage, which is often wrongly reduced to their religion, Islam, is frequently perceived by the outside world as the only factor that determines the lives of these immigrants and their children. Yet it is subject to constant change and reinterpretation.

For Nazneen, this process takes a long time and is self-conscious, and occurs via language. Ali introduces the religious character Karim in the narrative in order to demonstrate the changing nature of the characters' cultural heritage, including their religion, in a non-Muslim environment.

> 'Salaat alert,' [Karim] said.
> 'What do you mean?' [Nazneen] was so surprised she slipped into Bengali.
> 'On th-th-the phone. It's a service you can get. To warn you of prayer time'.
> 'Will you do namaz here?' She said it without thinking, in the same way that another time she had switched instinctively to English. [...]
> 'Allahu Akbar'. [...]

> She tried to stop the prayer words forming on her lips. To pray with an unrelated man, it was not permitted. She would pray later. (ABL 234)

As a woman for whom her faith plays a major part in everyday life, reinterpretations of her religious practices are highly significant in Nazneen's translation process. By letting Karim pray in her house, Nazneen appears to break the conservative Islamic rule that forbids prayer with a strange man; yet she does not pray with him and thus adheres to this restriction. Furthermore, the mix of the languages they have in common, Bengali and English, which Nazneen has meanwhile begun to learn, describes their relationship: it swings between a deeply religious mutuality and an increasing openness in their relationship, demonstrated by Nazneen's willingness to let a strange man pray in her house. They are both believers who share the same religious values, and these values (as represented by the act of prayer) bring them closer together. However, when Nazneen slips into Bengali, which is clearly the language she feels most comfortable in, and when Karim stutters uncomfortably in this language, his actual mother tongue, it suggests that problems arise regarding the understanding and subsequent reinterpretation of their relationship: Nazneen seems to be the stronger person in their relationship, whereas Karim tends to require strict rules of behaviour, especially when outside his religious realm. Language serves as an indicator for the diverse perceptions of the characters' relationship with regard to roles that shift or are even abandoned (Nazneen becomes Karim's lover, after all). Cultural translation is initiated on a personal level and is then transferred into the wider context of the Muslim Bengali community where radical changes are underway: their old set of rules of behaviour incorporates more and more aspects of the formerly foreign, that is, British, or also commonly referred to as Western, culture.

Arabic is also part of this family's religious life. 'How would [the Qur'an] sound in Arabic? More lovely even than in Bengali, she supposed, for those were the actual words of God' (ABL 20). Yet, as in *Das Leben ist eine Karawanserei*, Arabic is only an abstractly familiar element in religious practice, a phenomenon which can be found across religions, such as in the relationship to Latin for Catholics or to Hebrew for Jews. This may be different for Muslims from Arabic-speaking countries. The Arabic of the Qur'an is incomprehensible for Ali's Bengali characters (which may also be true for Arabic native-speakers) and is only imagined rather than used. Especially in a predominantly non-Muslim society such as the UK it becomes more and more difficult for the characters to remember their heritage.

However, this heritage still serves as an element of differentiation from non-Muslim 'Others', as shown by the establishment of the Tower Hamlets' Muslim association, the 'Bengal Tigers'. Although they define themselves exclusively through their Muslim identity, they do not base it linguistically on 'the actual words of God' (ABL 20), but on the language that derives from their national identity. During the first meeting of the 'Bengal Tigers' this issue is raised:

> 'Why don't we do this all in our own language?'
>
> [...]
>
> Karim stood with his arms folded. 'I will answer. This meeting is open to all Muslims. I am talking about the ummah here. Every brother and every sister, wherever they come from'.
>
> The Questioner stood up and looked elaborately around the hall, even at the empty chairs. '*Ekhane amra shobai Bangali?* Anyone here not speak Bengali?'
>
> There was a moment's silence before a chair scraped back and a black man in a wider-sleeved swirly-print shirt stood up. 'Do I look like a Bengali to you, brother?' (ABL 238, italics Ali's)

Ali humorously represents religious identity as a double-sided issue here: on the one hand, it is based on where one comes from, namely a Muslim country such as Bangladesh, yet on the other, it theoretically embraces all Muslims, the *umma*. By calling themselves 'Bengal Tigers', the members of this group express a strong affinity with their country of origin and are seemingly excluding Muslims from other countries. Ali looks at this issue with an ironic eye: in their keen ambition to establish a religious group, the 'Bengal Tigers' completely overlook the black man, that is, the fact that Muslims can have various appearances and not only the Bangladeshi one they are used to. English is the language that the Muslims living in East London are likely to have in common. As the language of the West, the Other of the radical Muslims such as the 'Bengal Tigers', it is paradoxically needed as the tool of translation and mediation between Muslims of different origins.

In *Brick Lane*, Ali constructs linguistic identity as Muslim identity on the basis of the language of the country of origin, Bengali, rather than the language of Islam, Arabic. Her characters define themselves primarily in terms of a specific kind of Islam, the Islam that is culturally and linguistically influenced by Bangladesh. With her novel, Ali emphasizes the diversity of versions of Islam, which is often overlooked in the West. She deliberately contributes to a differentiated understanding of Islam as part of British culture.

Language as a form of cultural translation and self-definition is a two-way operation: firstly, the new culture is translated by means of known signifiers in order to find a place that can be called 'home' and secondly, cultural translation affects the cultural baggage brought into the new country: it is reconsidered and re-valued in the light of the new surroundings and cultures that gradually become familiar to the migrants. Language is also a means of referring back to and comprehending one's heritage and possibly of differentiating oneself from non-immigrants and non-Muslims. In this sense, it provides stability as an emotional home. 'Home' as stability can also be given by obeying fixed roles in an initially unfamiliar environment, which is significant in relation to perceptions of gender.

***

Although Özdamar and Ali present cultural diversity as a positive factor in their novels, their characters also need stability in order to experience this diversity as an asset. They show one form of stability through the presence of women and their ability to conform to different roles — especially those expected by men. The West often assumes that Muslim women in particular are affected by their Islamic heritage. According to Horrocks, in Turkey, they are confronted with

> on the one hand the liberating influence of Atatürk's reforms, the introduction of a new family code based on that of Switzerland, the outlawing of polygamy, the granting of new rights to women in both the political and the educational sphere; on the other hand the persistence of patriarchal structures combined with the in practice, if not in theory, oppressive nature of many religious customs. (33)

In the novels studied here, women, more than men, are therefore situated between Muslim and Western perceptions of their roles, primarily as wives. However, the novels display differences in the expectations placed on women, especially between the generations. With her protagonist's maternal grandfather Ahmet, for instance, Özdamar uncovers a traditional view of gender roles.

> Dann sagte Großvater: 'Mein Hals ist trocken, bring mir Wasser, Stadtmädchen'. Als ich lief, sagte Großvater Ahmet: 'Meine Tochter, lauf, aber tritt mit deinen Füßen nicht so fest auf die Erde, dein Schmuck wackelt, das gibt den Männern Wollust'. Mein Busen sollte nicht wackeln. Er erzählte, als unser Prophet Mohammed lebte,

> kamen viele Männer in sein Haus, sie störten Mohammed und seine Frauen. [...] Es kam ein Koranvers auf die Erde. [...] Habe Angst vor Allah, höre meine Worte mit deinem ganzen Körper, ich will, daß du schöne Sachen ißt und trinkst, das schaffe ich für dich heran, sei mir gehorsam, dein Gehorsam ist Allahs und seiner Propheten Wunsch. Wer seinem Ehemann entgegentritt, tritt Allah und seinen Propheten entgegen. [...] Er darf an ihre groben Stellen hauen, am besten auf die Hüften. [...] Manchmal, beim Essen, nahm mir Großvater mit seiner Hand das Obst weg und aß es selbst, ganz langsam, dann sagte er: 'Mädchen sein, heißt Geduld haben'. Großmutter sagte mir heimlich: 'Der unbarmherzige Ahmet Ağa'. (ÖLK 309-11)
>
> [Then Grandfather said, 'My throat is dry, bring me some water, city girl'. As I ran off, my grandfather Ahmet said, 'My daughter, you may run, but don't take such hard steps, it makes your treasure wobble and that makes men lustful'. My bosom was not supposed to move. He told us that when our prophet Mohammed was alive, many men used to come to Mohammed's house, they bothered him and his wives. [...] A verse for the Koran arrived on earth [...]. Fear Allah, and listen to my words with your whole body, I want you to eat and drink good things, I provide these things for you, do as I tell you, your obedience is the wish of Allah and his prophet. If you oppose your husband, you oppose Allah and his prophet. [...] He can beat her in her coarse places, preferably her hips. [...] Sometimes at mealtimes, Grandfather would take the fruit out of my hand and eat it himself, very slowly, and say, 'Being a girl, [*sic*] means being patient'. Grandmother would say quietly, 'Merciless Ahmet Ağa'. (ÖLC 240–41)]

Although the narrator generally refrains from direct criticism, she uses her grandmother Ayşe as a representative of the older, supposedly more traditional generation to raise objections. This character also gives Özdamar the opportunity to be critical of gender-related practices in her cultural heritage and to show that women question and subvert them in Turkish society. Ahmet perceives women as servants and does not see any potential for the changing role of women in modern society. However, the girl, though displaying the 'patience' her grandfather prescribes for her by not complaining, will grow into one of those 'female figures of strong-minded independence who have carved out lives of their own, often in the face of powerful social and religious pressures to conform' (Horrocks, 33). Özdamar's women are not subservient objects. A case in point are the novel's crazy women who live on the margins of society. They perform a form of resistance by subverting well-known suppositions of how a woman should behave. One could see the protagonist as a 'milder' form of crazy woman as she leaves Turkey behind at the end of the novel in search for a new home abroad. (It was usually men who immigrated to Germany, with their families following later.) And it is in this new home with a new language, German, that she can reflect on her previous self to find flaws in the patriarchal nature of her country of origin. The girl's strong will to determine her life by herself does not need to be supported by raging against her grandfather. Her form of 'rebellion' — her leaving Turkey — is of a more subtle and therefore effective nature.

Although Özdamar's women tend to be independent and strong-minded, they cannot escape the expectations imposed on them by the patriarchal society they live in. Though 'patriarchal custom goes hand-in-hand with religious influence' (Horrocks, 35), the narrator's underlying criticism is directed to the patriarchal system rather than religion. Özdamar demonstrates this by pointing out the different interpretations of the most controversial symbol of Muslim femininity, the headscarf: in the novel, the women wear headscarves when they think it is appropriate and not primarily when it is presented as something rooted in Islam.

> Wir hüpften, bis aus vier Häusern vier Frauenköpfe aus den Fenstern rausschauten, die vier Frauen hatten alle Kopftücher, eine war meine Mutter, sie hatte auch ein Kopftuch [...]. Ich ging [...] ins Haus rein. Meine Mutter Fatma hatte jetzt kein Kopftuch. 'Wo ist das Kopftuch, Mutter?' Sie sagte, das Kopftuch werde sie nur für fremde Leute tragen. Ich hatte sie bis heute noch nicht mit Kopftuch gesehen. Nur meine Großmutter trug zwei Kopftücher übereinander. 'Warum trägst du für die Leute Kopftuch, Mutter?' Fatma sagte: 'Hier ist eine religiöse Straße, man muß die Menschen nicht stören'. Wenn Vater unsere Villa fertig gebaut hat, braucht sie dort kein Kopftuch tragen, weil dort nur die Memurs (Bürokraten) wohnen werden. (ÖLK 66)

> [We hopped until four women's heads looked out of four windows; the four women were all wearing headscarves, one of them was my mother, she had a headscarf too [...]. I came into the house [...]. My mother Fatma didn't have her headscarf on. 'Where's your headscarf, Mother?' She said she would only wear the scarf for strangers. I had never seen her with a scarf before. Only my grandmother wore headscarves, two of them, one over the other. 'Why do you wear a scarf for the other people, Mother?' Fatma said, 'This is a religious street. You mustn't upset people'. As soon as father finishes building our villa she won't have to wear a headscarf because only memurs (bureaucrats) will be living around there. (ÖLC 46-47)]

By clearly showing that wearing a headscarf is a conscious decision, Özdamar dismantles 'de[n] westliche[n] Mythos des Kopftuches als

Zeichen religiöser und gesellschaftlicher Unterdrückung' (Wierschke, *Schreiben als Selbstbehauptung*, 191) [the Western myth of the headscarf as symbol of religious and societal oppression]; it is simply

> ein Kleidungsstück, dessen Gebrauch neben religiösen auch praktische oder pragmatische Gründe haben und in unterschiedlichen Kontexten eine Vielfalt spezifischer Bedeutungen signalisieren kann. [...] Das Kopftuch ist ein kulturelles Emblem, das bewußt eingesetzt wird, um der Umwelt Gruppenzugehörigkeit und Anpassung an gewisse Normen zu signalisieren und um sich dadurch einen Handlungsspielraum zu schaffen.
>
> [a piece of clothing which is used for practical and pragmatic reasons as well as religious ones. It signals specific meanings in different contexts. [...] The headscarf is a cultural emblem which is used consciously in order to signal that the wearer belongs to a specific group and adapts to certain norms in order to increase her range of action.]

The women wear their headscarves out of respect — the girl's mother out of respect for the religious people who live in the same street as her family and her grandmother out of respect for God — yet not because it is imposed onto them. This is a rather positive interpretation of the notion of 'respect', a concept which can equally be imposed onto women by men, and the women follow it unquestioningly. If one sees the headscarf as part of a non-Western lifestyle, then 'Özdamar [...] is implicitly questioning the notion [...] that the only way for Muslim women to improve their status is to abandon their native culture and adopt the ways of the West' (Horrocks, 36), that is, to reject the headscarf completely. However, the narrator clearly demonstrates the necessity, rather than rejection, of traditional habits that emphasize the comfort of an emotional home, which makes it possible for people of different beliefs and value systems to live together. Narrating these episodes from the perspective of a German Turkish woman is especially interesting, as headscarf debates in Germany have recently dominated discussions about the integration of Muslim women. Muslim women's insisting on wearing the headscarf in public office has not only triggered public outcries against the visibility of supposedly conservative Islam in a non-Muslim Western country, but also entailed legislative issues. As Seyla Behabib points out, '[t]he two dimensions of [Fereshta Ludin's] citizenship rights — the entitlement to the full protection of the law and her cultural identity as an observant Muslim woman — clashed with one another'.[26] Although *Das Leben ist eine Karawanserei* does not engage with the political dimension of wearing headscarves in either Germany or Turkey — something which has been on the political agenda ever since Atatürk banned the headscarf in the public sector in 1924 — with episodes as the one described above the novel points to the loaded meanings of the headscarf as a symbol of traditional Islam and the heated debates surrounding it.

The example of the headscarves demonstrates that cultural translation does not mean the absolute replacement of one set of cultural entities by another. On the contrary, it contributes to a hybrid understanding of one's identity by choice, especially in such a diverse place like Turkey with its mixture of Muslim and Western traditions.

Although the girl heroine seems to enjoy the comforts of a home based on the diversity of cultures and personal relationships such as the ones between the women, Özdamar depicts her as a migrant who is always drawn to the outside, to a life beyond her immediate experiences. The freedom she enjoys when playing with boys in Bursa can be read as a symbol of her migration, of her distancing from home, which results in her leaving for Germany: 'Ich lief hinter den Jungen und dem Himmelsgürtel her, unsere heilige Brücke lief mehr und mehr weg von mir, mit dem Geruch unserer geruchlosen, seelenlosen Gasse, wo ich meine Mutter mit ihrer neuen Tochter in einem Bett im Schlaf gelassen hatte, als ich sie das letzte Mal sah' (ÖLK 143-44) ['I ran after the boys and the skybelt, our holy bridge ran farther and farther away from me along with the smell of our odourless, soulless street where I had left my mother asleep in bed with her new daughter the last time I saw her' (ÖLC 108)]. The heroine is clearly desperate for a change. (Her desire is also indicated by her attempted suicide towards the end of the novel.) She actively wants to run away from Turkey, yet simultaneously feels that her country is also withdrawing itself from her (the 'holy bridge runs away'). Özdamar presents the solution to her protagonist's discontent, the ultimate migration to another country and the adoption of another language in which she tells her story, in a positive, yet not romanticized or mystified light. As this means meeting people with different cultures and ways of living, it opens the protagonist's eyes — as a woman and a Turkish, transcultural migrant.

In *Brick Lane*, Ali's characters, primarily the women, initially perceive migration as a negative factor, since it creates a distance

26 S. Benhabib's discussion of 'The German Scarf Affair: The Case of Fereshta Ludin', in *The Rights of Others: Aliens, Residents and Citizens* (Cambridge: Cambridge University Press, 2004), 198–202, quotation here 200–01.

between memories of a happy, idealized past and a miserable present. Nazneen had to follow her husband to London and into the secluded life as a Bengali housewife in the 'diaspora' of a tower block. Chanu, however, made his decision to marry a girl from the countryside deliberately. It was based on his existence as an immigrant in a foreign country. As he explains: '"When I married her, I said: she is a good worker. Girl from the village. Unspoilt. All the clever-clever girls —" He broke off and looked at [his daughter]. "All the clever-clever girls are not worth one hair on her head"' (ABL 207). Ali portrays a representative of the first generation of male migrants for whom moving to a new country meant establishing an economically more secure future. In showing Chanu as someone who constantly fails in his enterprise to be successful, she reveals the hopeless situation of some of those migrants. Chanu increasingly bases his self-expectations on unstable dreams, for example, of being promoted in his job. In this sense, his masculinity, which is focused on the role of the breadwinner and father, is threatened. Chanu builds his and his family's (not so) new life on traditional values, which he sees still preserved in the Bengali countryside. He perceives the city as a decadent place. Ironically, he chose to live in London, which could be regarded as an even more decadent place than the cities in Bangladesh: London is a Western city and seems to support 'loose' lifestyles. For Chanu, living in a new place does not mean a new life altogether. On the contrary, as I have already pointed out, it is primarily the men who re-create their new home on the basis of their old home, and install their wives as mothers and housewives.

Bearing this observation in mind, Nazneen, often hopelessly homesick, which is demonstrated by her 'hallucinations' of seeing her village Gouripur in Bangladesh, initially flees into a comfort zone, her 'home', that she finds in what she knows from Bangladesh: everyday items such as Bengali food.

> Nazneen [...] took a tub of yoghurt from the fridge and sprinkled it with sugar. She leaned against the work surface and ate. 'Eat! Eat!' her husband told her at mealtimes. But for him she would not eat. She showed her self-restraint like this. Her self-denial. She wanted to make it visible. It became a habit, then a pleasure, taking solace in these midnight meals.
>
> Amma used to make yoghurt: thick and sweet and warm. Nothing like these plastic pots from the plastic English cows. But still. With the sugar, it went down. And it was very convenient. When she thought about Gouripur now, she thought about inconvenience. (ABL 77)

As in *Das Leben ist eine Karawanserei*, Ali mainly portrays 'home' as an accumulation of small or simple items rather than as a whole. Yet unlike in Özdamar's novel where 'home' consists of moments gathered while the protagonists travel and migrate, in *Brick Lane* these everyday items trigger a nostalgia which the women increasingly put into perspective since Bangladesh also has negative aspects such as 'inconvenience'. Initially, the women, who spend most of their lives in the house, are more passive and less strong-willed than the women in *Das Leben ist eine Karawanserei*. This point is supported by Nazneen's assumption that a woman's task is to endure.

> 'We will suffer in silence,' [...] said Amma. [...] What were they suffering? Nazneen wanted to ask. [...] 'That is all that is left to us in this life,' said Auntie. [...]
>
> 'We are just women. What can we do?'
>
> 'They [men] know it. That's why they act as they do'.
>
> 'God has made the world this way'. (ABL 102–03)

Her endurance results in a self-imposed structured lifestyle: 'regular prayer, regular housework' (ABL 51). It needs an outer influence to break through this rigidity. Ironically, Karim, who gradually changes into an 'Islamic fundamentalist', focuses his life on 'regular prayer' as well, yet for completely different reasons: while Nazneen prays primarily as a form of comfort, Karim sees regular prayer as a means to return to the 'right' way of life. For Nazneen, this man whose life is centred on Islam, a religion that, in a superficial Western perception, does not leave any space for the self-development of women, shows her possibilities beyond her secluded life. By starting to attend the meetings of the 'Bengal Tigers', for example, she leaves her familiar space and ventures towards new horizons: she starts to think for herself and to express her discontent with her life as a Bengali housewife. Thus, Islam becomes the driving force for her 'liberation', which results in her ultimate decision to stay in the UK and not to follow her husband, as she once passively did, to his ideal place of residence.

Ali also depicts women as strong-willed and independent, but in a different way from Özdamar: being out of touch with their country of origin — unlike the women in *Das Leben ist eine Karawanserei* who live in their country of origin — they feel dislocated and search for and also find a place of refuge, despite their lives as subordinate wives. By conceptualizing and comprehending London as their home they establish ways of breaking away from their husbands' longing for a home long gone and finally separate from them — spatially, yet not necessarily emotionally.

As a result, even though it takes longer for Nazneen to realize where her home is and it is with the help of a man whose religious ideas stereotypically place women in a subservient position, she manages to overcome her passivity and find her own version of home without the 'guardian' who was not able to live the life of a (successful) migrant. Ali's portrayal of women as more flexible and adaptable migrants than men goes hand-in-hand with her portrayal of successful female migrants who create homes of their own by incorporating the old into the new. They do not forget where they came from; but while the men's nostalgia for a past long gone prevents them from finding a home and makes them passive, women change from their position as passive housewives into active women, whose life is not centred on their past but on their present. Ali's migrant women choose the future, the essence of a migrant's success.

Both Özdamar and Ali take a critical stance towards migrant men: they good-naturedly poke fun at their novels' self-important and insecure male characters who fail. In the process of migration as these authors perceive it, women move from the position of the passive followers of their husbands to the active and open-minded doers, sometimes to the extent that they reject the old just as their husbands are trying to recreate it. Their willingness to embrace the present and the cultures that surround them proves to be the more practical and, consequently, successful tool in creating a comfortable home in an initially alien environment.

***

The novels *Das Leben ist eine Karawanserei* and *Brick Lane* deny the myth of a fixed home based on a long-lost past and a form of Islam that does not invite any cultural influences, yet Özdamar and Ali employ different means. Özdamar evokes 'home' as continuous movement and as an accumulation of moments rather than as a comforting wholeness: her characters never arrive at a fixed point, either physically or emotionally.[27] She creates identity as linguistic and cultural plurality, and as constant change which, after a painful learning process, is positively connoted. In this sense, Özdamar

27 K. Konuk, *Identitäten im Prozeß: Literatur von Autorinnen aus und in der Türkei in deutscher, englischer und türkischer Sprache*, Literaturwissenschaft in der Blauen Eule, 28 (Essen: Verlag Die Blaue Eule, 2001) (= doctoral thesis, University of Paderborn, 1999), 84.

describes 'das Leben als ein[en] Ort, wo man ein bißchen bleibt und dann wieder weggeht. Ja, und dann kommen viele Figuren rein und raus, wie in der Karawanserei. Sie wechselt dauernd Gäste' (in interview with Wierschke, *Schreiben als Selbstbehauptung*, 249) [life as a place where one stays for a little while und then leaves it again. Many people come and go like in a caravanserai. It constantly changes guests]. These guests, along with the movement of 'passing through', form the identities of migrants as 'discontinuities' and 'bridges'.[28] The protagonist's — literal and metaphorical — migrations are her chance to negotiate multiple identities based on complicated translation processes and the (deliberate) ambiguities they leave behind. Thus, Özdamar portrays a girl becoming a young woman who learns to perceive her migration not as loss but as the chance to accumulate more cultural and linguistic elements for her identity. She reveals her protagonist's religion, Islam, as part of Turkey's multifaceted heritage; she does not perceive it in opposition to the country's official secularism. While the heroine is dealing with her Arab Islamic heritage and the consequences it has for her as a girl, she discovers the hybrid components of her identity and even adds another one by spatially, though not emotionally, leaving it behind to migrate to Germany where she will tell her Turkish story in German, the language that exemplifies her ultimate migration.

The process of identity formation is of a different nature in *Brick Lane,* and the protagonists' religion plays a vital role in their finding stability in an initially alien place. Although Ali also depicts migration as the negotiation of unstable identities, the notion of loss and the painful realization — especially for the men — that the past cannot be regained is more prominent than in Özdamar's novel and creates major difficulties for the characters. In this context, Islam frequently serves as a vehicle that reveals unfulfilled dreams and desires. In *Brick Lane,* the notion of home is based on the need to belong somewhere. Stability is partly given by the religious practices demanded of a faithful Muslim as part of their culture. The family, who live in a predominantly Muslim environment, try to lead a religious life. Yet Ali exposes this way of living as a refuge rather than a conscious examination of their Muslim roots. On this basis, the feeling of loss and fragmentation may be limited, yet not totally

28 R. Müller, '"Ich war Mädchen, war ich Sultanin": Weitgeöffnete Augen betrachten türkische Frauengeschichte(n): Zum Karawanserei-Roman von Emine Sevgi Özdamar', in *Denn du tanzt auf einem Seil: Positionen deutschsprachiger MigrantInnenliteratur*, ed. S. Fischer and M. McGowan (Tübingen: Stauffenburg, 1997), 136, 143–44.

overcome: Chanu returns to Bangladesh. Nazneen, however, stays behind with her daughters. She — like the women in the novels in general — learns to see migration in a positive light. Women are, therefore, the stronger and more flexible characters who are able to adapt more easily without denying their heritage. As the men tend to refer back constantly to their past as an ideal home instead of trying to build a new home situated in the present and pointing towards the future, they do not overcome their suffering from a feeling of division that results in their invention of an immovable home.

It is the imagination of the male migrants that is the reason for their constant longing for their past and roots, which is opposed by the female flexibility and openness to invite other cultures into their everyday lives. The history of the migrant is inescapable,[29] and both novels suggest that it should be treated as one part of one's identity rather than the only determining factor of one's self.

Having gone through 'ethnographic operations' themselves,[30] having experienced and creatively dealt with migrations and the feeling of being 'different', Özdamar and Ali address the difficulties of transculturality and challenge Western perceptions of passive and closed-minded migrants, primarily from the perspective of women. Their transcultural novels suggest, therefore, that the idea of a stable home based on a certain way of living needs to be overcome. The assumption that cultures are fixed entities consequently becomes obsolete. Özdamar and Ali demonstrate that the choice of one culture is neither desirable nor possible. Migrants do not have to live in an in-between state — between religions, cultures and languages — but can use the creative potential of their migrant, transcultural situation.

29 L. Moss, 'The Politics of Everyday Hybridity: Zadie Smith's *White Teeth*', *Wasafiri*, 39 (Summer 2003), 11.

30 I borrow this term from Wolf, 182.

2. Travelling to Islam
Pilgrimage and Hajj: V. S. Naipaul's *Among the Believers and Beyond Belief*, and Ilija Trojanow's *Zu den Heiligen Quellen des Islam*

The last chapter discussed the notion of moving with Islam, and analysed the interrelation between Islam, migration and the creation of 'home'. However, Muslims as well as non-Muslims also travel to Islam — to its original sites as well as to the places where it is lived. The travellers I am concerned with here go on pilgrimages, in both a traditional and a metaphorical sense. This chapter explores this kind of movement and asks how significant travelling and, as a result, the immediate interaction with Islam are for the traveller's identity. It focuses on the hajj as one of the Five Pillars of Islam and thus a Muslim way of travelling, yet also on the metaphorical pilgrimage of the traveller-writer as a form of self-exploration.

Migration writing was the focus of the first chapter. This chapter considers the travel writers' experiences as former migrants and the influences of these on the journey as well as their reflections in the texts: V. S. Naipaul and Ilija Trojanow have undertaken the transition from migrant to traveller. Migration is normally not a movement of choice (it tends to be caused by the migrant's need or desire to find a better home); whereas a traveller chooses to go on their trip — and returns home. This significant difference in movement has consequences for the perceptions of the travellers' environment. Travellers, like migrants, employ techniques of translation, yet the aim of their journey (the discovery of other countries and cultures) tends to be determined by a 'quest for knowledge', not an urge to settle in. As a result, travellers translate in a different way from migrants, since making sense of the new surroundings is not an essential part of their travelling. This chapter will develop the notion of translation further in travel texts written by former migrants.

Traditionally, travel writing establishes relations between peoples of different cultures — within as well as beyond the text[1] — and thus enables both writer and reader to view themselves in the mirror of the Other. In travel texts, the act of travelling is more than just physical movement. It is simultaneously 'ein Muster der Welterschließung und der Persönlichkeitsbildung' [a mode of exploring the world as well as the self],[2] which starts by locating the self in opposition to the unknown or the Other. This process helps create order for the traveller on the basis of hierarchies whereby the familiar tends to be connoted positively and the unfamiliar negatively.[3] Karin Hlavin-Schulze emphasizes that travel writing describes not so much *what* is being perceived and experienced but *how* this process takes place.[4] As a result, the reader engages more deeply with the traveller and less with the country written about. The latter often serves as a platform for the cultural self-representation of the traveller.[5] In this context, Homi Bhabha emphasizes that the Other as 'the object of identification is ambivalent' ('DissemiNation', 162). The Other can be constructed as a positive as well as negative 'counter-picture' or as a 'completion' (Schäffter, 19, 22).[6] However, the Other is usually 'auf Distanz antizipiert und toleriert' [anticipated and tolerated from a distance],[7] whilst the task of travel writing is to find a balance between

1 See D. Porter, *Haunted Journeys: Desire and Transgression in European Travel Writing* (Princeton: Princeton University Press, 1991), 3.

2 H. Schlösser, 'Reiseliteratur als Literatur der Reisenden', in *Reiseformen des Geschriebenen: Selbsterfahrung und Weltdarstellung in Reisebüchern Wolfgang Koeppens, Rolf Dieter Brinkmanns und Hubert Fichtes*, Literatur und Leben: Neue Folge, 34 (Wien: Böhlau, 1987), 15.

3 O. Schäffter, 'Modi des Fremderlebens', in *Das Fremde: Erfahrungsmöglichkeiten zwischen Faszination und Bedrohung*, ed. O. Schäffter (Opladen: Westdeutscher Verlag, 1991), 12, 14.

4 K. Hlavin-Schulze, *'Man reist ja nicht, um anzukommen': Reisen als kulturelle Praxis* (Frankfurt a.M.: Campus, 1998), 11.

5 P. J. Brenner, *Der Reisebericht: Die Entwicklung einer Gattung in der deutschen Literatur* (Frankfurt a.M.: Suhrkamp, 1989), 18.

6 See also T. Todorov, *Die Eroberung Amerikas: Das Problem des Anderen* (Frankfurt a.M.: Suhrkamp, 1985; originally publ. as *Conquête de l'Amérique* (Paris: Éditions du Seuil, 1982)).

7 E. Obendiek on Zygmunt Bauman in *Der lange Schatten des babylonischen Turmes: Das Fremde und der Fremde in der Literatur* (Göttingen: Vandenhoeck & Ruprecht, 2000), 23. See also Z. Bauman, 'From Pilgrim to Tourist — or a Short History of Identity', in *Questions of Cultural Identity*, ed. S. Hall and T. Youngs, 18–36.

'das Fremde vertraut [zu] machen und gleichzeitig die Fremdheit [zu] erhalten' [making the foreign familiar and, simultaneously, preserving it as foreign].[8] Thus, according to Emanuel Lévinas, 'the Other as Other is not only an alter ego: the Other is what I myself am not'.[9] This relationship between self (the individual) and Other is the requirement for travel writing.

Klaus R. Scherpe and Alexander Honold analyse the travel writer's first encounter with the Other and describe it as the 'Verstehensdilemma [aufgrund kultureller Unterschiede], das in einen Schreibakt mündet' [dilemma of understanding [due to cultural differences] which results in the act of writing].[10] Travel writing deals with this gap of understanding. However, the means of approaching this gap are diverse. As Hermann Schlösser points out, a genre of 'travel writing' does not exist (9). It appears, rather, as a mode in a constant process of redefinition and readjustment according to the travel writer's needs and wishes. In this context, Peter Brenner emphasizes travel writing's 'Nähe zur Fiktion' (14) [closeness to fiction]. It seems that the 'foreign' can often only be grasped and explained with the help of the writer's imagination, which influences both the writer's perception of the country visited and the subsequent travel account. The book is the result of the traveller's examination of what they hope and wish to see and what they actually experience. Although travel writers take true experiences as the basis for their accounts and often wish to quote reality, they cannot achieve an 'authentic' report. Travel writing constructs a particular country: this act is preconditioned by the writer's own cultural background and imagination and their place in society. These preconditions rarely leave room for new approaches to the unknown. There is an urge to merge the unknown with the known in order to understand the foreign world (Brenner, 27, 30). This turns into an 'ethnographische[r]

8 V. Crapanzano, 'Das Dilemma des Hermes: Die verschleierte Unterwanderung der ethnographischen Beschreibung', in *Kultur als Text: Die anthropologische Wende in der Literaturwissenschaft*, ed. D. Bachmann-Medick, 162–63.

9 E. Lévinas, *Time and the Other*, trans. R. A. Cohen (Pittsburg: Duquesne University Press, 1987); here qtd from E. Lévinas, 'Time and the Other', trans. R. A. Cohen, in *The Levinas Reader*, ed. S. Hand (Oxford: Blackwell, 1989 [1999 printing]), 48 (lectures originally publ. in *Le Choix — Le Monde — L'Existence*, ed. J. Wahl (Grenoble-Paris: Arthaud, 1947), 125–96), then separately with a new preface (Montpellier: Fata Morgana, 1979)).

10 K. R. Scherpe and A. Honold, 'Auf dem Papier sind Indianer weiß, im Ritual die Weißen farbig: Fremdheitsforschung in der Literaturwissenschaft', *Humboldt-Spektrum*, 4 (1995), 29.

Prozess' [ethnographic process] whereby the act of re-producing the Other in the text contributes to its comprehension.[11]

These techniques tend to be employed in what is regarded as Western travel writing (it developed as a 'Western form of literature').[12] In contrast, being a non-Western tradition of travel writing, hajj literature (writing about the Muslim pilgrimage to Mecca) is not about discovering a new country and the interaction with a foreign Other. It aims to recapture the spiritual experiences of the pilgrim in the text: the progressive loss of individuality in a crescendo of unquestioning belief; it is a renewed experience of the journey, an inner reflection of the pilgrim. On their hajj, all pilgrims are on a similar spiritual level; the opposition between self and Other loses its significance. The journey and its textualization are a celebration of the unity of believers and not the construction of a country or culture.

Dale F. Eickelman and James Piscatori stress that there is a 'specific importance of travel and its significance as a process of social action in understanding "Islam" and ideas of Muslim community' ('Social Theory in the Study of Muslim Societies', 3). The pilgrimage as a celebration of religious belief reinforces the traveller's feeling of belonging to the Muslim community. The Prophet Muhammad emigrated from Mecca to Medina in 622 (*hijra*), fleeing persecution 'by the Meccan aristocracy, who regarded Muhammad's claim to prophecy and reformist agenda, with its implicit criticism of the political and socio-economic status quo, as a challenge to their leadership and interests' (Esposito, *The Islamic Threat*, 27). In Medina, Muhammad established the first Muslim community (*umma*). This significant event marks the beginning of Muslim history and the Muslim calendar. The pilgrimage establishes a close tie to Islam's origin and 'marks the believer's identity and her or his membership of the community of Muslims' (Melman, 115). Although the pilgrimage is an essentially communal form of travelling, it also makes each traveller aware of their individuality as a believer. This twofold experience may shape their identity, both consciously and unconsciously.

11 D. Bachmann-Medick, 'Einleitung', in *Kultur als Text: Die anthropologische Wende in der Literaturwissenschaft*, ed. D. Bachmann-Medick, 32.

12 P. Holland and G. Huggan, *Tourists with Typewriters: Critical Reflections on Contemporary Travel Writing* (Ann Arbor: The University of Michigan Press, 1998), viii. See also B. Korte, 'Exploring Without a Mission? Postcolonial Travel in a Global World', in *Colonies — Missions — Cultures in the English-Speaking World: General and Comparative Studies*, ed. G. Stilz, ZAA Studies: Language, Literature, Culture, 12 (Tübingen: Stauffenburg, 2001), 383.

Writing about the hajj has a strong tradition. Writers such as the philosopher and theologian Al-Ghazāli, who undertook the hajj in 1097,[13] and Ibn Jubayr, who travelled between 1183 and 1185, have influenced the genre of hajj writing, *rihla* (journey), named after Ibn Jubayr's travel account (1184).[14] One of the most important and widely read writers is Ibn Batuttah, who travelled extensively between 1325 and 1354, and went on his pilgrimage to Mecca in 1326.[15] In his foreword to *The Travels of Ibn Battutah*, Tim Mackintosh-Smith emphasizes the learning process of the Muslim pilgrim. He quotes Ibn Khaldun and the Prophet Muhammad in this context:

> 'Travelling in search of knowledge,' wrote Ibn Battutah's younger North African contemporary, Ibn Khaldun, 'is absolutely essential for the acquisition of useful learning and of perfection through meeting authoritative teachers and having contact with scholarly personalities'. The Prophet Muhammad had put it more snappily, 'Travel in search of knowledge, even though the journey takes you to China'. (x)

'Travel in search of knowledge' is at the centre of the hajj.

The pilgrimage to Mecca acquires, however, a different meaning for disguised Muslims, nineteenth-century Western travellers such as the Swiss traveller Johann Ludwig [John Lewis] Burckhardt, whose hajj took place in 1814,[16] or Sir Richard Francis Burton, who travelled to

13 Al Ghazāli, *The Revival of Religious Science*, A Translation of the Arabic Work *Ihyā 'ulūm al-dīn* by Bankey Behari, with a Foreword by Shree Humayun Kabir (Farnham: Sufi Publishing, 1972 [1964]), specifically 'Book One: Worship', 1–35, Section '7: The Esoteric Import of Pilgrimage (Haj): Virtue Behind Pilgrimage to Medina and Mecca', 16–17.

14 *The Travels of Ibn Jubayr: Being the Chronicle of a Mediaeval Spanish Moor Concerning His Journey to the Egypt of Saladin, the Holy Cities of Arabia, Baghdad the City of the Caliphs, the Latin Kingdom of Jerusalem, and the Norman Kingdom of Sicily*, trans. R. J. C. Broadhurst, with an Introduction and Notes (London: Jonathan Cape, 1952).

15 *The Travels of Ibn Battutah*, abr., intro. and annot. T. Mackintosh-Smith (London: Picador, 2003 [2002]). Ibn Battutah's memoirs were called *Tuhfat al-nuzzar fi ghara'ib al-amsar wa aja'ib al-asfar*, or *A Gift to Those Who Contemplate the Wonders of Cities and the Marvels of Travelling* (T. Mackintosh-Smith, 'Foreword', in *The Travels of Ibn Battutah*, ix).

16 *Travels in Arabia: Comprehending an Account of Those Territories in Hedjaz Which the Mohammedan Regard as Sacred*, by the late John Lewis Burckhardt, published by the Authority of the Association for Promoting the Discovery of the Interior of Africa (London: Colburn, 1829; repr. in Publications of the Institute for the History of Arabic-Islamic Science, ed. F. Sezgin, The Islamic World in Foreign Travel Accounts, 43 (Institute for the History of Arabic-Islamic Science at the Johann Wolfgang Goethe University Frankfurt am Main, 1995)).

Mecca in 1853. Imperial travellers such as Burton aimed to get behind the secrets and mysteries of Muslim belief by experiencing them themselves and relaying them to an audience that stayed at home.[17] Despite their perfect disguise, their observations remained those of outsiders, of ethnologists who recorded rather than spiritually participated in the rituals of their fellow pilgrims. Here, travelling as learning means acquiring knowledge in order to grasp the Other rather than as a form of worship.

In the twentieth century, Malcolm X was one of the most prominent Muslims to undertake the hajj. His conversion to Islam meant more than a personal decision to embrace a particular faith: his affiliation to the 'Nation of Islam' represented a step towards solving the 'race problem' in America by fighting for the African American's 'complete separation from white American and European hegemony'.[18] Yet this movement later became too radical for Malcolm X when it proposed an 'independent nationhood for African Americans' (226), and he eventually distanced himself from it.

On his hajj, which he undertook in 1964, Malcolm X vividly experienced the 'Oneness of Man under One God', which is highlighted by his celebration of the Muslim community, of 'brotherhood'.[19] For Malcolm X, Islam, including the duties of the devout Muslim, acquires another, political and thus secular meaning: it becomes a means for his personal struggle against racial inequality and discrimination by consciously referring to the idea of Islam as an all-embracing religion.

There are, then, multiple forms of the hajj and journeys to Islam. This chapter compares two different ways of travelling to Islam and writing about this journey. Ilija Trojanow's account of his traditional hajj, *Zu den Heiligen Quellen des Islam: Als Pilger nach Mekka und Medina*

17 R. F. Burton, *A Secret Pilgrimage to Mecca and Medina*, intro. T. Mackintosh-Smith (London: The Folio Society, 2004), 1 (originally publ. as *Personal Narrative of a Pilgrimage to El-Medinah and Meccah* (London: Longman, Brown, Green, and Longmans, 1855–56)). Ilija Trojanow has had a long-term interest in Burton which he fictionalized in two publications: *Der Weltensammler* (Munich: Hanser, 2006), translated as *The Collector of Worlds*, trans. W. Hobson (London: Faber and Faber, 2008), and *Nomade auf vier Kontinenten: Auf den Spuren von Sir Richard Francis Burton* [*Nomad on Four Continents: Tracing Sir Richard Francis Burton*] (Frankfurt a.M.: Eichborn, 2007).

18 K. Natambu, *The Life and Work of Malcolm X* (Indianapolis: Alpha, 2002), 127.

19 Malcolm X, *The Autobiography of Malcolm X*, with the assistance of A. Haley. With an introduction by P. Gilroy (London: Penguin by arrangement with Hutchinson, 2001 [1965]), 443, 452.

(2003),[20] portrays his immediate experience of Islam. As a Muslim, Trojanow not only performs the hajj as part of his religious duties, but also as the fulfilment of his longing for the experience of being a member of the *umma* (the community of believers) that celebrates its unity in its original 'homeland'. This relationship between the individual and the community is explored from a different perspective in V. S. Naipaul's accounts of his travels to non-Arab Muslim countries, *Among the Believers: An Islamic Journey* (1981) and *Beyond Belief: Islamic Excursions Among the Converted Peoples* (1996).[21] Naipaul is a secularized Hindu who became a Western writer, and his desire to find out why Islam has been able to gain such a significant status is at the centre of his books.

We need to keep in mind that both writers possess a concept of experience which operates within Western frameworks where — and this needs to be questioned — Islam does not admit the singularity of relative experience; these frameworks are rooted in ideas that relate back to the European Enlightenment: the emancipation of thinking, the autonomy of reason, secular autonomy, belief in progress and, above all, individuality, awareness of the self. We need to ask what meanings the writers attach to individuality on their journeys.

Both Trojanow and Naipaul are of migratory backgrounds, which they partly reflect on in their travel writing. Although they only visit selected countries, they also interact with the notion of migration, through the people they meet and through their own considerations of 'home'. However, despite sharing a peripatetic lifestyle, the writers have opposing ideas of travelling and perceiving the world.

Trojanow explicitly reacts to and comments upon Naipaul's work. A comparison between the two writers will therefore highlight the writers' different stances on being a traveller and writer and on their positions as such while on their journeys. As a Muslim, Trojanow does not hide his critique of Naipaul. According to him, Naipaul does not have the 'kulturelle Einfühlungsvermögen' (TZH 160) [cultural empathy],[22] which he (as a widely travelled writer of the twentieth and twenty-first centuries, with a supposed awareness and acceptance of

20 I. Trojanow, *Zu den heiligen Quellen des Islam: Als Pilger nach Mekka und Medina* (Munich: Malik, 2004). Translations taken from I. Trojanow, *Mumbai to Mecca*, trans. R. Morrison (London: Haus Publishing, 2007).

21 V. S. Naipaul, *Among the Believers: An Islamic Journey* (London: Picador, 2003 [1981]); *Beyond Belief: Islamic Excursions Among the Converted Peoples* (London: Abacus, 1999 [1998] [2002 printing]).

22 'Kulturelles Einfühlungsvermögen' [cultural empathy] and the passage on V. S. Naipaul are not translated in *Mumbai to Mecca*.

cultural difference) should bring out in his travel writing. Trojanow emphatically does not see himself in line with Naipaul as a travel writer: he does not feel a 'Brüderschaft' (TZH 159) ['brotherhood' (TMM 199)] with him as he does with other hajj writers. Trojanow makes a clear moral distinction between writers who travel in order to truly interact with the Other and writers who seem to use the Other for their own purposes as — so Trojanow thinks — Naipaul does.

It needs to be pointed out, however, that Trojanow does not encounter the Other on his hajj; he travels with his 'brothers' and, similarly to Western travellers like Naipaul, finds what he sets out to encounter — brotherhood with fellow Muslims. Furthermore, Naipaul is a non-Muslim writer with a less emotional attachment to his travel destinations, indeed to Islam, which might suggest a more critical and less sympathetic view on Islam.

***

Any journey that results in a written account is likely to have a particular objective and might even be undertaken entirely in order to produce a piece of writing. In the West, the interest in the Middle East has a long tradition: as the biblical Holy Land it has attracted Christian pilgrims and explorers.[23] It was also part of various imperial aspirations and thus also often revealed the colonizer's and traveller's desires and needs. The Eurocentric view of the Orient has been challenged since then but certain ideas of what the (Middle) East means still persist: even the collapse of the European empires and subsequent immigration movements to the former 'mother countries', which has entailed a growing interest in travel writing, could barely loosen fixed ideas of the Oriental Other.[24]

V. S. Naipaul's visits to non-Arab Muslim countries are a travel writer's journeys which aim at discovering and revealing knowledge and 'truth' through both the actual journey and the subsequent acts of taking notes and writing. The mutual dependency of travelling

23 For further information on the Christian pilgrimage and the importance of holy places in a Christian context, see B. Korte, *English Travel Writing from Pilgrimages to Postcolonial Explorations*, trans. C. Matthias (Basingstoke: Macmillan Palgrave, 2000), 24–25 (originally publ. as *Der englische Reisebericht: Von der Pilgerfahrt bis zur Postmoderne* (Darmstadt: Wissenschaftliche Buchgesellschaft, 1996)).

24 See M. Baine Campbell, 'Travel Writing and its Theory', in *The Cambridge Companion to Travel Writing*, ed. P. Hulme and T. Youngs, 261.

and writing is significant for Naipaul. In the prologue of *Beyond Belief* he tells us:

> This is a book about people. It is not a book of opinion. It is a book of stories. [...] This book is a follow-up to a book [...], *Among the Believers* [...]. When I started on this journey in 1979 I knew almost nothing about Islam — it is the best way to start on a venture — and that first book was an exploration of the details of the faith and what looked like its capacity for revolution. The theme of conversion was always there; but I didn't see it as clearly as I saw it on this second journey. (NBB 1)

Naipaul suggests that it was his aim to gain knowledge about Islam with a particular focus on the 'theme of conversion' (this central notion even appears in the subtitle of *Beyond Belief*). He consciously revisits the places known from his first journey, which resulted in a text, *Among the Believers*. Yet the focus of his exploration in *Beyond Belief* seems to have shifted slightly. This shift in emphasis appears to have been caused by the actual act of writing, of reflecting on the journey as well as by the simple idea that, particularly after a time gap of several years, one never sees a place with the 'same eyes' again. Suman Gupta points out that the central question of *Among the Believers* is: 'in what way do Muslims expect Islam to facilitate the creation of an ideal Islamic state, and what sort of concrete shape (in economic, technological and political terms) is the latter likely to take?'[25] Naipaul's objective in both books is the exploration of what he describes as 'Muslim rage',[26] 'rage about the faith, political rage' (NAB 400), against which he — a Western-educated cosmopolitan traveller — sees himself in relief. His writing explores, therefore, not simply the Other (the Muslims) but also the self (the secular 'Westerner' Naipaul) in relation to the questions of religious revivalism, individuality and reason. He modifies his method of exploration between the first and second travel accounts as he increasingly perceives the notion of conversion as a possible answer to his questions regarding 'Muslim rage' and as the thematic focus for his travelling and writing. Furthermore, Naipaul set out on his second journey as a more established writer than on his first trip. This might make us understand, as Gupta points out, why *Among the Believers* has 'an exploratory air [...]: it comes to its subject matter with

25 S. Gupta, *V. S. Naipaul* (Plymouth: Northcote House in association with the British Council, 1999), 67.
26 V. S. Naipaul, 'Our Universal Civilization' (1992), in *The Writer and the World: Essays*, ed. P. Mishra (London: Picador, 2003 [2002]), 507.

an assumption of ignorance, and the process of putting together and thinking about observations as they occur forms the substance of the book', whereas *Beyond Belief*, written fifteen years later, carries 'an air of retrospection [...]: it is more statemental in approach, and presents a concretised and confirmed thesis about Islam itself and about the general issues in question' (66). Naipaul's methodology shifts from 'the writing of enquiry'[27] to what I call 'the writing of confirmation': Naipaul's second book in particular appears to make non-Arab Muslim countries available by drawing on what he has learnt and seen since his first journey. Incidentally, hajj writing is also a form of 'writing of confirmation': it confirms the idea of the *umma* and unquestioning belief. We therefore need to ask whether Trojanow's confirmation aimed at in his hajj account reinforces a celebratory image of Islam and blanks out possible negative images of Islam.

Naipaul's desire to visit non-Arab Muslim countries is triggered by watching news about the Iranian Revolution on television. One could regard this news item as the kind of 'pretext' (Kabbani, 37), which, in colonial times, unleashed the wish in imperial travellers to see the colonies with their own eyes in order to gain knowledge about them and their people. Additionally, Naipaul's travel accounts express a political aspect, which can be one focus of colonial travel writing. Peter Hulme points out that '[g]iven that the world is constantly in flux, there is still a prominent place for the mixture of personal reportage and socio-political analysis which has been a component of travel writing since its earliest days'.[28] Naipaul's initial objective (the inquiry into the religiousness of 'the converted peoples') implies this kind of link between personal interest and political analysis. In 'Our Universal Civilization', an address that Naipaul gave at the Manhattan Institute of New York, he describes this connection by reflecting upon the use of the word 'fundamentalism' in the media and the growth of Islam in some non-Arab Muslim countries.

> 'Fundamentalism' — in connection with the Mohammedan world — was not a word often used by the newspapers in 1979; they hadn't yet worked through that concept. What they spoke of more was 'the revival of Islam'. And that, indeed, to anyone contemplating it from a distance, was a puzzle. Islam which had apparently so little to offer its adherents in the last century and in the first half of this — what did

27 R. Davidson, 'Introduction', in *The Picador Book of Journeys*, ed. R. Davidson (London: Picador, 2001), 5; this is Naipaul's own term qtd by Davidson.
28 P. Hulme, 'Travelling to Write (1940–2000)', in *The Cambridge Companion to Travel Writing*, ed. P. Hulme and T. Youngs, 94.

> it have to offer an infinitely more educated, infinitely faster, world in the later years of the century? (Naipaul, 'Our Universal Civilization', 507–08)

Naipaul seems to claim that he wants to reach beyond the superficial representation of Islam in the media by travelling to the parts of the Muslim world that 'revive' Islam. However, one needs to take into account what Patrick Holland and Graham Huggan emphasize: that 'travel writing frequently provides an effective alibi for the perpetuation or reinstallment of ethnocentrally superior attitudes to "other" cultures, peoples, and places' (xiii). Naipaul's statement can be read in this light: the word 'Mohammedan' nowadays is obsolete as it reduces Islam exclusively to its origins and denies its development, transformation and adaptation in other parts of the Muslim world. Furthermore, the statement that the media have not worked through the concept of 'fundamentalism' gives the impression that Naipaul, by contrast, understands this concept as he has seen the places where it flourishes. He perceives himself as a knowledgeable traveller, a position that, however, does not seem to correspond with what he perceived as the role of the travel writer. He states: 'I had trouble with the form. [...] I had trouble with the "I" of the travel writer; I thought that as traveller and narrator he was in unchallenged command and had to make big judgements. [...] Travel had taken me further'.[29] It remains to be seen whether, and how, travel takes Naipaul further, and whether he resists the temptation of 'making big judgements'.

Ilija Trojanow's objective is of a different nature from Naipaul's. He goes on the hajj primarily for religious purposes and subsequently writes about his experiences on this journey. The book is not presented as pre-planned: unlike Naipaul, he appears to travel without a notebook yet, since he is a writer by profession, this is questionable. The journey itself and the spiritual experience of the pilgrim appear to be more significant than answering particular questions, which is an equally valid aim of a journey. The religious duty of going on the pilgrimage to Mecca at least once in a Muslim's lifetime stands at the forefront of Trojanow's text. The hajj places the pilgrim more consciously in the community of believers. Trojanow has travelled widely in both the Muslim and the non-Muslim world, and has always aimed 'nicht von der Heimat in die Fremde und wieder zurück zu reisen, sondern die Fremde in Heimat zu verwandeln, sinnlich, sprachlich' [not to travel from home to foreign lands and back, but

29 V. S. Naipaul, 'Reading and Writing, a Personal Account' (1998), in Naipaul, *Literary Occasions: Essays*, intro. and ed. P. Mishra (London: Picador, 2003), 7.

to turn the foreign into a home, sensually, linguistically].[30] Being a Muslim, on the one hand, he knows all the rules he needs to follow (on the hajj as well as in everyday life), yet on the other, he acquires a more conscious understanding of the meaning of the religious rituals when he performs them in the land of Islam's origin. He writes: 'Jede Reise beginnt vor ihrem Antritt, auf die Hadsch aber, die Pilgerfahrt nach Mekka, bereitet sich der Gläubige ein Leben lang vor' (TZH 14) ['Every journey begins before one sets off on it; preparation for the Hajj, however, for the pilgrimage to Mecca, is a believer's vocation and the rewards for his life's work' (TMM 12)]. This sentence already summarizes the significance of the Muslim pilgrimage as opposed to other forms of travelling. The perpetual awareness of the existence of Mecca and of one's religious roots that is maintained by, for example, praying towards this place, and the constant knowledge from a very early age that one has to go on this pilgrimage to fulfil the duties of a devout Muslim appear as a lifelong preparation for this journey. Trojanow also uses the word 'sehnen' (TZH 14) ['yearn[ing]' (TMM 13)], an indescribable, mystical love for or feeling of desire for experiencing his religion at its roots, to describe his mental preparation. The pilgrimage starts long before the actual boarding of the plane. It starts and continues as a journey of the mind of the believer. Yet 'die Hadsch ist nicht nur eine individuelle Pilgerschaft, sondern auch eine Versammlung Gleicher, eine Beschwörung der Umma, der muslimischen Gemeinschaft' (TZH 15) ['the Hajj is not only an individual pilgrimage, it is a communal congregation, an entreaty of the Ummah' (TMM 13–14)]. It is this relationship between the individual Muslim and their role in the community of believers — the effective dissolution of the Western concept of the self — that Trojanow explores, taking himself as an example.

***

Both Trojanow and Naipaul mention people in their titles ('Pilger' [pilgrim], 'believers', 'converted peoples') and interpersonal relations provide the basis for their experiences of Islam on both a personal and a political-historical level.

Naipaul primarily meets carefully selected people by appointment. He is a rich traveller who can afford to interview the people who appear to be useful for his 'quest for knowledge'. Despite his

30 Trojanow in C. Bock, 'Ortswechsel: Interview mit Michael Ebmeyer und Ilija Trojanow', *Parapluie*, no. 19: *Worte, Worte, Worte*, http://parapluie.de/ archiv/ worte/ortswechsel [accessed 28 June 2010] (para. 9 of 53).

confidence in his previously acquired knowledge, he also relies on the people he meets on his journeys as mediators, translators[31] and helpers – a notion he recognizes himself: '[I]t became clear that I needed help, that by myself I would see nothing' (NAB 117). They sometimes even change Naipaul's perceptions of places. Naipaul's encounters with Behzad in Iran are significant here. He writes: 'Without Behzad, without the access to the language that he gave me, I had been like a half-blind man in Tehran. [...] Now, with Behzad, the walls spoke; many other things took on meaning; and the city changed' (NAB 7). Naipaul's reliance on people who provide access to the places he visits results in a translated view of the countries he travels in. Behzad literally translates Persian words into English, yet the question is whether he can communicate to Naipaul the specific cultural meanings behind those words. It is a translated view that fills the gaps in Naipaul's previously acquired knowledge. Naipaul has some sort of sense of the cultural implications of graffiti in a post-revolutionary country, and he communicates to his readers how he interprets these translations. Yet the reader does not know whether Naipaul's interpretations are the same as the Iranian Behzad's perception of these 'speaking walls'.[32]

Naipaul also functions as a translator for his own cause. He directs and extensively comments on the conversations he conducts with his interlocutors. Dialogues dominate the books – a common feature in travelogues. For example, in Malaysia, when talking to Shafi who 'worked for the Muslim cause' (NAB 266), Naipaul controls the conversation with his questions:

> I said, 'Do you think those white women are pretty?'
>
> He looked at them one after the other, with the same serious expression: he was trying hard to find out what he thought.
>
> He said, 'We don't have a sense of comparing'.
>
> 'But white men and others find Malay women pretty'.
>
> 'I have heard that. But is it true? Is that really what they feel?'
>
> [...] It was not easy for Shafi, though the effort of thought and memory excited him. The narrative that came out was shaped by my questions. (NAB 274)

31 See Cronin's *Across the Lines* on the role of translation in travel. Cronin points out many aspects of translation, for example, 'the fear of ridicule, vulnerability and helplessness' of the traveller who does not know the language (43) and the help of informants (54). Cronin also refers to Naipaul's use of interpreters (72–73).

32 Cronin refers to this problem: 'When a cultural reality is interpreted by the interpreter, is the traveller getting the benefit of measured judgement with general applicability or personal opinions disguised as cultural generalities?' (74).

This kind of conversation, which aims to tease out particular pieces of information, frequently appears in Naipaul's texts. He admits that 'the narrative [...] was shaped by [his] questions' and is therefore aware of the distorting effect of the interviewer-interviewee relationship. This practice gives him authority not only as a traveller but also as a writer: Naipaul asks in order to lead the conversation in a particular direction. He modifies the representation of his interlocutors with his questions, thereby placing them and himself in the positions of represented and representer. These practices are not specific to Naipaul and have always (more or less obviously) been part of European travel literature.[33] Naipaul appears to make use of them when he already seems to think about the narrative that will be the result of his journey.

A further notion behind the use of dialogue needs to be considered. Susan Bassnett observes that 'the increasing use of dialogue in travel writing has further closed the gap between travel account and fiction, making the travel text resemble the novel much more closely'.[34] She relates this observation to the use of language in travel accounts since '[t]he reader is expected to believe that such conversations which apparently transcend any language barrier are recorded rather than invented'. Naipaul solves this problem by the frequent reference to translators who superficially erase communication difficulties and to the use of his notebook which will later bridge any gaps of his memory and any gaps of understanding for his readers who have not been to these countries and met these people. Naipaul's relationship to translation is, therefore, twofold: on the one hand, he needs translators as providers of access to the form of Islam as it is lived in particular countries; on the other, he takes on the role of translator himself, by filtering his and his companions' experiences

33 See as an example of earlier travel writing Montesquieu's *Lettres Persanes* (originally publ. Amsterdam: PAGE Brunel, 1721). Although supposedly describing Europe from an 'Eastern' point of view, the *Lettres* primarily give an Orientalist, well-known and familiar picture of Persia by combining 'the exotic and the erotic' thus helping 'to build up the fascination of the East by concentrating on the cruelty and strangeness of Persian customs, often adding to the effect by means of what was then considered to be a flowery Eastern style [...]. Persia is sometimes horrifying, sometimes admirable' (C. J. Betts, 'Introduction', in Montesquieu, *Persian Letters*, trans. with an Introduction and Notes by C. J. Betts (London: Penguin, 1973 [2004(?) printing]), 21). See also M. L. Pratt's *Imperial Eyes: Travel Writing and Transculturation* (London: Routledge, 1994) for further discussion of travel writing's colonialist heritage.

34 S. Bassnett, 'Travel Writing and Gender', in *The Cambridge Companion to Travel Writing*, ed. P. Hulme and T. Youngs, 235.

for his readers through the act of writing. He teaches his readers what he knows, and simultaneously teaches the people he talks to whilst relativizing their knowledge: he often sets his knowledge in opposition to theirs.[35] Naipaul gives the impression that he already knows his interlocutors; Edward Said calls this 'knowledge reinforced by the colonial encounter as well as by the widespread interest in the alien and unusual' (*Orientalism*, 39–40). The notion of knowing goes hand-in-hand with what Naipaul regards as the role of the writer and the importance of this profession. On the one hand, Naipaul sets out to learn about Islam but on the other he introduces his own knowledge to the people he talks to, as well as to his readers by producing a travel account.

Naipaul's writing is reminiscent of an anthropologist's approach to his subjects. Melman observes that in the 'ethnography of modern everyday life', the 'experience of travel is primarily textual' (110), which also holds true for Naipaul: like an ethnographer, he interprets what he sees and simultaneously follows a 'desire for systematicity and precision'.[36] As he represents the people he meets, he produces and reproduces their culture[37] — as far as his conversational partners let him:

> And yet, after an hour of eating fruit and drinking tea and talking, I had got nothing new from Abbas, had not been able to get beyond his gaze and what seemed to be his formality and pride; had not been moved to make a note or even to take my notebook out from the breast-pocket of my jacket. And when the electricity failed in the neighbourhood, and everything was suddenly dark all around, it seemed time to leave. (NBB 202)

Naipaul frequently points out that taking notes is a significant part of his journey. In this instance, however, Naipaul fails to 'read' his interlocutor and therefore to take notes, or his 'subject' fails to give him the material he could use for his book. This is a temporarily

35 These techniques of teaching both the people the travel writer meets on his journeys and his readers is a common feature in travel writing. See as an earlier example Adam Olearius's *Moskowitische und persische Reise: Die Holsteinische Gesandtschaft beim Schah 1633–39* [*Moscowian and Persian Journey: The Holstein Delegation Visiting the Shah 1633–39*] (Schleswig 1647), ed. D. Haberland, Alte abenteuerliche Reiseberichte (Stuttgart: Edition Erdmann in Thienemann, 1986).
36 J. Pau Rubiés, 'Travel Writing and Ethnography', in *The Cambridge Companion to Travel Writing*, ed. P. Hulme and T. Youngs, 252–53.
37 Bachmann-Medick, 'Einleitung', in *Kultur als Text*, 28: 'Kultur wird produziert und reproduziert, indem sie repräsentiert' [culture is produced and reproduced in the process of representing].

disturbing experience for Naipaul, as he likes to get to the bottom of the consciousness of the countries he visits. Said suggests that

> many writers of travel books and guidebooks compose them in order to say that a country *is* like this, or better, that it *is* colorful, expensive, interesting, and so forth. The idea [...] is that people, places, and experiences can always be described by a book, so much so that the book (or text) acquires a greater authority, and use, even than the actuality it describes. (*Orientalism*, 93, italics Said's)

Naipaul as travel writer and the books he produces demonstrate a great authority: the declarative nature of his writing becomes particularly apparent in *Beyond Belief*. By describing how he takes notes and transfers his experiences into a piece of writing, he emphasizes the process of producing a book. He thereby gives the impression that the result of his journey, the book, is at least as significant as the actual journey.

Naipaul primarily requires translators as a vehicle for gaining access to inside knowledge. By contrast, Trojanow, who claims to perceive himself as a writer to a limited extent only, acts as a translator-teacher for his readers as he takes them through the rituals of the hajj: he explains what rituals a Muslim has to perform, and when and why. However, he also consciously seeks the help and advice of people he meets on his journeys. Throughout his travel account, Trojanow describes encounters with more experienced Muslims who help him find a more immediate access to his religion than he currently has. Trojanow appears as a less experienced Muslim, but he is fully embraced by the more experienced believers. Before he leaves he seeks advice in India where he is preparing for the hajj. The notion of translation (as a form of transferring and reappropriating knowledge and experience from one person to another rather than a one-to-one transmission) is positively connoted for Trojanow: he is eager to learn about Islam through the transferral of spiritual understanding by more experienced Muslims. By relating to 'translators', Trojanow stresses the importance of teachers and education in Islam:[38]

> Badrubhai betete, als ich das Zelt betrat. Sein Kopf schwang rhythmisch von einer Seite zur anderen, die Worte wurden heftig gesetzt, rasant betont, die Stimme schien aus der Brust zu brechen.

38 Cf. Sardar, 209, italics Sardar's: 'Thus, Islam does not only make the pursuit of knowledge obligatory but also connects it with the unique Islamic notion of worship: *ilm*, the term for knowledge, is a form of *ibadah* (worship)'.

> Zeige mir dieses Gebet, bat ich ihn, als er sich aus der Sitzstellung gelöst und auf seiner Decke ausgestreckt hatte.
>
> Ich kann es dir nicht beibringen, du bist dafür noch nicht weit genug fortgeschritten, sagte er, erklärte es mir dann aber doch: Das Gebet fängt im Herzen an. Du mußt alles aus deinem Herzen verbannen außer Allah. (TZH 114)

> [Badrubhai was praying when I entered the tent. His head was swinging rhythmically from one side to the other, the words were pronounced with precision and terrific emphasis; his voice came from deep within his chest.
>
> 'Show me this prayer,' I asked him when he moved [*sic*] from his seated position and stretched out on his blanket.
>
> 'I can't teach it to you, you are not advanced enough yet,' he said, but then he explained it to me nonetheless: 'The prayer begins in the heart. You have to cleanse your heart of everything apart from Allah'. (TMM 143)]

A point that is strongly associated with the role of teachers and the kind of (spiritual) experience they initiate is the different attitudes Trojanow and Naipaul maintain towards education: whereas Naipaul, a non-Muslim whose Western education brought him to England and later helped him become a successful writer, focuses on Western education, or secular reason, that may lay claim to universally binding world knowledge; Trojanow, as an educated Westerner and Muslim, consciously values other forms of knowledge, such as Islamic knowledge which does not have the same status for Naipaul. This may be due to the fact that Naipaul, not being Muslim himself, could not have encountered it in the same way as Trojanow. He writes:

> Mr Wahid praised him while he stood before us and said he was thirty and knew a lot of the Koran by heart. I said it was marvellous, knowing the Koran by heart. 'Half,' Mr Wahid said. 'Half'. And, considering the hunched man before us who had little else to do, I said with some sternness that it wasn't good enough. (NBB 29)

With his jovially 'stern' comment 'it wasn't good enough', Naipaul humours Mr Wahid's appraisal of the man's knowledge of the Qur'an. He uses irony as a way to distance himself from what he regards as his interlocutor's seriousness and exaggerated pride. Having moved to the UK for his education, Naipaul, the former colonial subject, cherishes the intellectual engagement with the wider world that is detached from religious doctrine as a means to overcome his supposed inferior position.[39] Since he managed to leave his former naïve self behind by studying and learning in a Western context, his humour seems to suggest an intellectual superiority based on his estimation of knowledge. He does not question that there is such a thing as valuable Islamic knowledge, yet he does not see his expectations of knowledgeable Muslims fulfilled in this instance.

Trojanow, by contrast, takes a more naïve approach to the Islamic heritage than Naipaul, the approach of the believer who is less critical of his religion than an outsider. His book appears as an advocate for Islam, which is partly justified as an affirmative counterweight to Naipaul's sceptical account. That does not, however, make Trojanow a more open traveller and writer about Islam — he is closed in a different, less reflective way than Naipaul: the hajj is the ultimate celebration of being part of the Muslim community and he would therefore like to return to the overwhelming atmosphere of the hajj through the act of writing as if to remind himself of what it was like to be a Muslim on this journey. He writes: 'Nicht nur aus Neugier sollte ich einige Monate später nach Deoband reisen; ich hoffte, zu der beglückenden Stimmung der Hadsch, zu Ruhe und Konzentration zurückzufinden' (TZH 126) ['It wasn't curiosity alone that led me to Deoband a few months later [...]; I was hoping to recapture some of the serenity and the contented state of mind I had experienced on the Hajj' (TMM 158)]. 'Ruhe und Konzentration' ['serenity and contented state of mind'] are concepts which are part of most religions and thereby do not distinguish one religion from another, such as Islam from Christianity. Back in India, Trojanow is primarily trying to find ways of re-imagining serenity, the quintessentially Muslim experience of the hajj, which is another indicator of the lifelong effect of the hajj (its preparation and afterglow) on a Muslim's existence.

Trojanow travels in order to experience the celebration of the community of believers and thus, one could argue, also wishes to see his positive attitude towards the *umma* confirmed. Similarly to Naipaul, he lets people talk in his book who do not doubt his positive view on Islam. (We need to ask, however, whether a doubter would go on the hajj at all, indeed whether the hajj allows room for doubters.) In contrast to Naipaul, Trojanow largely regards the relationships with the people he meets on his journey as a uniting and not as a dividing experience. This notion is already externally emphasized by the same dress, the *ihram*, a seamless white two-piece garment covering the

39 Naipaul describes his move to England and his education as a way of gaining acceptance in Britain in *The Enigma of Arrival: A Novel in Five Sections* (London: Picador, 2002 [1987]), 93.

upper and lower parts of the body that all (male) Muslims have to wear on the hajj. This dress enables each pilgrim to reach the state of purity, of inner immersion, which is the prerequisiste for performing the rituals of the hajj, and which works against the Western concept of individuality based on autonomy as advocated by Naipaul.

***

Both Trojanow and Naipaul meet their companions and interlocutors in 'contact zones'.[40] For Naipaul, contact zones are created by the common experiences that his younger, narrated self shares with many of his interlocutors: a kind of naïvity and ignorance that Naipaul has overcome but can still identify with. However, there are occasions when these contact zones do not work; this prevents Naipaul from gaining the inside knowledge that he aims for:

> I couldn't enter his [Idrees's] faith. But in that room, as he lost his anxieties, I felt tenderer towards him. I liked seeing him relaxed on the bed, snatching at peace, carrying the stupendousness of his faith, his belief in the Promised Messiah who had come to cleanse and reveal anew the true religion. [...] [I]t was like being taken far aback. (NAB 256)

Idrees is a member of the Ahmadis (the 'purest of Muslims' [NAB 247]) in Lahore. Naipaul is a secular Hindu with a strong sense of his Indian, Caribbean and Western backgrounds and their different value systems. Yet as a writer who writes from a Western vantage point he seems to find it difficult to meet his interlocutors on common ground: he cannot 'enter' their belief system. On the one hand, Naipaul observes his conversational partner very closely — he describes how Idrees gradually relaxes in his presence — yet, on the other, he deliberately keeps a (mental) distance to try to secure his objectivity and ability to assess events. This is the 'phenomenon of *distance*' (Ashcroft *et al.*, 186, italics theirs) which characterizes travel writing as a literary genre of personal detachment, a genre which focuses on the traveller as writer. In this conversation, it is the 'stupendousness of the faith' (NAB 256) — a concept that Naipaul defines as the unconditional acceptance and unquestioning celebration of the

40 I borrow Pratt's term in order to describe only a space where the traveller and their 'subjects' come into contact, and not 'the space of colonial encounter, the space in which peoples geographically and historically separated come into contact with each other and establish ongoing relations, usually involving conditions of coercion, radical inequality, and intractable conflict' (6).

tremendousness and might of Islam, rather than the greatness of the faith itself — which, to some extent, he also associates with a younger, less experienced and now detached self who was as impressionable and unquestioning as Idrees now is.

At first sight, Trojanow's contact zone is defined in a more egalitarian way: it is a space for all Muslims, but the hajj does not allow for contact between Muslims and non-Muslims, and we only read about the encounter of people who share the same belief. Mecca and its Great Mosque, the Masjid al-Haram, as the focal point of Islam are at the centre of every Muslim's consciousness.[41] Muslims acknowledge this place as part of their lives: they pray towards the Ka'ba and remember the Muslims on the hajj by slaughtering an animal at exactly the same time as the pilgrims do in Mina. Trojanow's contact zone reaches beyond a physically separating space. He approaches people's minds, because he claims to be one of them:

> Die heulenden Stimmen […] erklangen aus allen Richtungen. […] Keiner der zwei Millionen stand in dieser Stunde außerhalb des Gebets. Wir nutzten die Zeit […], um noch einmal um Vergebung zu flehen […].
>
> […] Hadsch Mabruk. Die Hadsch galt mit dem Ende dieses islamischen Tages als erfüllt. Unsere Sünden waren vergeben, wir waren wie neugeborene Kinder, und wir durften uns von nun an Hadschis nennen. (TZH 97–98)

> [The wailing voices […] rang out from every direction. […] Not one of the two million people was distant from the prayers at this time. We used the time […] to plead for forgiveness […].
>
> *Hajj Mabruk.* The Hajj is considered complete at the end of this day. Our sins were forgiven, we were like new-born babies, and from this moment on we could refer to ourselves as Hajjis. (TMM 119–20)]

Trojanow identifies with his companions (he uses the collective personal pronoun 'we', something the distanced traveller and writer Naipaul, who aims for objectivity, would not do): as pilgrims, they are all in the same position and, physically, in the same space. One could even go as far as to say that a notion of individualism based on Enlightenment ideas is dissolved here, indeed, that differences between Muslims from all over the world are eradicated: the hajjis are united in the religious rituals and have the same aim, the fulfilment of the hajj.

41 G. Endress, *Einführung in die islamische Geschichte* (Munich: Beck, 1982), 93–96.

Trojanow claims that his interest in his travel companions is about his self-definition as collective and Islamic. He thus places himself in opposition to what he regards as Western travel writers. He writes: 'Der Reiseerzähler, der die Welt um seine Physis und Psyche kreisen läßt, ist ein neueres, westliches Phänomen, das wesentlich dazu beigetragen hat, die Reiseerzählung als literarische Form zu diskreditieren' (TZH 8) ['The travel writer who allows the world to revolve around his own person and psyche is a more recent Western phenomenon [which has in no small part contributed to travel writing being discredited as a literary form]' (TMM 2)].[42] Trojanow prefers to be seen as part of the Muslim tradition of writing about the hajj, as a form of reflecting upon what it means to be part of the *umma* and not as a form of self-exploration in opposition to an Other. However, writing as a 'wir' [we] can be problematic, as Trojanow claims a collective experience here and thereby makes some vast assumptions: he exercises the authority of the writer which, in this context, is not dissimilar to Naipaul's authority over his subjects and readers. Trojanow is, like Naipaul, a professional writer, and books are always published with an eye to the market. Nevertheless, the question of the audience appears less significant for Trojanow than for Naipaul: he claims to be writing for 'anyone who can read'.[43] His travelogue, which only sold five thousand copies and was, in contrast to Naipaul's travel books, commercially unsuccessful, falls between audiences: as Trojanow states, Muslims tend to seek hajj guides, whereas non-Muslims seem to regard *Zu den Heiligen Quellen des Islam* as too spiritual in nature, and possibly as too much in favour of Islam. Despite Trojanow's claim to write in a specific hajj writing tradition, it needs to be questioned whether he is free of Western practices of travel writing, that is, an expression of self. Furthermore, as a Western writer, Trojanow can go on the hajj and then return to being a Western writer with freedom of speech, an option not open to writers and intellectuals in most predominantly Muslim countries. This position contributes to the contradiction between claiming to write in a particular way and, in fact, being a different kind of writer. Taking a closer look at the interaction between travelling and writing in Naipaul's and Trojanow's travel accounts can help reveal such contradictions more clearly.

***

42 Last phrase translated by F. M.

43 This and the following statements: Trojanow in an unpublished interview with Frauke Matthes conducted prior to his reading at the Goethe Institute Glasgow, 14 November 2006 (abbreviated version publ. as 'Die Fremde muss wie ein Stein sein', *Kreuzer*, 1/2007, 57).

In this mobile age, notions of travelling, migrating and nomadism are part of life. The interaction with the Other thus encountered, or an 'other' side which travellers discover in themselves, increasingly shapes people's identities.[44] Yet it seems that it is not until the textual realization of the journey that the latter is fully experienced. Barbara Korte emphasizes that, in the twentieth century, '[i]f the journey is found to be significant, this often happens not during the act of travelling itself, but rather at the moment when the journey is textualized. Meaningful travelling experience, for many postmodern travellers, will only emerge with the act of travel *writing*' (*English Travel Writing*, 144, italics Korte's). As Michel Butor points out, 'travelling' also takes place 'in order to write'.[45] By going abroad, writers can find new subject matter and/or develop different perspectives on previously formed opinions. Naipaul places great emphasis on the relation between travelling and writing: the former is almost a prerequisite for the latter. He expresses this mutual relationship in 'Our Universal Civilization' as follows:

> And if I have to describe the universal civilization I would say it is the civilization that both gave the prompting and the idea of the literary vocation; and also gave the means to fulfill that prompting; the civilization that enabled me to make that journey from the periphery to the centre [...] on whom — as on me — the outer world had worked, and given the ambition to write. (506–07)

For Naipaul the profession of the writer is closely connected to the migration from the 'periphery' to the 'centre', where he gradually gained the privileged position of the individualist Western writer. Later he started travelling back to the 'periphery', where he thought he could not have become a writer, in order to write about it (507).[46] It seems, therefore, that particularly at the beginning of his career he represents a 'prototypical' travel writer, for whom 'Reisen ist ein Muster der Welterschließung und der Persönlichkeits-Bildung,

44 R. Bonadei, 'Theory into *écriture*: Travel Literature Encounters Touring Cultures', in *Cross-Cultural Travel: Papers from the Royal Irish Academy International Symposium on Literature and Travel, National University of Ireland, Galway, November 2002*, ed. J. Couroy, Travel Writing Across Disciplines, Theory and Pedagogy, 7 (New York: Peter Lang, 2003), 418.

45 M. Butor, 'Travel and Writing', trans. J. Powers and K. Lisker, *Mosaic*, 8.1 (1974), 14 (repr. in *Temperamental Journeys: Essays on the Modern Literature of Travel*, ed. M. Kowalewski (Athens: The University of Georgia Press, 1992), 67; originally publ. as *Le voyage et l'écriture*, *Romantisme*, no. 4 (1972), 4–19).

46 See also Naipaul's semi-autobiographical novel *The Enigma of Arrival* in which he explores how he grew into the existence of the writer.

"Literatur des Reisens" wird so zum Ausdruck eines Erfahrungs- und Gestaltungsprozesses, in dem Reisen und Schreiben einander bedingen' (Schlösser, 15) [travelling is a mode of exploring the world as well as the self. 'The literature of travel' thus becomes the expression of a process of experiencing and re-forming in which travelling and writing depend on each other]. In *Among the Believers* and *Beyond Belief*, however, the notion of 'exploring the world' seems to be more prominent that that of 'exploring the self'. Naipaul describes this process in practical terms after having met Shahbaz, a Marxist and revolutionary, in Pakistan:

> But I felt that the narrative had become too fast here. I felt when I considered my notes that certain things had been elided. I telephoned Shahbaz; he didn't make difficulties. I went to see him again. I wanted to hear more about him. I wanted to hear more about those very early days in Baluchistan. I wanted to hear more about the first day. (NBB 300)

With this incident, Naipaul describes the act of writing as physical movement to his subject matter (going back to Shabhaz). Travelling enables him to meet people and write about what he is looking for through individual encounters. Naipaul is looking for knowledge through his companions and interlocutors, and he strongly connects the act of travelling with the act of finding writing material.[47] The travel accounts focus on Naipaul the writer, rather than on Naipaul the individual. This might be due to the nature of Naipaul's Western travel writing: Trojanow's hajj writing is supposedly about personal change, whereas Naipauls's travel accounts aim to focus on countries and their people. Although Naipaul is the lynchpin of his travelogues, his primary goal is to communicate to his readers the characteristics of the countries he visits (as he perceives them) and not his own character.

Trojanow's merging of travelling and writing is of a different nature. He firmly situates himself in the tradition of hajj writing, *rihla;* this comes across as a personal journey, yet through the publication of this travel account — a book that he, paradoxically, claims not to have had in mind when travelling to Mecca and Medina (unpublished interview) — Trojanow, being a writer, does wish to convey his experiences to a larger audience. As he does not question Islam as such, we might expect a proselytizing aspect in the book: by

47 B. King, *V. S. Naipaul,* 2nd edn (Basingstoke: Palgrave Macmillan, 2003 [1993]), 137.

encountering the peace and brotherhood he sets out to find on the hajj, he implicitly criticizes Naipaul's individualistic West in favour of the Muslim world. Trojanow writes:

> Dieser Bericht steht in einer alten Tradition. Seit mehr als tausend Jahren existiert der literarische Typus einer Reiseerzählung über die Hadsch, auf arabisch Rihla, auf persisch Safarnameh genannt — Zeugnisse einer Pilgerschaft als Kulmination aller Sehnsüchte, als einzigartige Aus-Zeit, so reich an Mühsal und Zermürbung wie an Belohnung und Beglückung. (TZH 7)
>
> [Ancient both as a form as well as a tradition, literary travel writing about the Hajj — *Rihla* in Arabic, *Safarnameh* in Persian — has been in existence for over one thousand years. These are the accounts of the Muslim pilgrimage as the culmination of all desires, the unique time-out that is rich in trial and tribulation as it is in rewards and delights. (TMM 1, italics Morrison's)]

Writing about the hajj has a long tradition: *rihla,* travel for learning and other purposes, emphasizes the interrelation between travelling and writing. It is a means of retrospective reflection which enables the writer to relive the experience of the pilgrimage. It becomes a journey of the mind. Trojanow comments on his revived experience of the hajj as follows:

> Als Ramadan erneut begann [...], las ich meine Notizen durch und war fast überwältigt von der intensiven Vergegenwärtigung. Ich sehnte mich nach der Hadsch zurück, und ich wußte von einem Weg, wie ich die Reise noch einmal begehen konnte. Das war die stärkste Motivation, dieses Buch zu schreiben. (TZH 165–66)
>
> [When Ramadan began again [...] I re-read my notes and was almost overwhelmed by how intensely I could still visualise it. I longed to be back on the Hajj, and I knew I could embark on that journey once more by writing about it: [t]his was the most powerful motivation for this book. (TMM 203–04)]

Yet publishing a book confirms the writer's ego, which is at the centre of Western travel writing. Trojanow cannot escape his profession with its root in individualistic Western traditions; by making his account available to a wider audience, he breaks out of the crowd of pilgrims and becomes a Western individual. Yet throughout his travel account, Trojanow clearly sees himself in the tradition of both the hajj and its accounts, *rihla,* which define him as a Muslim. This notion of self-dissolution in brotherhood is significant, particularly in relation to modern ideas of states and nations, and the experience of migration that challenge such (occasionally artificially created) categories. Nowadays, migration — the crossing of and conscious dealing with national, linguistic and cultural borders — seems to be part of the 'human condition'. Trojanow combines his experiences of migration with both the idea of 'going home' to one's origins, to a universal 'Muslim home', and the hajj account as a form of self-exploration and thus autobiography, which provides the framework for his journey.[48] He seems to personify a challenging relationship between Islam (submission to God and collectivity) and the West (secular autonomy).

Both Trojanow and Naipaul are itinerant writers in the true sense of the word: they explore their peripatetic life in literature and have a migrant and/or colonial background. It therefore also needs to be asked whether or how travel writing and postcolonialism, which I understand as a manifold and hybrid approach to perceiving the Other (the writer's openness to letting other voices be heard), can harmonize. Does the choice of genre rule out any form of non-patronizing writing? Since travel writing is usually regarded as a Western form of writing, the search for (postcolonial) alternatives might begin by examining travel writers of a postcolonial or migrant background and, based on their transcultural experiences, a possibly more differentiated view on their surroundings.

In contrast to migrants, travel writers must return home. This presupposition enables them to engage actively with their awareness of difference (Naipaul) as well as similarity (Trojanow), since they do not vitally need to integrate into a new society, but are exploring the new environment in relation to themselves.

This postcolonial consideration of travel writing raises questions about techniques of representation and interpretation, and about the acknowledgement that every traveller is influenced by their culture(s), religion, history and other aspects of their background.[49] In 1979, shortly after the Islamic Revolution in Iran, Naipaul went on a journey in order to find reasons for what he regarded as the destructive force of Islam. He also visited places of Muslim worship and pilgrimage where his position as a non-Muslim and his differentiation from Muslims particularly came to the fore. His difficulty in understanding Muslims has its roots in his early

48 B. D. Metcalf, 'The Pilgrimage Remembered: South Asian Accounts of the *hajj*', in *Muslim Travellers*, D. F. Eickelman and J. Piscatori, 100–01, 88.
49 See S. Hall, 'New Ethnicities', in *Black Film, British Cinema*, ed. K. Mercer, BFI/ICA Documents, 7 (London: Institute for Contemporary Arts, 1988), 29.

childhood in the Indian (Hindu) diaspora in Trinidad:[50] 'We knew nothing of Muslims. This idea of strangeness, of the thing to be kept outside, extended even to other Hindus' (188). Naipaul grew up with a strong sense of difference; nonetheless, when he started travelling, he seems to have been looking for similarities between him and other migrants regardless of their religious and cultural backgrounds: 'I thought, when I began to travel in the Muslim world, that I would be travelling among people who would be like the people of my own community' ('Our Universal Civilization', 508). Naipaul's comment could be read as his awareness of a similar colonial background for Hindu and Muslim migrants (after all, many Indians are Muslims). However, this kind of identification based on his former Trinidadian community as well as a common experience of migration with Muslims is a limited one, and his perception of the Muslim world is guided by dichotomies such as East — West, Muslims — Hindus. Yet it is his inquiry about the unfamiliar side of the dichotomy that helps him gain access to his surroundings.

Trojanow's multi-layered background equally affects his travel experience: he is of Bulgarian origin, but has lived in Germany, Kenya, India, South Africa and, at the time of the writing of this book, Vienna. However, he becomes less aware of cultural difference as he travels among and with Muslims who share the same goal: the pilgrimage as spiritual experience and celebration of the *umma*. It determines his interaction with fellow pilgrims. As they are united in their belief on the hajj, there is no space for divisions.

***

The writers' 'self-production' (as respectively curious and engaged traveller and writer) also comes to the fore when considering two fundamental questions raised by their texts: firstly, how do the writers explore Islam's past, and secondly, how do the writer and the community of the believers interact?

Islam is often associated with a strong sense of tradition and a focus on the past and the Prophet Muhammad. Although it is the youngest of the three 'religions of the book', whose self-awareness arose out of the *hijra* and is reflected in the hajj as a Muslim's conscious reflection on their religious roots, secular Westerners often perceive it as a religion that looks back to its origins as a means of justifying

50 V. S. Naipaul, 'Two Worlds (The Nobel Lecture)' (7 December 2001), in Naipaul, *Literary Occasions*, 181–95.

or explaining the present. However, both Naipaul and Trojanow address originality and diversity in Islam.

Naipaul travels in order to find out how 'fundamentalism' could have grown into such a significant issue in the non-Arab Muslim world. He sees one answer to his inquiry in the conversion from culturally different, non-Islamic cultures to a religion whose new believers do not share the associations of 'original', that is, in his view, Arab Muslims. Naipaul undertakes 'excursions among the converted peoples' (as the subtitle of *Beyond Belief* claims), whose form of Islam he identifies as a transformed one. Conversion implies an idea of the common origin on which Islam is built, yet also a sense of leaving non-Islamic traditions and customs behind. In his prologue to *Beyond Belief* he states:

> Islam is in its origin an Arab religion. Everyone not an Arab who is a Muslim is a convert. Islam is not simply a matter of conscience or private belief. It makes imperial demands. A convert's world view alters. His holy places are in Arab lands; his sacred language is Arabic. His idea of history alters. He rejects his own; he becomes, whether he likes it or not, a part of the Arab story. The convert has to turn away from everything that is his. The disturbance for societies is immense, and even after a thousand years can remain unresolved; the turning away has to be done again and again. People develop fantasies about who and what they are; and in the Islam of converted countries there is an element of neurosis and nihilism. These countries can be easily set on the boil. (NBB 1)

According to Naipaul's interpretation, the forms of Islam he encounters on his journeys are mediated ones: Islams without a past, or rather with a reconstructed past unconnected to Arabia. Thus Naipaul explores how Islam itself has been 'converted' in the countries he visits: from a belief system to a form of politics (primarily to 'fundamentalism').

Naipaul argues that these 'converts' strive for the appropriation of a new, Islamic past to feel complete as Muslims. He says that in non-Arab Muslim countries '[t]he faith abolished the [non-Islamic] past. And when the past was abolished like this, more than an idea of history suffered. Human behavior, and ideals of good behaviour, could suffer' (Naipaul, 'Our Universal Civilization', 509). These countries wanted to become 'pure(ly) Muslim' by cutting their ties with their non-Islamic heritage completely, which is also partly

Naipaul's own background, the Hindu traditions of his ancestors,[51] and Naipaul does not fail to bemoan the loss of 'his' religion in some of the countries he visits due to the contemporary dominance of Islam. (He particularly feels that way in Indonesia [NAB 435].) The revival of Islam and its 'fundamentalist' form of expression in particular serve as a counterpoint to Naipaul's perception of an 'original' past which was often forcefully removed through the people's gradual conversion to Islam. He describes in great detail how non-Arab Muslims 'invent' history and an Arab ancestry in order to overcome this loss of cultural 'originality' and to feel 'purely', 'authentically' Muslim:[52] 'I was among people whose identity was more or less contained in the faith. I was among people who wished to be pure' (Naipaul, 'Our Universal Civilization', 512). This religious history is closely tied to the political history of the countries he visits: here, Islam — maybe more so than in 'originally' Muslim countries — tends to be not only a religion but a complete way of life.

> So I not only began to understand what people in Pakistan meant when they told me that Islam was a complete way of life, affecting everything; I began to understand that — though it might be said that we had shared a common sub-continental origin — I had travelled a different way. I began to formulate the idea of the universal civilization — which, growing up in Trinidad, I had lived or been part of without quite knowing that I did so. (NBB 511–12)

Despite their common sub-continental origin, Naipaul sees a great divide between himself and South Asian Muslims, for he 'travelled a different way', away from cultural and religious roots and to the West. His image of the West is based on the idea of modernity, a process which, in Couze Venn's words, co-emerged with 'rational' capitalism and European colonialism, all three of which 'map out the history of the modern world' (19), and secularism, which, according to critics such as S. Sayyid who do not hide their ironic criticism of the West, 'is presented as one of the key achievements of western cultural formations'.[53] If one bases secularism exclusively on 'the excision of religion into a "private" zone where it can't interfere

51 For further details on Hinduism in the Caribbean, see S. Vertovec, *Hindu Trinidad: Religion, Ethnicity and Socio-economic Change* (London: Macmillan Caribbean, 1992) and *The Hindu Diaspora: Comparative Patterns* (London: Routledge, 2000).

52 For a discussion of notions of authenticity, see Gupta, 72.

53 S. Sayyid, 'Contemporary Politics of Secularism', in *Secularism, Religion and Multicultural Citizenship*, ed. G. Brahm Levey and T. Modood, 188.

with the common life',[54] then Islam, or Islamic societies, cannot be part of Naipaul's 'universal civilization'. However, such a simplified opposition between intolerant secularism and religiosity denies what Jürgen Habermas regards as a 'postsecular society' ('Ein Bewußtsein von dem, was fehlt', 27), in which the religious side and secular reason need to acknowledge each other and accept each other's validity (29). This being the case Naipaul's idea of modernity allows for informed and reflecting religiosity, but not for unquestioning belief as a 'complete way of life'.

Naipaul perceives 'Islam [as a] religion with a glorious past but an impoverished present'.[55] One could argue, however, that Naipaul is trying to compensate for his own lack of past. Naipaul's background and his own sense of (non-)belonging need to be considered in this context. Having been brought up in the Indian diaspora of Trinidad, his sense of non-belonging contributes to his understanding of notions of origin. Naipaul often refers to his — a migrant's — sense of loss of his old tradition as well as a sense of not being part of a new tradition after having moved to the UK. Indeed, as a former colonial subject, he bemoans his lack of tradition,[56] and as a result he appears to have created 'a myth of origin'.[57]

Naipaul constructs the West as the driving force behind positive change. His position in the West needs to be considered once again: having come from a British colony, he adopted Western ideas of individualism. The British Empire undertook similar conversion processes with its colonials to Islam with its 'all-embracing' nature. However, Western individualism can be and has been used to challenge Western thinking, something Muslims or Muslim converts can rarely do as openly with Islam in predominantly Muslim countries. Naipaul's examination of the notion of conversion (in relation to the past) could, therefore, be read as yet another example of self-recognition in the face of the Other (which is part of his former self and which, in retrospect, he rejects). This self-re-discovery (which Trojanow, by contrast, practises through identification with his fellow believers and not differentiation from them) comes especially to the fore when Naipaul examines the Muslim countries' relationship with

54 C. Taylor, 'Foreword: What is Secularism?', in *Secularism, Religion and Multicultural Citizenship*, ed. G. Brahm Levey and T. Modood, xx.

55 T. Weiss, *On the Margins: The Art of Exile in V. S. Naipaul* (Amherst: The University of Massachusetts Press, 1992), 148.

56 V. S. Naipaul, 'Jasmine' (1964), in Naipaul, *Literary Occasions*, 48.

57 J. Levy, *V. S. Naipaul: Displacement and Autobiography* (New York: Garland, 1995), xi.

the West. He increasingly establishes his position as the privileged and more knowledgeable traveller from the West, whilst paradoxically the concept of 'the West' appears ambiguous in the context of his own colonial heritage: his origin is not as clear-cut as he seems to pretend, and the West is as 'inauthentic' as the Islam he encounters.[58] Naipaul's heritage – and I specifically include his experience as a migrant to the UK here – serves as a means to establish his superiority. He describes his (and the West's) difficult and complicated relationship with a number of non-Western countries and also points out how the West is needed especially for science and modern technology, for instance in Tehran:

> I said, 'Mr Parvez, you are a good Muslim and a good Shia. Your paper [the *Tehran Times*] used to be full of criticism of materialist civilizations. Why are your sons studying in the United States?'
>
> It wasn't time to push the question. He was too weary. He said [...], 'It's his future. He's studying computer engineering. [...]'
>
> So, deep down, he was divided. [...] It was in that division of the mind – as much as in the excesses of the Shah – that the Islamic revolution had begun in Iran. And it was there that it was ending. (NAB 493–94)

In this conversation, Naipaul portrays Mr Parvez as an explicitly Muslim man and through him reveals the paradox of Islamic countries: shunning everything non-Islamic, Western is not possible. The West, particularly Western education and expertise, is needed and used in order to – paradoxically – establish these Islamic societies. This observation feeds into Naipaul's critical view that Islamic values alone cannot hold a country together. In the countries he visits, Naipaul sees what Rob Nixon lists as follows: 'insecurity [...] from a weak sense of history, the shock of partial modernization, habits of dependent idleness inculcated during the colonial era, and grandiose dreams'.[59] Naipaul does not discuss how Western colonialism in these areas worked to prevent progress, and how the West still both exploits the non-Western world and forces it into an inferior position. He also ignores the fact that as a result of this disappointment in 'Western modernization' and as a form of

58 See Melman, 116: 'The word "authentic" has different meanings: historical (denoting the descendents of the inhabitants of the peninsula before Islamisation), biological and even racial (indicating Arab racial purity), or socio-cultural (defining a nomadic and pastoral life and economy)'.

59 R. Nixon, *London Calling: V. S. Naipaul, Postcolonial Mandarin* (New York: Oxford University Press, 1992), 130.

counter-reaction to European colonialism, radical Islam appeals to the frustration caused by that condescension and hypocrisy, and many formerly colonized countries start to regard 'Islamic solidarity' 'as the correct alternative'.[60]

For instance, in Pakistan, Naipaul observes: 'Step by step, out of its Islamic striving, Pakistan had undone the rule of law it had inherited from the British, and replaced it with nothing' (NAB 195). Naipaul's standpoint seems naïve, as he does not acknowledge the contradiction between European ideals of rule of law and the reality in the colonies where these were bent to further European interests. He criticizes the colonizing effect of Islam and seems to suggest that, in comparison, British imperialism was better than 'Islamic imperialism': the positive effects of British imperialism (such as institutions) were deliberately eradicated to set the stage for a local, Islamic way, yet, for Naipaul, functioning alternatives were not offered. Naipaul has critically dealt with the effects that British imperialism had on him as an individual and a writer in previous texts, for example, *The Enigma of Arrival*. Having experienced British imperialism and the positive effects himself, he feels justified to judge the consequences when British institutions were ruled out in Pakistan. Overall, Naipaul seems to want to communicate that the non-Arab Muslim countries' reconstruction of the 'originality' of their faith as a counter-reaction to British imperialism is not the right alternative. It leads to 'fundamentalism' and ultimate destruction.

The attachment to the Islamic past can, however, be interpreted in a different, more positive way. For any Muslim, but particularly for a pilgrim who is going to Mecca, the past is primarily symbolized by one place: the Ka'ba, which is the physical centre for every Muslim believer. As a place of worship which goes as far back as Abraham, it carries a great sense of history. The past is also experienced as physical time: the Muslim calendar starts with Muhammad's *hijra* from Mecca to Medina in 622. Trojanow's travel account is structured according to the days of the Muslim month of pilgrimage, *Zuul Hijjah*, which all require particular rituals. These rituals refer back to Islam's past and its ancient land, and remind the pilgrim of significant incidents in the religion's development. They are followed by all Muslims all over the world (with individual, often culturally determined variations) and have the same implications. As well as being the focal point for Muslim belief, Mecca provides each pilgrim with a unique spiritual experience in the light of Islamic history.

60 J. A. Williams, ed., *The Word of Islam* (London: Thames and Hudson, 1994), 215.

As all Muslims pray towards the Ka'ba, they create a strong sense of unity among themselves. However, the actual act of prayer is an individual one. Despite this, praying simultaneously creates a collective experience, particularly on the hajj and in Mecca, when pilgrims are closest to the Ka'ba: 'Das Gebet, eine Struktur aus geraden und ungeraden Zahlen [...], vervollständigt die angelegte Symmetrie. In keiner anderen Religion ist dem Gebet ein so fester Rahmen vorgegeben, für den einzelnen wie für die Gemeinschaft' (TZH 55) ['The prayer, a structure of even and odd numbers [...]: the created symmetry is rendered complete. In no other religion is prayer given such a structured framework, for the individual and for the community' (TMM 62)]. Symmetry has a positive connotation and has little in common with Naipaul's perception of a uniform Islam. Trojanow returns to the idea of symmetry when describing Islamic architecture, which frames the spaces of Muslim worship. It enhances Trojanow's awareness of the beauty of Islam, and is part of his feeling of being a Muslim, which is arguably increased in and by the mosque. Art as something divine and, particularly in Mecca, as a means of connecting to the past, stands in a direct relationship to those who create and worship it, yet also worship in and with it.[61] This interaction refers back to Islam's past. Trojanow explains:

> Die Gänge, die Bögen, die Kuppeln, die Galerien [der Masjid al-Haram, der Großen Moschee zu Mekka], sie sind imposant, aber ohne die Kaaba, eindrucksvoll ob ihrer Einfachheit, wären sie wirkungslos. Die goldene Stickerei auf dem schwarzen Stoff erscheint einem fast ein Zuviel an Ornament, eine Ablenkung von der reinen, kubisch gefaßten Idee. Das Symbol wird fortwährend bestätigt durch die Pilger, die zu jeder Tages- und Nachtzeit wie Planeten diese Sonne umkreisen (oder wie Elektronen den Atomkern) und mit jedem ihrer Schritte das rechteckige Objekt menschlich aufladen. Aus dieser Wechselwirkung entsteht erst das Bayt Allah, das Haus Gottes, und die Umma, die Gemeinschaft der Gläubigen. Es ist wie mit dem heiligen Text: Er benötigt die Hingabe, die Moralität des Lesers, um lebendig zu werden. Die Offenbarung ist in ein menschliches Gefäß gegossen, die Sprache, und somit abhängig von der Kraft und der Wirkung, die ein jeder aus ihr schöpfen und ihr verleihen kann. (TZH 41–42)
>
> [The passageways, the arches, the domes, and the galleries [of the Masjid al-Haram, the Great Mosque in Mecca] are indeed imposing,

61 For further details on the aesthetic experience of Islam, see O. Leaman, *Islamic Aesthetics: An Introduction*, The New Edinburgh Islamic Surveys (Edinburgh: Edinburgh University Press, 2004).

> but without the Kaaba, impressive despite the simplicity of its architecture, they would be without effect. The golden embroidery on the black material seems almost too ornamental, a distraction from the purity of the simple, cubically conceived idea. The symbol is constantly affirmed by the pilgrims who night and day circle this sun like planets [(or as electrons circle the atomic nucleus)[62]], each of their steps charging the right-angled structure with human power. It is through this interaction that *Bayt Allah*, the House of God, and the Ummah, the community of believers, emerges [*sic*]. It is like the holy text: it requires the devotion and the morality of the reader to come to life. The revelation is poured into a human vessel, language, and is thus dependant [*sic*] on the power and the effect each one creates from it and lends it. (TMM 44)]

The pilgrims are united by their religion's past which is centred in Mecca and also expressed by the architecture of the Masjid al-Haram. Their past is the living past of Arabia, a past revived by them continuing to relate back to it in their consciousness (through the act of prayer towards Mecca, for instance) as well as by the actual journey to the original sites of Islam. On his journey, Trojanow is consciously looking for the unity of believers, which is positively connoted for him. This unity, the *umma*, is an historic concept which reaches into the present and beyond: it was formed by movement (the *hijra*), a journey which led to the self-recognition of the believers as a community. This might come across as a naïve concept as Trojanow does not discuss Muslim sectarianism, an issue that might challenge his perception of Muslim brotherhood and might lead him to discuss individuality and religious difference within Islam more attentively. However, Trojanow does criticize Islam when reflecting on what he perceives as its current crisis, its instrumentalization for political purposes and the rather unbrotherly behaviour of some of his fellow pilgrims during the ritual of the stoning of the devil.

***

The different interpretations and definitions of Islam also come to the fore when we take a closer look at the believers — as individuals and as community. For Naipaul, Islam seems almost incomprehensible, and he reduces the religion to the concept of 'submission' (the Arabic word *islām* means 'submission' or 'self-surrender to God') which for him means its literal translation, a lack of individuality, whereas Trojanow unquestioningly celebrates the unifying force of the *umma*.

62 This phrase translated by F. M.

As we might expect, the writers develop two extreme standpoints here.

There appears to be a dichotomy between Western individualism and the idea of the *umma* as a form of what Benedict Anderson calls 'imagined communities'. Naipaul holds a critical stance towards the idea of the *umma*. He comments on the internationality of Islam — here in Pakistan — rather cynically:

> It was organized; every row had a number. I was passed from person to person, snatched at one stage from a developing conversation, and taken to the foreign enclave, where there were Arabs, Indonesians, and even Africans (clearly old hands at these international Muslim gatherings, unashamedly enjoying the ethnic sensation they and their costumes and their language were exciting). (NAB 245)

Naipaul distinguishes between his idea of Western individualism and the possibility of preserving individuality within a larger community. He perceives the Muslim version of community (and the symmetry as described by Trojanow) as the negatively loaded idea of an 'enclave' rather than the positively connoted idea of brotherhood as '[f]acelessness [which] had begun to seem like an Islamic motif. [...] Individualism was to be surrendered to the saviour and avenger. But when the revolution was over, individualism — in the great city the Shah had built — was to be cherished again' (NAB 28). Naipaul appears to champion the notion of Western individuality rooted in the Enlightenment which leaves little space for other ways of experiencing individuality.

One interesting aspect and point of comparison is the nomadism that both writers have gone through in their lives. It serves as a metaphorical contact zone. Naipaul notices that 'a peasant or nomadic longing stirred within me. [...] But what to me was the impulse of the moment was for them a way of life. I would move on, do other things; they would continue as I saw them' (NAB 217). As a 'former nomad' Naipaul can be regarded as a postcolonial writer with a migrant, transcultural experience.[63] Yet he is not able to share the experience of dislocation and marginality with the Muslims he meets on his journeys. He now comes as a privileged traveller, someone with a 'home' to return to, who nonetheless often uses his previous experience of migration as a starting point for the conversations

63 Korte defines postcolonial travel writing as follows: 'as referring to travel writing produced after the Second World War by such travellers/writers whose origin is located in the world formerly colonised by Britain' ('Exploring Without a Mission?', 385).

he has with people. Their travelling (from country to city, to other, mainly Western, countries for education, and, historically, from polytheism and a diverse understanding of religion to monotheism and organized religion) has significant effects on the development of Islam — a notion which is frequently referred to by both Naipaul and Trojanow. As James Clifford points out, 'if contemporary migrant populations are not to disappear as mute, passive straws in the political-economic winds, we need to listen to a wide range of "travel stories" (not "travel literature" in the bourgeois sense)'.[64] Naipaul perceives these 'travel stories' (the life-stories of his conversation partners) with a curious eye, as these migrations remind him of his own migration from Trinidad to England as an anxious young man. Through education, he overcame this anxiety and developed into the self-assured writer who is now travelling the non-Arab Muslim world. Naipaul creates the aloof position of the outsider, as the following example demonstrates: 'Masood's panic now, his vision of his world as a blind alley (with his knowledge that there was activity and growth elsewhere), took me back to my own panic of thirty or thirty-five years before' (NAB 224–25). Naipaul enjoys two privileges in this instance: he can identify with Masood as he sees his former self reflected in him; yet, as he moved to the West, he could gain Western knowledge and experience which differentiates him now from his non-Western interlocutor. Knowledge becomes Naipaul's means of superiority and reveals what Bhabha uncovers as 'unequal relations of power' (Huggan, *The Postcolonial Exotic*, 11).[65] Fawzia Mustafa links his 'obsessive privileging of the Word and the Book and the "coherence" and "order" leading to "knowledge" they represent' to his Orientalist perception of the non-Western world.[66] Like many other critics, she uncritically regards this as an expression of Naipaul's position as a *Mimic Man*: not originating from the UK, he is 'not allowed' to represent the West,[67] as if Western critics wanted to distance themselves from his resolute ideas. Yet Naipaul

64 J. Clifford, *Routes: Travel and Translation in the Late Twentieth Century* (Cambridge, MA: Harvard University Press, 1997), 38.

65 Huggan is referring here to H. K. Bhabha, 'Postcolonial Criticism', in *Redrawing the Boundaries: The Transformation of English and American Literary Studies*, ed. S. Greenblatt and G. Gunn (New York: Modern Language Association of America, 1992), 437–65.

66 F. Mustafa, *V. S. Naipaul* (Cambridge: Cambridge University Press, 1995), 27.

67 For example, E. W. Said, 'An Intellectual Catastrophe', *Al-Ahram Weekly Online*, no. 389, 6–12 August 1998, http://weekly.ahram.org.eg/1998/389/cu1.htm [accessed 28 June 2010] (para. 3 of 9): 'He [Naipaul] is a man of the Third World'.

has struggled to become part of the West,[68] where he has lived since 1950. It seems that a Western origin allows a writer to take on a critical stance on non-Western cultures. This does not include writers such as Naipaul, who is — rather disapprovingly — said to have a '*Weltanschauung* of a secular Hindu West Indian would-be-Victorian (obsessed with finding confirmation for his judgements)' (Nixon, 45) and has been referred to as 'an outsider in England' (Levy, xv). Although being of non-Western origin, Naipaul's writing is grounded in Western traditions such as travel writing which the prolific writer has contributed to with the 'double vision' (Bhabha, 'Of Mimicry and Man', 88) of the former colonial. Naipaul is all too often criticized for 'having made it' in the West and for not keeping his peripheral position as a writer. Although he is a highly acclaimed writer, he has attracted much criticism with his publication of *Among the Believers* and *Beyond Belief*. He has been reproached for his seemingly partial perception of the countries he travels in. His 'bookishness' and, by extension, his aloofness after having experienced what it means to come from the non-Western world and to 'make it' in the West, is often regarded as the cause of Naipaul's pro-Western attitude. This goes hand-in-hand with his emphasis on the 'writer's "authority"', which is not part of the '*ethics* of writing and reading about non-western worlds' (Mustafa, 27, italics Mustafa's). Muslims in particular have felt that Naipaul misrepresented their religion as well as themselves as believers; he did not give them enough credit.[69] Consequently, many literary critics in Muslim countries have felt the need to defend their religion.[70] Yet these critics may have overlooked that Naipaul's position is a rather personal one: it seems that for Naipaul Western knowledge is progress; yet it is also a vehicle for reaching towards open-mindedness from a politically peripheral point of view and beyond cultural boundaries, both geographically and intellectually.

68 See Bhabha, 'Of Mimicry and Man', 85–92, where he discusses the '*ambivalence* of mimicry', the 'almost the same, *but not quite*' (86, italics Bhabha's) of the former colonial subject. Bhabha's title is derived from Naipaul's novel *The Mimic Men: A Novel* (London: Picador, 2002 [1967]) which describes the dilemma of the former colonial subject of wishing to conform to the imperial centre's standard and to become part of it. Naipaul himself went through this process as he illustrates in his semi-autobiographical novel *The Enigma of Arrival*.

69 For example, M. Ayub Khan, 'A Nobel for Islamophobia', *The Milli Gazette*, 2.22, www.milligazette.com/Archives/15112001/29.htm [accessed 28 June 2010] (10 para.).

70 For example, M. Saad El-Din, 'Plain Talk', *Al-Ahram Weekly Online*, no. 556, 18–24 October 2001, http://weekly.ahram.org.eg/2001/556/cu3.htm [accessed 28 June 2010] (10 para.).

Trojanow's approach to nomadism is based on his own experiences of migration. His peripatetic life triggers the question of origin, which serves as a leitmotif throughout his journey, only to refer back to Islam, not a state or a nation, as the place of origin. This is expressed in various answers to the question where he is from, and in the different answers he gives according to his conversation partners. He never replies definitely, but leaves deliberate gaps:

> Bruder Ilias, warte! Ich habe von dir gehört. Ich wollte dich unbedingt kennenlernen. Endlich jemand von meinem Kontinent!
>
> Ein knochiger Mann meines Alters stand vor mir und stellte sich auf englisch als Arif vor.
>
> Welcher Kontinent mag das wohl sein? fragte ich.
>
> Er war verunsichert. Stammst du nicht aus Deutschland?
>
> Doch, sagte ich, ein wenig.
>
> Na, also, ich meinte Europa, ich bin aus England. Dort geboren und aufgewachsen.
>
> [...]
>
> Arif träumte davon, nach Indien heimzukehren (er sagte 'heimkehren', obwohl er in England geboren war), sobald seine Kinder erwachsen seien, auf eigenen Beinen stünden. Aber er hatte keine Antwort auf die Frage, ob das reine islamische Leben sich in Gujarat, woher seine Familie stammte, um so viel leichter verwirklichen ließe. (TZH 89–91)
>
> ['Brother Ilias, wait!' someone called. 'I have heard about you. I really wanted to meet you. Someone from my own continent at last!'
>
> A bony man about my age stood in front of me and introduced himself, in English, as Arif.
>
> 'And which continent might that be?' I asked.
>
> He looked uncertain. 'You're from Germany, aren't you?'
>
> 'Yes,' I said, 'sort of'.
>
> 'Well, then, Europe, I meant. I'm from England, born and grew up there'.
>
> [...]
>
> Arif dreamed of returning home to India (he said 'returning home' even though he'd been born in England), as soon as his children had grown up, and could stand on their own two feet. But he had no answer to my question of whether it was easier to lead a pure Islamic life in Gujarat where his family was from. (TMM 109–11)]

Later on Trojanow tells us: 'Ich erklärte ihnen, daß ich aus Indien stamme und daher keine Ahnung hätte von Fußball, aber wenn sie sich über Kricket unterhalten wollten ...' (TZH 151) ['I explained that I came from India and didn't have a clue about football but if they wanted to discuss cricket ...' (TMM 188)]. He makes clear that the question of origin is a secondary issue for him: in the first quotation, it is the continent of Europe that connects these two Muslims who have completely different backgrounds; in the second quotation, Trojanow presents himself as an Indian on the basis of his current place of abode, but he shows his ironic side here as his answer appears as a way of avoiding a boring conversation about football. Trojanow's and other people's view of origin change constantly according to the people they encounter and their backgrounds and cultures. However, this instability does not create a longing in Trojanow for a geographical place of origin, a 'home' as it does for Arif. Trojanow does not share this aspiration, and we need to ask whether he has the same notion of origin as many of his fellow pilgrims. On the hajj, the community of believers should stand above the idea of nationhood (which is a political entity), but it becomes clear that nationality serves as an 'ordering device' to help differentiate people in the vastness of pilgrims: individuality within the faith is expressed through nationality, which in itself is based on cultural differences. Trojanow observes a need among pilgrims for differentiation and individuality by commenting on the country sections in the tent area in Mina, the differences in wearing the *ihram* and the various national dresses. Yet, for Trojanow, cultural differentiation is contained within the unity of believers and Islam as an all-embracing religion that goes beyond cultural and national boundaries and 'originality'.

Like many pilgrims before him, Trojanow experiences 'heightened identification with Islam and fellow Muslims' (Eickelman and Piscatori, 'Preface', xii), but he makes us aware of the heterogeneity of Islam. Naipaul travels through diverse countries and encounters a number of versions of Islam, but his perceptions are shaped by the idea of Islam as a self-contained religion and not by, for instance, Muslim intellectuals who want to engage with the West yet still remain Muslim.

Trojanow is looking for a transnational or transcultural dimension in Islam. Although he does not discuss how he became a Muslim, there is a sense in the book of how Islam, in conquering and converting Europeans, presents a challenge to Western concepts of European might, and how Islam can offer a 'home', a sense of (spiritual) origin in a deracinated world. Unlike Naipaul, Trojanow does not see a clear-cut differentiation between Muslims with an Arab background, as 'original', and Muslims from 'colonized', that is, 'converted', countries. This differentiation relates back to the Arab expansion far beyond the Arabian Peninsula and subsequent incorporation of other cultural influences into Islam (Endress, 122–23). Trojanow's religion is a lived one through the experience of the *umma* in Mecca and Medina, that is, through travelling to Islam's 'homeland': that does not mean that Muslims give up their individuality, but rather that their sense of being Muslim is strengthened by the experience of the Other who shares the same religious background whilst keeping a personal faith. Trojanow clearly describes what Eickelman and Piscatori refer to as 'a direct causal relationship between the act of travel and a heightened sense of being Muslim' ('Social Theory in the Study of Muslim Societies', 16). Trojanow develops a stronger feeling of community by going on this pilgrimage — with Muslims and with other hajj writers: 'Ich spürte eine Brüderschaft [...] mit den Muslims, die Zeugnis abgelegt, und mit den Christen, die Bericht erstattet hatten' (TZH 159) ['I felt a brotherhood [...] both with the Muslims who had testified as with the Christians who had reported on it' (TMM 199)]. His travel account reaches beyond an Orientalist experience of the East. He recognizes the Other as part of himself: religion, for Trojanow, serves as a way of connecting to people, whereas Naipaul sees it as a separating device. (One should note, however, that Trojanow connects with his 'Muslim brothers', not 'sisters', thus distinguishing himself, the male writer, from women writers and initiating a different form of separation.) The question of individuality and community is, thus, not only differently perceived by Trojanow and Naipaul but also differently interpreted. This derives partly from the fact that the former is a Muslim and the latter is not, and partly from their different objectives for their journeys. The results are different versions of Islam.

***

Trojanow and Naipaul perceive Islam primarily in relation to themselves — as travellers and writers. Yet each writer puts a different emphasis on these roles. Being a Muslim, Trojanow travels foremost as a pilgrim who is part of the *umma*, claiming to be the writer again only after the journey; he literally performs Islam (through rituals) in order to learn but also in order to stylize himself deliberately as a Muslim with a transcultural background and an open-minded perception of cultures and religions. He can thereby create what Eickelman and Piscatori refer to in relation to Muslim travellers in general as an 'image of a flexible Islam' ('Preface', xiv). In this sense, Islam can be lived anywhere and is not tied to an 'original' place. Iain Chambers suggests that, on migratory journeys, there is 'no fixed identity or final destination' (25). This idea coincides with Trojanow's reading of the hajj as a celebration of Muslim diversity in unity: in its accumulation, Islam appears as a culturally diverse religion. Trojanow's Islam as a one-sidedly positive experience permits subjective modes of experience as well as transculturalism, and thereby implicitly questions whether Naipaul's individualist West grants more cultural difference on the basis of secular autonomy. Translation (the transferral of knowledge from more experienced Muslims to the learner Trojanow as well as the interaction of different forms of Islam in its 'homeland') becomes a tool of education, possibly even indoctrination, and understanding oneself as a Muslim, both individually and — and this is the primary aim of the hajj — collectively; yet although the pilgrims perform the same rituals that have been practised for centuries, they are able to keep and constantly change their individuality by primarily focusing on cultural, non-religious differences.

Naipaul, by contrast, performs something completely different: the role of the inquiring writer. He perceives Islam as unity in diversity in the non-Arab countries he visits. As he primarily wants to understand why and how 'fundamentalism' came into existence, he puts himself in the position of an exploring and curious outsider. Naipaul regards (literal) translation as access to other languages and cultures. It serves, effectively, as the sole means of getting to the bottom of 'Muslim rage'. Naipaul wants to achieve rather than experience: he gains knowledge, and his journey becomes a pilgrimage to knowledge and understanding, rather than to Islam itself.

These diverse treatments of individuality and collectivity raise the following crucial questions: does the West, by contrast to Islam, demand difference and thus does not allow people to be different, or rather does it allow difference only to the extent that this difference is accepted as flawed, backward and inferior? Can choosing individuality over collectivity ever be based on reasoned ethics rather than simple psychological preference?

The writers cannot, and certainly never claim to be able to, give definite answers themselves, but we can detect hints that reveal their attitudes towards notions of individuality when considering the role of each writer and the production of his text on Islam. This is revealed when we take a closer look at the writing styles of Naipaul and Trojanow. For Naipaul, the task of writing a stylistically sophisticated book is as fundamental as the content of his travel accounts. He frequently reflects upon the act of writing and, in contrast to his earlier travel books, perceives himself as a 'manager of narrative', someone who claims to let 'the people of the country come to the front' (NBB 2) (as we have seen, this claim is not entirely fulfilled). As a high-profile and prestigious writer, Naipaul takes a stance of authority on the people he meets. His highly sophisticated use of English can convince the Western readership of the relevance of the non-Muslim former colonial's perceptions of Islam.

Trojanow's engagement with his readers is of a different nature from Naipaul's. As a less high-profile writer, he does not have to fulfil his readers' expectations in terms of style — and content, for that matter. He aims to contribute to the tradition of hajj literature. Trojanow underlines this ambition, as well as his engagement with the culturally diverse *umma* in the places of Islam's past in stylistic terms. For instance: 'Gemeinsam ist allen muslimischen Autoren, daß sie die eigenen Gefühle nicht in den Vordergrund stellen, daß sie nur selten aus dem Brunnen der eigenen Befindlichkeiten schöpfen' (TZH 7–8) ['A common feature for all Muslim narrators who write about their Hajj experience is that they do not place their own feelings in the foreground and only on occasion delve into their own sensitivities' (TMM 2)]. Trojanow begins the sentence with 'gemeinsam' [common], thus emphasizing the idea of community; he repeats 'daß' [that] rather than connecting the two sub-clauses with a conjunction, and he uses the archaic metaphor 'aus dem Brunnen der eigenen Befindlichkeiten schöpfen' [to draw from the well of one's sensitivities], 'sensitivities' being paradoxically a phrase redolent of early, Orientalist travel writing. As shown in this example, he reflects his embrace of the *umma* and earlier hajj writers with a partly archaic, partly plain, yet highly metaphoric style which, potentially, can reach more people and believers. However, this observation reveals a problem: at what point can we perceive a difference between Trojanow, the Muslim brother, and Trojanow, the Western intellectual individual? In his travel account he seems to suggest that he never faces any problems caused by this twofold, partly contradictory identity; on the contrary, Trojanow claims to re-experience the feelings of Muslim brotherhood evoked by the hajj, through the mental journey of writing, thereby merging these two identities seemingly seamlessly.

This self-positioning within (as traveller) as well as outside Islam (as writer) enables Trojanow to convey an almost exclusively positive image of Islam and to situate himself in contradistinction to Naipaul's sceptical view of Islam. The latter's conclusion is as follows: 'Islam meant "submission", and in an Islamic republic, such as the people of Iran had passionately wanted and had voted for in a referendum, everyone had to submit' (NBB 163). For Naipaul, conversion triggers a false sense of belonging (Weiss, 155). As he rarely differentiates between different forms of Islam, he creates an 'idea Islam' (cf. Said, *Orientalism*, 5), which is primarily defined and fixed by its violence, 'fundamentalism', dependency on the West and the unquestionable acceptance of the faith. His texts do not give any hints of a changed, more positive perception of Islam as a result of his journey.

In contrast, Trojanow constructs himself as an open traveller. He is specifically looking for flexibility, also through the people he communicates with: 'Es mag paradox erscheinen, meinte der Ältere, aber manche Ideale des Islam sind im Westen eher verwirklicht' (TZH 153) ['"It might sound paradoxical," the older one said, "but some of the Islamic ideals are more of a reality in Britain [in original: the West]"' (TMM 190)]. This is the point where we can establish a difference between Islam as a religion of tolerance, love and understanding (which Trojanow conveys to his readers) and Islamism as a vicious backlash against an unfair and often hypocritical world (which Naipaul explores). The writers clearly differ in their portrayal of Islam and in their perceptions of, or even preferences for, a seemingly freely thinking, individualistic West that Naipaul advocates and the ideals of Islam that Trojanow brings closer to his readers. Above all, the texts reveal that Islam encompasses a variety of visions of faith; and once a year one of Islam's Pillars brings the diversity of believers back to Mecca to be Muslims only.

***

Chapters 1 and 2 have focused on movement and translation processes. The following two chapters will concentrate on the notion of 'having arrived' in transcultural writing. Although translation processes are also significant for the post-migrant generation, they are regarded differently: in the texts, translation becomes a process of defining one's position in an environment that is no longer new. It is no longer necessary as a means of making sense of the unknown, or of settling in; rather it contributes to the self-awareness of many post-migrants as being 'different', yet part of German and British culture. The post-migrant protagonists make use of the results of translations undertaken by the previous generation — the 'gaps' and 'impurities' which shape their identities and become the basis for the creation of something new. In these translation processes, gender is the site of struggle (as already partly explored in Chapter 1, 'Moving with Islam'). Two kinds of translation, the maintenance of difference as a means of self-definition in the case of male post-migrants and the significance of language in the case of female post-migrants, will guide my reading of transcultural literature in the next two chapters.

3. Islam, 'Difference' and Masculinity Male Perspectives from the 'Margins of Society': Feridun Zaimoğlu's *Kanak Sprak* and Hanif Kureishi's *The Black Album*

The image of Muslims in the media in the new millennium is primarily of young, radical men. These Muslims are seen as trouble-makers situated at the margins of a Western society that is looking for security and stability in a time of an increased fear of 'terrorism' and 'Islamic fundamentalism'. These prescribed margins are both rejected and peculiarly embraced by those in the German and British Muslim communities. Young and, in their individual ways, radical Muslims are excluded by dominant society, yet they increasingly use this imposed exclusion as a means of self-identification and self-definition.

This chapter focuses on the portrayal of young male Muslims in texts from Germany, or rather 'Kanakistan, ein[em] unbekannten Landstrich am Rande der deutschen Gesellschaft' (ZKS 2) [Kanakistan, an unknown area at the margins of German society], as Feridun Zaimoğlu puts it in his *Kanak Sprak: 24 Mißtöne vom Rande der Gesellschaft* (1995);[1] and in the British writer Hanif Kureishi's *The Black Album* (1995) and 'My Son the Fanatic' (1997).[2] Both books centre on young males who are also, if not necessarily primarily, defined by

1 F. Zaimoğlu, *Kanak Sprak: 24 Mißtöne vom Rande der Gesellschaft*, 6th edn (Hamburg: Rotbuch, 2004 [1995]).

2 H. Kureishi, *The Black Album* (London: Faber and Faber, 1996 [1995]); 'My Son the Fanatic', in *Love in a Blue Time* (London: Faber and Faber, 1997), 119–31. I do not have the scope to include Zaimoğlu's novel *Abschaum: Die wahre Geschichte von Ertan Ongun* [*Scum: The True Story of Ertan Ongun*], 5th edn (Hamburg: Rotbuch, 2003 [1997]) or any other of his publications here. Like *Kanak Sprak*, *Abschaum* tells the story of a young German Turk and is, according to the author, based on interviews.

their Muslim identity. This enforces or reinforces their identity as 'different' and in opposition to the West in general, and to the German or British mainstream in particular. With the focus on male – and in the next chapter on female – protagonists, the discussion in these two chapters will reach beyond cultural and national differences and include the consideration of a gender dimension which often determines perceptions of Islam, both within and outside Muslim communities.

Zaimoğlu's and Kureishi's texts have to be read against the social and political context of the late 1980s to mid-1990s. This decade, which was far removed from the immigration of the 1950s and 1960s, is characterized by increasing self-awareness in former immigrants and, even more so, in their children as part of German or British society. However, under Margaret Thatcher's conservative government in the UK and the Conservative Christian Democrat government led by Helmut Kohl in Germany, former immigrants were seen as a possible economic as well as cultural threat to these prospering societies.[3] This is exemplified by the 'Rushdie affair' and its aftermath.[4] In 1988, Salman Rushdie published his novel *The Satanic Verses*. The novel was seen as a 'parody of Islamic history', a 'sharp anticlerical satire' (Gorra, 151) that caused riots in Islamabad (Pakistan) and other places in the Muslim world. It was subsequently banned in India, Pakistan, South Africa and several other Muslim countries. *The Satanic Verses* also caused book-burnings among the Muslim population in Britain, most famously in Bradford (14 January 1989). Events such as these brought Muslims negative attention, and images of Muslims as 'fanatic' and 'backward' were circulated in the media. On 14 February 1989, Ayatollah Khomeini of Iran issued a fatwa 'that Rushdie should be executed as an apostate who has blasphemed against Islam' (Sardar and Davies, 185). Rushdie subsequently went into exile in the USA, reacting with open letters in newspapers that caused further attacks from journalists. Ziauddin Sardar and Merryl Wyn Davies argue that

3 See, for example, J. S. Nielsen, *Muslims in Western Europe*, 2nd edn, Islamic Surveys (Edinburgh: Edinburgh University Press, 1995 [1992]).

4 The following details on the 'Rusdhie affair' are based on M. Gorra, '"Burn the Books and Trust the Book": *The Satanic Verses*, February 1989 (Appendix to Chapter Three)', in *After Empire: Scott, Naipaul, Rushdie* (Chicago: University of Chicago Press, 1997), 149–56, and Z. Sardar and M. Wyn Davies, *Distorted Imagination: Lessons from the Rushdie Affair* (London: Grey Seal, 1990). See also S. Akhtar, *Be Careful with Muhammad! The Salman Rushdie Affair* (London: Bellew, 1989). For a more general approach to the 'Rushdie affair', see Lewis, *Islamic Britain*, 26, 153 in particular, and Nielsen, 158–60.

> [t]he Rushdie affair is proof that a genuine plural society does not exist. More sadly, it demonstrates that, as yet, there is little desire in Western society to create a plural society. There is diversity in both Western society and the modern world order, but diversity is not necessarily plurality. (8)

Another event which exacerbated the tensions between Islam and the West was the Gulf War in 1991. The media coverage of this war contributed to a general perception of the Muslim world as tense and politically unstable, which — it was feared — could also lead to problems within the Muslim communities of Germany and the UK as well as between these communities and the mainstream society.

All this coincided with increasing self-awareness among second- and third-generation immigrants in both Germany and the UK. Since the late 1980s the children of former immigrants have noticeably turned away from their parents and the latter's need to integrate (to adjust to the new abode without giving up their own cultural identity) or even to assimilate (to conform completely to the customs of the 'host country'). Many young Muslims living in Germany and the UK have looked for alternative, transcultural spaces where they have been able to prosper and redefine their identity according to their own rules (see Nielsen, 47–96, and Lewis, *Islamic Britain*, 24–27).

Zaimoğlu's 'protocols' of interviews with German Turks reflect on ways in which supposedly real young Muslim men situate themselves in active contradistinction to the German (male) population, as well as to assimilated, 'Germanized' Turks. Zaimoğlu's protagonists see themselves as angry young men and Muslims in an essentially hostile environment.[5] Their 'foreignness' is reinforced by their working-class background, that is, their economically and socially disadvantaged position; many German Turks, and many of Zaimoğlu's characters, live on the edge of poverty, and this social status causes anger. Their anger may also be related to the fact that until the replacement of the *Staatsangehörigkeitsrecht* [(German) nationality law] by the *Staatsangehörigkeitsgesetz* [nationality act] in 2000 and the abolition of the *Ausländergesetz* [aliens act] and its replacement by the *Aufenthaltsgesetz* (*Zuwanderungsgesetz*) [residence act (immigration act)] in 2005, German Turks were regarded as 'foreigners'. Although

5 See Zaimoğlu's organization *Kanak Attak* which was founded in 1998 as a 'national network of anti-racist cultural political activists, accepting members of all backgrounds but dominated by migrants' (T. Cheesman, 'Akçam — Zaimoğlu — "Kanak Attak": Turkish Lives and Letters in German', in *Emerging Writers*, ed. F. Finlay and S. Taberner (= Special Number, *German Life and Letters*, 55.2 (April 2002), 191).

this attribution of status as 'foreigners' may have changed since then, today German Turks are confronted with another part of their identity that makes them 'different': coinciding with the Islamic suicide attacks in New York, London and Madrid in the early 2000s, German Turks are now increasingly seen as Muslims,[6] and being a follower of Islam is widely regarded as 'an obstacle of integration' (Karakasoglu, 159).

Zaimoğlu's characters live in a Germany that is less concerned with Islam as a possible threat to Western civilization as is the case at the beginning of the twenty-first century. Leslie A. Adelson points out: 'The figural counterpart to the newly emboldened woman in a headscarf is that of defiantly aggressive Turkish men, especially young ones. Zaimoğlu's iconic *Kanaken* are interpellated by this figure, though they are not generally represented as Muslims' (*The Turkish Turn*, 130). Although 'Muslim identity as a source of Turkishness contrasts with Turkish state definitions of identity' (Helicke, 185), this chapter will show that their Muslim identity does play a role, mainly in cultural, less in religious terms. It will outline the roots for today's increasing perception of young German Turks as Muslims.

Zaimoğlu's interlocutors are identified by their *Kanak Sprak* — the language that the writer chose as the title for his book — and its feminine equivalent *Kanaka Sprak* as used in the subtitle of *Koppstoff*. It needs to be pointed out that, in *Kanak Sprak*, we are reading a 'Kunstsprache' [artificial language] created by Zaimoğlu.[7] In his preface to *Kanak Sprak*, Zaimoğlu claims to have recorded the language of 'authentic' German Turks, yet he makes clear that he has manipulated the material for his 'protocols': '*Kanak(a) Sprak*' is no longer the language of real-life German Turks. Tom Cheesman emphasizes that '[r]eaders should bear in mind that what apparently claims to be a protocol of spontaneous speech may perhaps in part be just that, though we will never know; far more importantly, it is a script for dramatic performance' ('Akçam — Zaimoğlu — "Kanak Attak"', 185).[8] The style in his 'protocols' is, therefore, Zaimoğlu's

6 See Y. Yıldız, 'Turkish Girls, Allah's Daughters, and the Contemporary German Subject: Itinerary of a Figure', *German Life and Letters*, 62.4 (2009), 465–81. Yıldız is focusing on the perception of German Turkish women as Muslims here.

7 D. Skiba, 'Ethnolektale und literalisierte Hybridität in Feridun Zaimoglu's Kanak Sprak', in *Migrationsliteratur: Schreibweisen einer interkulturellen Moderne*, ed. K. Schenk *et al.* (Tübingen: Francke, 2004), 184, 197–203.

8 Similarly, the subtitle of Zaimoğlu's novel *Abschaum* is *Die wahre Geschichte von Ertan Ongun*. Zaimoğlu claims Ertan's story is authentic. In his 'Nachwort' [epilogue], the author tells his readers about Ertan after the publication of the book and situates his story in the context of migration (183–84).

own rather than his interviewees' style and his interlocutors appear as the creative property of the writer and *Kanake* Zaimoğlu.[9]

The question of language relates to that of genre: are we reading fiction or documentary protocols?[10] Elements of both genres can be found in the short texts; this is, for example, expressed in how Zaimoğlu and critics refer to them: as 'Protokolle' (ZKS 15) [protocols], 'Reportagen' [reports],[11] 'Nachdichtungen' (ZKS 14) [free renderings] or even 'Übersetzungen' (ZKS 18) [translations]. Zaimoğlu plays a significant role in this context: as editor, translator, writer and allied fighter, he forms the material coming out of the characters' heads (the 'Koppstoff' [headstuff], which constitutes the title of Zaimoğlu's collection of 'protocols' of interviews with German Turkish women) into 'Kunstwerke' [works of art] (Skiba, 195–97).[12] He uses supposedly authentic documentary material and shapes it into pieces of writing.[13] Although this is a highly problematic enterprise as Zaimoğlu is of a different class than most of his interlocutors, he emphasizes his authority as editor in order to 'prove' the verity of the experiences reported in the texts which enables him to raise awareness among his middle-class German readers for the difficulties of young migrants in the 1990s.[14] Yet he also keeps his readership and thus the commercial aspect of his book

9 Gary Schmidt raises the question of Zaimoğlu's 'authorial identity' and 'the problem of authorial legitimacy', which have changed since *Kanak Sprak* as he has gained 'recognition as an author'; Schmidt focuses on *Liebesmale, scharlachrot* and *Leyla* in his article. He also usefully mentions the notion of 'performance in the German sense of *Leistung* — achievement in a particular field of activity [...], or in the case of Zaimoglu himself, the performance of an author who constructs his own legitimacy through the voice of a gendered narrator' (G. Schmidt, 'Feridun Zaimoglu's Performances of Gender and Authorship', in *German Literature in a New Century: Trends, Traditions, Transitions, Transformations*, ed. K. Gerstenberger and P. Herminghouse (New York: Berghahn, 2008), 202, 200).

10 For an analysis of Zaimoğlu's text as part of the tradition of protocol literature, see Skiba, 187–91.

11 S. Peters (*Frankfurter Rundschau*) on the back cover of *Koppstoff*.

12 Skiba also points out the relation between the compound 'Koppstoff', the material covering the head, and the headscarf (190).

13 See Cheesman, *Novels of Turkish German Settlement*, 137, for a discussion of the question of the authenticity of Zaimoğlu's texts.

14 This technique is reminiscent of eighteenth-century novels such as Daniel Defoe's *The Life and Adventures of Robinson Crusoe* (ed., with an Introduction by A. Ross, Penguin English Library (1965); repr. in Penguin Classics (London: Penguin, 1985; first publ. London: Taylor, 1719)). The alleged editor Defoe supplies his readers with a preface to give them the impression that the story they are about to read is authentic (27) and written by Robinson Crusoe himself (25). See also Zaimoğlu's comments in his preface 'Kanak Sprak', in ZKS, 18.

in mind: the fairly limited use of Turkish, for example, clearly shows that he aims to reach a non-*Kanak* audience. Furthermore, Zaimoğlu's 'translations' of the 'symbolische Jargon' [symbolic jargon] into a less flowery German are meant to avoid the 'Folklore-Falle' [folklore trap] (Zaimoğlu, 'Kanak Sprak', ZKS, 14),[15] to convince his readers of the serious dimension of the struggle of his interlocutors.

Kureishi's novel *The Black Album* portrays young Muslims as a radically religious group establishing their identity in opposition to the West. Often regarded as a *Bildungsroman*,[16] *The Black Album* tells the story of Shahid Hasan,[17] an undergraduate student of Pakistani origin studying at a college in London. Newly arrived in the big city, he meets the political activist Riaz and his religious group. Initially, Shahid is impressed by the group's activities and gets involved in their struggle for social justice. Yet in the course of the novel Shahid is increasingly disturbed by the group's 'fundamentalist' ideas, and extreme measures in their fight against the West (such as the burning of *The Satanic Verses* at the end of the novel). Simultaneously, Shahid is having a love affair with his lecturer Deedee Osgood, a white Left-liberal feminist. He is in constant conflict with himself on whether

15 For a detailed linguistic analysis of Zaimoğlu's *Kanak Sprak*, see C. W. Pfaff, 'Kanaken in Alemannistan: Feridun Zaimoglu's Representation of Migrant Language', in *Sprachgrenzen überspringen: Sprachliche Hybridität und polykulturelles Selbstverständnis*, ed. V. Hinnenkamp and K. Meng, Studien zur deutschen Sprache: Forschungen des Instituts für deutsche Sprache, 32 (Tübingen: Narr, 2005), 195–225; for the use of Turkish, see particularly 206–07.

16 Roy Sommer emphasizes the 'Motiv der Suche' [motive of search] in *Fictions of Migration: Ein Beitrag zur Theorie und Gattungsgeschichte des zeitgenössischen interkulturellen Romans in Großbritannien*, ELK (Studien zur Literatur- und Kulturwissenschaft) / ELCH (Studies in English and Cultural History), 1 (Trier: Wissenschaftlicher Verlag Trier, 2001) (= doctoral thesis, Justus Liebig University, Gießen, 2000), 117. See also Mark Stein's approach to 'novels of transformation' in *Black British Literature: Novels of Transformation* (Columbus: Ohio State University Press, 2004), particularly the chapter 'Of Aunties and Elephants: Kureishi's Aesthetics of Postethnicity', 108–42.

17 The name 'Shahid' in both Arabic and Persian means 'martyr'. In the Qur'an, *shahid* is identified as someone who 'fight[s] on the path of God [...]; for whoever fighteth on God's path, whether he be slain or conquer, we will in the end give him a great reward' (Q4: 76). This name emphasizes an active, fighting element, and reveals the relation between 'struggle' (jihad) and martyrdom (see website of the Zentrum für Literaturforschung, Berlin, Research Focus: 'Figurationen des Märtyrers in nahöstlicher und europäischer Literatur' [Figurations of the martyr in Middle Eastern and European literature], www.zfl.gwz-berlin.de/forschung/europaeische-kulturgeschichte/maertyrer/ [accessed 28 June 2010]).

he should support the group or his lover (and their contradictory political attitudes). The story ends with Shahid and Deedee finding reconciliation in their provisional relationship.

The characters of both Zaimoğlu and Kureishi are situated at the 'margins of society' — and, to different degrees, welcome this condition. As Graham Huggan points out, '[t]he embrace of marginality is, above all, an oppositional discursive strategy that flies in the face of hierarchical social structures and hegemonic cultural codes' (*The Postcolonial Exotic*, 20).[18] This 'oppositional discursive strategy' is highlighted by the different genres previously mentioned: semi-fictional, textualized interviews (*Kanak Sprak*), and the fictional novel (*The Black Album*) and short story ('My Son the Fanatic'). Zaimoğlu's asserted pretence of authenticity reveals his agenda: he wishes to be seen as a mouthpiece for young German Turks who, as 'marginal' Germans, significantly influence German culture,[19] and he aims to create an immediate, 'authentic' experience for his readers who are part of a Germany which can still be hostile to 'others'.[20] Kureishi, in contrast, deliberately keeps a distance from his characters, which gives him and his readers the space to reflect more openly and critically. The stylistic differences also capture the writers' diverse emphases in their representations of Islam: Zaimoğlu focuses on an outspokenly radical stance held by a section among German Turks, those he calls *Kanaken*,[21] while Kureishi's concern is

18 See also M. Günter, '"Wir sind bastarde, freund ...": Feridun Zaimoglus Kanak Sprak und die performative Struktur von Identität', *Sprache und Literatur in Wissenschaft und Unterricht*, 30.83 (1999), 15–28, for an examination of 'margins' (as 'Rand' [fringe], 'Grenze' [border] and 'Naht' [seam]) in relation to performativity in Zaimoğlu's *Kanak Sprak* and *Koppstoff*.

19 See footnote 46 in this chapter.

20 Zaimoğlu's work of the 1990s needs to be read in the context of the racist attacks on 'foreigners' in Mölln, Solingen and Rostock in 1991 and 1992. Furthermore, in 1993, the German government introduced changes in the asylum law which put more restrictions on who could seek asylum.

21 To simplify matters, I use the terms '*Kanake*'/'*Kanaka*' as umbrella terms for all Zaimoğlu's interviewees, whether they describe themselves as such or not. I thus follow Zaimoğlu's own reappropriated, originally pejorative term, but I am aware of the fact that these men and women cannot be generalized in that way. Similarly, I use the terms 'German Turks' or 'Muslims' since, whether they are believers or not, they have an at least culturally defined Muslim background. I thereby differentiate Zaimoğlu's interviewees from 'mainstream Germans', a term that I use to refer to the part of the German population whose xenophobic attitudes and general 'floating-with-the-current' the *Kanaken*/*Kanakas* reject and struggle against. I am aware of the problematic of this — like any — dichotomy,

with British Muslims who define themselves through their religious purity turned into Islamism.[22]

It is useful to examine these different valuations and representations of Islam with reference to notions of opposition, difference and belonging. In what way do these notions, which imply and build on linguistic, geographic and/or religious segregation, contribute to the creation of masculine spaces? And to what extent are these spaces connoted with concepts of violence, religion and sexuality as markers of difference?

***

In the colonial histories of Germany and the UK, the subjugation of the colonized peoples involved their Orientalization: according to Edward Said, 'the Orient [became] an idea that has a history and a tradition of thought, imagery, and vocabulary that have given it reality and presence in and for the Western misconstruction of the "Oriental"' (*Orientalism*, 5). Orientalization became a means of domination: by attaching certain roles (such as 'the despotic or violent Oriental') to the colonized, the colonizers could easily exercise power and allege cultural superiority (38–40). As Rana Kabbani points out, '[a]mong the many themes that emerge from the European narration of the Other, two appear most strikingly. The first is the insistent claim that the East was a place of lascivious sensuality, and the second that it was a realm characterised by inherent violence' (6). This chapter is concerned with these themes: 'Oriental' sexuality and violence and their instrumentalization in the process of securing colonial — and post-colonial — control. As discussed by Kabbani and Said, feminizing the 'Oriental' in particular was a significant step in the establishment of colonial power (67; *Orientalism*, 182). Within the discourse of self-justification, the masculine West was described as physically and intellectually, but also metaphorically 'stronger', and thus more positively connoted than the feminine Orient (207). A similar dichotomy can also be seen in relation to 'race': 'black' (non-

but refer to it throughout this and the following chapter as it is also applied in *Kanak Sprak* and *Koppstoff*.

22 In the following, I refer to Kureishi's protagonists widely as 'British Muslims': as Islam plays a fundamental role in their creation of masculine spaces, I regard it as necessary to include the religious element in my reference to Kureishi's characters who live in London. See also M. Gorra, 'Conclusion: Notes Towards a Redefinition of Englishness', in *After Empire*, 157–75. The debate on nationality (British or English) among 'minorities' living in the UK is a controversial one, which, however, is not my focus here.

British) subjects were 'feminized', disempowered and thus more controllable (and in need of control), whereas the 'white' colonizers retained control of their maleness (226–28). These dichotomies served as a rationale for the colonizers' oppressive practices and supported their feeling of superiority.

Zaimoğlu aims to break such dichotomies by highlighting the individuality of his *Kanaken*; he thereby denies Germany's domination over its citizens with a Turkish background: in his preface to *Kanak Sprak*, Zaimoğlu lists the different roles *Kanaken* can play, thus breaking the group perceived collectively as 'foreigners' or 'Turks' by mainstream Germans into subgroups and individuals:[23]

> Über einen Zeitraum von zwölf Monaten gelang es mir, das Spektrum weit zu öffnen: vom Müllabfuhr-Kanaken bis zum Kümmel-Transsexuellen, vom hehlenden Klein-Ganeff, dessen Geschenke ich nur mühsam zurückweisen konnte, bis zum goldbehängten Mädchenhändler, vom posenreichen Halbstarken bis zum mittelschweren Islamisten. Sie alle eint das Gefühl, 'in der Liga der Verdammten zu spielen', gegen kulturhegemoniale Ansprüche bestehen zu müssen. Noch ist das tragende Element dieser Community ein negatives Selbstbewußtsein, wie es in der scheinbaren Selbstbezichtigung seinen oberflächlichen Ausdruck findet: Kanake! Dieses verunglimpfende Hetzwort wird zum identitätsstiftenden Kennwort, zur verbindenden Klammer dieser 'Lumpenethnier'. Analog zur Black-consciousness-Bewegung in den USA werden sich die einzelnen Kanak-Subidentitäten zunehmend übergreifender

23 '*Kanaken*' is not an exclusive term for German Turks and can include everybody who is politically active in race-related issues. See Cheesman, 'Akçam – Zaimoğlu – "Kanak Attak"', 187: '"Kanak" is a parody identity, a flagrantly artificial and intentionally slippery construct: Zaimoğlu denies that only "Turkish Germans" or "German Turks", or only "ethnically non-German" German denizens and citizens can be "Kanaken" or "Kanakstas". Instead it is a political category: "Viele Deutsche sind Kanakstas. Du bist in dem Moment Kanaksta, wo du die Gesellschaft durchschaust." [Footnote: Joachim Lottmann, "Kanak Attack!", *Die Zeit*, 14 November 1997, p. 88. "Kanaksta" crosses "Kanake" with "gangsta" (as in "gangsta rap") or, Zaimoğlu claims, with "youngster".] The launch of "Kanak" as a cultural label aimed to make visible the artificiality and rigidity of the conventionally ascribed identities derived from the history of colonialism and of post-colonial migrations.' See also 'Kanak Attak's' manifesto 'Kanak Attak und basta! Manifest gegen Mültikültüralizm, gegen demokratische und hybride Deutsche sowie konformistische Migranten' [Kanak Attak and Basta! Manifesto against Multiculturalism, against Democratic and Hybrid Germans as well as Conformist Migrants], www.kanak-attak.de/ka/down/pdf/textos.pdf [accessed 28 June 2010] (originally publ. in *die tageszeitung* (28 January 1999)), for a comment on who they are and who they include. However, being of Turkish origin himself, Zaimoğlu focuses on German Turks in *Kanak Sprak*.

Zusammenhänge und Inhalte bewußt. Die Entmystifizierung ist eingeleitet, der Weg zu einem neuen Realismus gelegt. Inmitten der Mainstreamkultur entstehen die ersten rohen Entwürfe für eine ethnizistische Struktur in Deutschland. (ZKS 16–17)

[Over a period of twelve months I managed to open up the spectrum wide: from the garbage removal-*Kanake* to the *Kümmel* [cumin]-transsexual, from the dealing petty-ganef, whose presents I could only reject with difficulty, to the white sex-trafficker covered in gold, from the yob abundant with poses to the semi-radical Islamist. They are all united by the feeling of 'playing in the league of the damned', of resisting culturally determined hegemonic demands. So far the fundamental element of this community is a negative self-awareness as it is expressed superficially in the seeming self-accusation: *Kanake*! This defaming abusive word is turned into a code word which creates identity, into a uniting brace for this 'ethnic underclass'. In analogy to the Black Consciousness movement in the USA, the various *Kanak* subidentities become increasingly aware of overarching contexts and contents. Demystification has started, the way to a new realism has opened up. Amid mainstream culture, there emerge the first rough concepts for an ethnicistic structure in Germany.]

Zaimoğlu takes an anthropological approach to the *Kanaken* he meets, thus reappropriating and reclaiming the traditionally Western role of the observer and classifier:[24] he claims to have observed and 'studied' them, which resulted in his recording and categorizing the *Kanaken*. İnci Dirim and Peter Auer identify an exoticizing element in Zaimoğlu's approach:

Die 'Kanaken' wurden also in ihrer ethnischen Sonderart für die Deutschen — sprachlich und inhaltlich — unverständlich (gemacht). Dass Zaimoğlu diese Distanz durch seinen Schreibstil selbst kreiert, wurde dabei übersehen [...]. [...] *Kanak Sprak* hat wesentlich dazu beigetragen, die (jungen, großstädtischen) Türken in Deutschland in der Öffentlichkeit zu ethnisieren und sogar zu exotisieren.[25]

24 F. Zaimoğlu, 'KümmelContra', in *Kursbuch Jugendkultur: Stile, Szenen und Identitäten vor der Jahrtausendwende*, ed. SPoKK (Arbeitsgruppe für Symbolische Politik, Kultur und Kommunikation) (Mannheim: Bollmann, 1997), 174; Zaimoğlu also speaks of 'kanak-kunde' [*kanak* science] here, thus making the satirical nature of his enterprise clear.

25 İ. Dirim and P. Auer, *Türkisch sprechen nicht nur die Türken: Über die Unschärfebeziehung zwischen Sprache und Ethnie in Deutschland*, Linguistik — Impulse und Tendenzen, 4 (Berlin: de Gruyter, 2004), 7.

> [The *'Kanaken'* were, therefore, (made) — linguistically and textually — unintelligible for Germans within their ethnic distinctiveness. Readers ignored the fact that Zaimoğlu created this distance himself through his writing style [...]. [...] *Kanak Sprak* has significantly contributed to the public ethnicization or even exoticization of (young, urban) German Turks.]

However, I read Zaimoğlu's alleged ethnicization as a deliberate form of subversion.[26] It is analogous to the self-imposed exclusion or exclusivity that many of the *Kanaken* assert because they do not want to be mistaken for mainstream Germans or for assimilated and therefore (in their eyes) weak or emasculated Turks. They are all united in the fight against cultural hegemony, and this gradually shifts their negative self-perception to a positive one. Stuart Hall points out that 'cultural hegemony is [...] always about shifting the balance of power in the relations of culture; it is always about changing the dispositions and the configurations of cultural power, not getting out of it'.[27] The *Kanaken* shift the balance of power by breaking (Turkish-)German culture into subidentities based on the fight against 'Mültikültüralizm' (the *Kanak* term for 'multiculturalism'),[28] while criticizing homogenizing tendencies amongst both the mainstream and any subculture.[29]

26 B. Venkat Mani discusses the notion of authenticity in his chapter on Zaimoğlu's novel *Abschaum*, stating that by focusing on *Lumpenethnics*, 'Zaimoğlu concedes the importance of ethnicity' (B. V. Mani, *Cosmopolitical Claims: Turkish-German Literatures from Nadolny to Pamuk* (Iowa City: University of Iowa Press, 2007), 132). He thereby pays particular attention to the notion of hybridity (118–45). Although I do not entirely disagree with Mani, I regard it as important to consider other cultural, social and religious factors when discussing the identiy of the *Kanaken* as constructed by Zaimoğlu.

27 S. Hall, 'What Is This "Black" in Black Popular Culture?', in *Stuart Hall: Critical Dialogues in Cultural Studies*, ed. D. Morley and K.-H. Chen (London: Routledge, 1996), 468.

28 Manifesto of 'Kanak Attak'. The exaggerated use of 'ü', which is also a sound/letter in Turkish, appears as linguistic subversion that immediately draws attention to the Turkish component of *Kanak Sprak*.

29 See F. Zaimoğlu, 'sicarim süppkültürünüze, züppeler! Ich scheiße auf eure Subkultur, ihr Schmöcke!', in *Mainstream der Minderheiten: Pop in der Kontrollgesellschaft*, ed. T. Holert and M. Terkessidis (Berlin: Edition ID-Archiv, 1996), 86–95, and T. Cheesman, 'Talking *"Kanak"*: Zaimoğlu contra *Leitkultur*', in *Multicultural Germany: Art, Performance, and Media*, ed. D. Göktürk and B. Wolbert (= Special Issue, *New German Critique*, 92 (Spring/Summer 2004)), 84. See also the public debate on 'Deutsche *Leitkultur*' triggered by Friedrich Merz's (then chairman of the CDU in the German *Bundestag*) comment on rules for immigration and integration in the newspaper *Die Welt* on 25 October 2000. For a discussion of subculture and youth see S. Hall and T. Jefferson, eds, *Resistance Through Rituals:*

Zaimoğlu's approach goes hand-in-hand with the reappropriation of the term '*Kanake*'. Similarly to the terms 'nigger' or 'niggah', it is usually used pejoratively by the mainstream to describe a gap between themselves and 'foreigners'. However, Zaimoğlu, the author, as well as most of his characters redefine '*Kanake*' as a means of expressing proud difference from the privileged, middle-class German population. In the Hawaiian/Polynesian language *kanaka* means 'human being', and denotes the native population of the South Sea Islands, particularly New Caledonia.[30] The German word '*Kanake*' has a derogatory meaning referring to immigrants and foreigners from Southern and Eastern Europe, and from the Middle East.[31] Similarly, some German Turks refer to themselves as '*Kümmel*' [cumin] (derived from the pejorative expression '*Kümmeltürke*' [Cumin Turk]) to subvert a common perception of Turks as distinctly foreign in their cooking and eating habits (their allegedly high consumption of cumin).[32] I also regard '*Fremdländer*' [someone from a strange country] as opposed to the more commonly used '*Ausländer*' [someone from another country] as a deliberate form of protest: *Kanaken* who use this word make the mainstream aware of its deliberate and ridiculous detachment from people of a 'different' background. They can — according to Kiên Nghi Hà — 'durch den "Mißbrauch" des rassistischen Begriffs auch seine rassistischen Konnotationen verdrängen und deaktivieren' [also suppress and deactivate its racist connotations by the 'misuse' of the racist term].[33] This is the point where performative processes can begin: the *Kanaken* reappropriate an historically determined term and redirect historical oppression into a political struggle whose ultimate aim is to regain

Youth Subcultures in Post-War Britain (London: Routledge, 1993 [2000 printing]; first publ. as *Working Papers in Cultural Studies*, 7/8 (Birmingham: Centre for Contemporary Cultural Studies, University of Birmingham, 1975)), esp. J. Clarke *et al.*, 'Subcultures, Cultures and Class: A Theoretical Overview', 9–74.

30 Entry on 'kanaka', in *Oxford English Dictionary Online*, www.oed.com [accessed 19 June 2006].

31 F. Kluge, *Etymologisches Wörterbuch der deutschen Sprache*, 22nd edn, with the assistance of M. Bürgisser and B. Gregor, fully rev. E. Seebold (Berlin: de Gruyter, 1989 [1883]), 351: 'eine abwertende Bezeichnung für südliche Ausländer' [a pejorative term for southern foreigners].

32 According to Kluge, in the late eighteenth century, '*Kümmeltürke*' referred to 'a student from Halle' in whose surroundings cumin was grown. This area was also called '*Kümmeltürkei*' [Cumin Turkey]. Today, '*Kümmeltürke*' is an abusive term for Turkish *Gastarbeiter* (418).

33 K. N. Hà, *Ethnizität und Migration* (Münster: Westfälisches Dampfboot, 1999), 166–67.

their masculinity as a form of power.[34] Jonathan Culler's examination of the performative can be usefully applied when looking into the struggle of the *Kanaken*. He writes, summarizing Judith Butler:

> But this historical dimension of performative implies the possibility of deflecting or redirecting the weight of the past, by attempting to capture and redeploy the terms that bear an oppressive signification, as in the adoption of 'Queer' by homosexuals themselves, or in a citation of norms of femininity in drag performances. (515)

Yet despite the fact that Zaimoğlu freely appropriates these terms to label the young German Turks he interviews, some of his Turkish German readers have identified potential problems with the expression '*Kanake*':[35] it is still often perceived as a racist term and thus an insult. Furthermore, it is felt to be a creation of the writer Zaimoğlu. By choosing the name '*Kanak Attak*' for his anti-racist network mentioned earlier, Zaimoğlu both reinvented the term '*Kanake*' and imposed it upon a group of people (namely primarily young German Turks) who would not necessarily call themselves that or identify with this group. This raises the question who is allowed to use the word and who is not:[36] are only German Turks in a position to employ it as a form of subversion, and are ethnic Germans not allowed to use it, as their use would imply racism?

Other German Turks suggest that the word '*Kanake*' strengthens the community as it brings the common experiences of migrants, or rather migrants' children (post-migrants), to the fore. Nationality and ethnicity become less significant. *Kanaken* create their own 'nation'.

34 Zaimoğlu himself is aware of the fact that he performs the role of the subverting writer. See F. Zaimoğlu, 'Eure Coolness ist Gigaout: Eine Gespräch mit Jutta Winkelmann', in *Kanaksta: Von deutschen und anderen Ausländern*, ed. J. Lottmann (Berlin: Quadriga, 1999), 28: 'Ich bin ein Sonderfall, auch unter den Kanakstern. Ich bin einer, der sich das alles angekuckt hat und der gesagt hat: "Ihr Scheißer, ihr falschen Propheten da oben! Was ihr könnt, kann ich schon lange! Ihr wollt Macht, ihr demonstriert Macht, da liefere ich euch eine Macht, die anziehender und sexier ist als euer Scheingemurmel"' [I am a special case, even among the *Kanakstern*. I am someone who had a look at all that and then said: 'You shitheads, you false prophets up there! Whatever you can do, I have been able to do for ages! You want power, you demonstrate power, I'll show you power which is more attractive and sexier than your pretentious mumbling'].

35 The following discussion of the differences in meaning and connotation of the term '*Kanake*' is based on M. Güngör and H. Loh, *Fear of a Kanak Planet: HipHop zwischen Weltkultur und Nazi-Rap* (Höfen: Hannibal, 2002), 27–40.

36 See Cheesman, *Novels of German Turkish Settlement*, 26–27, on Zaimoğlu's contradictory use of the word '*Kanake*' and '[t]he cultural and political significance of [his] early work' (27).

The term is also used to shed light on the relationship of the *Kanaken* with their parents (former *Gastarbeiter*): '*Kanake*' describes the second and third generations' active rebellion against the mainstream, and '*Gastarbeiter*' relates to a passive acceptance of Germany's superiority. Thus '*Kanake*' expresses a political attitude: in this case, the word's meaning literally shifts from racist connotations to a political form of protest. It embraces the 'Solidarität in einem gemeinsamen Kampf' (Güngör and Loh, 31) [solidarity in a common struggle] by telling 'die Geschichte des migrantischen Widerstandes' (37) [the history of migrant resistance]. *Kanaken* have an aim: 'die Geschichte [...] anzueignen, sie zu verbreiten, weiterzuerzählen, um aus ihr zu lernen und andererseits uns selbst in diese bestimmte Tradition zu stellen' (39) [appropriating this history, broadcasting, retelling it, in order to learn from it and on the other hand to put ourselves in this particular tradition]. This point is crucial: on the one hand, the *Kanaken* actively fight against the passivity of their parents and against the stigmatization forced on them by the mainstream; on the other, they use — in Murat Güngör's and Hannes Loh's terms — their 'Geschichtsbewußtsein' [awareness of history] and their 'kollektives Gedächtnis' [collective memory] as a means of creative struggle. It is this interaction between past and present, group and individual which determines the position of the *Kanaken* in German society.

Zaimoğlu's characters seem to be used to being different, perhaps because there is a less complicated relationship between Germany and Turkey in terms of colonial interests.[37] Zaimoğlu's interlocutor Akay tells us: 'Den Fremdländer kannst du nimmer aus der Fresse wischen' (Akay, 29, vom Flohmarkt [from the flea market]; ZKS 23) [You can't wipe foreign off your mug]. These young German Turks'

37 However, Emine Sevgi Özdamar points out that one can describe the relationship between Germany and Turkey as that between colonizer and colonized (in D. Horrocks and E. Kolinsky, 'Living and Writing in Germany: Emine Sevgi Özdamar in Conversation with David Horrocks and Eva Kolinsky', in *Turkish Culture in German Society Today*, ed. D. Horrocks and E. Kolinsky, 52–53). See also Özdamar's story 'Fahrrad auf dem Eis' [Bicycle on the Ice] in her collection *Der Hof im Spiegel* [*The Courtyard in the Mirror*] (Cologne: Kiepenheuer & Witsch, 2001), 77–112. Here the protagonist tells her interlocutor: 'Mir kommen die Männer so weich vor. Sie haben am Meer gestanden und haben gesehen, daß die Welt groß ist. Und Deutschland ist ein Wald. Bis sie den Weg rausgefunden hatten, war die Kolonialzeit vorbei. Man sagt, deswegen haben die Deutschen die Kolonien im Land selber geschaffen, die Gastarbeiter' (95) [I think the men are really soft. They stood by the sea and saw that the world was huge. And Germany is a forest. By the time they had found the way out of it, the colonial period was over. It is said that this is the reason why the Germans have created colonies in the country itself, the *Gastarbeiter*].

parents came to Germany as 'foreigners' — and usually remained in that position. Growing up in Germany, their children often tried to become 'German', but then came to realize that the mainstream still regarded them as foreign, as either Turkish or Muslim. Zaimoğlu's protagonists have learned to accept this label as something that one has to deal with — and ultimately be proud of. Judith Butler's exploration of gender performativity serves as a valuable tool to understand the objective behind this.[38] The notion of acting out a role comes into play. According to Butler, '[p]erformativity is [...] not a singular "act", for it is always a reiteration of a norm or set of norms, and to the extent that it acquires an act-like status in the present, it conceals or dissimulates the conventions of which it is a repetition' (*Bodies That Matter*, 12). Although *Kanaken* also reiterate a set of norms, namely those of the subversive, non-conventional, often radical German Turk, they are aware of the conventions they are following and make them explicit. By contrast to Butler's notion of performativity, Zaimoğlu's *Kanaken* have chosen their *Kanak* identity. Although Butler also points out that 'the acts by which gender is constituted bear similarities to performative acts within theatrical contexts,'[39] in the material discussed in this chapter, performance is, rather than resembles, a show. Most of the young Muslims 'stage' their identities. But this 'dramatic performance' has an empowering effect. As Hà says: 'Durch den Akt des Redens versuchen die Marginalisierten ihr eigenes Ich, ihre Geschichte und einen Ort des befreiten und befreienden Sprechens zu finden' (165) [through the act of speaking, the marginalized try to find their own self, their history, and a place of liberated and liberating speech] which results in a 'grundlegende Verschiebung der Perspektive' [fundamental shift of perspective]. They increasingly make use of their 'Recht auf Selbstkonstruktion' (165–66) [right to construct themselves]; they — as Butler puts it — 'do' their bodies ('Performative Acts and Gender Constitution', 404) and their speech.

In this context it is noticeable that the men initially perform roles within sets of norms and expectations imposed on them; later they

38 Cf. Günter, esp. 19–22. Schmidt has also examined the interrelation between performance and performativity, and gender, that is, 'assertive ethnic masculinity', in Zaimoğlu's work, although not focussing on *Kanak Sprak* (see esp. 199–202).

39 J. Butler, 'Performative Acts and Gender Constitution: An Essay in Phenomenology and Feminist Theory', in *Writing on the Body: Female Embodiment and Feminist Theory*, ed. K. Conboy *et al.* (New York: Columbia University Press, 1997), 403.

reappropriate these roles consciously as parts of their identities. There is a movement from the rejection of the role of the 'foreigner' to the idea of choice: the role is increasingly perceived as a chance for subversion (for example, in the form of parody or mimicry).[40] Butler relates to this fact when she points out that 'it is only *within* the practices of repetitive signifying that a subversion of identity becomes possible' (*Gender Trouble,* 185, italics Butler's). Zaimoğlu's *Kanaken* are also shown to repeat the practices of being a *Kanake* continuously, but they are conscious of the provocative and thus subversive potential of their behaviour. One could argue that the young men in these texts negotiate what Gayatri Chakravorty Spivak refers to as an 'exmarginal' position:[41] they are aware of their situation at the 'margins of society' and deal with it consciously. On the one hand, they reject 'margins', they are forcing their way into the 'centre' (the consciousness of the mainstream); on the other, they purposefully use these 'margins', their 'new positive sense of difference',[42] as a liberated position from which they can challenge the 'centre' and its perceptions of them.

Kureishi's young Muslims, too, are defined by their, or their parents', exclusion from the British mainstream. The historical experience of the British Empire led colonized peoples to regard the UK as (as they were taught) the 'mother country', but when they moved to this 'centre' they came to realize that they were not welcome there.[43] For the children of those immigrants, this inner division (which their parents could compensate by a longing look towards

40 For parody, see Butler, *Gender Trouble,* 176–77; Butler refers to gender parody or pastiche (as gender 'acts') here, but it can equally be applied to the parody of any role that is socially acquired and then subverted. For mimicry, see Bhabha, 'Of Mimicry and Man', 85–92. See also Ashcroft *et al.* The authors point out numerous subversion processes, primarily in terms of language and literature. Schmidt also takes this idea up when he writes that Zaimoğlu 'narrates, analyzes, even mocks the ways in which Turkish-German men construct their masculinity and ethnicity through clothing, speech, gesture, and so on' (200).

41 G. C. Spivak, 'Theory in the Margin: Coetzee's Foe Reading Defoe's *Crusoe/ Roxana*', *English in Africa,* 17.2 (1990), 1.

42 Begemann, 218: 'Darüber hinaus erwächst Identität hier lediglich aus der Negation und dem Bewußtsein der Differenz' [Furthermore, here, identity arises merely from the negation and the awareness of difference].

43 See H. Kureishi, 'The Road Exactly: Introduction to *My Son the Fanatic*' (1986), in *Dreaming and Scheming* (London: Faber and Faber, 2002), 219: 'Yet all along it was taken for granted that "belonging", which means, in a sense, not having to notice where you are, and, more importantly, not being seen as different, would happen eventually. […] The "West" was a dream that didn't come true. But one cannot go home again. One is stuck.'

their former home and/or a great effort to integrate) can result in a continuous feeling of being excluded everywhere — in their parents' country of birth as well as in their own country of birth. This seems to be a particularly pressing issue for young British Muslims, many of whom reach for their religion as a way of finding the stability of a 'home'; Kureishi puts it thus: '[F]undamentalist Islam could do this [provide spiritual comfort, or community and solidarity] in a country that was supposed to be home but which could, from day to day, seem alien' (220–21). Consequently, Kureishi's Muslims in *The Black Album* develop an increasing self-awareness as Muslims, rather than immigrants or 'Pakis' (KBA 128). Unlike Zaimoğlu's *Kanaken*, they do not wish to reappropriate the xenophobic term as the focus of their identity. They emphasize the religious aspect of their identity rather than their cultural roots instead and thus develop their radical Islamist agenda to fight the decadent West.

In a similar way to Zaimoğlu's *Kanaken* though, Kureishi's Muslims have chosen and consciously perform their identities as a result of their social exclusion. As strictly religious young men they follow the rules of Islam pedantically; regularly repeated rituals such as praying together turn into performative acts that bind them together as a group. These practices ultimately give them self-esteem in their now chosen difference as well as power over those — in their eyes — decadent non-Muslims who react to their provocative behaviour. Thus they find their position as 'different men' on their own terms in a United Kingdom that shuns them.

The subversion processes of Kureishi's young Muslims also take place when communicating with non-Muslim British people, most notably when Western expectations of exoticism related to ethnicity and not to religion are appropriated as a tool to demonstrate the superficiality of labels for the children of South Asian immigrants.[44] By recognizing racial, rather than religious, stereotypes as a means of subversion, some of Kureishi's Muslims learn to identify their 'different' position within British society as a 'de-exoticising category' (Huggan on Said, *The Postcolonial Exotic*, 19), that is, as the opportunity to act against racial stereotypes.

> [Shahid:] 'Please, Strapper, you said the whites are selfish. I need your help. I thought you loved Asian people.'

44 Cf. Huggan, *The Postcolonial Exotic*, 13–14: 'Exoticism [...] might be described as a kind of semiotic circuit that oscillates between the opposite poles of strangeness and familiarity. [...] As a system [...] exoticism functions along predictable lines but with unpredictable content.'

> [Strapper:] 'Not when they get too fucking Westernized. You all wanna be just like us now. It's the wrong turnin'.' (KBA 195)

Muslim immigrants are pushed into a racial corner. They were – and still are – referred to as 'Asians' and defined by their origin, but also (at least in the 1980s and 1990s) by the darker colour of their skin rather than by their religion. By reiterating Strapper's racist attitude based on the dichotomy of 'the whites' vs 'Asian people', Shahid both becomes part of this discourse in order to gain a position (and ultimately a voice) in the mainstream and (speaking as somebody from the 'inferior race') uses this dichotomy as a means to an end. He wants Strapper's help to find his brother Chili, who is involved in drugs – even by means of racist discourse whose conscious appropriation is a form of speech act and thus performative. Although this particular subversion process is a limited one, it nonetheless shows that the children of former immigrants appropriate racist discourse as a tool for survival and, under certain circumstances, as an instrument for engaging in their radically religious activities. Racist discourse thereby loses some of its original force as verbal and, by implication, physical oppression.

Kureishi's Muslims construct an idea of Islam as a force that fights Western dominance and social exclusion, and thereby also separate themselves from less devout Muslims. One critic claims that Kureishi has a 'desire to "explain" the contemporary resurgence of Islam in Britain' (Ranasinha, 82). He himself has explained his interest in the revival of Islam among young British Muslims as follows: '[I]n *The Black Album*, I suppose, I want to share what it might be that makes people become fundamentalists. I portray book burning as being foolish, but that fact is also banal; I want to show, too, why it may be that people get involved in it.'[45] Although Kureishi comes from a mixed race background, he, like the later Zaimoğlu,[46] emphatically rejects the notion that he is a spokesman or cultural translator for

45 Kureishi's comment in K. C. Kaleta, *Hanif Kureishi: Postcolonial Storyteller* (Austin: University of Texas Press, 1998), 193.

46 As Cheesman points out, at the time of the publication of *Kanak Sprak* Zaimoğlu did see himself as a 'mouthpiece' for the *Kanaken* ('Talking "*Kanak*"', 94). However, Zaimoğlu has later rejected this position (Zaimoğlu in an interview with *Islamische Zeitung*, '"Die Polemik vergiftet das soziale Klima": Gespräch mit dem Regisseur Neco Çelik und dem Schriftsteller Feridun Zaimoglu über ihr Stück "Schwarze Jungfrauen"', *Islamische Zeitung*, 6 April 2006, www.islamische-zeitung.de/?id=7106 [accessed 28 June 2010] (24 para.)), and 'Gespräch zu *Schwarze Jungfrauen*' on NDR Kultur, 2 April 2008, www.ndrkultur.de/media/gespraech196.html, URL no longer available).

the racially despised. Nonetheless, he has had a long-term interest in race-related issues, which he also expresses in *The Black Album* (Ranasinha, 12).[47]

How do Zaimoğlu's *Kanaken* and Kureishi's young Muslims define their difficult relationships to the German and British mainstreams? As their subversive attitudes suggest, these children of former immigrants tend to have a deep mistrust for anything Western, which may be based on (in the case of British Muslims) their parents' humiliating colonial history or (in the case of German Muslims) their parents' equally humiliating *Gastarbeiter*-history; thus it is mainly the less affluent (post-)migrants who have no desire to be like German or British people. As Büyük Ibo puts it in Zaimoğlu's account: 'Den deutschen traust du nich übern weg, weil sie, die haben durchblick in ne andre richtung, und da willst du ums verrecken nich hin' (Büyük Ibo, 18, Packer; ZKS 45) [You don't trust the Germans, because they're just looking in another direction, and there's no way you want to go there]. This attitude implies a reversal of old colonial patterns and a '[R]epuzzeln [der] Geschichte' (Güngör and Loh, 58) [repuzzling of history] which 'erzeugt Sicherheit und führt zu neuem Selbstbewusstsein' [creates security and leads to new self-esteem]. The effort to integrate socially, economically, linguistically and, to some extent, culturally, that is, to overcome the marginal (and potentially dangerous) position,[48] occurs to a limited extent and as a means to an end: the West is only desirable as a dwelling place; its values are increasingly replaced by radically different or more traditional values, or reappropriated for the needs and desires of a generation that feels more consciously excluded than its parents did. In Zaimoğlu's account, for example, Hasan who as a young teenager is particularly keen to figure out who he is, expresses his feeling of social and cultural exclusion:

> Auch mit der familie und auch mit nem namen bleibst du ein bastard, du hast krause haare und benimmst dich nicht wie die deutschen, denen das licht längst ausgegangen is, du hast was vor, aber ne menge arschlöcher möchten dich aus der gegend haben, und wenn du dich nicht wehrst, kappen sie dir die leitung und machen dich zur

47 See also Kureishi's essays 'The Rainbow Sign' (1986) and 'Bradford' (1986), in *My Beautiful Laundrette and Other Writings* (London: Faber and Faber, 1996), 71–102, 121–44.

48 For more information on integration of second-generation migrants, see H. Weiss, ed., *Leben in zwei Welten: Zur sozialen Integration ausländischer Jugendlicher der zweiten Generation* (Wiesbaden: VS Verlag für Sozialwissenschaften, 2007).

> dunklen memme [...]. (Hasan, 13, Streuner und Schüler [tramp and pupil]; ZKS 93)
>
> [Even with the family and even with a name you remain a bastard, you have frizzy hair and you don't behave like the Germans whose light has been switched off long ago, you've planned something, but a lot of arseholes want to get rid of you, and if you don't struggle, they'll cut you off and turn you into a dark coward.]

In *Kanak Sprak*, opposition to the *alemannen* [German people] becomes the determining factor in Turkish German self-positioning. The choice of word for the Germans derives from Turkish (*alman*) but is linguistically Germanized — another form of subversion. Zaimoğlu's interlocutors assert a particular linguistic power: they have the advantage of being bi- or even multilingual (often as opposed to their parents) and are able to show disrespect for the Germans who may not understand this term, or where it comes from.

Although we can also detect opposition to mainstream society in *The Black Album*, as we might expect, there is a more religious dimension to it. Kureishi's 'fundamentalist' characters regard the West as decadent and hence deplorable: Riaz asserts that 'we have to guard against the hypocritical and smug intellectual atmosphere of Western civilization' (KBA 99). Riaz's reaction is based on a complex relationship between Muslims and the UK that derives from colonial history. One aspect illustrates this particularly well — education. Formerly colonized peoples tend to have a double relationship with the knowledge they gained from the colonial power: it was — more or less — openly received, but now the younger generation are increasingly seeing its faults (primarily the exclusion of the knowledge of the colonized) and are turning against it:

> [Riaz:] 'We are educated, a little. We are not slaves day and night in some shop or factory. But that means we have other duties, doesn't it? We cannot just forsake our people and live for ourselves.'
>
> [Shahid:] 'No.'
>
> [Riaz:] 'If we did, wouldn't that mean we had totally absorbed the Western morals, which are totally individualistic?' (KBA 173)

Riaz makes use of his Western education to support a subversion process without falling into the trap of 'Western individualism' (cf. Ranasinha, 88). He nourishes the idea that there is a duty to help those who could not 'enjoy' a Western education (which is, after all, an advantage when living in the West). It can be argued that Riaz himself exercises superiority and patronage: throughout the novel, he perceives himself as a leader, which is a form of individualism and (mainly intellectual) power. He unconsciously shows that he himself has adopted a certain degree of 'Western individualism' (as an educated leader he acts on his own terms) and that Western influences cannot be dismissed altogether.

The use of standard English also comes into play. It was taught by the colonizers, the colonized absorbed it, but now, when there is some distance from linguistic imperialism, it can be mimicked by their children. In *The Black Album*, Shahid 'asserted that Papa's generation, with their English accents, foreign degrees and British snobbery, assumed their own people were inferior' (KBA 91–92).

However, Kureishi's Muslims do not engage in acts of linguistic subversion. This practice is more prominent amongst Zaimoğlu's *Kanaken*: they create their own linguistic spaces based on a mixture of German, slang, colloquialisms and other languages — their transcultural *Kanak Sprak* [Kanak-speak]. According to Zaimoğlu, the result is 'eine Art Creol oder Rotwelsch mit geheimen Codes und Zeichen' (ZKS 13) [a kind of creole or *Rotwelsch* [thieves' slang] with secret codes and signs], which deliberately excludes those who do not understand.[49] (Standard Turkish, incidentally, does not play a significant role in the creation of *Kanak Sprak*.)[50] These processes seem to be more effective in German- than in English-language texts reflecting the life of young Muslims of the 1990s: the reason might be

49 As the secret language of thieves, *Rotwelsch* has negative implications. I assume Zaimoğlu employs the term sociologically in order to show the criminal element of some *Kanaken*, yet also linguistically in order to emphasize the exclusivity of this language which is only understood by a specific group of people. The linguistic aspect of the language *Kanak Sprak* is underlined by Zaimoğlu's equal use of the term 'creole', a hybrid language created through the merging of various languages.

50 For a linguistic analysis of *Kanak Sprak*, see Y. Yildiz, 'Critically "*Kanak*": A Reimagining of German Culture', in *Globalization and the Future of German*, ed. A. Gardt and B. Hüppauf (Berlin: Monton de Gruyter, 2004), 319–40; Yildiz focuses on the use of English, Turkish, German, North German vernacular, rap, *Rotwelsch* and Yiddish. She claims that Zaimoğlu 'has created a distinctive style and language that is neither found on the streets, nor elsewhere in language' (320). She also draws attention to 'fraternal relationships' and the 'emphasis on masculinity' that is inherent in *Kanak Sprak* (325). See also Cheesman, 'Akçam — Zaimoğlu — "Kanak Attak"', 183, on the untranslatability of *Kanak Sprak*, and 184 on the inventive use of language in *Kanak Sprak*. Hà takes a postcolonial standpoint and regards the language *Kanak Sprak* as an '*unreine, kreolisierte Sprache*' [*impure, creolized language*] and points out the '*Karnevalisierung und Dezentrierung* der herrschenden Herrensprache' [*carnivalization and decentring* of the ruling master-language] (165, italics Hà's).

that the *Kanaken* are less tied to an ideal of producing the standard language as a result of (linguistic) colonization which even today has an impact on a number of postcolonial people, and therefore are freer to play with language as a form of struggle.

***

Both Zaimoğlu's *Kanaken* and Kureishi's Muslims know then what they are *not* in relation to the German and British population. Yet the texts reveal their characters' need to belong. Belonging can be expressed through religious values and their implementation in both a pious or secular context, enabling the characters to establish a counter-attitude towards both Western Christians (in Zaimoğlu's texts) and Western immorality (in Kureishi's texts). In this way, Islam can become the main factor of identification: it only belongs to these young Muslims and is not shared by the secular or Christian West. On a political level, it can also contribute to the idea of a nation. For example, the 'Nation of Islam' with Malcolm X as its most prominent representative emphasizes the transnational and transcultural nature of Islam.[51] It embraces Muslims of all cultural backgrounds and unites them as the community of believers, the *umma*. It is a virtual substitute for a real nation; but it needs to be kept in mind that Zaimoğlu's and Kureishi's Muslims do not have a choice. As pointed out earlier, they largely feel that Germany and the UK do not welcome them as part of the nation.

Yet the link with the Black Consciousness Movement in the USA and its close connection to the 'Nation of Islam',[52] is made by the *Kanaken* and the British Muslims. The reference not only serves the purpose of creating a unity among themselves as male Muslims but also a wider connection and solidarity with African-Americans in the USA:

> [W]ir sind hier allesamt nigger, wir haben unser ghetto, wir schleppen's überall hin, wir dampfen fremdländisch, unser schweiß ist nigger, unser leben ist nigger, die goldketten sind nigger, unsere

51 See Natambu, particularly 'Chapter 10: Malcolm Discovers the Nation of Islam', 127–42. Personally, Kureishi does not approve of the separatist nature of the 'Nation of Islam' (Ranasinha, 3), and nor, in the end, did Malcolm X (Natambu, 299–302).

52 The 'Nation of Islam' was part of this movement and appropriated the idea of religious 'brotherhood' (Malcolm X, 452). The *Kanaken* and British Muslims discussed here use this idea to some extent, but they mainly apply it for expressing their masculinity.

zinken und unsere fressen und unser eigner stil ist so verdammt nigger, daß wir wie blöde an unsrer haut kratzen, und dabei kapieren wir, daß zum nigger nicht die olle pechhaut gehört, aber zum nigger gehört ne ganze menge anderssein und andres leben. Die haben schon unsre heimat prächtig erfunden: kanake da, kanake dort, wo du auch hingerätst, kanake blinkt dir in oberfetten lettern sogar im traum, wenn du pennst und denkst: joker, jetzt bist du in deiner eigenen sendung. (Akay, 29, vom Flohmarkt [from the flea market]; ZKS 25)

[We're all nigger, we have our ghetto, we drag it along wherever we go, we're foreign out of every pore, our sweat is nigger, our lives are nigger, the gold chains are nigger, our conks and our ugly mugs and our own style are so damn nigger that we scratch our skin like mad and then we get it that there's more to nigger than this old pitch-black skin, but you need a whole lot of being-different and living differently to be a nigger. They've invented our home marvellously: *kanake* here, *kanake* there, wherever you end up, *kanake* flashes in huge letters even when you're dreaming, when you're sleeping and thinking: joker, now you're in your own show.]

In this quotation, 'nigger' serves as an all-embracing term for ethnically different people who fight for social justice, but it also refers to the 'black brothers' of the 'Nation of Islam'. As their struggle was partly successful in the USA, *Kanaken,* more specifically those who, due to their lack of education and access to wider society, cannot relate to a large number of identity options, seem to regard their 'black brothers' as a kind of role model for the struggle. This is also expressed in their use of the English language (for example, 'nigger', 'joker'): cultural differences no longer play a role; it is the position of social inferiority and their Muslim heritage that unites them[53] — and turns them into proud, not victimized young men. The *Kanaken* create a transcultural space for their struggle for self-determination and power.

The identification of the *Kanaken* with the race struggles in the USA is also related to exclusive spaces for *Kanaken,* their society within German society:

Gaarden is knochenbrecher, 'n sperrbezirk, das hier das olle ostufer und dort der reiche westen, und dazwischen reckt sich wie'n langer

53 See Yildiz, 'Critically "Kanak"', 321–30, on the use of English in *Kanak Sprak*: 'As a third term and language, English breaks down the binary between sole affiliation with either Turkish or German' (329). She describes the interaction between globalization and the 'threat of cultural Americanization' (321) when the *Kanaken* use 'English and the *local* appropriation of English' (322, italics Yildiz's). Yildiz also points out the transnational role of rap (327–30) (see also Hà, 165, for this aspect).

> arm die gablenz-brücke, doch du denkst die vermaledeite brücke is tag wie nacht und ewig hochgeklappt, so is es in gaarden, wo ja prall unzählige kümmel hausen [...]. (Bayram, 18, Breaker; ZKS 39)

> [Gaarden is bone-cruncher, a prohibited area, right here the damn East bank and over there the rich West, and in between the gablenz-bridge stretches out like a long arm, but you're thinking this damn bridge is raised forever, day and night, it's like that in gaarden where countless *kümmel* live.]

The image of the bridge is of particular significance here; it describes the divided attitude of the *Kanaken* to their exclusion: on the one hand, Turkish immigrants were put into 'ghettos' (in Kiel this is the Gaarden-district) and thus separated from the rest of the German society, who may or may not have been prejudiced against German Turks of a lower social status and of a different religion than theirs. Thus, initially, *Gastarbeiter* were not allowed to 'bridge gaps': to become part of 'the German ethnic group or *Kulturnation*, the German state society, and the German citizenry'.[54] Their physical marginalization has led to their separation on the level of ideology, culture and law, to inequality at work, in social welfare, education, housing and legal status.[55] To this day Turks are the most affected by poverty among minorities (122) as many of them have 'limited protection through employment', may also suffer from 'status uncertainties', that is, the fear of having to leave the country, and are excluded from support functions (123). These migrants experience a sense of security through familial networks, through friends and family who were brought over from Turkey instead (116–17).

On the other hand, the *Kanaken* are now reappropriating this space as their own, thus creating a *Kanak* society within the German mainstream society and thereby challenging German integration politics with its fear of a Turkish 'Parallelgesellschaft' [parallel society]. This *Kanak* society can be regarded as a society within Turkish society within German society.

In *The Black Album*, distinct spaces associated with the young Muslims portrayed here are less prominent. This reflects the fact that former immigrants are often living alongside less well-off British people in deprived areas. However, in Kureishi's depiction, there is no interaction between the 'Asian' and the 'white' communities,

54 W. A. Barbieri Jr, *Ethics of Citizenship: Immigration and Group Rights in Germany* (Durham, NC: Duke University Press, 1998), 9.

55 E. Kürsat-Ahlers, 'The Turkish Minority in German Society', in *Turkish Culture in German Society Today*, ed. D. Horrocks and E. Kolinsky, 118.

who share the same space. On the contrary, these areas are places of physical struggle. In *The Black Album*, religion serves as a separating force creating 'intellectual spaces'. As these young Muslims seem to be on a jihad (both an intellectual and physical struggle for the spread of Islam), they deliberately divide themselves off from the allegedly atheist mainstream:[56] '"Atheism won't last," Riaz explained. "Without religion society is impossible. And without God people think they can sin with impunity. There's no morality"' (KBA 33). For Riaz, Islam serves as a means of protection against the West's immoral influences. He aims, therefore, to create his and his people's own mental spaces free from 'the evil West' (despite living in the middle of it), and defined by religious purity.

In 'My Son the Fanatic', Ali, the 'fanatic', relates the West's immoral influences directly to his father Parvez: 'Parvez knew he was getting drunk, but he couldn't stop himself. Ali had a horrible look on his face, full of disgust and censure. It was as if he hated his father. [...] He leaned across the table. [...] "You are too implicated by Western civilisation"' (KMS 125). The father is immorality personified. He is the graspable object, not simply a general notion of the West that Ali can fight against. This makes Ali's struggle real and personal.

For Zaimoğlu's *Kanaken*, defining exclusive spaces helps uncover a 'double consciousness',[57] which they increasingly perceive as something positive, but not necessarily in religious terms: it is the result of living with many cultures, which are not exclusively Turkish and German but also include rural and urban cultures. In contrast to some of Kureishi's characters, Zaimoğlu's *Kanaken* move away from a self-perception as 'feminized' 'new Jews' (KBA 201),[58] demonized outsiders that in this day and age are all too often young Muslim men, and develop a strong self-awareness: 'Und die sagen: du bist auf'm damm, mann, wie willst du, daß wir dich nennen? Und du sagst: ich bin, der ich bin!' (Hasan, 13, Streuner und Schüler [tramp

56 See Kureishi's comment in Kaleta, 203: 'One couldn't have predicted in the sixties that in the nineties young people who were born and brought up here would be asserting their Muslim identity in quite such a right-wing way. Who would have thought such an odd thing could happen? ... the young are less likely to take any shit.'

57 See P. Gilroy, *The Black Atlantic: Modernity and Double Consciousness* (Cambridge, MA: Harvard University Press, 1993), 1: 'Striving to be both European and black requires some specific forms of double consciousness.'

58 See Kureishi's short story 'We're Not Jews', in *Love in a Blue Time*, 41–51. In this story, one of the characters, a mother married to a South Asian 'immigrant', uses the sentence 'We're not Jews.' as a defence against a racist attack against her son and herself on a bus (45).

and pupil]; ZKS 92) [And they say; you're alright, man, what do you want to be called? And you say: I am who I am!]. Despite the group identity as *Kanaken* that Zaimoğlu creates on the basis of the concerns they have in common, most of them create their personal identity: belonging to a group is important but not the ultimate aim. Seen from that perspective they maintain a more individualistic attitude whose roots may be found in Western secular societies. In contrast, Kureishi's young Muslims create a culture of community: the anti-individualistic group is needed for their religious rediscovery — again as an effective means of opposition to the decadent and individualist West.

However, trying to become part of the religious community is often connected to emotional struggle and personal doubt; it is not a 'straight path' that automatically leads to fulfilment.[59] In *The Black Album*, Shahid who did not receive any religious input at home, has serious doubts when he is away from his religious friends:

> Shahid felt he had passed the point when he could question Riaz about the fundamentals. Shahid frequently fell into anxiety about his lack of faith. Observing the mosque, in which all he saw were solid, material things, and looking along the line of brothers' faces upon which spirituality was taking place, he felt a failure. But he was afraid that enquiry would expose him to some sort of suspicion. He could at least discuss the doubts with Hat, who said, not to worry, let it happen. And when Shahid did relax he grasped that faith, like love or creativity, could not be willed. This was an adventure in knowing. He had to follow the prescriptions and be patient. Understanding would surely follow; he would be blessed. (KBA 96)

Previously, Shahid was surprised by 'the religious enthusiasm of the younger generation, and its links to strong political feeling' when visiting relatives in Karachi (KBA 91). This feeling of surprise is now replaced by 'anxiety' and a sense of 'failure'. His education at home was Western, that is, less focused on religion, and this experience is released when interacting with Riaz and his new friends. These doubts, which can be seen as an opportunity to express his individuality, are based on Western influences such as his education, his parents'

59 In the first sura of the Qur'an, the *fātiha* [opening], we read: 'Guide Thou us on the straight path, / The path of those to whom Thou hast been gracious; — with whom thou art not angry, and who go not astray' (Q1: 5–7). God is described as 'someone to whom people look for help and guidance' in order 'to find their way onto the "Straight Path"' (M. Cook, *The Koran: A Very Short Introduction* (Oxford: Oxford University Press, 2000), 9, 14). See also J. L. Esposito, *Islam: The Straight Path*, 3rd edn (New York: Oxford University Press, 1998 [1988]).

more secular attitude to life, and primarily his love relationship with Deedee. The more he feels peer pressure ('prescriptions' and 'patience') the more he is afraid of 'suspicion', but simultaneously hopeful of help which will result in 'understanding' and 'pure belief'. The question remains, however, whether faith can be acquired, and whether being part of a group is essential in this learning process.

In 'My Son the Fanatic', Ali is finding his path to Islam entirely on his own, and only seems to be part of a virtual group, the 'millions of others [... who] will gladly give [their] lives for the cause' (KMS 126). He is, according to Kureishi, 'at war with [the clash of cultures] *internally*, trying to evacuate it, but never succeeding'.[60] Kureishi shows that his protagonist's struggle is an eternal one as he will never be able to shed his culturally and religiously mixed background and present (the cause of his confusion and struggle). He should simply learn how to come to terms with it instead.

***

Both Zaimoğlu's *Kanaken* and Kureishi's Muslims form 'imagined communities' of their own kinds, and for both groups the city plays a significant role as a dwelling place and site of resistance.

The German Turks in *Kanak Sprak* live in Kiel, which is situated in the 'provinz aleman' (Zaimoğlu, 'sicarim süppkültürünüze, züppeler!', 89) [German provinces]. Although some of the *Kanaken* refer to themselves as 'big city-anatolier' (Zaimoğlu, 'KümmelContra', 174) [big city Anatolians], it is the local affiliation with this North German city that serves as an alternative to a political nation, which is clearly expressed in the use of the local dialect (see Yildiz, 'Critically "Kanak"', 326). It seems to be easier for *Kanaken*, particularly for those of a lower social rank, to gain acceptance in a smaller unit than in Germany as a whole: 'Wir sind wüchsige aus gaarden' (Bayram, 18, Breaker; ZKS 39) [We've grown up in gaarden], the '*Kanaken*-ghetto' within the city of Kiel which is marked by struggle.

Kureishi's novel is set in London where belonging is also an issue. Bart Moore-Gilbert points out that 'the modern inner city is an easier "England" to identify with for diasporic populations than rural, industrial and suburban "Englands"'.[61] Initially, belonging seems

60 H. Kureishi, 'Sex and Secularity: Introduction to *Collected Screenplays One*' (2002), in *The Word and the Bomb* (London: Faber and Faber, 2005), 86, italics Kureishi's.

61 B. Moore-Gilbert, *Hanif Kureishi* (Manchester: Manchester University Press, 2001), 10.

easy for Shahid: 'In London, if you found the right place, you could consider yourself a citizen the moment you went to the same local shop twice' (KBA 193). As a metropolis, London seems to welcome everybody. Yet in order to make it a home, other factors (such as finding a group of like-minded people) need to come in.

It appears, therefore, that in both texts the young Muslims' culture is an urban culture. The *Kanaken* and Kureishi's young British Muslims clearly do what Hà refers to as 'die imaginative *Rekonstruktion* kultureller Räume, die *Relokalisierung* spätmoderner Urbanität und die *Reterritorialisierung* städtischer Landschaften' (164, italics Hà's) [the imaginative *reconstruction* of cultural spaces, the *relocalization* of late-modern urbanity and the *reterritorialization* of urban landscapes]. One approach to these processes is consciously living in a gang culture. Gangs or posses are a significant aspect in the process of regaining masculinity for Zaimoğlu's and Kureishi's protagonists. Groups give a sense of belonging, strength within the group as well as against others, and security in a hostile environment.

> Die jungs streunen durch die stadt, sie rotten sich zusammen, weil sie große teile des tages einsam sind. Im rudel findet man früher oder später zu einem kodex, in der gang erhält man die feuertaufe, und mit dem neugewonnenen sinn im leib gehen sie in kleinen scharen auf die suche. Das geld ist eine sorge, das outfit nicht minder. [...] Sie sind das wahre lumpenproletariat [...]. Sie sind menschenmüll, eine verschwendung in den straßen der metropolen, sie haben das spiel verloren, weil die karten gezinkt sind, die man ihnen in die hand drückt. Deshalb sind sie kanaken, deshalb bin ich ein kanake, deshalb bist du ein kanake. Wir sind bastarde, freund [...]. (Memet, 29, Dichter [poet]; ZKS 109–10)

> [The guys roam the city, they gang up because they're lonely for most of the day. Among the pack, sooner or later they find a code, in the gang you get a baptism of fire, and with the new found meaning causing through their veins they go hunting in small posses. Money is one concern, threads are another. [...] They're the true masses [...]. They're human waste, sucked dry in the streets of the metropolis, they've lost the game because they've been dealt marked cards. That's why they're *kanaken*, that's why I'm a *kanake*, that's why you're a *kanake*. We're bastards, friend.]

The city encourages the formation of groups as a means of belonging. Memet expresses a strange mix of attachment and detachment in his description of *Kanaken*: on the one hand, he describes them in an anthropological way, which emphasizes his high level of education, yet, on the other, he includes himself in this 'wir' [we]. Yet Memet emphasizes that the gang is a unifying device against the mainstream and thus represents a conscious choice to belong.

Gangs are part of a masculine world, a 'gangsta culture'.[62] As Zaimoğlu indicates in his preface: 'Am öffentlichen Leben in den Szenen der Kanaken-Ghettos nimmt hauptsächlich der Mann teil, der Frau dagegen wird bedeutet, sie habe sich aus der männlichen Welt herauszuhalten' (ZKS 15) [It is mainly men who take part in public life in the scenes of the *Kanaken*-ghettos. The woman is told that she has to keep out of the male world]. Male exclusivity is expressed in the formation of gender-specific groups at the expense of women. Women, particularly Western women, and especially prostitutes, are regarded as 'fair game', as an exchangeable trophy,[63] and are only passively part of the men's activities.[64] This is a return to gender stereotypes (which can also be found in hypocritically conservative interpretations of Islam that favour men) and the idea that physical fighting is exclusively masculine behaviour, an attitude which is also expressed in the constant reference to drugs, crime and violence: gangs operate in an 'Unterwelt' (KZS 100) [underworld] where the struggle between power and law is conducted.[65] Many of the *Kanaken*, especially the strong and hypermasculine ones, deliberately go against any law as an expression of their identity. For example, as a pimp, Cem clearly experiences elements of power and male prowess, and certainly not of religiosity; his profession serves as a tool to catapult him out of the Muslim stereotype and, consequently, masculinize him: 'Die erste devise heißt: der hahn kräht nur nach dem starken' (Cem, 25, Zuhälter [pimp]; ZKS 54) [The first motto is: we only care about the strong]. Living in the city demands the survival of the fittest which is personified by the *Kanakster/Kanaksta* (a

62 b. hooks, *We Real Cool: Black Men and Masculinity* (New York: Routledge, 2004), 15–32.

63 Cf. B. Mennel, 'Bruce Lee in Kreuzberg and Scarface in Altona: Transnational Auteurism and Ghettocentrism in Thomas Arslan's *Brothers and Sisters* and Fatih Akin's *Short Sharp Shock*', in *Postwall Cinema*, ed. E. Rentschler (= Special Issue, *New German Critique*, no. 87 (Fall 2002)), 150.

64 See the way Cem talks about 'his' prostitutes in *Kanak Sprak*, 49–54. See also the written conversations the characters Serdar (on holiday in Turkey) and Hakan (in Germany) have in Zaimoğlu's epistolary novel *Liebesmale, scharlachrot* [*Love Bites, Scarlet*] (Cologne: Kiepenheuer & Witsch, 2002 [2000]). They tend to speak about women in a disparaging way. The number of their trophies (German women they have been able to seduce) is proof of their masculinity.

65 Cf. M. Foucault, *The Will to Knowledge: The History of Sexuality, Volume 1*, trans. R. Hurley (London: Penguin, 1998 [1978]), 87 (originally publ. as *La volonté de savoir* (Paris: Gallimard, 1976)).

combination of *Kanake* and gangster) 'as a new and effective strategy of survival'.[66] It is noteworthy that Butler, too, notes that 'as a strategy of survival, gender is a performance' ('Performative Acts and Gender Constitution', 405); this view parallels bell hooks's observation that the role of the strong young men is less of a free choice than is usually thought, but rather a product of 'a biased imperialist white-supremacist patriarchal mass media' which 'teaches [*sic*] young black males that the patriarchal man is a predator, that only the strong and the violent survive' (27). The question remains whether the *Kanaken* follow this media image subconsciously or whether they consciously recognize the potential of metaphorical and physical fights to make them visible. Yet — apart from the interlocutor Yücel, the Islamist — fighting is for the *Kanaken* not an action motivated by fundamentalism. To Kureishi's British Muslims, by contrast, fighting has become a useful tool to gain visibility in today's West with its major fears of fundamentalist attacks.

In *The Black Album*, the group around Riaz is also partly transgressing civil law whilst upholding religious law: they are fighting against what they regard as Western immorality and injustice. Women are included in activities such as protecting a Bangladeshi family in a housing estate against racial attacks. However, these stereotypically male actions seem to de-gender or even masculinize them: they are not recognized as women but purely as Muslims, and thus become part of the struggle, of the group. This is the only way for Muslim women in this environment to gain visibility.

> Chad squatted back down on his haunches with his armoury around him, as far from Nina and Sadiq as possible. The pair volunteered for the maximum duty. Forbidden to kiss or touch, they liked to fight: Sadiq had pinched her and now Nina was poised for the chance to pinch him back, regarding Chad and Shahid suspiciously, as if they were teachers. Chad didn't like the sisters accompanying them, though it was they, being devoted to the cause, who insisted; it was they, encouraged by Riaz, who had to make excuses to their parents. (KBA 126)

66 Cheesman defines *Kanakster* as a combination of the words *Kanak* and 'youngster' or 'gangsta' ('Talking *"Kanak"*', 83, and *Novels of Turkish German Settlement*, 3). S. Hestermann, 'The German-Turkish Diaspora and Multicultural German Identity: Hyphenated and Alternative Discourses of Identity in the Works of Zafer Şenocak and Feridun Zaimoğlu', in *Diaspora and Multiculturalism: Common Traditions and New Developments*, ed. M. Fludernik, Crosscultures: Readings in Post/Colonial Literatures in English, 66 (Amsterdam: Rodopi, 2003), 364.

The relationship between the men and the women here is based on struggle, which is a familiar, secure field of communication. The women are regarded as 'sisters', a role which is non-sexual and thus — again — safe. This role is encouraged by their leader Riaz: it appears that it is only by being an asexual companion that the women can achieve respect within the group. By acting like men, they develop the desire to prove their strength — their only opportunity to gain a place within the masculine world of the city.

Using and boasting of physical strength is another reaction against the way others perceive and categorize them. The urge to find a space away from assimilation might also be the result of a general exclusion from Turkey where 'Germanized' Turks are often referred to as *alamancı* or *Deutschländer* (a pejorative term for Turkish people who live in Germany and who, in the eyes of their family and friends in Turkey, have become 'Germanized' over the years and thus do not belong to Turkey any more). The self-determination of the *Kanaken* is based on their assumption that dominant society puts them in certain categories to be enabled to 'deal' with them. Many *Kanaken* react against this:

> Der einheimische hat für'n kümmel ja zwei reservate frei: entweder bist du'n lieb-alilein, 'n recht und billiger bimbo eben [...]. So'n lieb-alilein ist der wahre kanake, weil er sich dem einheimischen zwischen die ollen arschbacken in den kanal dienert, und den kakaoüberzug als ne art identität pflegt. 'n kanake is sowas wie ne rothaut, die man mit bunten glasperlen und feuerwasser bescheißt, und der grient dazu wie'n tourist auf'm schnappschußfoto. Dann gibt's noch'n zweites reservat, in dem der fremdländer den part des verwegenen desperados übernimmt, ein richtiger mannskerl eben, der wie'n blitz aus der hüfte schießt, und sonst auch'n feiner stecher is, und in diesem reservat lümmeln sich die goldkettchen-bimbos und die schneuzerkümmel und machen jagd auf blonde weibchen, weil die krücken brauchen und jede menge stützgeräte, um auf den beinen zu bleiben. In beiden fällen, bruder, wirst du als luschengaul ins tote rennen geschickt [...], und dann steckt man dir mürbe zuckerwürfel ins maul und krault dich herrisch an der mähne. (Ali, 23, Rapper (von 'da crime posse'); ZKS 31–32)

> [The native has, well, two spaces reserved for the *kümmel*: you're either a nice little ali, a right and proper uncle tom [...]. Such a nice little ali is the true *kanake* because he brown-noses the native right between the cheeks of his ass and looks after his own chocolate-covered skin like some sort of identity. A *kanake*'s something like a redskin who's being cheated with colourful glass beads and fire-water, and he smirks like a tourist on a snapshot. Then there's the second reserve in which the

> foreigner takes over the part of the reckless desperado, a real bloke who shoots from the hip like a thunderbolt and is also a fine stud in other ways, and in this reserve the gold chained brother and the moustachiod *kümmel* are slouching and are chasing blonde bitches because they need crutches and an awful lot of support to stay on their two feet. In both cases, bro, you're sent into the dead race as a dud horse [...], and then they shove dry sugar cubes into your mouth and give your mane a masterful ruffle.]

Kanaken, particularly the most radical, but interestingly also the most creative ones such as the rapper Ali, reject assimilated Turks, who 'dienern' [brown-nose] their way into an identity based on 'false consciousness': this identity is something that one puts on like a piece of clothing that does not fit properly. These Turks also support 'exotic' elements without subverting them (like the 'friendly Turk' or the 'womanizer'). *Kanaken* fight against 'klein-ali-träume' (ZKS 74) [little ali dreams], the dream of 'making it in Germany' (which automatically means observing the law), that is, to become part of middle-class Germany. The assimilation of the infantilized and emasculated *Lieb-Alilein* [Nice Little Ali] means submitting to the German mainstream — and ultimately becoming feminized, as male Muslims still feel. His rejection verbalizes not only the fight against those who do not accept 'other' Germans, but also the struggle within the group: Zaimoğlu's *Kanaken* heavily criticize assimilated Turks because in their view, only a *Kanake* fights and can subvert, and can raise awareness of different ways of being (Turkish-)German within the dominant German society. The *Kanaken* think an 'authentic' identity can only be arrived at through a conscious and ultimately political decision.

This kind of exclusivity gives the *Kanaken* a sense of belonging which is also expressed in their name or 'title'. Ulku, for example, says: 'Ich kann dir man auflisten, was'n kanake echt sein läßt [...]' (Ulku, 28, arbeitslos [unemployed]; ZKS 136) [I can tell you what makes a *Kanake* real]. 'Echtheit' [authenticity] seems to be based on not accepting anything exclusively German. It is a social and political category as well as a group-identity with individual peculiarities.

In *The Black Album*, authenticity is expressed in terms of religion (and thus moral purity) and set against the Western generalization of 'Pakis', a label that makes the West feel superior to 'Asian' immigrants. Chad says: 'No more Paki. Me a Muslim. We don't apologize for ourselves neither. We are people who say one important thing — that pleasure and self-absorption isn't everything!' (KBA 128). Chad reacts against Western practices of labelling and differentiates himself from

'Pakis', who include people of different religious backgrounds, on the grounds of his Muslim religion (the 'important thing'). For him, only the label 'Muslim' is acceptable as it directly draws attention to what it stands for: honour and self-restraint. Chad simultaneously refers to Islam as an idea that goes beyond nations and is all-embracing.

These reactions against labelling show that Zaimoğlu's *Kanaken* and Kureishi's Muslims are involved in masculine struggle – for oneself as well as for other, weaker people of the same religion.[67] This struggle is directed against the 'centre' that frequently shuns away from engaging with poverty and violence. Yet the *Kanaken* and British Muslims make the 'centre' aware of the problems arising out of poverty and violence, of the inequality between 'centre' and 'margin'. This kind of struggle also serves as a way to define and strengthen their sense of belonging to the community of *Kanaken* or British Muslims. Hall has suggested that

> the term 'community', in this context, also reflects certain shared self-understandings by people who are in it: a strong sense of group identity; the binding ties of common language, religious practices, history, social customs and customary types of relationship, especially those maintained in familial and domestic settings.[68]

In this sense again, fighting is strongly associated with having a common attitude towards life and a goal to fight for the 'right' way of living, with honour and respect. This is connected to a code, a certain kind of behaviour and way of speaking as a separating device – and it is related to religious ideas of 'good behaviour' and honour. One's own and one's family's honour, which is often represented by the idea of sexual purity, need to be protected, if necessary by means of violence. However, as I will discuss further down, for some *Kanaken* this is a highly problematic belief associated with their parents' generation. There are further religious connotations: the *umma* embraces all Muslims from around the world and it keeps Islam alive with a code. This reminds us of how the *Kanaken* reach out to everybody who wants to be a *Kanake*, that is, who behaves according to the *Kanak* code. The *Kanaken* clearly show their Muslim background in this context: they have reappropriated religious concepts to define

67 Cf. Gilroy, 174–75: 'Violence articulates blackness to a distinct mode of lived masculinity, but it is also a factor in what distinguishes blacks from whites.' (Gilroy is referring here to Richard Wright (in e.g. *The Outsider*) and the ideology of family).

68 S. Hall, *The Multicultural Question*, Pavis Papers in Social and Cultural Research, 4 (Milton Keynes: The Open University, 2001), 5.

a *Kanak* identity that is associated with some cultural elements of Islam. As Ali in *Kanak Sprak* explains,

> und ich nahm gleich auch den guten kodex an, der da heißt: wirf dein leben nicht weg, wenn du echt bronx sein willst, pfoten weg von dem, was dich und die gemeinde schwächt, no drugs, no crime, und stärke und respekt vor schwestern und brüdern, und schutz nur in der gemeinschaft derer, die sich clean halten aus purer überzeugung. (Ali, 23, Rapper (von 'da crime posse'); ZKS 28)
>
> [And i immediately adopted the good code which is: don't throw your life away if you want to be real bronx, hands off what weakens you and the community, no drugs, no crime, and power and respect for sisters and brothers, and protection within the community only for those who keep themselves clean out of true conviction.]

Paradoxically, the group's restlessness, their struggle, provides stability, as they are creating something of their own, namely a counter-movement to the Western mainstream: 'wir schwimmen nicht mit dem strom, wir machen nen eigenen strikten strom, wo jeder'n fluß is und aufhört 'n gottverschissenenes rinnsal zu sein' (Bayram, 18, Breaker; ZKS 42) [we're not going with the flow, we're making our own strict flow, where everybody is a torrent and stops being a goddamn shitty trickle]. It is this unifying idea of being and struggling together which determines their self-definition as 'different' young men.

Struggle also stands for fighting against Christianity — a religion that Riaz regards as passive:

> 'We're not blasted Christian,' Riaz replied with considerable aggression for him, though the effect was rather undermined by the fact that he was, as usual, carrying his briefcase. 'We don't turn the other cheek. We will fight for our people who are being tortured in Palestine, Afghanistan, Kashmir! War has been declared against us. But we are armed.' (KBA 82)

It is once again noticeable how dichotomies inform Riaz's thinking: they serve conveniently as support for his struggle, his jihad. This suggests that the West is needed as a means of identification through opposition; it is questionable whether Riaz's Muslim identity could be formed from within himself and his religion.

The idea of religious struggle needs to be examined in relation to generational issues and the different versions of Islam discussed here: South Asian Islam in the UK as opposed to a Turkish form of Islam in Germany. 'Turkish Islam', or rather Ottoman Islam, incorporated many pre-Islamic (tribal, nomadic and shamanic) traditions and customs into its heterodox belief system, something which Mustafa Kemal Atatürk stressed when building his Turkish, Westernized, Republic.[69] Atatürk's reforms in the 1920s had an enormous impact on the perception of Islam as a private religion and culture rather than as a way of life or political movement.[70] However, 'the Sunni, orthodox form of the faith' was administered by the state (Shankland, 22) which ensured that the practice of Islam was explicitly Turkish and had nothing to do with 'fundamentalism' (*kökdendincilik*) which was associated with Arab or Iranian Islam (10). Thus, in Turkey one could find what David Shankland refers to as 'parallel worlds': on the one hand, '[t]he state declares that is it irrevocably secular'; on the other hand, '[i]t uses freely the idea of being Islamic to appeal to national sentiment' (33). In the course of the twentieth century, the state's control over religion was gradually relaxed (36–37, 39–40). With the victory of Prime Minister Recep Tayyib Erdoğan's conservative-democratic AKP in the general election in June 2011, the growth of the importance of religion in Turkey is particularly noticeable and it remains to be seen what role secularism will play in the country's future.

By contrast, in South Asia, Islam is a heterogeneous religion shaped by cultural influences from other religions such as Hinduism.[71] Many South Asian Muslim migrants came from more educated backgrounds and as a sign of integration and becoming British they rejected Islam. In both cases, the migrants' children often rebel against their parents' interpretations of Islam in non-Muslim environments.

69 Y. Atasoy, *Turkey, Islamism and Democracy: Transition and Globalization in a Muslim State* (London: I. B. Tauris, 2005), 40. The role of Turkish Islam in German transcultural writing has been discussed mainly in relation to Emine Sevgi Özdamar's work: B. Haines and M. Littler, 'Emine Sevgi Özdamar, "Mutter Zunge" and "Großvater Zunge" (1990)', in *Contemporary Women's Writing in German: Changing the Subject* (Oxford: Oxford University Press, 2004), 135, and Seyhan, 'Lost in Translation', 422.

70 F. Şen, 'Der Islam in Europa', in *Der Islam: Eine Einführung durch Experten.* Christoph Burgmer spricht mit Reinhard Schulze, Baber Johansen, Yann Richard, Gudrun Krämer, Annemarie Schimmel, Faruk Şen und Gernot Rotter (Frankfurt a.M.: Suhrkamp, 1998 [1996]), 82–84.

71 C. S. Sprung, 'Aspekte der Heterogenität des Islam in Indien', in *Islam in Südasien*, Themenschwerpunkt des Südasien-Informationsnetz e.V.: *suedasion. info*, ed. N.-C. Schneider *et al.* (2006), www.suedasien.info/analysen/1611 [accessed 28 June 2010] (17 para.).

Many of Kureishi's Muslims rediscover their religious roots as a way of turning away from the older generation and of finding an alternative 'family':

> At home Papa liked to say, when asked about his faith, 'Yes, I have a belief. It's called working until my arse aches!' Shahid and Chili had been taught little about religion. [...]
>
> Now, though, Shahid was afraid his ignorance would place him in no man's land. These days everyone was insisting on their identity, [...] brandishing whichever features they could claim, as if without a tag they couldn't be human. Shahid, too, wanted to belong to his people. But first he had to know them, their past and what they hoped for. Fortunately, Hat had been of great help. [...] [C]learing a space on the floor, he had demonstrated what to do. (KBA 92)

For the older generation, work was frequently substituted for religion because it gave them the means to do well and be accepted by the dominant society, and thus to create a new home. (Kureishi also puts this issue at the centre of 'My Son the Fanatic'. Parvez, who 'love[s] England' for the freedom it gives people (KMS 126) thinks his son is taking the 'wrong turning' (KMS 120) by choosing the supposedly backward way of religion instead of going forward to progress and prosperity. He wants his son to do better than him.) Yet as this endeavour does not seem to have worked, the younger generation has felt the consequences. The turn to religion makes clear that the role of teachers is no longer fulfilled by the fathers, who have become obsolete, but by generational peers. The latter recruit other Muslims to ensure the continuity of their religious endeavours,[72] and teach the meaning of Islam which guarantees the preservation of a group defined by religion.

Exemplifying this, the central theme of Kureishi's short story 'My Son the Fanatic' is the controversy between father and son regarding the son's rediscovery of Islam as a form of purity — and ultimately personal satisfaction and happiness — in a culturally and religiously hostile world. The story is about Parvez and his dream of 'making it' in England and, consequently, his will to integrate rather than about Ali who is fighting against the 'persecution' of 'his people' (KMS 126). Ali substitutes the Muslim community for his family of birth since his father is no longer able to provide an emotional home for him. The notion of having lost a 'home' is dealt with differently by the

72 Cf. Sardar. Throughout *Desperately Seeking Paradise,* Sardar describes how various Muslim organizations tried to recruit him and how he later recruited new members himself.

younger generation from the older one: young people are looking for something 'higher'. This may be a form of rebellion against what they see as the humiliation of their fathers' cowing to Western domination, yet it is primarily regarded as something that distinguishes them from the 'rest'.

Thus religion in *The Black Album* becomes a way of finding security and expressing manliness. Ruvani Ranasinha points out that the male characters in Kureishi's novel have no 'strong sense of self' (18), but seem to want to strengthen it by the outer frame given by rituals and regular practices. Even the talks of Riaz at the mosque are deliberately delivered for an audience, partly to strengthen his self-esteem:

> Sitting barefoot and cross-legged on a low podium in grey salwar, with a bowl of flowers in front of him, Riaz didn't use notes and he never hesitated. The momentum of his conviction made him fluent, amusing, passionately coruscating. He appeared more comfortable addressing a crowd than being with one person. (KBA 80–81)

The leader needs his group in order to transmit his religious ideas, just as the group needs its leader for religious guidance: on the one hand, the leader would not be able to assert his position without the group, on the other, the group requires a leader as a role-model for its religious practice. This relationship is also demonstrated by performative acts that support both the group and, through it, the religion, such as the symbolic act of praying together which is led by Riaz (KBA 91). It is also confirmed by the role of teachers, or imams, who pass on knowledge to the community by, for example, lecturing, a task Riaz clearly enjoys.

Purity is a form of differentiation from the 'unclean' West that they are fighting. However, it also means less play with identity. Kureishi says of his characters: 'If you are a Muslim, you can't play with your identity in that way [dressing up and playing with gender boundaries]' (Kureishi qtd in Kaleta, 140). Purity is expressed through rituals, for example the ritual washing before prayer, regulations in the preparation of food or sexual abstinence. These are outer signifiers that serve as signs for inner cleanliness (in opposition to the 'decadent' West).

The notion of purity is also significant for the development of 'My Son the Fanatic'. While finding his way back to religion, Ali tries to reach a state of spiritual purity by dressing modestly, getting rid of excessive 'stuff' in his room, and structuring his days (and life) more strictly. He shows how he views Parvez as 'impure' by the way he speaks to him and his choice of vocabulary: 'Ali sounded as if he'd swallowed someone else's voice' (KMS 126). This clash between father and son, 'impure' West and 'pure' belief, is what creates the tension in Kureishi's text that deals with Islamic 'fundamentalism'.

The question remains whether the return to religion can be regarded as a form of conservative rebellion. It clearly provides a structure in a life that is otherwise determined by uncertainty and restlessness. This is a feeling that the older generation did not have in the same way: they knew exactly where their roots were. However, religion — in these young Muslims' definition — also deliberately causes unrest (such as the burning of *The Satanic Verses*) and in this case it becomes a means of active rebellion. Religion does not have to be a sign of passive nostalgia, but can be turned into active nostalgia, the struggle for a better life without negative Western influences.

Religion carries a very different meaning and occupies a very different place in the lives of Zaimoğlu's young German Turks. Where British immigrant Muslims turned to work, Turkish settlers often regarded religion as a means to find stability and warmth in an alien and cold Germany:

> Ich sehe sie [die Alten] niederknien vor einem gott, der immerfort in der wüste sprach. Ich weiß, daß sie diesen ihren gott bitternötig haben, sonst würden sie zerbröckeln wie starre salzsäulen, die man einfach umwirft. Sie haben, getäuscht und abermals getäuscht, eine fremde, aber komischerweise naheliegende version verdient. Man soll sie in ruhe lassen. Die jungen dagegen fuchteln mit zu langen gliedern, sie wissen nicht wohin mit der überschüssigen energie [...]. Dabei sind wir bloß besessen von der idee, besser zu sein als der eingeborene, der uns sehr früh einbläut, daß nur besonders tüchtige oder besonders intelligente kanaken die zielgerade erreichen. (Memet, 29, Dichter [poet]; ZKS 112–13)
>
> [I see them [the old] kneeling down before a god who spoke constantly in the wilderness. I know that they desperately need this god otherwise they'd crumble like stiff pillars of salt that are simply knocked over. They have, after deception upon deception, deserved an alien yet bizarrely natural version. They should be left alone. The young, by contrast, are brandishing limbs which are too long, they don't know where to with this excess energy [...]. But we're only obsessed by the idea of being better than the native who, from the very first moment on, drills into us that only extremely efficient or extremely intelligent *kanaken* can reach the finishing straight.]

Memet refers here to their fathers' God, not theirs, thus establishing a distance from the previous generation. Kadir even speaks of a 'fehlerhafte[] orthodoxie' [flawed orthodoxy] by which he means the nostalgia for a more stable life, which can also be expressed in terms of religion: '[S]ie warten auf das mystische zeichen, das ihnen anzeigt, ihre zelte abzubrechen und heimzukehren. Auch dann würden sie, diese alten männer, ein gottseibeiuns murmeln [...]' (Kadir, 32, Soziologe [sociologist]; ZKS 103) [They're waiting for a mystical sign which will tell them to pull up their stakes and go home. But even then they, these old men, would mumble a godbewithus]. For the *Kanaken*, return, including a return to Islam, is not an option; the question is 'where to', since they — at least by birth — belong to Germany. In this sense, their parent's religion cannot be of help, as it carries a sense of nostalgia for something better that actually never existed. The parents' Islam was brought unquestioningly from Anatolia, and it was only in Germany that it was 'unwrapped': unlike in their familiar, largely secular Turkey it was needed as a form of stability and 'protection'[73] in an alien, non-Muslim environment. As James Helicke points out, '[f]rom their earliest arrival in Germany, Turks have gathered together as Muslims' (185). When is became clear that *Gastarbeiter* would settle in Germany, and would bring their family over from Turkey, Islam was also needed as a form of social control that ensured family values such as respect, honour, obedience and acceptance of structures of authority. It cannot be denied that traditional values were also interpreted rather arbitrarily as it suited male social control (Tan and Waldhoff, 162). Furthermore, organizational networks such as the *Zentralrat der Muslime in Deutschland* (ZMD) [Central Council for Muslims in Germany] and the *Islamrat für die Bundesrepublik Deutschland* (IRD) [Islamic Council for the Federal Republic of Germany], which are responsible for schools and mosques (Karakasoglu, 168), on a larger scale, and the Turkish language press, but also a largely religious-fundamentalist Islamic video market, on a smaller scale have their roots in Islam (158). They 'make it easier for migrants to integrate into their new social environment', but can also build a barrier to German society. The *Kanaken* — primarily the more formally educated ones like Memet, the poet, or Kadir, the sociologist — no longer believe in Islam as a form of stability or social control. They are partly disillusioned,

73 D. Tan and H.-P. Waldhoff, 'Turkish Everyday Culture in Germany and its Prospects', in *Turkish Culture in German Society Today*, ed. D. Horrocks and E. Kolinsky, 141.

partly extremely realistic about their 'different' position in Germany; this difference is their reality.[74]

The difference of the *Kanaken* relates to their struggle for their acceptance in Germany, something which is thought to have been neglected by the older generation, 'aber da draußen tobt ne fehde, die alten sind ohne saft, das is jetzt ne zeit nach den alten' (Büjük Ibo, 18, Packer; ZKS 47) [but out there a feud's raging, the old are without any zest, their time's past]. Old family structures and their values such as those based on religion that are meant to keep families intact do not seem to work any more. Despite frequent disappointments when trying to be accepted in the new 'mother country', the first generation of male migrants mainly aimed at integrating into it (arguably at the price of their masculinity). Zaimoğlu's German Turkish men increasingly move away from this and gain a renewed self-awareness: to be different is regarded as something positive and a way of finding an identity based on their own ideas of how they should be, and not what the 'centre' tells them to be. Through their physical as well as personal struggle, they seem to regain a different kind of power — a power based on pride and not on submission, which is contrary to the Islamic concept of the submission to God. Islam as a religion plays therefore a subordinate role in the lives of the majority of *Kanaken*.

As young radicals *Kanaken* want to overcome their parents' passivity, which is partly based on strictly following religious rules, by asserting their own identity. Hà comments:

> Ohne ein starkes männliches Vorbild aufgewachsen, das mit allen Eigenschaften patriarchalischer Gewalt ausgestattet ist, müssen die männlichen Jugendlichen, um sich ihrer *Maskulinität* zu vergewissern, auf dem einzigen Terrain, das ihnen in ihrer gesellschaftlichen Stellung offen steht, sich als besonders 'männlich' darstellen. (48, italics Hà's)

74 A discussion of dual citizenship would go beyond the scope of this chapter. However, this issue is of greater significance for the post-*Gastarbeiter* generations as they have to face the fact that they cannot easily return to their 'home country'. Their parents often dreamed about it, but rarely made this dream come true. They never consciously asked themselves whether they would stay in Germany permanently and hence tended to be tied to their Turkish citizenship. Their children need to deal with the question of nationality and citizenship more thoroughly in the light of the ongoing debates on these issues in German migration politics, particularly since the change of legislation in late 1999, which made dual citizenship more possible. For more information, see Helicke, 175–91.

> [Having grown up without a strong male role model equipped with every characteristic of patriarchal violence, male adolescents, in order to assure themselves of their *masculinity*, have to portray themselves as particularly 'manly' in the only terrain open to them given their position in society].

In *Kanak Sprak* masculinity is performed though physical, not religious struggle, an idea the older generation do not share. In contrast to their fathers, the sons are not averse to demonstrating their manliness publicly in the form of physical strength.

It therefore does not come as a surprise that Zaimoğlu's *Kanaken*, particularly those who do not debate religion on an intellectual level, only refer to religion when it serves as one among many means of opposition to the *alemannen*: 'Ich bin'n freier, und knecht nur vor gott, dem herrn, und sonst keener blondsau was schuldig' (Hakan, 22, Kfz-Geselle [mechanic]; ZKS 86) [I'm a free person and a servant only before the lord, god, and i don't owe anything to any blond muthas]. It becomes clear that, for most of Zaimoğlu's *Kanaken*, Islam is only part of the process of self-identification where we can detect 'eine vollkommen neue Aneignung bestimmter religiöser Vorstellungen und Riten' [a complete reappropriation of certain religious attitudes and rituals].[75] Generally having reservations about 'halbmondfreaks' (Zaimoğlu, 'KümmelContra', 179) [crescent freaks], they tend to use Islam as a vehicle of expressing difference rather than belonging. If Islam plays a role in the life of those *Kanaken* at all, it has solely cultural significance.

Zaimoğlu presents his readers with one outspokenly religious interlocutor: 'Yücel, 22, Islamist' (ZKS 137–41) voices a strongly religious view on his life in a non-Muslim and therefore 'unholy' environment. His 'protocol' is the last one in *Kanak Sprak*; because it may thus stay longer in the reader's mind, Zaimoğlu may be implying that Yücel's attitude needs to be given more serious attention and may even be read as a herald for the fundamentalist attacks in the early 2000s and the increasing perception of German Turks as Muslims. Yücel considers himself to be fighting a war against the 'unbelievers', particularly in their sexual behaviour, and is proud to be seen as a 'fundamentalist'. However, he merely talks: 'Ich, der ich mich seinem [Gottes] wort ergeben' (ZKS 141) [I who am devoted to his [God's] word]. Yücel does not do anything about his religiously motivated

75 R. Mayer and M. Terkessidis, 'Retuschierte Bilder: Multikulturalismus, Populärkultur und Cultural Studies: Eine Einführung', in *Globalkolorit: Multikulturalismus und Populärkultur*, ed. R. Mayer and M. Terkessidis, 11.

discontent with German society. According to what some other *Kanaken* declare in their statements, Yücel's surrender is regarded as a failure as a radical, active *Kanake*.

If anything, Islam makes the majority of *Kanaken* Turkish (in cultural terms): the less formally educated ones follow a 'folk Islam', a form of religion with some reinterpreted values such as honour, which serves as a device of distinction from the German mainstream. This 'folk Islam' is distinct from the Islam their parents brought with them from Turkey. Karakasoglu describes this Islam as follows: 'Based on the somewhat naive popular faith of the Turkish homeland that contained strong elements of Sufism, this kind of religious observance was not grounded in an orthodox Islamic theology, especially since few of the migrant workers were themselves strictly religious' (160). Although their children often rebel against this use of religion, they often hold a moral position based on religious values and honour. This is especially true for young men such as Zaimoğlu's *Kanaken*. They incorporate certain religious concepts such as rituals and rules into their culture and everyday lives, often at the expense of women. Thus this 'folk Islam' becomes a form of control again — because it suits the *Kanaken*, not because they are religiously-minded or genuinely engage with their religious background. They stand in contrast to more formally educated Muslims, such as Kureishi's characters who meet at college and who have the intellectual means to engage critically with their religion, thus to embrace or to reject it consciously.[76] It is for that reason that Islam makes Kureishi's consciously Muslim characters Muslims in entirely religious terms.[77]

***

As we have seen, both Zaimoğlu's *Kanaken* and Kureishi's British Muslims consciously construct their identities as *Kanaken* and religious Muslims respectively, but they also perform their maleness

76 Ranasinha also stresses this aspect: 'Butler's concept contrasts with Kureishi's representations of the conscious performance of ethnicity, wherein a notion of a residual sense of the self behind the performance, however elusive, remains' (69).

77 Recent developments among German Muslims show, however, that they too are approaching Islam more intellectually, for instance by learning Arabic. Karakasoglu regards this as a chance to 'generate more points of contact between the two cultures (172). These young Muslims reinterpret Islam as a religion that embraces both religious observance and modern living (174), which may be one of the reasons why German Turks are increasingly perceived as Muslims these days.

and sexuality, albeit to varying degrees. Returning to Butler, a further implication of gender performativity is the fact that gender, more specifically in the context of this chapter, masculinity, 'is a performative accomplishment compelled by social sanction and taboo' ('Performative Acts and Gender Constitution', 402). The young Muslims in this chapter clearly depend on their social surroundings with their sanctions and taboos; it is on this basis that they can act in opposition to the society they live in. The *Kanak* identity depends on the provocation within the German mainstream which includes their sexual seduction of German women; without the Germans' reaction, the *Kanaken* could not create their identity. By contrast the British Muslims in Kureishi's novel express their masculinity in terms of religious purity, less of their sexuality; it is therefore less dependent on non-Muslims' reactions and their performativity of sexual prowess.

Despite the different attitudes toward sexuality, in both *Kanak Sprak* and *The Black Album*, sexuality brings to the fore a strong connection between race and masculinity as well as between Islam and sexuality which takes on a particular meaning in the relationship of the 'Oriental' with Western women and men. This relates to a long tradition of Orientalist discourse introduced earlier: the West associated the East with sexuality, particularly with, in Kabbani's words, 'the embodiment of it in a woman or a young boy' (67). This turned 'Orientals' into outsiders and thus into a 'weak partner for the West' (Said, *Orientalism*, 208). However, the performances of the young Muslims portrayed in this chapter's texts as young 'foreigners' match neither the expectations of the West nor — once again — those of their traditionally-minded fathers who wish to conform to 'Western law' yet who do not wish to appear threatening as men. Zaimoğlu's *Kanaken* in particular play with these expectations: 'Sie verzeihen ihren söhnen nicht, daß diese über plastikklosschüsseln gebeugt oder unter stromzählern masturbieren, sie lieben ihre söhne als zeuger von dicken enkeln' (Kadir, 32, Soziologe [sociologist]; ZKS 100–01) [They don't forgive their sons that they masturbate bending over plastic toilet bowls or underneath electricity meters, they love their sons as begetters of chubby grandkids]. The younger generation increasingly turns to Western, secular lifestyles, in relation to their sexuality too. Their fathers also perform a role: they perceive themselves as protectors of their tradition (including their religion), and expect their sons to follow them.[78] Although sexual intercourse

78 Interestingly, mothers are hardly mentioned in the texts discussed here. It seems that the dispute between the generations is an entirely male concern. The

between Muslim spouses is encouraged, the fathers perceive their sons' openly lived sexuality as 'wrong'. An element of control, therefore, determines the relationship between fathers and sons, but it also brings the fathers' repression of their own sexual desires to the fore (cf. Foucault, 8–13). Furthermore, as Karakasoglu notes, it also shows that 'fathers lose some of their dominance and young people use their superior command of the German language and their familiarity with German society to act as intermediaries between Turkish and German social norms, thus assuming nontraditional leadership functions inside and outside the family' (162). Sexuality is one way of challenging traditional social norms of both the country of their fathers and Germany, and rejecting patriarchal control.

Some *Kanaken* reclaim the desires their fathers supposedly deny themselves. Sex simultaneously becomes part of masculine identification: they define their status according to the (white) women they have access to, and in contradistinction to German men who are, they assert, sexually less successful. These *Kanaken* are coopting, indeed taking advantage of, the stereotype of the sexually hyperactive southerner. In the context of race and sex, hooks has noted that '[s]ex becomes the ultimate playing field, where the quest for freedom can be pursued in a world that denies black males access to other forms of liberating power' (74); it is one way to 'gain visibility' (80). In this process, some of them play with notions of exoticism; these young Muslims use their 'exotic' features to seduce women and to be more successful than Western men. This is a subtle subversion process: they know exactly why they are supporting the racist stereotype of the 'exotic lover'.

> Erst mal isses in der branche gold wert, wenn du als besorger mit'm spezi-bonus kommst [...]. Du bist nur ne fleischpartie, 'n äffchen [...]. Die lady hat dich für ne ganze nacht gekauft, deinen schwanz hat sie gekauft, und der ist mir mein bonus, weil ja'n hautstück fehlt, und ich laß man damit die hölle jodeln. [...] und als sie sich halt über mir die pralle eichel beugt, sagt sie: du mein schöner jude, und als ich ihr sag, ich bin nur'n schlichter kümmel, wird die lady potzblitz ärgerlich und sagt, ich soll die man nicht zerstören, lieber's maul halten und

exclusion of women or, as described previously, their reduction to certain roles, is a sign of their oppression; they are not taken seriously and their obedience is simply taken for granted. (Chapter 4, however, puts women's self-perception in texts written by both men and women at the centre.) It is only in later texts primarily by Zaimoğlu (and this is a particularly recent phenomenon to be discussed briefly in the conclusion to this book) that women are depicted and celebrated as the heroines of the *Gastarbeiter*-generation.

> sie man machen lassen [...], wo die lady man annehmen tut, sie würd jetzt'n verbotenes spiel treiben mit nem judengringo [...]. Sonne schicke lady hat eben ne latte von klugbüchern gelesen [...]. (Ercan, 24, Gigolo; ZKS 69–71)
>
> [First of all it's great in this industry if as a stud you have a special bonus [...]. You're only a piece of meat, a monkey [...]. The lady has bought you for a whole night, she's bought your prick, and this is my bonus because a bit of skin is missing, and i let hell yodel with it. [...] and when she's bent over the big strong bell-end, she says: you my beautiful jew, and when i tell her, i'm just a simple *kümmel*, the lady, blimey, becomes angry and says, i shouldn't destroy it, rather shut up and leave her to it [...], where the lady assumes she's playing a forbidden game with a jew-gringo [...]. Well, such a posh lady's read a stack of clever books.]

Young German Turks like Ercan, whose profession is marketing their sexual abilities, talk openly about their sexual adventures. That triggers the question whether, in talking about sex, they are trying to explain or defend their promiscuous behaviour (cf. Foucault, 53). They are certainly playing with taboos that are partly based on religious ideas (cf. 84), and thus they are initiating a subversion process in relation to both their parents and the mainstream: it is a rebellion against the constraints of their parents' life (including those that are the result of Islam) as well as a way of reclaiming power. In analogy to Butler's 'girling' of girls (*Bodies That Matter*, 7), they 'man' themselves as men in exclusively sexual terms by ritualized repetitions of clichés. By emphasizing their sexual virility, Zaimoğlu's *Kanaken* — again — initiate an 'operation of exclusion' (11): men are judged according to their sexual abilities. As a performance that is meant to oppose the behaviour of German men, the overemphasis on sexuality changes the power relations between 'foreigners' and Germans: power is measured by the sexual power these men have over women and, as a result of that, over Western men. The latter's alleged sexual weakness leads to their feminization: Orientalist discourse is reappropriated as a means of claiming back the masculinity of the *Kanaken* — at the expense of women who serve as a projection for the competition between the *Kanaken* and the *alemannen*: ''n alemanne mimt gern 'n verwegenen flegel im busch, unartig will er sein', but '[d]er alemanne, bruder, frißt krise, scheißt krise' (Fikret, 25, arbeitslos [unemployed]; ZKS 80 and 83) [a german likes miming the reckless lad in the bush, he wants to be naughty, [but] the german, bro, eats crisis, shits crisis]. There is a feminization of the *alemanne* who tries hard to be sexually exciting and interesting, yet, by contrast to the sensual Muslim *Kanaken*, without success; it is the aim of the *Kanaken* not to become part of this crisis and to maintain their masculinity by transforming Western men's alleged sexual weakness into their strength.

According to Moore-Gilbert, in *The Black Album*, '[t]he sexuality of the "Oriental" male [...] also plays ironically (if sometimes uncomfortably) with the figure of the colonized male subject as over-sexed, even a potential rapist of white women, which is an enduring trope in metropolitan literature of empire' by 'stressing the active side of white women for exotic sexual "Others"' (123–24). Deedee Osgood subverts the stereotypical role of the woman who is passive and 'taken' by putting herself in an active, masculine and 'taking' position:

> Sadiq said: '[... Deedee] Osgood is taking lovers among the Afro-Caribbean and Asian students. Definitely. [...] For political reasons she selects only black or Asian lovers now.'
>
> Tahira adjusted her scarf. 'Our people have always been sexual objects for the whites. No wonder they hate our modesty.' (KBA 228)

Here, the relationship between race and sexuality is analyzed from a different perspective. The 'modest' Muslims use the West's alleged attitude to sexual pleasure as something that is not meant to last; this is part of their politics against the 'decadent' West. They then apply it as a vehicle to explain the fundamental differences between 'good Islam' and the 'bad West'. These Muslims are shown almost to enjoy seeing themselves as victims of Orientalist perceptions. (Shahid, who is the object of Deedee's sexual desire, is an exception in this case. He is happily feminized by Deedee who undresses him, and then dresses him in women's clothes and makes him up as a form of role and gender play, but also as sexual pleasure [Stein, 126].)

Zaimoğlu's *Kanaken* also recognize the Orientalist discourse of sexuality as condescending, but use different means to transform it into their own tool of power. They try to break the 'Kreislauf der Viktimisierung' (Hà, 48) [vicious circle of victimization] by trying to be 'schneller und härter als der Mainstream' [faster and harder than the mainstream]. Ha reads this attitude 'als nachträglicher Widerstand stellvertretend für die überangepaßte Elterngeneration, als verspätete Rache gegenüber dieser Gesellschaft' (49) [as subsequent resistance on behalf of their over-assimilated parents' generation, as belated revenge on this society]. The 'victim' becomes the 'doer', and ultimately an active performer.

Zaimoğlu's and Kureishi's Muslims demonstrate 'the racialised subject's violent subjugation as body and voice' (Cheesman, 'Akçam – Zaimoğlu – "Kanak Attak"', 189), but they reclaim their bodies and voices. Performing a particular role (as 'Islamic fundamentalist' or 'sexualized exotic') seems to enable them to set their mark on the mainstream. Both the *Kanaken* and Kureishi's characters are aware of their roles as 'foreigners' or 'exotic others', and turn acting these roles into a tool of power. However, these acts of performance seem to be exhausting, and some of the *Kanaken* develop a desire for peace: '[I]ch frag mich, wann ich das olle zähnefletschen endlich lassen kann, weil ich doch nicht aus'm tierreich bin, und meine ruhe haben will im menschenreich' (Faruk, 26, arbeitslos [unemployed]; ZKS 77) [I ask myself when i can finally stop this damn snarling, because i'm not from the animal world, and i want peace in the human world]. Faruk wants a place among the mainstream: he wants to move up from being perceived as an animal to being respected as a human being. (He applies old colonialist vocabulary by referring to his animal-likeness, thus pointing out the obvious: that nobody can completely escape from the influence of the mainstream. Yet it is exactly the mainstream that initiates Faruk's performance as *Kanake*.) The characters in Kureishi's and Zaimoğlu's texts hope to achieve peace by finding and defining who they are — as virtuous Muslims in *The Black Album*, and as deliberately sexualized and secularized men in *Kanak Sprak*.

***

Regaining and then proudly emphasizing masculinity — whether by means of religion or sexuality — appears as a way of answering the 'question of knowing who we are' (Foucault, 78). As Büyük Ibo in *Kanak Sprak* points out, '[e]rste sorge: identität, ne person sein' (Büyük Ibo, 18, Packer; ZKS 44) [first concern: identity, being someone]. He emphasizes both the collective experience of *Kanaken* and their individuality. The majority of Zaimoğlu's and Kureishi's Muslims recognize the fluidity and ever-changing nature of identity: 'There was no fixed self; surely our several selves melted and mutated daily?' (KBA 274). They negotiate ways of escaping from a fixed identity as 'Oriental': they do not accept being '*first* an Oriental, *second* a human being, and *last* again an Oriental' (Said, *Orientalism*, 102, italics Said's). Both the *Kanaken* and Kureishi's main protagonist Shahid, who adopts the idea of fluid gender identities from Deedee, uncover constructions and fictions of identity.[79] Ranasinha argues that the discovery of 'identity as performance' is the result of 'experiment[s] with a range of identities, because they are not allowed to be English' (70) — or indeed German.[80]

Yet Zaimoğlu makes clear that 'ich will keine parallelwelt zum mainstream' ('KümmelContra', 176) [I don't want a parallel world to the mainstream]. The subversion processes of his *Kanaken* might contribute to a new understanding of Turkish-Germanness as a transcultural identity. The *Kanaken* use the gaps in previously imposed identities as 'foreigners' or children of *Gastarbeiter* as a form of resistance and change: they are fighting against the 'Märchen von der Multikulturalität' (ZKS 11) [the myth of multiculturalism] and their 'Opferrolle' (ZKS 12) [role as victims]. The result is an alternative to 'pure' ethnicities: Zaimoğlu hopes '[d]aß diese Kanaksterbewegung eine richtige Alternative wird zu all diesen Entgleisungen wie der Reethnisierung' ('Eure Coolness ist Gigaout', 30) [that this *Kanakster* movement will become a real alternative to all those aberrations such as re-ethnicizing]. With his 'protocols' of interviews, Zaimoğlu wishes to offer alternatives to 'diese scheiße mit den zwei kulturen' (ZKS 95–96) [this shit about the two cultures], thus counter-acting the liberal-benign attitude of some of his German readers that determines the public debate on multiculturalism in Germany.[81] Identity is fluid and can be fixed neither in the *in-between* nor in the *either/or* (this aspect is of great significance in *The Black Album*) (see Stein, 12). Like Kureishi's Muslims, Zaimoğlu's semi-fictionalized *Kanaken* are looking for stability away from notions of cultural in-betweenness.

79 *The Black Album* takes its title from a title of one of Prince's albums, thus immediately drawing attention to the instability of (gender) identities (Moore-Gilbert, 128).

80 See also Ranasinha's comment: 'Many black Britons prefer to describe themselves as "British" citizens rather than as "English": the latter is more overtly imbricated in exclusive monocultural terms to signify whiteness. In contrast, Kureishi and his characters identify themselves primarily with Englishness. [...] Both terms are used problematically to exclude' (4).

81 Paying attention to the 'problematic symbiosis between the author [Zaimoğlu] and the public/media persona' (120), Mani offers a more critical view on Zaimoğlu's statements that should be read as 'annotations to his works' (131): 'Zaimoğlu reutilizes the very terms that dominate the mainstream discourse of multiculturalism, even as he claims distinction and distances from those terms' (135). However, Mani concedes that '[a]gainst these recently reinforced categories that continue to dominate the public image of the Turks forty years after the first wave of Turkish immigration to Germany, Zaimoğlu's assertion of difference in their assimilatory equation and the reasons for his journalistic fascination are not difficult to understand' (130).

Yet as this security is not provided by the country they are 'at home' in, they need to define their own spaces of transcultural belonging.

The young Muslims in *Kanak Sprak* pursue a cultural definition of their religion; they tend to turn away from the older generation's strong sense of religion that revived in the new environment as a means of stability. On the surface, Islam is not visible as an influence on their self-perception; they come across as secular Turks. However, the *Kanaken* have inherited certain values from Islam whose religious origin they might no longer recognize; these values contribute to the construction of their 'folk Islam', their cultural interpretation of Islam, or are debated in an intellectual context. As pointed out earlier, at the beginning of the twentieth century, there has been an increasing awareness and intellectual interest in Islam among young, well-educated German Muslims, which may be regarded as a reaction against the Islamophobia encountered in certain Western societies after 9/11. Using Islamic knowledge in discussions about Islam in the West may serve as an alternative, postsecular form of struggle and challenge the widely-spread image of young, radical Muslims.

The *Kanaken*'s is primarily a sexualized masculinity, constructed largely at the expense of women. Women are used to support male fantasies of power, and of sexual and physical strength, which men seem to regard as the prerequisite for self-determination. The *Kanaken* often reappropriate racist and religiously motivated patriarchal stereotypes of their power over women in order both to have a voice in mainstream discourse and to initiate subversions.

In *The Black Album* reconstructions of masculinity are mainly created via religion: Kureishi's protagonists return to their 'Arab roots', which he can examine critically from a distance he achieves by his choice of fictional genre. He invites his readers to engage with what he sees as his characters' 'fundamentally backwards' movement towards what their parents gave up (or voluntarily or forcefully suppressed) when they came to the UK in order to integrate more successfully. For Kureishi's Muslims, Islam becomes a form of struggle against the West as a corrupt and over-sexualized, 'Occidentalized' entity.[82] Kureishi's characters construct masculinity as priesthood, abstinence and sexual self-restraint, which the protagonists think leads to mental strength and ultimately to power.

Through their choices of genre Kureishi and Zaimoğlu show how differently they perceive 'Mißtöne' (*Kanak Sprak* subtitle) [dissonances] – attitudes and opinions the mainstream does not want to hear,

82 H. Kureishi, 'The Word and the Bomb', in Kureishi, *The Word and the Bomb*, 10.

produced by young Muslim men. Although differently textualized, the 'disobedience' of both the UK's and Germany's young Muslims becomes part of the performative side of Muslim masculinity. It redefines power (cf. Foucault, 86) and demystifies ethnicity (see Hà, 166) — away from repression and towards creativity. In this sense, marginality becomes 'a self-empowering strategy within minority discourse' (Huggan, *The Postcolonial Exotic*, 103), just as the title of Kanak Attak's manifesto suggests: 'Kanak Attak und Basta!' [Kanak Attak and that's that!].

4. Islam, Writing and Femininity Female Perspectives from the 'Margins of Society': Emine Sevgi Özdamar's *MutterZunge*, Feridun Zaimoğlu's *Koppstoff*, and Leila Aboulela's *The Translator* and *Minaret*

The mass media image of Muslim women tends to be made to fit the Orientalized picture of the submissive, veil-wearing and oppressed woman which puts them even more distinctly at the margins of Western society than Muslim men. A number of recently published literary texts by Muslims try to shed a different and multifaceted light on Muslim women: Emine Sevgi Özdamar, Feridun Zaimoğlu and Leila Aboulela show how female and Islamic identity can interact.

In Islam as in some sections of Christianity and Judaism, women are widely seen as 'physical markers of social norms'; their 'physical absence [...] from public space occupied by men' denies their active participation in society.[1] As 'women and the family [are perceived] as the foundation of the Islamic community, the heart of Muslim society' which is 'reflected in Islamic law',[2] they, in particular, are rule-bound and connected with 'notions of the sacred'.[3] Even though men and women are equal before God and have the same rights and duties in Islam, it is often the men's interpretation of the Qur'an and ultimately their exercise of power, rather than Islam itself, which segregates women from both the public and religious domains and binds them to the traditional roles of housewives and mothers.

1 M. Cooke, *Women Claim Islam: Creating Islamic Feminism Through Literature* (New York: Routledge, 2001), 118.

2 J. L. Esposito, 'Introduction: Women in Islam and Western Society', in *Islam, Gender, and Social Change*, ed. Y. Yazbeck Haddad and J. L. Esposito (New York: Oxford University Press, 1998), xii.

3 M. Ruthven, 'Women and Family', in *Islam: A Very Short Introduction* (Oxford: Oxford University Press, 2000 [1997]), 92.

It is because of this exclusion from the public and religious spheres that women tend to be doubly weakened and marginalized. John McLeod refers to this situation as the 'double colonisation' of women:[4] colonized women, who were *made* Oriental by the Western colonizers, tend to have the weakest voice — if they have one at all in their own culture, let alone in the colonizers' culture. Particularly hijab (headscarf)-wearing Muslim women become 'icons of Muslim otherness' (Cooke, 131). The veil represents '*essential* "Orientalness"' for Westerners who reduce Islam to its hijab-wearing women.[5]

A number of Muslim women living in both Muslim countries and the West have started to challenge these fixed perceptions. These social developments have influenced literary representations of women. Like the literary representations of Muslim men in the last chapter, the women in the texts selected for this chapter create their own spaces for negotiating their identities beyond societal and religious restrictions and conventions.

***

Aboulela's fiction examines Muslim women living in the West (Aboulela has lived in various countries; for example, she has spent many years in London and Aberdeen.[6]) I read Aboulela's texts in the light of Islamic feminism, a form of feminism which includes addressing the encounter between East and West in relation to the role of Muslim women in patriarchal societies.[7]

4 J. McLeod, *Beginning Postcolonialism* (Manchester: Manchester University Press, 2000), 175.

5 M. Yeğenoğlu, *Colonial Fantasies: Towards a Feminist Reading of Orientalism* (Cambridge: Cambridge University Press, 1998), 47, 48, italics Yeğenoğlu's. For a discussion of the veil as something quintessentially 'Oriental', see Chapter 2, 39–67.

6 It is difficult to classify Aboulela as a writer in terms of nationality. For example, she won the Caine Prize for African writing in 2000, yet is also often seen as an Arabic or Scottish writer. See, for example, the collection of multicultural writing from Scotland *Wish I Was Here: A Scottish Multicultural Anthology*, ed. K. MacNeil and A. Finley, Pocketbooks, 5 (Edinburgh: Pocketbooks, 2000), or the numerous reviews as they are reprinted on the front pages or covers of her books.

7 In the following, I refer to this kind of feminism as 'Islamic feminism' to emphasize its religio-political aspect, which is significant for Aboulela's work. As in other forms of feminism there are a range of feminisms coming from Muslim countries, focusing on specific aspects, for example, politics (Islamist), culture (Arab), religion (Muslim) or Lebanese secular feminism. I thank Dr Christine Lindner (University of Balamand) for clarifying some aspects relating to feminism and Islam. In secondary literature, the differences between Arab and Islamic feminism are often blurred (see titles in following footnotes).

Although the tensions between Islam and the West are already inherent in the very definition of what feminism means, and is supposed to stand and struggle for, there are women who call themselves Islamic *and* feminist.[8] Feminism is often regarded as something that developed in the West and that campaigns for such issues as the equality between men and women or the liberation of women from patriarchal notions of womanhood. It is frequently assumed that these concepts are not negotiable within an Islamic framework, and the question arises whether an Islamic version of feminism is possible at all.[9] Furthermore, the supposed oppression of 'the poor Muslim woman' can result in tensions with Western feminists who, assuming that she has no voice, may try to speak for her.[10] For Islamic feminists, the term 'feminism' describes the struggle of Muslim women fighting for social equality, which is not dissimilar from Catholic or orthodox Jewish feminists. In contrast to Western forms of feminism, Islamic feminism is firmly grounded in religion. Islamic feminists thus reappropriate the term 'feminism' and create their own 'tradition' in a post-colonial framework. Islamic feminist critics such as Egyptian-American sociologist and historian Leila Ahmed or Moroccan feminist sociologist Fatima Mernissi analyze a 'feminised space which may be said to operate between the continuing pressure of Western cultural imperialism, and conservative, anti-modernist cultural Islamism';[11] yet they also question what 'so-called Islamic practices, such as veiling, segregation and seclusion'

8 For an analysis of the tension between the terms 'Islamic' and 'feminist', see H. Moghissi, *Feminism and Islamic Fundamentalism: The Limits of Postmodern Analysis* (London: Zed, 1999), 65–66.

9 M. Badran and M. Cooke, 'Introduction', in *Opening the Gates: A Century of Arab Feminist Writing*, ed. M. Badran and M. Cooke (London: Virago, 1990), xx. See also there for a history of Arab feminism.

10 See some Western feminists' comments on, for example, 'headscarf debates', debates and court hearings on whether Muslim women should be allowed to wear headscarves in official posts in Germany or burqas in France; for instance, Alice Schwarzer's articles such as 'Ludin — die Machtprobe: Die Kopftuch-Entscheidung des Verfassungsgerichtes ist für uns alle von großer Bedeutung', Editorial, *Emma*, 31.4 (July/August 2003), 3. See also Emine Sevgi Özdamar's story 'Die neuen Friedhöfe in Deutschland' [The New Graveyards in Germany] in the collection *Der Hof im Spiegel*, 122, where she critically addresses the Western notion of wanting to help 'the poor Muslim woman'.

11 G. Nash, 'Re-siting Religion and Creating Feminised Space in the Fiction of Ahdaf Soueif and Leila Aboulela', *Wasafiri*, 35 (Spring 2002), 28. For further details on the development of Islamic feminism, see D. Kandiyoti, 'Contemporary Feminist Scholarship and Middle East Studies', in *Gendering the Middle East: Emerging Perspectives*, ed. D. Kandiyoti (London: I. B. Tauris, 1996), 1–27.

(Badran and Cooke, xxvii), actually mean. They combine the fight for equal access to rights and education, which provides the basis for the conscious engagement with Islam, with *ijtihād* (independent reasoning) and a reinterpretation of Islam, its practices and the Qur'an as a potential defining factor of the identities of women living in Muslim countries. Islamic feminism thus entails the reclaiming of Islam for women based on its egalitarian ethics.[12] Leila Ahmed claims that there are different 'Islams' for women and for men.[13] She asserts that for Muslim women to act freely, Islam needs to be liberated from its culturally influenced patriarchal attitudes and practices. Islamic feminists aim to overcome fixed interpretations and ideas of Islam, including how women should behave under the 'rule' of Islam – the patriarchal application of jurisprudence. Thinking about Islam in this way is based on a conscious acceptance of Islam, and suggests a genuine belief in its values as it is not forced upon these believing women. The path is where choice leads. Miriam Cooke points out that '[t]he term "Islamic feminist" invites us to consider what it means to have a difficult double commitment: on the one hand, to a faith position, and on the other hand, to women's rights both inside the home and outside. [... It celebrates] multiple belongings' (59).

The notion of 'multiple belongings' and the difficulties associated with them are also addressed in Aboulela's novels *The Translator* (1999) and *Minaret* (2005).[14] Both her protagonists originally come from Sudan. Islam is the dominant religion in northern Sudan. In the south in particular, there are a variety of ethnic groups and languages. The northern Arab Muslims have dominated the politics and economics of the country since the country's independence in 1956. In 1991, the regime of the National Islamic Front announced that they were imposing the shari`a (Islamic legislation) everywhere except the south.[15] This has brought about religious divergence and civil war, with the southern, non-Arab Muslims perceiving themselves

12 N. Tohidi, 'The Issues at Hand', in *Women in Muslim Societies: Diversity Within Unity*, ed. H. Bodman and N. Tohidi (Boulder, CO: Rienner, 1998), 283–85.
13 Leila Ahmed in Cooke, xiii. Ahmed has published various books on women and Islam, for example, *Women and Gender in Islam: Historical Roots of a Modern Debate* (New Haven, CT: Yale University Press, 1992); see particularly the section 'The Discourse of the Veil', 144–68.
14 L. Aboulela, *The Translator*, new edn (Edinburgh: Polygon, 2005 [1999]); *Minaret* (London: Bloomsbury, 2005).
15 There is a distinction between *shari`a*, 'God's external and immutable will for humanity, as expressed in the Quran and Muhammad's example (Sunnah), considered binding for all believers; ideal Islamic law', and *fiqh*, 'the remainder of Islamic law [as] the result of jurisprudence', yet, in this context, *shari`a* 'is applied

as second-class citizens.[16] On 9 January 2005, the Government of Sudan and the Sudan People's Liberation Movement signed the Comprehensive Peace Agreement. Following a referendum in early 2011, Southern Sudan became an independent state in July 2011.

These issues do not feature in Aboulela's novels. Furthermore, in her Sudan, Arabic is the official language. Indigenous languages, such as Nubian, the second widely spoken language in Sudan (see Holt and Daly, 1–10), are not dealt with in her writing. Aboulela follows an 'Islamic agenda' which excludes the ethnic conflicts and the religio-political development of her country of origin: she wants to portray 'ordinary Muslims trying to practise their faith in difficult circumstances and in a society which is unsympathetic to religion'.[17] The tensions created by the interaction of her fictional Muslim characters with their non-Muslim environment and their examination from a Muslim (rather than Western) point of view are of interest to Aboulela.

Aboulela chose a female translator as the protagonist of her first novel *The Translator*. Sammar, who lives and works as an Arabic translator in Aberdeen, comes to terms with the apparent contradiction between her Sudanese past and her Scottish present, between her religious personal life and the secular life surrounding her in the UK. Although Aboulela does not primarily address language issues, the missionary role of her Muslim main character is based on the Arabic language (the language of her faith, origin, past and emotional security) whose meaning, along with its religious connotations, she conveys to Rae, her boss, a non-Muslim, thus providing a linguistic basis for their relationship.

In her second novel *Minaret*, Aboulela also puts a Muslim woman, Najwa, at the centre of her narration. Having lived a Western-style life in Sudan, which she had to leave after a military coup, Najwa moves to London where she finds herself emotionally lost after the deaths of her parents and the imprisonment of her brother. After years of financial and emotional struggle, she finds her way back to religion as a means of emotional support. In this novel, Aboulela asks specifically how it is possible to lead a Muslim life in the West. Thus

to Islamic legislation' (J. L. Esposito, entry on 'Shariah', in *The Oxford Dictionary of Islam* (New York: Oxford University Press, 2004 [2003]), 287–88).

16 P. M. Holt and M. W. Daly, *A History of the Sudan: From the Coming of Islam to the Present Day*, 5th edn (Harlow: Longman, 2000 [1961]), 3, 187–94.

17 Aboulela in S. Eissa, 'Interview with Leila Aboulela', *iWitness*, July 2005, www.iwitness.co.uk/features/0705fe03.htm [accessed on 4 July 2006] (para. 4 of 24), URL no longer available.

her text focuses on the experiences of alienation and exclusion, as they are often part of the lives of immigrants. Aboulela shows how, after many years of feeling emotional emptiness in the UK, a culturally Muslim woman may undergo a drastic change from 'freedom'-loving young girl (AMi 165) to observant Muslim woman, which becomes a freedom of a different kind. We can trace this development by looking at how protagonist Najwa perceives other visibly Muslim, veiled women in the novel. In accordance with the Orientalist notion of the 'mysterious Orient', the West often associates the veil with secrecy, which comes particularly to the fore in a non-Muslim environment:

> We passed a couple of Arab women dressed in black from head to foot; their faces were veiled. Anwar made a face and, when they were out of earshot, he said, 'It's disgusting, what a depressing sight!'
>
> His expression made me laugh. 'Aren't you curious about all the beauty they're hiding?' (AMi 167)

This combination of curiosity and the veiled woman is Orientalist thinking that Aboulela is critically examining as part of a Western lifestyle which her protagonist used to have in Sudan. Originally from a wealthy background, her protagonist now finds herself on a lower social level in the UK. Her migration and subsequently lonely life in London gradually make her redefine her religion: in Sudan, Najwa strongly connected religion with the life of the working class; in the UK it has a more intellectual association as she increasingly perceives 'Western freedom' as 'empty space' (AMi 175). By making Najwa regard learning as an essential component of her life, strongly linked to intellectual exchange with other Muslims living in the UK, Aboulela emphasizes the fact that Islam is also a religion of education, something which Najwa apparently did not see in Sudan. This is reminiscent of the Islamic feminists' call for equal access to education, as it is education that gives women the ability and power to make informed decisions regarding the role Islam should play in their lives. Islam is partly isolated reflection and contemplation, but the community of the believers and learning from as well as with other Muslims are highly significant. Through Najwa and her other characters' well-informed religious confidence, Aboulela reveals her conception of Islam: it rejects the Western idea of 'backward fundamentalism' (AMi 179) and embraces the notions of guidance and intellectual exchange.

It is noteworthy that Aboulela displays her protagonist's transformation into a devout Muslim and her personal redefinition of Islam through signifiers that define a visibly devout Muslim woman. In *Minaret*, she turns dress (the wearing of the hijab) and modest, restrained behaviour into tokens of Muslim femininity and thus seemingly offers a stereotypical portrait of Islam to her readers.

The hijab or veil is a powerful symbol, particularly in relation to colonialism, and resistance and independence movements.[18] The question of what this item of clothing might reveal or hide is important in this context. As Meyda Yeğenoğlu points out,

> the veil was seen as the concrete manifestation of the colonized's resistance to an imposed reciprocity: veiled women are able to see without being seen. Orientalist desire was hence articulated as the desire to unveil the colony, for women's insistence on wearing the veil really meant the colony's resistance to being colonized. (142–43)[19]

The veil was perceived as a threat, and it became 'a Western product in the sense of the creation of a "colonial traditionalism"'.[20]

The hijab becomes part of the performance of a female Muslim's identity in *Minaret*. This identity requires the observation of rituals and guidelines (for example, praying and interacting with other Muslims) to create an 'authentic' religious self. Aboulela designs a character who, through the hijab, appears as a 'true' Muslim. Occasionally, the hijab also serves as a device of separation from Western 'indecency': it helps Najwa preserve her Islamic identity and female dignity, and encourages the 'revitalization and restoration of the native [Muslim] culture'; it is a 'return to [an] original Islam' (Yeğenoğlu, 139). Even though Najwa lives in another culture, this does not have an effect on her perception of Islam: although Islam in *Minaret* adapts to a new environment, it is not open to 'foreign' influences. This is the reason why Muslims who are willing to include 'foreign' elements in

18 For example, many women in Algeria started to wear the hijab as a reaction against colonialism. Here, Islamic identity appears as their only resort in opposition to the French (Yeğenoğlu, 136–44).

19 For an analysis of the relationship between women and nationalism, see also V. M. Moghadam, ed., *Gender and National Identity: Women and Politics in Muslim Societies* (London: Publ. for the United Nations University World Institute for Development Economics Research by Zed, 1994), particularly V. M. Moghadam, Chapter 1, 'Introduction and Overview: Gender Dynamics of Nationalism, Revolution and Islamization', 1–17.

20 Yeğenoğlu is referring to Pierre Bourdieu and his anthropological work on Kabylia (Algeria), for instance, *Outline of a Theory of Practice*, trans. R. Nice, Cambridge Studies in Social and Cultural Anthropology, 16 (Cambridge: Cambridge University Press, 1998 [1977]; originally publ. as *Esquisse d'une théorie de la practique, précédé de trois études d'ethnologie kabyle* (Geneva: Librairie Droz, 1972).

their interpretation of Islam puzzle Najwa, and her path to religion turns into a struggle to define a believer's identity in a non-Muslim environment. This comes to the fore when, for instance, Najwa compares herself with younger British Muslims:

> Usually the young Muslim girls who have been born and brought up in Britain puzzle me though I admire them. They strike me as being very British, very much at home in London. Some of them wear hijab, some don't. They have individuality and an outspokenness I didn't have when I was their age, but they lack the preciousness and glamour we girls in Khartoum had. (AMi 77)

Najwa appears to be one generation 'behind': moving from one (a Western-style) to another (a religious) lifestyle, she is not able to reinterpret her religion under Western circumstances. She cannot transform or reappropriate her role as a Muslim woman. Retracing her religious roots includes a literal, traditional understanding of Islam. Here, Islam leads to a feeling of security, and Aboulela makes Najwa experience Islam as something powerful. For example, she puts these words into her protagonist's mouth during Ramadan: 'The rest of the year I have hope but in Ramadan I have confidence, the certainty that, if I keep plodding this path, Allah will give me back that happiness again, will replace the past with something grander, more potent and enhanced' (AMi 189). Thus Aboulela attempts to show how Islam offers definiteness in an ambiguous West that often provides too many options.

In previously discussed texts such as *Brick Lane*, Islam also serves as a tool for stability in an initially unknown West. However, Monica Ali shows us how, gradually, other cultures influence her female protagonists' lives and how this is necessary as a formula for successful migration and life in the UK. Aboulela lets her protagonist take the opposite route (from cultural diversity to religious strictness). Although this religious exclusivity partly isolates her character from her Western environment, Aboulela reveals the power of religion as protection against personal desolation. The opposing approaches to the roles of Islam of Ali's and Aboulela's fiction show that Muslim migrants have diverse views on religion, something which is often overlooked in the Western mass media.

Aboulela's novel raises the question whether her protagonist is going 'backwards' (as an Orientalist reading of her actions would suggest) by abandoning her former Western, supposedly more liberated life. However, Aboulela introduces her concept of choice here: Najwa chooses to be a servant of God. And this is where Aboulela's Islamic feminism comes in again: contrary to first impressions, the writer is describing a progressive form of Islam based on choice and conscious commitment.

In *The Translator*, Aboulela focuses on religion in terms of language interaction; this is her tool for describing her protagonist's migration from Sudan to Scotland. Sammar is shown to perceive migration as a restrictive process: she cannot see the positive potential in her life as a migrant. Sammar explains the meaning of her name: 'It means conversations with friends, late at night. It's what the desert nomads liked to do, talk leisurely by the light of the moon, when it was no longer so hot and the day's work was over' (ATr 5). Sammar's name contrasts her ancestors' nomadic past with her own migrant present. Nomadism implies constant movement, whereas migration is a movement in one direction, to one new destination. The fact that Sammar works as a translator represents her cultural and linguistic migration, the interaction between two places (Sudan and Scotland) and two languages (Arabic and English).[21] She knows where she belongs in this dichotomy: to an Arabic-speaking environment, which for her is a Muslim one. The language of her immediate environment, English, is simply a tool to secure her a living and not a means to connect to her non-Muslim surroundings beyond necessity. She does not mingle with Scottish people, and she is visibly Muslim — she wears the hijab.

'Home' can only be one place: her religion. Sammar connects her mother tongue Arabic closely with her religion and thus an emotional home: 'Yesterday when I spoke in Arabic to Fareed, I felt that home was close' (ATr 106). Her faith is her only fixed point in life. Aboulela is once again showing how Muslim people can turn their religion into a home: through living in a non-Muslim environment and speaking a language that she does not regard her own, Sammar learns more about Islam: 'Here in Scotland she was learning more about her own religion, the world was one cohesive place' (ATr 108). It is her work as a translator of mainly religious texts, the encounter between Arabic — 'the real thing' (ATr 29) — and English, that makes Sammar understand Islam more deeply than she did in Sudan.[22] As

21 Nadia Butt also discusses the relationship between travel and translation, and the impossibility of cultural translation in *The Translator* in 'Negotiating Untranslatability and Islam in Leila Aboulela's *The Translator*', in *Transcultural Modernities: Narrating Africa in Europe*, ed. E. Bekers *et al.* (Amsterdam: Rodopi, 2009), 168–70.

22 Brenda Cooper also points out how Scotland enables Sammar — as a woman — to interpret/translate Islam; for her, 'Islam has to be able to migrate

an educated young woman, Sammar masters the English language very well. Although she was born in the UK, Sammar grew up in a formerly colonized country where she was confronted with English on a daily basis. This privileged background enabled her to move back to the UK and, after her husband's death, to get closer to her religion there than in Sudan.

In *The Translator*, Aboulela again draws upon the link between a Muslim woman's education and her identity: Sammar is educated and consciously wears the hijab; she is a thoughtful Muslim woman with a progressive understanding of Islam, which relates to Aboulela's Islamic feminism since it is an active decision for religious belief. Her protagonist uses English as confidently as Arabic. This kind of multilingualism can also be used as a weapon: this highly educated woman is linguistically part of 'two worlds', a position that makes her stronger. She is, to some extent, a type of Homi Bhabha's *Mimic Men* who have the advantage of a multidimensional view on their environment ('Of Mimicry and Man', 85–92). In *The Translator*, this 'double vision' (88) is shown to be essential for Sammar's life: she is the connector between English and Arabic, and, on the basis of this position, the missionary who shapes her own destiny as a Muslim woman by trying to convince Rae to convert to Islam and to be her husband.

In her novels, Aboulela puts her 'Islamic agenda' into literary practice with two different interpretations of Islam. By describing how her protagonists find their way back to Islam, she shows the potential power of religious belief in both the traditional perception of Islam by an accepting, though learning believer in *Minaret* and a more progressive understanding of this religion by a highly educated believer in *The Translator*. Both women's Muslim identity comes to the fore in their non-Muslim environment: on the one hand, 'cold' Britain triggers the wish in her protagonists to live their religion openly; on the other, it is only in the West that they have the freedom to choose to live as Muslim women according to their own needs and desires. This startling paradox is also something Aboulela herself experienced. When asked in an interview whether there was 'more freedom for Muslim women to be religious in Britain?', she replies: 'Oh, definitely. But then you have to decide what you are going to do

and mutate, taking as its luggage its weighty words, mantras and spirituality' (B. Cooper, *A New Generation of African Writers: Migration, Material Culture and Language* (Woodbridge: James Currey; Scottsville: University of KwaZulu-Natal Press, 2008), 56, 55).

with all this freedom.'[23] Choice means freedom for Muslim women, but choice implies responsibility: it can lead to doubt and the question whether one has made the right decision. Aboulela's Islam comes across as a flexible and adaptable religion,[24] but it is also a religion one needs to take responsibility for.

***

As a determining factor of one's identity, when migrating between places and cultures, language is highly significant. Like other items of one's cultural identity, languages can either be taken with the migrant and adjusted to the new environment, or left behind. Migration is often associated with the latter: it is connected with losing one's mother tongue, either already in the country of origin or in the new country of residence.[25] Yet migration also offers the option to choose or gain a new language as the means of communication, both when interacting with one's immediate environment and also — on the meta-level of the migrant writer — when producing literature. I relate Gilles Deleuze and Félix Guattari's concept of *nomadicism* as the metaphor for a creative and dynamic process of 'becoming' to this section's writers:[26] Emine Sevgi Özdamar and Feridun Zaimoğlu. According to Deleuze and Guattari, nomadic groups have 'their own

23 Aboulela in an interview with Anita Sethi, 'Keep the Faith: Award Winning Novelist Leila Aboulela Tells Anita Sethi Why Her Religious Identity Is More Important Than Her Nationality', *Observer*, 5 June 2005, www.guardian.co.uk/books/2005/jun/05/fiction.features2/print [accessed 28 June 2010] (para. 8 of 14).
24 Butt has a less positive view on Aboulela's Islam as constructed in *The Translator*. According to her, 'the female protagonist remains determined that she cannot believe in a hybrid but only in a pure Islam' (170); '*The Translator* dismisses cultural mélange in favour of cultural authenticity' (177).
25 See Özdamar's concept of losing one's mother tongue whilst moving around. In *Seltsame Sterne starren zur Erde*, the protagonist describes how she already lost her mother tongue in Turkey (23), whereas in *MutterZunge*, this losing process is linked to moving to Germany.
26 G. Deleuze and F. Guattari, 'The Aesthetic Model: Nomad Art', in *A Thousand Plateaus: Capitalism and Schizophrenia*, trans. B. Massumi (London: Continuum, 2004 [1987]), 543–51, quotation here 547 (originally publ. as *Mille Plateaux*, II of *Capitalisme et Schizophrénie* (Paris: Minuit, 1980). Deleuze and Guattari's concept of *nomadicism* cannot be applied usefully in the context of Aboulela's writing. She does not highlight her or her characters' creative 'becoming' (547): they do not transform or influence the spaces they inhabit, that is, 'fill the space from within' (C. Colebrook, 'Nomadicism', in *The Deleuze Dictionary*, ed. A. Parr (Edinburgh: Edinburgh University Press, 2005), 182).

"will" to art', not 'imposed by a transcendent above'.[27] Both Özdamar and Zaimoğlu have a nomadic background in Deleuze and Guattari's sense: they do not have to conform to a standard but are able to 'become' the writers they wish to be. Deleuze and Guattari refer to this process as 'becoming-artist' (547). The two writers can enter creative operations which enable them to develop a language that mirrors transcultural experiences.[28] This process entails the mingling of the various languages which are available to them in order to suit their needs.

Language is closely connected to social dominance. Being able to articulate one's concerns — in the context of this chapter these are Muslim women's concerns — is highly significant. Gayatri Chakravorty Spivak's question whether the subaltern, or here more specifically whether the subaltern Muslim woman, can speak comes into play.[29] Yet verbal communication is often perceived as 'a woman's job': by functioning as linguistic mediators between people, women keep (family) relations going and play an important social role. Dale Spender has addressed this apparent contradiction between women's silence and their actual position in communication. In *Man Made Language*, she points out the discrepancy between the general perception of women as the 'talkative sex' and the empirical fact that men dominate mixed-sex conversation.[30] She suggests that the general assumption that women are more talkative is based on 'comparison not with men but with *silence*' in a 'patriarchal order' where 'any talk in which a woman engages can be too much' (42, italics Spender's). However, contrary to Spender's rather gloomy outlook migrant women do break the silence imposed by men (60).[31] In the texts selected they engage with their new surroundings more consciously than men. I relate the women's linguistic interactions to

27 E. Holland, 'Nomadicism + Citizenship', in *The Deleuze Dictionary*, ed. A. Parr, 183.

28 I do not use the Deleuzian/Guattarian philosophical term 'nomad' despite the creative potential implied in this term. I continue using the terms 'migrant' or 'post-migrant' whereby I emphasize the contextual rather than philosophical side of my reading of the texts. My selected writers (and their protagonists) either migrated to Europe ('migrant') or were already born there ('post-migrant').

29 G. C. Spivak, 'Can the Subaltern Speak?', in *Marxism and the Interpretation of Culture*, ed. C. Nelson and L. Grossberg (Basingstoke: Macmillan Education, 1988), 271–313.

30 D. Spender, *Man Made Language*, 2nd edn (London: Pandora, 1990 [1980]), x, 9; see also 41–50.

31 Spender revokes her previous claim that women cannot change established meanings to some extent (58).

the freedom that their new places of abode offer: here women may feel liberated from old structures and hence more daring.

Whereas men often rely on their physical strength more than on language in gaining or expressing dominance, verbal and symbolic resistance appear as women's best tool of struggle. Being able to articulate one's concerns and desires means having control and power over oneself. Language contains the possibility to resist and to subvert power relations. These processes are reflected in literature where linguistic spaces for the negotiation of Muslim women's identities are central.

Emine Sevgi Özdamar's *MutterZunge* (1990) is a fictionalized autobiography or semi-autobiography.[32] The text is based on her life in the divided city of Berlin, and is a conscious reflection on her personal life during this time. This includes the creative engagement with matters of language that exemplify her migratory and transcultural experiences. Özdamar's first person-narrator, a Turkish-born actor and writer like herself, is preoccupied with self-exploration in the light of different languages she encounters on her way and their cultural and religious implications. These are primarily German and Turkish, as well as Arabic which she explores as an influence on Turkey's — and implicitly her own — linguistic, religious and cultural heritage.[33]

The protagonist's linguistic journeys describe displacement and the implications of leading a peripatetic life. Margaret Littler connects the protagonist's 'sense of dislocation' to '[Mustafa Kemal] Atatürk's attempt to obliterate from the Turkish language all traces of the

32 E. S. Özdamar, *MutterZunge: Erzählungen*, 2nd edn (Cologne: Kiepenheuer & Witsch, 2002 [1990]). The stories 'Mutter Zunge' (9–14) ['Mother Tongue'] and 'Großvater Zunge' (15–48) ['Grandfather Tongue'] in the collection form a whole, telling the protagonist's history of engaging with Arabic in relation to Turkish (and German). Hence, in the following, I do not specifically refer to the individual stories. Translations taken from E. S. Özdamar, *Mother Tongue*, trans. C. Thomas, Passport Books, 3 (Toronto: Coach House Press, 1994).

33 I am aware that other languages such as Farsi, French etc. have had an influence on both Turkish and Özdamar's protagonist's linguistic environment. However, the protagonist's interest in language as part of her heritage and culture concentrates on Arabic and its script in particular. If, in the following, I describe Arabic as a 'predecessor' of Turkish, I do not wish to imply a linguistic connection between Arabic and Turkish, but I refer to the protagonist's perception of Arabic as one part of her cultural ancestry and as an expression of her religious background. Furthermore, I focus on the interaction of Turkish and Arabic in relation to German as these are the languages that feature in *MutterZunge*.

imperial Ottoman past'.[34] Atatürk's politics promoted secularization and a Western-oriented practice of religion. Islam was meant to be religion and culture, and not a way of life. This was also symbolized by the educated, thus unveiled woman who became the site of modernization and the formation of a national identity (Yeğenoğlu, 128).[35] The aim of Atatürk's reforms was to cut Turkey's ties with its Arab Islamic past and traditions in order to create a new Turkey as a modern, Western state. Özdamar, having received a Western education in Turkey, however, conceives of this as a fundamental loss in the identity of the people and suggests a fruitful interaction between secular and religious attitudes instead. Bearing analogy to Jürgen Habermas's concept of a 'postsecular' modernity, she seems to ask whether secularization, that is, the complete denial of religion is still possible, and she suggests that secular concepts and those rooted in the Enlightenment as well as religious doctrines should be examined critically.[36]

The linguistic search of her protagonist in *MutterZunge* also has a specific reason: she has lost her mother tongue Turkish whilst leading a peripatetic life and now finds herself in the position of someone with a 'gedrehten Zunge' (ÖMZ 9) ['twisted tongue' (ÖMT 9)], that is: a writer who, despite her temporarily confusing German environment, is able to express herself.[37] Simultaneously she is looking for the roots of her existence as someone who creatively deals with language. In order to regain Turkish language and culture, which strongly

34 M. Littler, 'Diasporic Identity in Emine Sevgi Özdamar's *MutterZunge*', in *Recasting German Identity: Culture, Politics, and Literature in the Berlin Republic*, ed. S. Taberner and F. Finlay (Rochester, NY: Camden House, 2002), 223.

35 See also F. Mernissi, *Beyond the Veil: Male-Female Dynamics in Muslim Society*, rev. edn (Cambridge, MA: Saqi Books, 2003 [1975]), and N. Göle, *The Forbidden Modern: Civilization and Veiling*, Critical Perspectives on Women and Gender (Ann Arbor: The University of Michigan Press, 1996).

36 See J. Habermas, 'Vorpolitische Grundlagen des demokratischen Rechtsstaates', in J. Habermas and J. Ratzinger, *Dialektik der Säkularisierung: Über Vernunft und Religion* (Bundeszentrale für politische Bildung: Bonn, 2005 / Herder: Freiburg im Breisgau, 2005), 16–17.

37 Seyhan, *Writing Outside the Nation*, 204: '"Zunge drehen" (twisting the tongue) is a literal translation of the Turkish idiom *dili dönmek*, often used in the negative as *dilim dönmüyor* (I cannot say or pronounce).' If the narrator sits in Berlin with a twisted tongue, it suggests she is able to express herself (Haines and Littler, 123). See also Konuk who relates *drehen* to the Turkish verb *çevirmek* which means 'to turn' or 'to rotate', but metaphorically also 'to translate'. For her, 'gedrehte Zunge' therefore means 'translated language' (K. Konuk, 'Das Leben ist eine Karawanserei: Heim-at bei Emine Sevgi Özdamar', in *Kein Land in Sicht: Heimat — weiblich?*, ed. G. Ecker (Munich: Fink, 1997), 146).

influence the German she is writing, the protagonist migrates back linguistically: she explores Arabic, the part of her Turkish origin that she describes as her 'grandfather tongue', the language whose script was used to write Ottoman Turkish, and which influenced Turkey's literary and cultural traditions until 1927. Referring to Arabic as her 'grandfather tongue', the protagonist points to the generational distance, yet not foreignness, between Arabic and Turkish. She is partly familiar with Arabic for she uses it in both everyday and religious life.

At this point it needs to be asked why the protagonist regards Arabic as her 'grandfather tongue' and not Ottoman Turkish, which is the actual predecessor of present-day Turkish. Azade Seyhan argues that this 'grandfather tongue' is in fact Ottoman Turkish, 'a hybrid language of the Ottoman court and the educated classes which was mostly made up of Persian and Arabic loan words and structures held together by Turkish connectors' (*Writing Outside the Nation*, 205); but I identify Arabic as the protagonist's 'grandfather tongue' mainly on the basis of its alphabet, in which Ottoman Turkish was written, and the limited familiarity with the language in everyday and religious life. The narrator comments:

> Ich werde Arabisch lernen, das war mal unsere Schrift, nach unserem Befreiungskrieg, 1927, verbietet Atatürk die arabische Schrift und die lateinischen Buchstaben kamen, mein Großvater konnte nur arabische Schrift, ich konnte nur lateinisches Alphabet, das heißt, wenn mein Großvater und ich stumm wären und uns nur mit Schrift was erzählen könnten, könnten wir uns keine Geschichten erzählen. (ÖMZ 14)
>
> [I am going to learn Arabic, which was once our system of writing. After our war of liberation, 1927, Atatürk outlawed the Arabic script and brought in the Latin letters. My grandfather only knew Arabic script, I only know the Latin alphabet, which means that if my grandfather and I had been unable to speak and could only tell each other things in writing, we'd have been unable to tell each other stories. (ÖMT 15)]

The exchange with her country's Ottoman past, which was interrupted by Atatürk's language reform, is at the centre of the protagonist's interest in the Arabic script. Her and Turkey's past is exemplified by her grandfather, who grew up in the culturally diverse Ottoman Empire. Being Turkish already involves knowledge of more than one language, more than one political system, and extremely variegated relations through history between religion and state. The protagonist chooses to examine closely one particular aspect of her hybridity, an aspect which is strongly linked to notions of past and heritage (as exemplified by stories carried over by her grandfather), elements that she cannot find in the German context but which might help her find her place in Germany. This is not an examination of foreignness but rather the attempt to overcome the politically enforced estrangement between Turkey's past and present after Atatürk's westernizing reforms of the 1920s and by extension to overcome her initial estrangement from Germany. This examination of parts of her linguistic heritage relates to her critical reevaluation of her religious background in the context of migration and her existence as a German-language writer.[38] Littler points out that although the protagonist 'sets out to excavate the past', she 'also raises questions as to the viability of this project' ('Diasporic Identity', 223). She works with a curious and, simultaneously, critical awareness of the language of Islam and is thus strongly connected with her religious and cultural past, while being severed from it by Atatürk's reforms. The protagonist's historical orientation towards her Islamic heritage now promises a sense of unity and security in an initially alien place. Yet the driving force behind her protagonist's approach to her heterogeneous Ottoman origins is to make sense of her hybrid present — with the help of her equally hybrid grandfather — rather than a longing for a lost homeland.

The protagonist's wish to rediscover part of her cultural heritage is a form of back-and-forth movement between languages and cultures, acts of translation which make particularly detailed insights into a migrant's identity possible. The relocation of language is the technique Özdamar's protagonist employs to explore Arabic in relation to herself as a migrant. This kind of displacement of language is the literal movement of items of a language into another linguistic and cultural context. Özdamar's protagonist explores her linguistic yet also literal displacement by negotiating the meanings of Arabic words in relation to her German Turkish present (Konuk, *Identitäten im Prozeß*, 84). She ventures on this backward journey to be able to move forward again as a German Turkish migrant writer with a redefined language.

After the publication of *Kanak Sprak*, many of his female readers and audience-members urged Feridun Zaimoğlu to publish a female pendant to the Muslim men's views on their position in German

38 For further discussions of this point, see Bird; Littler, esp. 'Diasporic Identity'; Haines and Littler; and Seyhan, esp. *Writing Outside the Nation*.

culture. He duly produced *Koppstoff: Kanaka Sprak vom Rande der Gesellschaft* (1998).[39]

In *Koppstoff*, Zaimoğlu's interlocutors recognize language as their tool of struggle. Their use of language reflects the women's overall higher, more educated status than that of the male *Kanaken*, and the question is whether, in that respect, they really are 'marginal' (Skiba, 190–91). Zaimoğlu tells us that most of his interlocutors approached him after public readings of his work (ZKSt 9). Their interest in his writing already reveals an educational level that many of Zaimoğlu's male interlocutors do not share, yet there are also differences in the Muslim women's positions in society which are partly expressed linguistically.[40]

One of the most prominent features of the *Kanakas'* language is the use of words that emphasize their toughness, something not normally associated with Turkish or Muslim women. This linguistic toughness is mainly expressed in the inventive use of language such as the creation of 'strong' nouns. Nouns, along with their capitalization which is not practised in the male *Kanak Sprak*, are a prominent feature of the German language. The *Kanakas'* creation of nouns suggests that they are fighting the German mainstream by linguistically using German 'weapons': pejorative words such as 'Alemangeschichtsfick', 'Insgesichtspucker', 'Radieschenvonuntenriecher' (ZKSt 32–33) [German history fuck, spitter in the face, smeller of radishes from below] reveal a creative resistance to the negative use of expressions such as '*Kanake*'. This postcolonial practice of reappropriating and transforming insulting names denies the privilege of German. Through his *Kanakas*, Zaimoğlu abrogates the 'centre's' linguistic authenticity and appropriates the language of the dominant culture to make the mainstream aware of their own one-dimensional attitude towards 'foreigners' or Muslims. His German Turkish women twist language and make it relevant to their situation as 'different' Germans. By creating their own 'reality' in this way, the *Kanakas*

39 F. Zaimoğlu, *Koppstoff: Kanaka Sprak vom Rande der Gesellschaft*, 3rd edn (Hamburg: Rotbuch, 2000 [1998]).

40 I have already pointed out that there are linguistic differences between *Kanak Sprak* (the female version being *Kanaka Sprak*) and the actual speech of young German Turks. For example, there is hardly any genuine code switching, which is one of the most prominent features of the language of children of former immigrants. The reason for that is that *Koppstoff* occupies the same position between literature and reportage as *Kanak Sprak*. However, it would go beyond the scope of this chapter to analyse the *Kanakas'* language in relation to the actual speech of young German Turkish women. For a detailed linguistic analysis, see Pfaff, 214–20.

reclaim their pride and power as cultural or religious Muslims or as Turkish or 'different' German women, at least in linguistic terms.[41]

Zaimoğlu also exposes the reclaiming of their linguistic power as the *Kanakas'* opposition to Muslim men whom they often perceive as 'zu soft' (ZKSt 11) [too soft]. This comes to the fore through their use of Turkish. Reappropriating Turkish as a tool for resistance is something the *Kanaken* hardly ever do, whereas the *Kanakas* are shown to enjoy their linguistic advantage over non-Turkish speakers. As opposed to most male *Kanaken* they do not simply 'reden gegen irgendwas' [speak against anything],[42] as one of the most eloquent *Kanakas,* Nesrin, a twenty-four-year-old rapper and streetfighter, states (ZKSt 11). Nesrin's use of Turkish as the language of struggle — several consecutive sentences are given in Turkish without translation — gives her the chance to assert herself as a German Turk, that is, a German woman with the potential to stir up fossilized perceptions of 'foreigners'. This comes across as resistance to nostalgia — to the longing for a lost homeland that is often associated with older male immigrants — and as a means of expressing discontent with the German mainstream at the same time: 'auf ne Bourgeoisie voller Künste geschissen' (Ferah, 24, Studentin (Film- und Fernsehen) [student (film and television)]; ZKSt 16) [shat on a bourgeoisie full of arts]. Here, it is mainly the Orientalism of the German public (which often includes having a 'foreigner' as a good friend, as a status symbol) that Ferah is angry about. Although she does not explicitly use Turkish in this sentence, her mother tongue also serves as a means of intentional exclusion.

Despite the fact that the *Kanakas* apply their mother tongue more consciously than their male counterparts, they do not long for a home linked to Turkey. On the contrary, their use of Turkish can be read as a means of avoiding cultural or religious nostalgia, because their 'home' is, somehow, present when they rebel by means of language. Their origin is part and parcel of their expression of their discontent with the Germany they were born and live in, which points towards another creative interaction between their linguistic origins and present. In any case, Zaimoğlu reveals his *Kanakas'* easy linguistic

41 These ideas are based on what Ashcroft *et al.* describe in relation to the abrogation and appropriation of English in post-colonial writing in *The Empire Writes Back,* 38–44.

42 Cheesman also points out 'the gendered division of testimonial modes' when stating: 'The commitment to struggle, with the hope for the eventual creation of a homeland or secure settlement in Germany, is all but absent in *Kanak Sprak,* but frequently voiced in *Koppstoff'* (*Novels of Turkish German Settlement,* 138).

transition from one culture to another and thus their cultural flexibility (cf. Dirim and Auer, 22).

Not all the *Kanakas* feel the urge to rebel linguistically. Referring to herself, Reşide says: 'Ihr Mund ist ein Wortmund. Eine Spalte, die keine Überwindung kennt. Ihr Mund bildet ganze Sätze in einer Sprache, die keine Öffnung hat und keinen Ausgang' (Reşide, 34, Lehrerin [teacher]; ZKSt 88) [Her mouth is a mouth of words. A slot which doesn't know conquest. Her mouth is building whole sentences in a language that has neither an entrance nor an exit]. Reşide is shown as an (at least linguistically) assimilated Turkish woman. Her standard use of language suggests a passive relationship to the German mainstream. However, Reşide uses German poetically; this is an equally valid and effective form of resistance to the German mainstream and a sign of an individual approach to language.

Whatever the differences between the *Kanakas'* approach to language and its use, they share the same attitude: 'Kämpfen oder Klappe halten' (Mihriban, 30, Gemüseverkäuferin [greengrocer]; ZKSt 41) [fight or shut up]. The waitress Seynur expresses this attitude as follows:

> Der Stumme, der ich bin, hat beuligen Sprech, hat Monsterdeitsch auf der Zunge. Spricht Kackmeierstammel. Und weil keiner sieht das Bild auf meiner Zunge, will's keiner wissen, von was ich sprech. Als wär ne fette Schleife gewickelt um mein Zungenmageres, wird mein Null-Assimil-Sprech gehalten für Gaga-Unsprech. Es fragen sich die Menschen: Hat ein Gaga mir zu sagen was? Mein Monsterdeitsch aber klarwortig, ist mit allen Schikanen gesegnet. Das meiste an meiner Zunge ist Weib, doch nicht gestöckelt und mit Nuttendiesel und nimmt keinen Männerschwanz innen Mund. Der kann ruhig hängen zwischen eines Mannes Beinen. Das meiste an meiner Zunge ist kein Unglimpf, und das meiste an meiner Zunge schabrakelt nicht. (Seynur, 25, Kellnerin [waitress]; ZKSt 115)
>
> [The mute one, that's me, has puss-filled speak, has monster-German on the tongue. Talks crapster-stammering. And because no-one notices the picture on my tongue no-one wants to know what I'm talking about. As if a giant ribbon was wrapped around my lean tongue, my zero-assimilated-speak is regarded as crazed unspeak. People ask themselves: has that gaga a thing to say to me? My monster-German yet clear-worded is blessed with all chicaneries. Most of my tongue is female but not high-heeled and with prossie perfume and doesn't mouth a man's cock. It can hang between a man's legs. Most of my tongue is no slight, and most of my tongue isn't vixenish.]

Seynur's German (mediated through Zaimoğlu) appears as an extreme version of Özdamar's German. In *MutterZunge*, Özdamar's German is a subversive language which is primarily the result of literal translations of Turkish sayings or 'highly metaphorical' expressions,[43] by which she is emphasizing the possibility of language-play. These translations combine different systems of signification. For example, through her literal translation of 'Sprache' into 'Zunge' (ÖMZ 9) ['language' into 'tongue' (ÖMT 9)], Özdamar draws attention to the differences between the languages and cultures that are available to her, and her relationship to them. Similarly, Seynur uses the expression 'das Bild auf meiner Zunge' [the picture on my tongue] to refer to her language as something she creates rather than repeats.

Supposed mistakes, or rather unusual expressions which tend to be the result of literal translations from Turkish, are part of the subversion process. Özdamar makes her readers 'stumble'.[44] Not only do 'mistakes' show the changing nature of the German language under the influence of a foreign language, but they also become a method of her protagonist's identification.[45] Özdamar, a native speaker of Turkish, is distanced enough from German to see its 'faults' (Brunner, 558), namely gaps in the language that give access to the creative potential for her transcultural writing.

Seynur, too, defines her own German by the unusual word order, the creation of new words (such as 'klarwortig' [clear-worded]), her application of slang ('Sprech' [speak]), the scoffing at spoken German dialect ('deitsch' [German]), the deliberate use of 'bad' German ('von was' [literally: of what], instead of 'wovon' [whereof]), and the transformation of sayings ('mit allen Schikanen gesegnet' [to be blessed with all chicaneries] based on 'mit allen Wassern gewaschen' [to know all the dodges]). However, she also applies formal German (indicated by the use of the genitive) which shows both her level of education and her linguistic flexibility. On a further level, by clarifying that she refuses to use her mouth for sex she makes readers aware of social and religious norms and expectations such as honour. Despite her linguistic aggressiveness, Seynur wants to come across as

43 A. Seyhan, 'Scheherazade's Daughters: The Thousand and One Tales of Turkish-German Women Writers', in *Writing New Identities: Gender, Nation, and Immigration in Contemporary Europe*, ed. G. Brinker-Gabler and S. Smith (Minneapolis: University of Minnesota Press, 1997), 245.

44 Özdamar in Horrocks and Kolinsky, 'Living and Writing in Germany', 49: 'They [mistakes] have to be made to stumble, as it were'.

45 A. Wierschke, 'Auf den Schnittstellen kultureller Grenzen tanzend: Aysel Özakin und Emine Sevgi Özdamar', in *Denn du tanzt auf einem Seil: Positionen deutschsprachiger MigrantInnenliteratur*, ed. S. Fischer and M. McGowan, 188.

a sexually pure (something associated with religiosity) and intelligent woman. Yet she is not made one by men, but chooses to be one: her mouth is not the place for a man's penis but for language, thus for subversion and rebellion. She portrays herself as a woman who is independent of men and lives according to her own standards and beliefs.

Both Özdamar's language and Seynur's *Kanaka Sprak* as reproduced by Zaimoğlu are an 'Akt des Widerstandes' [act of resistance].[46] Seynur in particular does not want to be seen as an assimilated German Turkish woman: she refers to her German as 'Null-Assimil-Sprech' [Zero-assimilated-speak]. Neither Özdamar and her protagonist nor Seynur through Zaimoğlu conform to the notion of the 'Ausländerin mit Akzent' [foreign woman with an accent],[47] but create their own versions of German. By playing with socially determined norms, they make clear that it is a female, yet individual language they speak.

However, it needs to be asked whether through the *Kanakas'* use of language Zaimoğlu exposes a form of weakness, a rebellion of the 'voiceless'. As I pointed out earlier, women are doubly marginalized. It seems therefore that, for many *Kanakas,* the high volume of their voices is the only effective way of speaking as a 'subaltern', since it means that the German mainstream they implicitly address cannot ignore them. In any case, the *Kanakas* are shown to have a unique relationship to language that breaks away from patriarchal practices of language — and from the 'social silence' that has constrained women.[48]

***

Leila Aboulela said in an interview with Saleh Eissa: 'Women are more sensitive and gloomy then [*sic*] men (if it is possible to generalise) — they internalise a lot of their troubles. At the same time they are more flexible and expressive — they do and want to adjust' (para. 16 of 24). Although this comment may seem tendentious, the women

46 E. Boa, 'Sprachenverkehr: Hybrides Schreiben in Werken von Özdamar, Özakin und Demirkan', in *Interkulturelle Konfiguration: Zur deutschsprachigen Erzählliteratur von Autoren nichtdeutscher Herkunft,* ed. M. Howard (Munich: Iudicium, 1997), 126.

47 K. Konuk, '"Identitätssuche ist ein [sic!] private archäologische Graberei": Emine Sevgi Özdamars inszeniertes Sprechen', in *AufBrüche: Kulturelle Produktionen von Migrantinnen, Schwarzen und jüdischen Frauen in Deutschland,* ed. C. S. Gelbin *et al.* (Königstein/Taunus: Helmer, 1999), 69.

48 C. Kaplan, 'Language and Gender' (1986), in *The Feminist Critique of Language: A Reader,* ed. D. Cameron, 2nd edn (London: Routledge, 1998 [1990]), 62.

characters in Monica Ali's *Brick Lane* and Emine Sevgi Özdamar's *Das Leben ist eine Karawanserei* could be seen to demonstrate the kind of flexibility that Aboulela describes. This flexibility, however, can also be defined as a struggle for identity that is carried out in various ways. Identities are shown to be shaped and performed through interpersonal relationships with both women, mainly as religious guides and teachers, and men, primarily as (potential) lovers. They are constructed through the characters' use of language: through the act of speaking, they reconstruct their previous histories to understand their current situations and establish their relations to their surroundings. These aspects, which will be the focus of the following section, should also be read in relation to the authors. The language use or creation in the texts also brings the authors' attitudes towards their writing to the fore; an element that helps to define their identities as writers.

The relationship between men and women in Islam is central to the practice of their religion. It is primarily regulated in the Qur'an.[49] In *The Translator*, Aboulela reveals how a relationship between a man and a woman can become an element of Muslim worship.

Aboulela describes the relation between a practising Muslim woman and an Orientalist Western man who gradually get closer to each other. It is through language and, more specifically through the bridging of gaps of meaning between English and Arabic, that Sammar and her boss Rae eventually find each other — as a Muslim, not as a mixed faith couple (see Cooper, 51–52). Their first scholarly then gradually private relationship is based on the translation of religious texts. Sammar completely engages with her task and discovers her strong side in this. In terms of language, which is significant for his work as a scholar of Middle Eastern history, Rae is largely dependent on her, which changes the stereotypical power dynamics between men and women. Sammar has the advantage of being fluent in both languages, and this gives her an element of power over Rae. Arabic serves as her safety net, something she is familiar with; she does not feel close to English, the language of her country of abode. However, it is English, and not the language of her faith that becomes her tool for explaining Islam to Rae.

49 For further details on the relationship between men and women in an Islamic context, see A. Bouhdiba, *Sexuality in Islam*, trans. A. Sheridan (London: Routledge & Kegan Paul, 1985; originally publ. as *La sexualité en Islam* (Paris: PUF, 1975)).

> He [Rae] said, 'Translations don't do it [the Qur'an] justice. Much is lost ...'
>
> [Sammar:] 'Yes, the meanings can be translated but not reproduced. And of course the miracle can't be reproduced ... But even then, hearing it from the prophet, peace be upon him, not everyone believed. Not everyone accepted that the source and wording of what they were hearing came from Allah. The first believers were mostly women and slaves. I don't know why, maybe they had softer hearts.' (ATr 124)

Sammar goes back to the roots of Islam, to its spread and development in the hostile environment of Mecca, which, according to believers, can only be rendered in the Arabic language: translations into other languages cannot capture the magic and beauty of the Qur'an (see Butt, 171). Aboulela shows that Sammar aims to convey to Rae much more than the essence of the Arabic language.

> She thought of what she would tell him, all the things she would translate for him. He knew a lot. Like others here, this world held his attention and the scope of his mind. But he did not know about the stream of Kawthar, the Day of Promises, or what stops the heart from rusting. And the balance he admired. He would not understand it until he lived it. (ATr 118)

Religion is closely connected to Sammar's identity, both as a woman and as a partner. As Aboulela aims to capture and describe female, specifically Muslim, identities, her characters regularly bring the question of believing to the fore: 'Rae, do you believe in God?' (ATr 95). Although, at that moment, he says that he does and therefore dismisses Sammar's dread of atheism, he later answers as follows:

> 'It's not in me to be religious,' he said. 'I studied Islam for the politics of the Middle East. I did not study it for myself. [...] In the middle of all the prejudice and hypocrisy, I wanted to be one of the few who was saying what was reasonable and right.'
>
> 'It's not enough,' she pressed her hands together. 'It's not enough. It's not enough for me.' (ATr 126)

Henceforth Sammar's goal becomes to convert Rae — this coincides with Aboulela's agenda to show her readers the power of Islam and its ability to give strength. She lets two different attitudes towards Islam clash: Rae is an Oriental scholar, although someone who is open to a believer's perception of Islam, whereas Sammar is a true believer who did not study her religion but grew up with it as part of her cultural heritage. Because Rae is an open-minded scholar, there is the possibility of him becoming a Muslim on the basis of knowledge and immersion in Islam, and this is the starting-point for Sammar's intervention.

> [Rae:] 'The reason why he [Fareed, his scholarly friend] goes on is that I view the Qur'an as a sacred text, as the word of God. It would be impossible in the kind of work I'm doing, in the issues I'm addressing for me to do otherwise but accept Muslims' own vision of the Qur'an, what they say about it. To Fareed, though, this is a tantamount to accepting Islam, and so he can't understand it when I say I am not a Muslim.' (ATr 89)

Aboulela provides the ground for Rae's conversion: his attitude towards Islam already reveals his closeness to and acceptance of this religion. It only needs some external intervention, personified by Sammar, to move him towards Islam — and to make him take the final step of conversion. Sammar believes in the strength-giving ability of her religion and wants to convey this to Rae: 'It [conversion] would be good for you, it will make you stronger' (ATr 89). She relates Islam to happiness, her own as well as others' — and thus takes on the role of a missionary. Sammar fights and becomes more than a translator: she acts as a teacher and a conveyor of meaning. This is her task: 'She thought, I have to explain things [the meaning of the *shahādah,* the Islamic creed] right, I have to be clear' (ATr 123). The notion that the translator has to be clear is essential, particularly since the Islamic creed, a speech and performative act that establishes Muslim identity, is central if the couple is to find each other as Muslims. Yet translation also takes place on an intermediate level, and certain concepts, such as the meaning of the *shahādah,* cannot be articulated. Translation includes interpersonal communication. Aboulela emphasizes this by revealing Sammar's ambition to convince Rae of Islam with the help of her translations. This is also part of Sammar's religious worship. Aboulela seems to follow the logic that 'in Islam, love is actually prayer' (Bouhdiba, 91).[50] Through the relationship between Sammar and Rae Aboulela unfolds what she regards as the beauty and power of Islam beyond cultural and linguistic boundaries.

Eventually, Rae converts to Islam. Aboulela's text suggests that this is based on Sammar's power and emotional strength drawn from her religion: yet Sammar initially fails as a missionary and a true believer, someone believing for 'no worldly reason', and she

50 Yet, as Cooper points out, '[s]he will only be able to translate these worlds for him through the energy of her released sexuality if he lives the spiritual balance that accepting Islam would provide for him '(54–55).

has to learn to 'clean her intentions' and to want conversion for the sake of Rae, not herself, thus making it 'true' missionary work (ATr 175). Rae, like Sir Richard Burton, 'looked exactly like an Arab' (ATr 60) and appears to be able to adapt easily to different circumstances (different cultures, languages and religions). This is the conciliation between the professional Orientalist man, who previously 'travel[led] the world in search of war and revolution' (ATr 62) and the Muslim woman.

The Translator portrays a woman who is powerful and has the strength to influence the man she loves and to prove that 'West' is not always 'best' (ATr 22). Despite her initial passivity, Aboulela's protagonist shapes her own fate and reacts against the traditional notion of the Muslim woman who is dependent on first her father and then her husband. Aboulela evokes a progressive form of Islam: employing Islamic feminist ideas, she portrays a woman who demands her right of pursuit of happiness by means of a well-informed understanding of religion.

In *Minaret*, Aboulela presents us with a Muslim who appears to be comfortable in the stereotypical role of the submissive woman. Language, or rather language interaction, is not as significant as in *The Translator*, yet it is at the root of the protagonist Najwa's identity-formation. Since believing Muslims regard Arabic as the original and only true language of Islam (this is the language in which the Prophet Muhammad received his revelations), Aboulela portrays Najwa as keen to learn about and to understand Islam via language, that is, learning how to pronounce the language of Islam properly: 'I want to read the Qur'an in a beautiful way' (AMi 79). The tradition of reciting and also listening to the Qur'an becomes a performative act of practising Islam and consciously regarding oneself as a Muslim. Aboulela reveals the learning of Arabic as a way of travelling to Islam and to oneself as a Muslim. In this sense, the study of Arabic and Islam constitutes her feminism: generally, Islamic feminists regard engaging with the past, the life of the Prophet Muhammad and foundational texts as a means of reinterpreting and reclaiming Islam for women (Cooke, 62). It makes them intellectually stronger and therefore capable of giving their discontent with the way the religion is practised by some Muslim men an intellectual foundation.

As I pointed out earlier, *Minaret* addresses the question of access to education and intellectual exchange, which is at the heart of Islamic feminism. What is particularly noteworthy in this novel then is that Aboulela introduces female teachers who show how a Muslim woman can gain access to her religion and its language; it is through women that Najwa finds her way back to Islam in the UK. Najwa is consciously submissive: by being a pupil, she becomes a 'servant' to God. Religion turns into the guiding tool in her life and is represented by women: 'She [Wafaa] was a guide, not a friend' (AMi 247). In her relationship with Wafaa, Najwa experiences a strong bond among (Muslim) women that provides stability. Aboulela suggests that men are not needed (or indeed wanted) when Muslim women reappropriate their religion. This is a self-imposed separation between the sexes (as it is practised among strict Muslims), yet Aboulela also reinterprets this separation as a device that gives security in an unstable life. She reveals the power that believing women can gain from Islam without being dependent on men. The novel therefore suggests a progressive way of understanding Islam by letting women define Islam according to their conceptions of this religion.

Aboulela also shows the challenges that believing Muslims face in non-Muslim environments. She brings this to the fore by introducing women characters (Najwa's employer Lamya in particular) who are culturally influenced by Islam but do not practise the religion, and who appear Western. These women deliberately nourish the dichotomy between their own independence and the role of obedient believer that Najwa used to look down upon in Sudan but that she has chosen for herself now. The novel's Westernized Muslim women are also shown to perceive devout Muslim women as competitors or a threat. This holds particularly true for Doctora Zeinab, Najwa's employer's mother, who is afraid of losing her son Tamer to a religious woman. Najwa is emotionally closer to Tamer than anybody else in the family who seem intimidated by the trust between these two believers. In the novel, the hijab-wearing woman becomes an object of jokes: by making fun of the Other (for example in the form of a theatre play at a party, AMi 222–23), the novel's non-believing Muslims no longer perceive the Other as a threat. The ridicule indicates that these Westernized Muslim women do not look at what is behind the hijab. Najwa observes: 'She [Lamya] will always see my hijab, my dependence on the salary she gives me, my skin colour, which is a shade darker than hers' (AMi 116). Najwa compares the distribution of roles with her own previous life: now it is clearly herself who is in a lower position, in the position her servants filled in Khartoum, and she learns what it feels like to be reduced to outer appearances. By turning the tables in relation to roles that believing and non-believing Muslims take on, choose or adjust, Aboulela assesses the challenges that Islam has to face in hostile surroundings. Yet, once again, she demonstrates how religion can make a believer stronger and what power faith can offer.

That does not mean, however, that her characters have actual power. Aboulela also shows the limits of a devout believer's ability to turn the tables, particularly in regard to the power balance between women and men. Here, we have to consider the notion of women as the bearers of Islamic culture and preservers of the family (which can be expressed through the veil) (Esposito, 'Introduction: Women in Islam and Western Society', xvi). In that context, *Minaret* addresses a conflict: Najwa is neither a mother nor does she live in a Muslim society. The closest she can get to this ideal is by working as a childminder in a Muslim family. Aboulela seems to suggest that a Muslim woman, as represented by Najwa in *Minaret*, 'naturally' has an impetus to fulfil the role of keeper of the family. If she cannot be a mother, she feels a sense of lack that she tries to overcome by being as good a Muslim as possible. The novel starts by Najwa telling us: 'I accept my sentence' (AMi 1). This opening shows a conservative attitude towards Islam (literal submission to one's fate as intended by God) which, however, Aboulela challenges by addressing notions of patriarchal society critically. This includes the approval of women's behaviour by men:

> [Tamer:] 'I don't approve of her [Lamya, his sister]. She hardly prays. She doesn't wear hijab. It's wrong. She has such bad friends. They go and see rude films together. They smoke and even drink wine — it's disgusting. I tell her but she doesn't listen to me. Her husband should tell her but he's just as bad. It's all to do with pride, the way she talked to you just now. She shouldn't ...'. (AMi 115)

Men's moral judgements have always been part of Najwa's life and she has never challenged them. Before her transformation into a devout Muslim, she was approved of as Western by Anwar, a young man she knows from Khartoum and with whom she has a brief relationship in London: '"I know you're Westernized, I know you're modern," he said, "that's what I like about you — your independence"' (AMi 176). Yet having a sexual relationship with him causes guilt, which will later partly contribute to her return to religion as the morally 'correct' way of living. Aboulela again foregrounds what she regards as the dilemma of the Muslim woman here: she perceives non-believing Muslim women as torn between Islamic values (that still have an effect even if the woman is not religious) and adopting Western values (such as personal sexual freedom). Aboulela continues to follow her 'Islamic agenda' by intimating that a Muslim woman will feel lost with an entirely Western lifestyle. It is Islamic values, including in relation to men, that will bring her mental stability.

According to Tamer, '[i]t's not very Islamic for a man and woman to be friends' (AMi 211). But in the course of the novel Najwa develops feelings for her employer's brother, and religion becomes sexy: she is attracted to the 'beautiful, devout youth with striking eyes' (AMi 100). As Tamer has a conservative attitude towards a Muslim woman's role and the path she should follow, Najwa too fosters a traditional, even Orientalist perception of her submissive role in this relationship: 'I would like to be his family's *concubine*, like something out of *The Arabian Nights*, with life-long security and a sense of belonging. But I must settle for freedom in this modern time' (AMi 215). Najwa perceives the 'freedom' of not being guided by a man as a failure. Here, Aboulela shows how a Muslim can transform the notion of freedom as availability to freedom as guidance, thus providing space for an identity as a (rather conservative) Muslim woman. Yet she has not shed her former Orientalist ideas of the Muslim woman as secretive (which is something the word 'concubine' implies), and she comes across as a Muslim woman who unquestioningly adopts an Islam based on patriarchal notions of womanhood. However, the end of the novel (Najwa is planning her hajj) shows a woman who, after many challenges, has developed her own definition of independent Muslim womanhood. Having eventually broken away from her conservative, even Orientalist perception of Islam, she — like Sammar, the protagonist in Aboulela's *The Translator* — also shapes her own fate, albeit in a very different way: she seeks the 'true' experience of Muslim identity by celebrating the Muslim community, the *umma*, in Islam's originating land on the hajj. By portraying strong Muslim women who learn how to live a successful life as Muslim migrants in the UK, Aboulela comes across as an advocate of a progressive form of Islam grounded in Islamic feminist ideas. She promotes an Islam that is based on conscious intellectual interaction (such as translating or learning Arabic), choice and determination.

***

Many German Turkish authors pay distinct attention to the relationship between language and interpersonal relationships in order to explore their characters' identity formation through moments of performativity in their texts. The protagonist of Özdamar's *MutterZunge* engages in the search for her self as a migrant writer through a translation process between the language she has lost

(Turkish) and the language she aims to acquire in order to recover this lost language (Arabic) with the help of a teacher. The language she is surrounded by, the language of her work (German) thereby serves as a useful translation tool.[51] In this process, language, or rather Arabic, is embodied by her teacher, Ibni Abdullah. He serves as a translator in more than one way: firstly, he delivers the script, the Qur'an, to the protagonist and, religiously speaking, acts as an imam. His service to god (Ibni Abdullah means 'servant to Allah') is worship through letters. Secondly, he symbolizes a physical approach to language: he has a love affair with his student, the protagonist.

The learning environment of Ibni Abdullah's study appears to the protagonist as 'eine kleine Moschee' (ÖMZ 15) ['a small mosque' (ÖMT 17)] where the conservative rules of Islam are redefined (see Haines and Littler, 124). The separation between herself and the other students, German scholars of Oriental studies, is represented by a curtain, a version of the Muslim veil. As a 'mosque', the teacher's study becomes a place of worship: through language, Islam as well as language itself are idolized. Ibni Abdullah teaches Arabic through reading the Qur'an which, for conservative Muslims such as him, regulates the relationship between men and women, 'die heilige Liebe, reine Liebe' (ÖMZ 42) ['holy love, pure love' (ÖMT 490)] (see Haines and Littler, 132).[52] The Qur'an is significant as religious text for Ibni Abdullah who fears the loss of his ability to teach the language of Islam if he continues to be with the protagonist. For her, the Qur'an is a means to an end, namely the ability to read and understand Arabic. Here, a secularized Turk meets a religious Saudi which leads to a

51 See Adelson's *The Turkish Turn* for an analysis of *MutterZunge* in relation to language with a useful overview of criticism on Özdamar and linguistic issues (149–58).

52 For a detailed analysis of the love relationship between the protagonist and her Arabic teacher as an exoticized and Orientalized element in Özdamar's writing, see B. Blahak, '"Du feine Rose meiner Gedanken ...": Orientalismen in der Darstellung von Liebe, Erotik und Sexualität als tiefere Ebene einer Hybridität in Emine Sevgi Özdamars *Mutter Zunge — Großvater Zunge*', *Wirkendes Wort*, 56.3 (December 2006), 455–74. With particular reference to 'Deleuzian becoming' Margaret Littler focuses on 'the sacred connotations of the sexual encounter between the narrator and her teacher', the corporeality of their love and eroticism in relation to Islam, in 'Intimacies Both Sacred and Profane: Islam in the Work of Emine Sevgi Özdamar, Zafer Şenocak, and Feridun Zaimoğlu', in *Encounters with Islam in German Literature and Culture*, ed. J. Hodkinson and J. Morrison, 222–24. See also her article 'Profane und religiöse Intensitäten: Die islamische Kultur im Werk von Emine Sevgi Özdamar und Feridun Zaimoğlu', in *Von der nationalen zur internationalen Literatur: Transkulturelle deutschsprachige Literatur und Kultur im Zeitalter globaler Migration*, ed. H. Schmitz, 146–48.

unique exploration of language and shows that there is no clear-cut division between secularism and religiosity.

The protagonist explores linguistic and cultural estrangement, yet also the unifying factors between the languages that determine her identity: she compares Turkish with Arabic words in German, the language that she and Ibni Abdullah have in common.

> Ich suchte arabische Wörter, die es noch in türkischer Sprache gibt. Ich fragte Ibni Abdullah: 'Kennst du sie?'
> *Leb* – Mund[53]
> *Ducar* – Befallen
> *Mazi* – Vergangenheit
> [...]
> *Yetim* – Waise
> 'Ja,' sagte: [*sic*] Ibni Abdullah, 'es hört sich ein klein bißchen anders an.' (ÖMZ 29)

> [I looked for Arabic words, [*sic*] that are still in the Turkish language. I asked Ibni Abdullah. 'Do you know them?'
> *Leb* – mouth
> *Ducar* – befall
> *Mazi* – past [...]
> *Yetim* – orphan
> 'Yes,' said Ibni Abdullah, 'that sounds a bit like it.' (ÖMT 34)]

By looking for and enunciating Turkish words of Arabic origin, the protagonist's engagement with language takes on a performative element, as she tries to find connections between the different aspects of her identity, Turkey's Ottoman past and her German Turkish present. However, this endeavour is thwarted as the pronunciation of the Arabic words differs from the pronunciation of the Turkish words due to the different phonological systems (Littler, 'Diasporic Identity', 228; Haines and Littler, 135): the words were transformed drastically when Turkish appropriated them from Arabic. Yet at least she is able to recollect part of her cultural memory which was influenced by Turkey's Arab Islamic heritage, to make sense of her current situation as an adult in the religiously and culturally different environment of Germany.[54] She associates certain differences between the various sides of her identity with the differences between Arabic

53 *Leb* is not Arabic but Persian in derivation. I am indebted to Dr Kamran Rastegar (Tufts University) for this information.

54 See B. Brandt, 'Collecting Childhood Memories of the Future: Arabic as Mediator Between Turkish and German in Emine Sevgi Özdamar's *Mutterzunge*', *Germanic Review*, 79.4 (Fall 2004), 294–315.

and Turkish that now help her recover her mother tongue. These differences are based on diverse language systems and language change (the different pronunciation of Arabic words and Turkish words of Arabic origin), and the protagonist compares them with her own development from childhood to adulthood, from her life in Turkey to her life in Germany, and from her existence as a migrant to her creative transformation of migrancy as a German Turkish writer.

Having come to the end of her Arabic lessons and to the end of her love affair with Ibni Abdullah, she reflects:

> Als ich zum ersten Mal vor Ibni Abdullahs Tür stand, hatte ich drei Wörter aus meiner Mutterzunge. Sehen, Lebensunfälle erleben, Arbeiter, ich wollte zurück zum Großvater, daß ich dann den Weg zu meiner Mutter und Mutterzunge finden könnte. Ich habe mich in meinen Großvater verliebt. Die Wörter, die ich die [*sic*] Liebe zu fassen gesucht habe, hatten alle ihre Kindheit. (ÖMZ 45–46)

> [When I stood for the first time before Ibni Abdullah's door, I had three words from my mother tongue. 'To see', 'to experience life's accidents', and 'workers'. I wanted to go back to my grandfather so that I could find the way to my mother and to my mother tongue. I had [*sic*] fallen in love with my grandfather. The words, whose love I tried to grab, all had their childhood. (ÖMT 54)]

The protagonist's love for her Arabic teacher unveils the complex relationship between Turkish and Arabic, and between different — modern and orthodox — views on Islam and the way they can intermingle. Through that, the different attitudes towards the kind of love the protagonist and her teacher want — secular or spiritual — come to the fore (Littler, 'Diasporic Identity', 224–25, 228; Haines and Littler, 126, 128–30). Yet despite these differences, this love enables her to find the 'childhood' of those Turkish words which have an Arabic heritage and to bridge supposed differences between religiosity and secularism. Having 'fallen in love with her grandfather', having found access to her past (even if this access is limited and not unbroken) through her love for Ibni Abdullah, her collection of words that are still similar in Turkish and Arabic can be read as an opposing act to the collection, reintroduction and even 'invention' of words of Turkish origin in the 1920s and 1930s in order to eradicate words of Arabic and Persian origin, and to purify Turkish.[55] The

55 For more detailed information on the Turkish language reform, see G. Lewis, *The Turkish Language Reform: A Catastrophic Success*, 2nd edn (Oxford: Oxford University Press, 2002 [1999]).

protagonist initiates a form of protest against the official purity of the Turkish language by defining the space of linguistic migration, of language exchange, as the site of language development. She notices: 'Bis diese Wörter aus deinem Land aufgestanden und zu meinem Land gelaufen sind, haben sie sich unterwegs etwas geändert' (ÖMZ 29) ['When these words rose and travelled from your country to my country, they were somewhat changed on the way' (ÖMT 34)]. This linguistic, yet simultaneously performative movement (Haines and Littler, 136–37) is also the site of the formation of her transcultural migrant identity — among Turkish, Arabic and the language of her immediate environment, German. Just as language is an ever-changing construct, a place of flux, so is her identity. Like the protagonist, words migrate. They change on their journey from one language to another — not only in phonology, pronunciation and script but also in terms of meaning (Bird, 169). The transformation of language resembles the protagonist's experience as a secularized Turkish migrant whose identity is shaped by the various cultural and religious encounters on her journeys.[56] She acknowledges the potential of her ambiguous position as a German writer with a Turkish heritage and Arabic (Ottoman Turkish) roots, an ambiguity Ibni Abdullah as representative of the 'original faith' does not share, and extracts her creativity out of this position.

Özdamar reflects her and her protagonist's creativity in language by emphasising its proximity to the visual arts (Haines and Littler, 125). In the following example, a visual experience results from the perception of Arabic letters as pictures. The metaphors created draw upon Arabic calligraphy, an Arabic already familiar from the Qur'an (Seyhan, 'Scheherazade's Daughters', 245).

> [Ibni Abdullah:] 'Lese, Gott hat es uns geschickt.'
>
> Es kamen aus meinem Mund die Buchstaben raus. Manche sahen aus wie ein Vogel, manche wie ein Herz, auf dem ein Pfeil steckt, manche wie eine Karawane, manche wie schlafende Kamele, manche wie ein Fluß, manche wie im Wind auseinanderfliegende Bäume, manche wie laufende Schlangen, manche wie unter Regen und Wind frierende Granatapfelbäume, manche wie böse geschreckte Augenbrauen, manche wie auf dem Fluß fahrendes Holz, manche wie in einem türkischen Bad auf einem heißen Stein sitzender dicker Frauenarsch, manche wie nicht schlafen könnende Augen. (ÖMZ 18)

56 For a detailed discussion on Özdamar's 'nomadic writing' in the context of 'feminine writing', see S. Ghaussy, 'Das Vaterland verlassen: Nomadic Language and "Feminine Writing" in Emine Sevgi Özdamar's *Das Leben ist eine Karawanserei*', *German Quarterly*, 72.1 (Winter 1999), 1–16.

> [[Ibni Abdullah:] 'Read, God has given this to us.'
> Letters came out of my mouth. Some looked like a bird, others like a heart pierced by an arrow, others like a caravan, others like sleeping camels, others like a river, others like trees flying apart in the wind, others like fleeing snakes, others like pomegranate trees freezing in the rain and the wind, [others like angry startled eyebrows],[57] others like a log floating on the river, still others like a fat woman's arse sitting in a Turkish bath on a hot stone, others like eyes that cannot sleep. (ÖMT 20)]

The protagonist's visual experience of language — language's performativity in the form of images — enables her to find access to the Arabic script — even though she does not understand it. Language is closely linked to the body (language, personified by Ibni Abdullah, actually 'enters' her body [Haines and Littler, 130]); it is a physical experience.[58] This approach to Arabic helps her to incorporate it into her Turkish heritage, thereby to find her mother tongue again, and on a further level to reappropriate the German language as she tries to transfer the Arabic letters into German. Thus, not only does she demonstrate a new, translated perspective on the Arabic language, but she also offers a new perspective on German by enriching it with this uncommon imagery. German thereby serves as a mediator between Turkish and Arabic; it becomes the language of the Muslim migrant writer.

With reference to postcolonial authors writing in English, Salman Rushdie suggests that '[t]o conquer English may be to complete the process of making ourselves free' ('Imaginary Homelands', 17). In *MutterZunge*, Özdamar's protagonist liberates herself by examining the migration of language as a performative symbol for her own migration — from an Ottoman-era Turkish context to a present-day Turkish context and finally to a German Turkish context. This might remind us of Rushdie's insistence on the notion that 'something can also be gained' by bringing languages and cultures into contact, but also by letting different interpretations of Islam, including the relationship between men and women, encounter one another. The protagonist of *MutterZunge* demonstrates that the Arabic language is not lost for the Turkish native speaker after the Turkish language

57 This phrase translated by F. M.

58 For further discussions of the physicality of language and the different interpretations of Islam exemplified by Arabic (and Ibni Abdullah) and Turkish (and the protagonist), see K. Roy, 'German-Islamic Literary Interperceptions in Works by Emily Ruete and Emine Sevgi Özdamar', in *Encounters with Islam in German Literature and Culture*, ed. J. Hodkinson and J. Morrison, 173–75.

reform of the 1920s. It comes alive again, not as a nostalgic reminder of a bygone era but as an object of learning on the basis of an interpersonal relation; it becomes a tool for the rediscovery of Turkish and an art form that enriches the language the narrator currently lives and writes in: German (cf. Littler, 'Profane und religiöse Intensitäten', 154).

Like their male counterparts, Zaimoğlu's *Kanakas* are shown to have a strong sense of being 'different' which is expressed in their struggle in and with Germany as a system and state. This is a mainly linguistic struggle based on the *Kanakas*' enhanced use of radical language when examining their relations with German men and women. Many of the *Kanakas* experience 'Düsternis und Wut' (ZKSt 10) [murk and anger] in Germany, primarily as the result of a sense of isolation after the country's unification and of racist attacks against 'foreigners' in the 1990s. Yet they now creatively transform their anger against social and racial injustice into something positive by reacting non-physically against physical attacks.[59]

The *Kanakas* develop a 'Gegenbewegung' (ZKSt 30) [counter-movement] which incorporates more individualistic, and in that sense stronger, approaches to struggle than the men's. They show a critical awareness of what they are supposed to be part of and as a result, individuality gains more significance for them than the support of a group. Not all of Zaimoğlu's interlocutors perceive themselves as '*Kanakas*', a term given by their interviewer (the observer and 'ethnographer'). This emphasizes Zaimoğlu's intervention as editor: only few of his interviewees use the term '*Kanaka*' for themselves which suggests a reaction against labelling and belonging to a group in general.[60]

As a response to being put into either the category of 'foreigner' or 'victim', the *Kanakas* create their own labels. These neologisms often include both a feminine and a strong component. They are,

59 This resembles Schmidt's cautious mention of Butler's 'hate speech' explored in *Excitable Speech: A Politics of the Performative* (New York: Routledge, 1997) in his analysis of the link between (masculine) gender performativity and language as well as authorship. He writes: 'As an author, Zaimoglu uses what might elsewhere be construed as hate speech to stake a claim to an area of representation and play with dangerous signifiers in which their dangerousness is ostensibly suspended: the literary space of the performance. Alternatively, it is an area in which the author can utilize politically incorrect speech by creating a fictional world in which such speech is directed at characters rather than real people' (202).

60 Butler also refers to the historicity of naming, 'the movement of a history that it [the name] arrests' (*Excitable Speech*, 36).

for example, 'Starkfrau' (ZKSt 13) [strong woman] and 'Kanak-Weib' (ZKSt 34) [*Kanak* woman]. These are individual 'titles'. They point up the *Kanakas'* idiosyncratic performances as young German Turkish Muslim women. Judith Butler's question 'What does it mean for a word not only to name, but also in some sense to perform and, in particular, to perform what it names?' (*Excitable Speech,* 43) illuminates the *Kanakas'* choice of labels: they deliberately choose names that reflect their position as strong, angry women to match their behaviour, their performance. In that sense, they 'perform what they name'. Whatever labels they use, they put themselves in clear opposition to mainstream German women, who are referred to as, for example, 'Sauertopf-Frauen' (ZKSt 117) [grumpy women], 'deutsches Liebchen' (ZKSt 119) [German sweetheart] and 'diese Bundesfrauen' (ZKSt 117) [those federal wives]. By naming mainstream German women in this derogatory way, the *Kanakas* empower themselves. This results in a new self-definition in — now deliberate — delimitation to non-*Kanak* women. Zaimoğlu's interlocutors want to be recognized and recognizable (cf. Butler, *Excitable Speech,* 5) — on their own terms. This is part of a subversion process that reclaims the act of naming from the German mainstream. It also comes across as an act of avoiding vulnerability (cf. 2–4): by turning the tables, by naming themselves as well as German women, which includes playing with gender stereotypes, the *Kanakas* circumvent the possibility of being hurt linguistically. They take the wind out of the mainstream's sails by being verbally aggressive themselves. They thus also practise a certain exoticization of German women. This reproduces and subverts Orientalist techniques of classifying and defining the Other.

On a further level, the *Kanakas'* opposition to the German mainstream is also directed against the Othering and Orientalization of Muslim women by Germans and their desire to help the allegedly oppressed Muslim woman where help is not wanted or indeed needed: 'Sie wollen mich als Schmerzweib in Fesseln und sehen meinen Befreiungskampf, aber ich kämpfe, weil ich in diesem verruchten Deutschlandhaus bin [...] dies scheiß "wo du Kopftuch gelassen?"' (Nesrin, 24, Rapperin und Street-Fighterin; ZKSt 13 and 15) [They want me suffering in chains and to witness my struggle for freedom, but I fight because I'm in this loathsome house of Germany [...] this shitty 'where's your headscarf?']. Struggling becomes a necessity: it is shown to be part of the *Kanakas'* life in Germany. Nesrin here reappropriates what linguists refer to as 'foreigner talk' (a way of communicating with non-native speakers in very simplified terms) in order to point up the German attitude towards 'foreigners'.[61] She also emphasizes the German women's need of the Other in order to enhance their own self-image and confidence through assisting Muslim women to 'liberate' themselves. This can result in a feeling of superiority, because helping Muslim women only works when they remain silent. Leslie A. Adelson reads this desire to help as an expression of German, or more generally, Western insecurity (*The Turkish Turn*, 129–30). The *Kanakas* have long recognized that they are exploited in this respect. They feel it is now time to challenge the stereotype of the helpless Muslim woman.

Zaimoğlu does, however, give one believing Muslim woman a voice, possibly in order to give as complete a picture of the diversity of Muslim women's attitudes as possible: she is 'Hatice, 22, Jura-Studentin [law student]' (ZKSt 67–71). Hers is the portrait of a self-confident religious woman whose belief is based on choice and her sense of worldly transience. Although she is highly educated, she does not interact with her German environment more than necessary — and thus shows her deliberate separation from the non-Muslim world. Hatice also exposes her religious attitude by wearing a headscarf and explaining its advantages for women. She has a conservative view of Islam. However, Hatice is shown to challenge the common Western view of the veiled woman who is confined to the house and does not speak: Zaimoğlu makes us believe that Hatice interacts with the 'outside world' (his audience) and offers a self-conscious perspective on devout Muslim women.

The *Kanakas'* gender performance is also explored through their relationships with German men. As the last chapter showed, sexuality, or rather the 'art' of seducing German women, is one of the major defining factors of male *Kanaken*. In that respect, their identity is performed at the expense of women. Some of the *Kanakas* reappropriate this technique for their own self-positioning in Germany; for them too, sexuality serves as one of the means of opposition to the mainstream. They use their sexual experiences with German men for their own purposes: they explore the tensions caused by these relationships and employ them as a form of fighting

61 See V. Hinnenkamp, 'Türkisch Mann, Du? Sprachverhalten von Deutschen gegenüber Gastarbeitern', in *Mehrsprachigkeit in der Stadtregion*, ed. K. H. Bausch, Jahrbuch des Landes NRW, Sprache der Gegenwart, 56 (Düsseldorf: Schwann, 1981), 171–93, and M. Bingham Wesche, 'Input and Interaction in Second Language Acquisition', in *Input and Interaction in Language Acquisition*, ed. C. Galloway and B. J. Richards (Cambridge: Cambridge University Press, 1994), 219–49.

against Orientalized perceptions of Muslim or Turkish women by playing with stereotypes:

> Deutsche Männer: Das ist ein Kapitel für sich. Ich werde mal offen reden: Sie halten sich ja für die Größten, wenn sie das schon nicht mehr über ihre Ottos denken. Da steht in den Statistiken, die Neger haben die größten. An so was glauben die, das ist ihre Bibel. Aber sie denken, sie wären die Besten im Bett. (Banu, 33, Barfrau [bartender]; ZKSt 51)
>
> [German men: that's another story. I'll speak openly: they think they're the greatest, if they don't think that about their willies any more. It says in the statistics that niggers have the largest ones. They believe in something like that, it's their Bible. But they think they're the best lovers.]

Banu's comment can be read in relation to what the *Kanaken* think of themselves: they consider themselves the better lovers in comparison with German men. The *Kanakas* seem to think the same. To some extent, the *Kanakas* are shown to support the exoticizing notion of the Turkish man as the better lover. However, this is also a form of opposition to the German mainstream, exemplified by German men, rather than a form of Orientalizing the *Kanaken* in the same way a German woman might do by praising a Turkish man's sexual abilities.

Banu also makes clear that most of the *Kanakas* grew up in a traditionally patriarchal society based on conservatively interpreted Islamic values. She notices that 'alle haben ihre Leiden, alle Frauen. Das ist nun mal ihr Schicksal. [...] Andere haben schon alles bestimmt für uns. Wir müssen es akzeptieren. [...] Die deutschen Frauen, sie sind nicht so wie wir. Sie lernen alles von klein auf' (Bonu, 33, Barfrau [bartender]; ZKSt 47–49) [all women suffer, all women. Well, this is their fate. [...] Others have already decided everything for us. We have to accept it. [...] German women aren't like us. They learn everything from an early age]. The notion of suffering is clearly connected to Muslim women and could be read as another example of Orientalist thinking, the assumption that Western women are more modern and self-confident and less likely to suffer than Muslim women. Banu shows that *Kanakas* are also dealing with stereotypes and prejudices. She, like most other *Kanakas*, does not deny that some of the stereotypes she and other *Kanakas*/*Kanaken* are exposed to are partly based on facts. The *Kanakas*' interaction with German women is not entirely based on rejection, which demonstrates the complicated nature of this relationship. It is this interaction as well as friction with their environment that determines the *Kanakas*' identity.

Zaimoğlu's *Kanakas* perform their role at the 'margins of society' individually and primarily through their empowering use of language. Their protest can only be effective if someone listens and responds to it. Özdamar, by contrast, does not overemphasize her marginal position but makes creative use of it without highlighting her difference from her surroundings. Her protagonist, too, uses her voice in public: she abandons the railway mission where she was stranded after leaving Ibni Abdullah's flat and actively enters into conversation with her own situation as a migrant: by talking to the distressed girl at the end of her linguistic journey, she recognizes herself as a 'Wörtersammlerin' (ÖMZ 48) ['collector of words' (ÖMT 57)], someone who, by collecting and then dealing with words that shape her (and Özdamar) as a migrant and transcultural writer, consciously interacts with her linguistic past, present and future (see Littler, 'Diasporic Identity', 229). Thus, through their interlocutors and narrator, Zaimoğlu and Özdamar raise a critical voice that is likely to reach and move people.

***

The fictional and semi-fictional Muslim women dealt with in this chapter engage in physical as well as metaphorical migration processes which are reflected in their use of language and their constructions of female identity. Özdamar, Zaimoğlu and Aboulela translate the interdependence of migration, language and identity into literature in distinct ways.

In *MutterZunge*, Özdamar connects migrancy to the creative reinvention of the self. Her protagonist tries to find connections between the various languages that surround her and create a path to her own language of the migrant writer. Özdamar thus depicts her protagonist's literal migration process as 'Migration auf stilistischer Ebene' (Konuk, 'Das Leben ist eine Karawanserei', 150) [migration on a stylistic level], a linguistic movement that refers not only to the protagonist herself but also to the language that she carries with her, Turkish. The protagonist's explorations demonstrate that linguistic as well as cultural homogeneity is neither desirable nor possible. Her search is a counter-reaction to Atatürk's language reform, and celebrates plurality and constant change as the condition of any migrant and any language. This seems to be possible only on neutral ground: Germany gives the protagonist the freedom to embark on her linguistic journey, which is reminiscent of Aboulela's characters who can only find the freedom to live their Muslim identity in the

West. Although part of Turkey's cultural and religious heritage was officially cut off, it forces its way back into people's consciousness, even if this — as in the protagonist's case — happens with a secular understanding. Thus, differences, heterogeneity and movements create identity — in fact identity is situated in movement (Konuk, *Identitäten im Prozeß*, 84). In *MutterZunge*, Özdamar reveals the process of creating a form of the German language that reflects her transcultural experiences by taking the detour of engaging with the interaction between Turkish and Arabic.

Something similar can be said of Zaimoğlu's *Kanakas*. Their *Kanaka Sprak* mirrors their struggle to find a position in Germany they feel comfortable with, a position that does not reduce them to 'the subservient Turkish girl' or 'the suffering Muslim woman'. Although Islam plays a subordinate role in the self-perceptions of most of the *Kanakas*, it is noticeable, how, similar to their male counterparts, religion filters through their lives, into their vocabulary and into their perceptions of concepts such as 'purity' and 'fate'. Yet it is above all their German environment that sees them as 'Muslims', especially since 9/11 (see Yıldız, 'Turkish Girls, Allah's Daughters', 465–81), and it is this outside perception they raise their voices against. By relating to their Muslim background in their verbal struggle, they may start subverting the image of the 'oppressed Muslim wife or daughter'.

However, neither Zaimoğlu nor Özdamar make it easy for their readers to consume their texts: Zaimoğlu does not provide glossaries for Turkish words, and neologisms in both writers' texts have to be interpreted by the readers. As writers, Özdamar and Zaimoğlu exercise power over their readers: their multicultural and multilingual audience is not provided with any explanations regarding the unusual use of language and become, as objects, part of the subversion process instead. Language becomes '[ein] Ort der Ambivalenz [und ...] Ort des Inauthentischen' (Konuk, 'Identitätssuche ist ein [sic!] private archäologische Graberei', 69) [a place of ambivalence and of the inauthentic] where clear-cut meanings are not the norm, but where redefinitions of established notions and ideas take place. Both writers address the question of language from a postcolonial perspective: language is reappropriated and partly alienated for the monolingual German reader who gains access to subject-matter rarely encountered in German-language writing before, and is forced to engage actively with Özdamar's and Zaimoğlu's issues.[62] As they seem to be less

62 For a detailed analysis of the various ways language issues are approached in postcolonial texts, see Ashcroft *et al.*, Chapter 2, 'Re-placing Language: Textual Strategies in Post-colonial Writing', 38–77.

concerned with accessibility, they can educate the German middle class who consume their books about (post-)migrant Muslim women's transcultural experiences and about their self-perceptions as Muslims. A German Turkish middle class has only slowly started to develop in Germany, and, sharing some of Zaimoğlu's and Özdamar's (post-)migratory experiences, they certainly do not need to be told what life as a 'different' German is like.

By contrast, Aboulela undergoes a different creative process when writing her novels. This author has a specifically religious agenda when approaching questions of Muslim female identity, which she expresses in the Western form of the novel, a genre which has the potential to reach many people.[63] She can minimise the possibility that readers might challenge her views on Islam: fictional characters speak in her texts, not the author Aboulela. As she said in an interview with Eissa: 'I am interested in writing about Islam not as an identity but going deeper and showing the state of mind and feelings of a Muslim who has faith. I also want to write fiction that follows Islamic logic' (para. 4 of 24). Her term 'Islamic logic' describes the way of living of her characters and their way of finding a path back to their Islamic roots, something which the writer experienced herself (interview with Sethi, para. 6 of 14). As Ferial J. Ghazoul explains, 'what makes her writing "Islamic" is not a religious correctness or didacticism. Rather, it is a certain narrative logic where faith and rituals become moving modes of living'.[64] On another level, Aboulela feels that '[t]he absence of Muslims from contemporary fiction, TV, radio etc. always makes them feel marginalized, as if they don't really exist in British society' (interview with Eissa, para. 9 of 24). The absence of Muslims in the media might have been an issue prior to the London July bombings in 2005; nowadays Muslims are more prominent in the media than ever before. However, they are usually not represented in a positive light, and Aboulela's fiction might contribute to a more differentiated picture of Muslims in British society.[65] Aboulela uses her personal

63 Aboulela has also written short stories published as *Coloured Lights*, new edn (Edinburgh: Polygon, 2005 [2001]). The stort story is not an exclusively Western genre, and Aboulela addresses similar issues discussed in her novels there. Aboulela's agenda can be detected in all of her work and is not a unique theme of her novels.

64 F. J. Ghazoul, 'Halal Fiction', *Al-Ahram Weekly Online*, no. 542, 12–18 July 2001, http://weekly.ahram.org.eg/2001/542/bo4.htm [accessed 28 June 2010] (para. 1 of 13).

65 However, Butt points out that Aboulela 'forgets that Muslims need to be ready for change in the form of cultural hybridization, too, by seeking some common ground in secular societies'; according to her, Muslims need to take

experiences of having rediscovered her religion in the West to foster her responsibility as a Muslim intellectual and an Islamic feminist to speak for and 'represent' the Other.[66]

Aboulela also addresses the notion of the 'margin' here: she aims to move Muslims from a marginal, usually negative position to a more central, positive one since they are part of British society. Yet she has a different attitude towards 'margins' from Özdamar and Zaimoğlu who apprehend their and their parotagonist's and interlocutors' marginal position as a position of redefined power and ultimate creativity.[67] In that respect, they are 'nomads' in the Deleuzian and Guattarian sense (Deleuze and Guattari, 547) and 'become' the writers they are by making creative use of their identity based on movement.

Unlike Zaimoğlu and Özdamar, who create forms of the German language that reflect their protagonists' and characters' transcultural experiences, Aboulela uses standard English. As a language that potentially reaches more people than her native language Arabic, English is the language of her work and living. The decision to employ standard English and not to let the various languages that constitute most formerly colonized writers' identities interact, that is, not to create a language that captures migratory experiences reminds us of another writer whose work has been discussed in this book:[68] V. S. Naipaul and his desire to become an 'English' writer. Aboulela too seems to follow an evangelical mission: she writes for Muslim and non-Muslim (British) people alike, that is, the middle classes who read novels. (The UK has had a Muslim middle class for longer than Germany, since post-war migration to the UK started earlier than in Germany.) As she has pointed out, she primarily wants

on more responsibility for a 'productive dialogue that can bridge the growing gulf between religious orthodoxy and secular cultures, between tradition and change, and above all between Islam and modernity' (178).

66 Cf. Spivak, 'Can the Subaltern Speak?', 288–89: 'To confront them is not to represent (*vertreten*) them but to learn to represent (*darstellen*) ourselves'. See also Cooper, 56.

67 For a classification of marginality, see R. Powell and J. Clarke, 'A Note on Marginality', in *Resistance Through Rituals*, ed. S. Hall and T. Jefferson, 223.

68 However, Cooper regards Aboulela's English as 'the English of migrant writers living in the West' (64); it is 'an English that absorbs traces of Arabic and is infused with Islam' (45). She does not analyse this English in great detail but, by focussing on everyday objects as 'part of Aboulela's, and by extension, her protagonist's spiritual mosaic' (54) in her analysis of *The Translator*, is able to state: 'Arabic sayings, meanings, word plays and names are solid signposts pointing to another culture and set of meanings, always invested in the minutiae of daily life' (52).

Muslims to 'relate and respond to what I'm writing' (interview with Eissa, para. 10 of 24).

Despite their differences in the innovativeness and radicality of their writing, the genre and form, all these writers portray or represent Muslim women as strong women who have become non-nostalgic and successful migrants and post-migrants. The writers emphasize choice as the determinant of Muslim femininity which they explore in interaction, even friction, with non-Muslims or Muslims with different perceptions of Islam. Thus, Özdamar, Zaimoğlu and Aboulela challenge the 'margins of society' and rectify the tale of the 'geschundene Suleika' [ill-treated Suleika].[69]

69 K. Yeşilada, '"Die geschundene Suleika": Das Eigenbild der Türkin in der deutschsprachigen Literatur türkischer Autorinnen', in *Interkulturelle Konfiguration*, ed. M. Howard, 95–114. See also Cheesman, *Novels of Turkish German Settlement*, 113–17.

Conclusion: Islam and its Audience

Since the reunification of Germany,[1] the first Gulf War, and particularly since 9/11, which is widely perceived as a political and cultural caesura, Muslim minorities have been forced to re-position, even justify themselves in a 'new world order'. Muslims have since been defined a visible minority under the Western gaze: their Muslim identity has reemerged as a battleground on which Western cultural and religious positions are reexamined.

This book has explored some literary reactions to these political and social developments from a primarily Muslim point of view. As I pointed out in my introduction, postcolonial criticism has largely overlooked the role of religion in postcolonial and post-migration societies (Malak, 17). My examples of English-language writing (as prototypical postcolonial) and German-language writing (as marginal postcolonial) highlight the creative potential of transcultural literature written in German without discounting the quintessentially postcolonial and transcultural literature written in English.

A comparative reading shows that the writers create different ideas of Islam through their characters, beyond Orientalist perceptions. Overall, religious modesty and 'purity' plays a more central role in British than in German Muslim writing which tends to understand Islam in primarily cultural terms. Many German Muslim writers promote transculturality as a form of the migrant writer's innovative mingling of various cultural and religious backgrounds and languages as a means to create the voice of migrants. British Muslim writers, by contrast, seem to regard Muslim identity principally in religious, less in cultural terms. This difference in defining Islam requires a reassessment of postcolonial criticism. In regard to religion,

1 For the impact of German unification on Turkish Muslims in Germany, see Helicke, 187–88.

transculturality has less currency in the examination of Islam in the British Muslim writing discussed here: being a British Muslim is shown to exclude non-Muslim influences that might fruitfully shape a multifaceted Muslim identity.

This observation leads me to conclude that the opposing perceptions of transculturality are the reason why Islam is more widely regarded as 'home' (a form of stability) in the British transcultural writing on Islam discussed here than in its German counterpart. An exception is the travel to the roots of Islam, the hajj, where the idea of community in the *umma* is celebrated but, as Ilija Trojanow emphasizes, a pilgrim's individuality is not dismissed. Movement actually implies transculturality, the mutual influencing of cultures which creates cultural 'impurity', something which the selected German transcultural writers reflect on more than the British ones. In this respect, they try to educate their German audience; with the exception of V. S. Naipaul who sets out to learn about Islam and to convey his newly acquired knowledge to his readership, the British writers in this book, by contrast, either mainly reflect on what is happening in Muslim communities in the UK in an entertaining way or reveal their evangelical mission. The slowly emerging German Turkish middle class, of which the writers in this book are part, has – unlike the longer established ethnically non-British middle class – only recently grasped the potential to make their German environment aware of a German Turkish identity beyond that of the *Gastarbeiter*. It seems that this enterprise may succeed by reflecting on religious and cultural 'impurities' creatively and by challenging simplistic identities of both 'foreigners' and Germans.

Notions of religious and cultural 'purity' come particularly to the fore in terms of language. The English-language texts examined in this study do not reveal a form of *english* (as in a number of former postcolonial texts) but are written in standard English.[2] A stylistic interaction between various languages (for both the writer and their characters) rarely happens in British Muslim writing of the 1990s and early 2000s, which has left the linguistic and textual innovations of earlier English-language postcolonial literature behind. Ashcroft *et al.* discuss those referring to the work of, for example, Gabriel Okara (*The Voice*, 1964), Ngũgĩ wa Thiong'o (*A Grain of Wheat*, 1967) and Michael Anthony ('Sandra Street', 1973) (38–115).[3] By contrast, many German

2 Ashcroft *et al.*, 8: 'english which the language has become in post-colonial countries'. I coin the term 'german' in analogy to Ashcroft *et al.*'s term.

3 G. Okara, *The Voice* (London: Heinemann, 1970 [1964]); Ngũgĩ wa Thiong'o, *A Grain of Wheat* (London: Heinemann, 1967); M. Anthony, 'Sandra Street', in *Cricket in the Road* (London: Heinemann, 1973), 9–18.

transcultural writers create a form of postcolonial *german* to capture the experiences of migrants and post-migrants. This is where German transcultural writing is at its most self-aware and self-confident: it is deliberately different, but also part of German literature. Through their innovative use of language, German transcultural writers question and redefine the idea of a homogeneous German language and literature. Their linguistic innovations are a conscious reaction against the *in-between* arguing instead for the productive interactions of various cultures that make up their and many other (post-)migrants' identities. Some British Muslim writers, however, (for instance, Leila Aboulela) emphasize the *in-between* of the Muslim who has to take sides, choosing either Islam or the West, religion or secularism. This is where the limits of British transcultural writing as it is discussed in this book are revealed most explicitly: this literature does not seem to promote its transcultural element or to overcome consciously the clash between intolerant secularism and self-responsible religiosity as much as its German counterpart.

Islam is the subject of (cultural) translation in the transcultural texts discussed here; this is related to the performance of Muslim identities (as migrants, travellers, converts, hajjis, cultural or devout Muslims) and gender. The communication between cultures, languages and religions, and between a migrant's or traveller's heritage and present existence seems more acute when moving to a new country; when migrants, and post-migrants in particular, have arrived translation becomes an act of self-positioning in an environment that is no longer new, and a challenge to notions of 'centre' and 'margin'. (Again, the German Muslim writers are more innovative and creative here in stylistic and linguistic terms.) Cultural translation in these texts reveals estrangement from previous generations and women emerge as the more successful migrants. The female characters in the texts deal with their migratory experiences more consciously. They act as translators, that is, they know how to tackle cultural differences to their advantage. It seems that the writers have a particular interest in (post-)migrant women. I suggest that this interest is based on a general mass media image of Muslim women as the 'losers' of Islam. Many Muslim writers prove that this does not have to be the case: their characters raise their voices and shape their lives independently. With their literary representations of Muslim women these writers challenge and criticize the static perceptions of Islam supported by the mass media.

These concerns (and writers' interests) are also reflected in the choice of genre. German transcultural writers tend to write semi-fiction, whereas we find more fiction in British transcultural writing. The choice of genre may be related to a degree of freedom which German Muslim writers enjoy: they do not need to 'fit into' a canon (many critics still do not read German transcultural writing as part of German literature). The innovative side of German transcultural writers captures their audience's attention effectively (the unusualness of their writing remains in people's minds) and they can leave their mark as educated German Turkish intellectuals. British Muslim writers also capture the attention of their readership, but mainly through the stories they are telling rather than radical style: *Brick Lane,* for instance, was shortlisted for the Man Booker Prize for Fiction in 2003. It appears that the greater concern with subject matter rather than with groundbreaking style is related to the fact that multiculturalism has been in British people's minds longer; art and literature have long contributed to multicultural concerns. The educated British Muslim middle class does not need to struggle for a place in society and – by extension – English literature any more, at least not as assertively (that is, stylistically creatively) as the developing German Turkish middle class and its writers.

With their different relationship to their audience, German transcultural writers make explicit that their writing goes beyond a *Third Space*: they deal with postcolonial concepts such as the relocation of language, hybridity, the relationship between self and Other more subversively and creatively than their British counterparts and thus challenge postcolonial criticism from its margins.

I see the different perceptions of transculturality as religious and cultural 'impurity' primarily as the result of the different points in recent history when British and German Muslim writers have started to engage explicitly with Islam. In the 1990s, British Muslims were increasingly faced with their identity as *Muslims*. This started with the 'Rushdie affair' in 1988. By contrast, it is only since 9/11 that more and more German Muslim writers have started to address Islamic issues such as the 'purity' of the faith as a consequence of an increasing public demand for the positioning of Muslims in the West. It is interesting then to point out that the investigation of cultural 'impurity' (which entails stylistic and linguistic innovations) has become a topic in more recent literature by British, and not German, Muslims, and to ask why this may be the case. Taking a closer look at examples of more recent literary perceptions of Islam and the different stylistic approaches to them will reveal not only a shift in terms of subject-matter and style but also differences in popularity within European transcultural writing. The still increasing interest in

Islam remains a powerful tool for defining positions of the self and the Other.

Issues of popularity are significant when discussing transcultural literature. I suggested that the German transcultural texts addressed in this book have mainly attracted academic interest, whereas their English-language counterparts were more broadly successful. Reasons given for this include the more challenging style of the German publications and the longer-established visibility of Muslims in the UK and their further-reaching establishment of a middle class. Yet, since 9/11, the German texts have become increasingly popular,[4] reflecting the growing demand in the West for 'authentic' Muslim voices: 'authentic' Muslims have been asked to comment on migration, multiculturalism and supposed problems related to them, or on the noticeable Islamic revival in both Europe and Muslim countries.[5] Many Muslim writers are also public figures and have taken up journalistic work. For example: Zafer Şenocak is one of the most prominent German Turkish intellectuals, poets, novelists and essayists.[6] Recently, he has identified a crisis within Islam as it is overlooking its past which was more open to other cultural influences. Şenocak suggests that contemporary Muslims should go back to their roots and cultural heritage in order to find 'Spielräume für Mehrdeutigkeit' [spaces for ambiguity] to be explored and used for the dialogue with non-Muslims.[7]

4 Notice their number of editions.

5 Jim Jordan also discusses the issue of 'the representative role (or not) of the diasporic writer' in 'Identity, Irony and Denial: Navid Kermani's *Kurzmitteilung*, in *Aesthetics and Politics in Modern German Culture: Festschrift in Honour of Rhys W. Williams*, ed. B. Haines, S. Parker and C. Riordan (Oxford: Peter Lang, 2010), 166. He continues: 'Diasporic writers have re-emerged as convenient mediators to a public which fails to grasp why such events [of 9/11] have been visited on them'. His article also offers an insightful analysis of Navid Kermani's *Kurzmitteilung*, which is briefly discussed below.

6 For a discussion of 'Muslim intellectual voices', that is, 'writers who had previously been perceived as migrant-German writers' but who now find themselves 'in a new role as public Muslims' (183), see K. E. Yeşilada, 'Dialogues with Islam in the Writing of (Turkish-)German Intellectuals: A Historical Turn?', in *Encounters with Islam in German Literature and Culture*, ed. J. Hodkinson and J. Morrison, 181–203. See also M. Shafi, 'Constructions of Islam: Select Voices from Germany and the Netherlands', in *Religion and Identity in Germany Today: Doubters, Believers, Seekers in Literature and Film*, ed. J. Preece *et al.*, Leeds-Swansea Colloquia on Contemporary German Literature, 2 (Oxford and Berne: Peter Lang, 2010), esp. 165–69.

7 Z. Şenocak, 'Glaube und Krise' and 'Spielräume für Mehrdeutigkeit I: Paradigmen für ein Gespräch mit den Muslimen', in *Das Land hinter den*

Being of 'special status', some transcultural writers make 'strategische[n] Gebrauch von [ihrer] Fremdheit' [strategic use of [their] foreignness].[8] This 'strategy' can be read as both a genuine creative interaction with their particular cultural heritage or as a selling-point which they effectively employ to catch readers' attention (and sometimes to educate them). Ilija Trojanow attracted much interest that way with his widely perceived novel *Der Weltensammler* [*The Collector of Worlds*] (2006). The book can be regarded as his self-stylization as cosmopolitan Muslim via Sir Richard Francis Burton, whose story Trojanow tells in this text.[9] Burton seems to have the 'cultural empathy' the writer misses in V. S. Naipaul, hence Trojanow can comment on things Muslim in a more positive light through his protagonist. (However, the chapter on Arabia, Burton's hajj, has — interestingly — not been received as enthusiastically as the chapters on British India and East Africa [Trojanow in unpublished interview]). Yet it seems that by conflating himself with Burton to some extent Trojanow loses distance to what he describes and runs the risk of glorifying 'transculturality'. We need to ask therefore whether Trojanow uses his transcultural experiences, which come across predominantly as positive, to market his book.[10]

Feridun Zaimoğlu's work can be seen in a similar light. He developed from a relatively unknown writer who was nonetheless highly acclaimed by critics, to a writer who enjoys great success.[11]

Buchstaben: Deutschland und der Islam im Umbruch (Munich: Babel Verlag Tulay, 2006), 91–93, 45–47. Anglo-American critics such as Ziauddin Sardar with his aforementioned *Desperately Seeking Paradise: Journeys of a Sceptical Muslim* should also be mentioned in this context.

8 H. Uerlings, *'Ich bin von niedriger Rasse': (Post-)Kolonialismus und Geschlechterdifferenz in deutscher Literatur* (Cologne: Böhlau, 2006), 9.

9 Shortly after *Der Weltensammler,* Trojanow published a personal journey following Burton's footsteps and intertwining it with his own biography: *Nomade auf vier Kontinenten: Auf den Spuren von Sir Richard Francis Burton.*

10 These last observations on Trojanow's *Weltensammler* are based on an unpublished paper delivered by Michaela Holdenried, '"Weltensammeln" — ein neues Hobby für Literaten und Literaturwissenschaft?', at the XII. Congress of the International Association for Germanic Studies, 'Vielfalt und Einheit der Germanistik weltweit' (University of Warsaw, 30 July–7 August 2010). See Julian Preece's analysis of *Der Weltensammler,* also with reference to *Zu den Heiligen Quellen des Islam* as a — in comparison — 'flat' description of the hajj (220–21), in 'Faking the Hadj? Richard Burton Slips between Lines in Ilija Trojanow's *Der Weltensammler*', in *Religion and Identity in Germany Today: Doubters, Believers, Seekers in Literature and Film,* ed. J. Preece *et al.*, 211–25.

11 Exemplified by the literary prizes Zaimoğlu has been awarded over the past years, such as the Hebbel Prize (2002), the Prize of the Jury at the Ingeborg

Zaimoğlu, who, of all the writers discussed in this study, has engaged with Muslim issues most actively in recent years, is no longer seen as a radical writer (as a — in his own terminology — *Kanake*) but as an 'expert' on questions relating to Muslims living in Germany.[12] This transformation is the result of Zaimoğlu's self-stylization: he now comes across as a post-migrant intellectual, and this is a marketable figure. Incidentally, he avows himself a Muslim openly now which is significant in this time of general hostility or uneasiness towards Islam.[13] This is also reflected in his post-*Kanak Sprak* writing. Having largely overlooked devout Muslim characters in his work until the early 2000s, he engages more critically with Islam now.[14] For him, Islam has more distinctly religious and less cultural significance in the lives of young German Turks in the early 2000s than in the 1990s.[15]

Has Islam become a fashion item? Zaimoğlu claims to have always been a believer;[16] however, it is conspicuous that he rarely talked about his belief in public prior to the publication of his novel *Leyla* in 2006 (see *Cheesman, Novels of Turkish German Settlement,*

Bachmann Competition in Klagenfurt (2003) and the Adelbert von Chamisso Prize (2005). In 2005, he was a fellow at the Deutsche Akademie Rom Villa Massimo.

12 For example, Zaimoğlu was asked to participate in the 'Deutsche Islam Konferenz (DIK)', which aims to evaluate the interaction between Muslims and the non-Muslim German population, www.bmi.bund.de/cln_165/DE/Themen/PolitikGesellschaft/DtIslamKonferenz/dtislamkonferenz_node.html [accessed 28 June 2010]).

13 Zaimoğlu in an interview with *Islamische Zeitung*. However, in a recent discussion broadcast on NDR Kultur on the same topic he claims the opposite ('Gespräch zu *Schwarze Jungfrauen*').

14 For example F. Zaimoğlu, 'Gottes Krieger' [God's Warrior], in *Zwölf Gramm Glück: Erzählungen* [*Twelve Grams of Happiness: Stories*], 2nd edn (Cologne: Kiepenheuer & Witsch, 2006 [2004]), 122–56.

15 For further details on 'Gottes Krieger', see Littler 'Intimacies Both Sacred and Profane', 230–32, and 'Profane und religiöse Intensitäten', 150–54; Cheesman, *Novels of Turkish German Settlement*, 78–79; and in comparison to *Kanak Sprak*, see F. Matthes, 'Of *Kanaken* and *Gottes Krieger*: Religion and Sexuality among Feridun Zaimoğlu's Young Muslim Men', in *Edinburgh German Yearbook*, 2: *Masculinities in German Culture*, ed. S. Colvin and P. Davies (Rochester, NY: Camden House, 2008), 250–61.

16 Zaimoğlu has mentioned his religious attitude in various interviews he has given since the publication of *Leyla*. For example, in an interview at the Leipzig book fair (March 2006), he regrets a 'neue[n] Bekenntniszwang' [new need to confess one's faith] imposed by post-9/11 society. He says that he is 'gläubig, aber nicht religiös' [believing, yet not religious] (in 'Bitte Bodenhaftung!', *ZEIT-online*, 4/2006, podcast www.zeit.de/online/2006/41/Buchmesse-Zaimoglu [accessed 28 June 2010]).

75–76),[17] which was the turning-point in his career as a 'serious' writer.[18] This is also reflected in his treatment of religion as a private affair, which is how the West tends to perceive religion, and to devoutness in his latest two novels *Liebesbrand* [*Love Fire*] (2008) and *Hinterland* (2009),[19] both of which are influenced by his perception of German Romanticism. He claims now that this engagement with religion can also be detected in earlier texts such as *Kanak Sprak* and *Koppstoff*.[20] More noticeably, Zaimoğlu has moved from stylistic innovation to traditional narrative.[21] He now avoids the kind of provocative confrontation he enjoyed as a *Kanake*. He has also managed to shift successfully his own experiences of his (and his parents') marginality to the attention of the 'centre': *Kanak Sprak* and *Koppstoff* were written more than ten years ago and at that time Zaimoğlu shook German literature with the creation of these texts. Nowadays, his impulse to struggle has calmed down to a great extent, or rather, he struggles in commercial terms by serving the public's taste: the mainstream audience seems to nourish a voyeuristic interest in the tale of 'the suffering Muslim woman' which the publishing industry supports.[22]

17 F. Zaimoğlu, *Leyla: Roman*, 2nd edn (Cologne: Kiepenheuer & Witsch, 2006). The allegation that Zaimoğlu had plagiarized sections from Özdamar's *Das Leben ist eine Karawanserei* in *Leyla* and the writers' dispute over this issue are not relevant for my discussion of their work. For more information and an overview over this controversy with reference to reactions in the press, see Cheesman, *Novels of Turkish German Settlement*, 190–94. For an example of such an article, see Z. Şenocak, 'Authentische Türkinnen: Der Streit zwischen Feridun Zaimoglu und Emine Sevgi Özdamar zeigt, wie sehr die so genannte Migrantenliteratur in der biographischen Falle sitzt. Sie spielt das Spiel der Typisierung mit', *Die Tageszeitung*, 10/11 June 2006, 13.

18 Schmidt has also observed this, paying particular attention to the question of authorship (198).

19 F. Zaimoğlu, *Liebesbrand: Roman* (Cologne: Kiepenheuer & Witsch, 2008); *Hinterland: Roman* (Cologne: Kiepenheuer & Witsch, 2009).

20 Zaimoğlu in discussion after the reading of *Liebesbrand* at Swansea University on 26 June 2008, www.swan.ac.uk/german/Video/#Zaimoglu [accessed 28 June 2010]. See also Tom Cheesman's unpublished paper 'Feridun Zaimoğlu on Religion' given at the conference 'Religion in Contemporary German Culture' (Swansea University, 9–11 July 2008).

21 Similarly, Selim Özdoğan developed from a rebellious writer to a 'serious' writer with a conventional subject matter and style in his novel *Die Tochter des Schmieds* [*The Smith's Daughter*] (Berlin: Aufbau, 2005). For a comparison between *Leyla* and *Die Tochter des Schmieds*, see Cheesman, *Novels of Turkish German Settlement*, 184–90.

22 The genre of (formerly) suffering Muslim women's 'autobiographies' is still in the hands of less prestigious publishing houses such as Ullstein or Goldmann. A number of them are translations, mainly from the French. Two examples

It is difficult to subvert fixed public views on Islam; yet texts such as *Leyla* do not contribute to the questioning of set opinions.[23]

Are 'Mißtöne' (*Kanak Sprak* subtitle) [dissonances] out of fashion or are they no longer necessary? This is probably not the case, but the 'margins' have largely been silenced again — or have silenced themselves and moved to the 'centre'. We should not call for a 'different' literature for its 'exotic' value, but subversive challenges to German literature are hardly audible right now. Yet there might be an exception: Imran Ayata's short stories *Hürriyet Love Express* (2005).[24] Ayata lends his characters the identities of *Kanaken*.[25] His stories' quality and relevance for the youngest generation of German Turks is questionable, however. The decreasing interest in 'radical difference' may also be a sign of an oversaturation of *Kanak*-like stories and a demand for more traditional genres such as Zaimoğlu's recent novels.[26]

Yet Zaimoğlu has been radical in a different genre, namely in his texts for the stage, which appears as a more innovative space for disenfranchized voices than prose. Despite being a commissioned work, *Schwarze Jungfrauen* [*Black Virgins*] (world premiere March 2006, Hebbel-Theater, Berlin) is Zaimoğlu's and his co-author Günter

should suffice: Ayşe, *Mich hat keiner gefragt: Zur Ehe gezwungen — eine Türkin in Deutschland erzählt* [*Nobody Asked Me: Forced to Marry — A Turkish Woman in Germany Talks*] , ed. R. Eder (Munich: Blanvalet, 2005), and C. R. Egbene, *Hinter goldenen Gittern: Ich wurde im Harem geboren* [*Behind Golden Bars: I Was Born in a Harem*] (Munich: Ullstein, 2005 [2001]), the latter published in its 9th edition, thus showing the popularity of these 'autobiographies'.

23 Cheesman mentions the '"mainstreaming" of Turkish German fiction', specifically referring to Özdoğan's *Die Tochter des Schmieds* and Zaimoğlu's *Leyla*, in his conclusion to *Novels of Turkish German Settlement* (185). Norbert Mecklenburg also discusses the significance of the market, but in relation to the quality of earlier migrant writing and comedy ('Eingrenzung, Ausgrenzung, Grenzüberschreitung: Grundprobleme deutscher Literatur von Minderheiten', in *Die andere deutsche Literatur: Istanbuler Vorträge*, ed. M. Durzak and N. Kuruyazıcı with the assistance of C. Şenöz Ayata, 27).

24 I. Ayata, *Hürriyet Love Express: Storys* (Cologne: Kiepenheuer & Witsch, 2005).

25 Ayata in '"Ich bin Teil der deutschen Literatur, so deutsch wie Kafka": Ist Fremd-Sein ein Problem, ein Thema oder ein Markt-Vorteil? Vier nicht ganz deutsche Autoren — Terézia Mora, Imran Ayata, Wladimir Kaminer und Navid Kermani — im Literaturen-Gespräch', *Literaturen*, 4/2005, 29.

26 A similarly traditionally narrated novel is Rafik Schami's novel *Die dunkle Seite der Liebe* (Munich: Deutscher Taschenbuchverlag, 2006 [2004]), translated as *The Dark Side of Love*, trans. A. Bell (London: Arabia, 2009). It tells his pre-story of immigration from Syria to Germany.

Senkel's literary answer to the political and societal debate on openly lived Islam in Germany.[27] Like *Koppstoff* — or the play *Almanya* (world premiere March 2004, Theater im Depot, Dortmund), which is loosely based on these texts — the Muslim women's monologues in the play rest upon supposedly authentic interviews with Muslim women who Zaimoğlu calls 'Neo-Muslima'.[28] They are angry, provocative and eloquent. As in *Koppstoff*, Zaimoğlu provides us with what he alleges is an inside view into the lives of female Muslims.[29]

Navid Kermani's novel *Kurzmitteilung* [*Short Message*] (2007) should also be mentioned in this context.[30] *Kurzmitteilung*, which is set in the aftermath of the London suicide bomb attacks on 7 July 2005, focuses on a German Iranian event manager who struggles between wanting to be true to his Shiite Iranian roots and using his 'exotic' value, both commercially and interpersonally, only to dismiss Islam altogether (he turns to scientology). Kermani, born in Germany of Iranian parentage, is a scholar of Islamic Studies as well as a writer. He has engaged with Islam (and religion generally) in his writing for some time.[31] Yet it is particularly his scholarly, and therefore academically more critical engagement with Islam, but also to some extent his religious upbringing, that have enabled him to offer a more differentiated view of Islam as object of (Christian) Western counter-identification —most recently in *Wer ist wir? Deutschland und seine Muslime* [*Who is We? Germany and its Muslims*] (2009)[32] — than many German-language writers of Muslim faith who have 'discovered' Islam since 9/11. Kermani's novel explores Western cultural and religious identification in relation to Islam after 9/11 and 7/7 critically,

27 F. Zaimoğlu and G. Senkel, *Schwarze Jungfrauen*, Stückabdruck, *Theater Heute*, 5 (2006), 46–55.

28 In an interview with Vera Gaserow, Zaimoğlu even proclaims an 'ethno-avantgarde', which mainly consists of 'junge selbstbewusste Frauen, die ihren Glauben mit großer Normalität vertreten' [young self-confident women who advocate their faith in the most natural way] ('Es gibt eine Ethno-Avantgarde', *Frankfurter Rundschau*, 2 May 2007, www.fr-online.de/_inc/globals/print.php?sid=3c2e2cb255acc9acf215774a0cal.html, URL no longer available (para. 15 of 21).

29 For further analysis of *Schwarze Jungfrauen* and the development of Zaimoğlu's writing on Islam, see F. Matthes, '"Authentic" Muslim Voices? Feridun Zaimoğlu's *Schwarze Jungfrauen*', in *Religion and Identity in Germany Today: Doubters, Believers, Seekers in Literature and Film*, ed. J. Preece *et al.*

30 N. Kermani, *Kurzmitteilung: Roman* (Zurich: Ammann, 2007).

31 See N. Kermani, *40 Leben* [*40 Lives*] (Zurich: Ammann, 2004); *Du sollst* [*You Shall*] (Zurich: Ammann, 2005).

32 N. Kermani, *Wer ist wir? Deutschland und seine Muslime* (Munich: Beck, 2009).

and in comparison to many other recent German-language texts on Islam, in a most sophisticated fashion.[33]

In recent publications by British transcultural writers of the mid-2000s a more innovative side can be detected than in much current German post-migration writing. These recent publications have been commercially less successful than mainstream novels such as *Brick Lane,* but they have been pushing linguistic boundaries in a fashion observed for instance in *Kanak Sprak* or Emine Sevgi Özdamar's German-language writing of the 1990s. Examples are Suhayl Saadi's *Psychoraag* (2004) and Gautam Malkani's *Londonstani* (2006). One explanation for the recent growth of linguistically innovative English-language writing might be a further removal from the experience of Empire: these writers seem to feel more liberated from the constraints of language than their parents and no longer have to prove that they are 'properly' British.

Saadi's novel *Psychoraag* is written from the perspective of a Scottish Muslim, Zaf, whose parents came from Pakistan.[34] This is also an experience Saadi discusses in his essays, speeches, poetry and short stories:[35] the notion of identity, of being Scottish and Muslim, is seen as a question of choice. Saadi defines himself as a Scottish writer.[36] This puts him in critical opposition to mainstream post-migrant writers from London many of whom have enjoyed an Oxbridge education and who write in standard English, whilst clearly keeping an eye on the market.[37] *Psychoraag* is a postcolonial and post-migrant novel in line with texts discussed in this book: it thematizes migration and its consequences for the migrants' children, which includes a consideration of generational issues; it subverts language by combining Punjabi, Arabic, standard English and Glaswegian dialect, which necessitates a glossary for the monolingual reader.[38]

33 For further analysis of *Kurzmitteilung,* see F. Matthes, 'Islam in the West: Perceptions and Self-Perceptions of Muslims in Navid Kermani's *Kurzmitteilung*', *German Life and Letters,* 64.2 (April 2011), 305–16.

34 S. Saadi, *Psychoraag* (Edinburgh: CHROMA, 2005 [2004]).

35 See, for example, Saadi's collection of short stories *The Burning Mirror* (Edinburgh: Polygon, 2000 [2003 printing]).

36 S. Saadi, 'Being Scottish', http://sarmed.netfirms.com/suhayl/NEW/ articles_ essays/being_ scottish/index.htm [accessed 28 June 2010] (5 para.).

37 S. Saadi, 'Psychoraag: An Interview', with N. Mitchell, www. spikemagazine. com?0406-suhayl-saadi-psychoraag-interview.php [accessed 28 June 2010] (para. 29–31 of 43).

38 Saadi reappropriates a technique typically employed by early postcolonial writers such as Chinua Achebe here. In *The Empire Writes Back,* Ashcroft *et al.* point out that 'such glosses foreground the continual reality of cultural distance'

Saadi's choice of language demonstrates his engagement with the various sides of his identity as an English-language writer with a Scottish Muslim identity.

Saadi's work focuses on borders and breakages, on the transitional space between Lahore and Glasgow, between his characters' ancestors and their present. This entails an exploration of their and their parents' Indo-Pakistani history, culture and religion in relation to their current situation which has been shaped by (post-)migratory experiences: the partition of India and Pakistan in 1947 and the ongoing conflict in Kashmir have intensified the experience of being a migrant, and left younger generations with a difficult inheritance. Saadi reveals close links between migration and family, their dreams and disappointments, their values and the reality they had to face when arriving in a new country. Furthermore, the recurring theme of relationships to women in connection with 'race' makes the reader aware of identity issues on a personal level. The fact that the narrator of *Psychoraag* refers to Scotland with its Latin/Gaelic name, 'Alba, the land of whiteness' (213), makes the challenges of an 'other' Scottish identity apparent. 'Race' becomes part of performativity, of performing one's identity. It is this interaction between place, race and language in his work that shapes Saadi's self-portrayal as a Scottish Muslim writer.

Gautam Malkani's debut novel *Londonstani* also plays with the interaction of place, race and language.[39] With its radical language and focus on masculinity, this text is reminiscent of Zaimoğlu's radical and innovative texts of the mid-1990s. Similarly to *Kanak Sprak*, Gautami's novel puts young men from the margins of society at its centre. Their identity is an urban one; the negotiation of their masculinity takes place in gangs whose members are strongly influenced by consumerism, which includes the trading and consumption of women like a commodity or a status symbol. Malkani too gives his characters a strong, radical language and, by contrast to Kureishi, lets them reappropriate the name 'Paki' (the novel's first section is entitled 'Paki'); like in *Kanak Sprak*, this is a label of pride. Once more language turns out to be an invaluable tool to capture the extreme mindsets of young, radical men. At the beginning of the twenty-first century, their religious identity (Muslim, Hindu and Sikh) has taken on a different meaning from the late 1980s and early 1990s: it serves

(61). In his text, Saadi also examines a void between cultures, yet turns this void into a significant moulder of his Scottish Muslim identity.

39 G. Malkani, *Londonstani* (London: Fourth Estate, 2006).

as a means of gaining acceptance among peers or elders rather than of violent struggle.

The question is how far Malkani's novel is a mainstream text. Saadi has called it a 'multicultural cult novel'.[40] He continues: 'Too often the latest groovy writer of South Asian origin comes to be worshipped by the (white) gatekeepers of the literary salons as a (bogus) cipher for colonial redemption' (para. 12). Like many of the English transcultural texts discussed in this book, *Londonstani* has enjoyed popularity among the wider reading public. This may suggest the largely white British middle-class readers' conscious, or, as Saadi suggests, self-righteous engagement with matters relating to 'multiculturalism', which ultimately are the result of British colonialism. This interest is, at least partly, steered by the publishing industry who decides what to bring on the market and which writers to hype. Malkani's innovative, though accessible writing style contributes to the commercialization of a specific consequence of colonialism for a white British middle-class: ethnicity has become a subculture and continues to change urban landscapes. *Londonstani* is an example of how the Other remains a marketable object for a mainstream culture that requires ethnical, cultural and religious differences as mirrors for its self-assertion.

These observations lead me to conclude that there is still mainly a voyeuristic interest in Muslim issues, which suggests that easily accessible styles and non-challenging contents make literature about Islam popular.[41] This is also underlined by the way in which post-migrant texts are discussed in the media: the vocabulary ('Oriental', 'colourful', etc.) in literary supplements is proof of a reluctance to accept what is now a transcultural reality.[42] One might think

40 S. Saadi, 'A Taste of Gangsta Sikh: *Londonstani*, by Gautam Malkani', *Independent*, 21 April 2006, www.independent.co.uk/arts-entertainment/books/reviews/londonstani-by-gautam-malkani-474920.html [accessed 28 June 2010] (para. 11 of 12).

41 We should not forget the immense popularity of films with a multicultural and/or Muslim subject matter. The scope of this book does not allow me to go into detail here. Some of my texts have been turned into films, thus capturing an audience that might not receive these texts otherwise: *Kanak Attack* (2000) based on Zaimoğlu's novel *Abschaum* (1997), and *My Son the Fanatic* (1997) based on Hanif Kureishi's short story of the same title. *Brick Lane*, whose filming has caused much controversy, has also been turned into a film (see R. Lea and P. Lewis, 'Local Protests over Brick Lane Film', *Guardian*, 17 July 2006, www.guardian.co.uk/books/2006/jul/17/film.uk [accessed 28 June 2010] (14 para.).

42 Yasemin Dayıoğlu-Yücel has analyzed Orientalizing reviews in the section '"Tausendundeine Geschichten: Die *Karawanserei* im Spiegel der Presse', in *Von der Gastarbeit zur Identitätsarbeit: Integritätsverhandlungen in türkisch-deutschen*

that the current publishing strategies meet public taste. It could, however, be the case that, on the contrary, they largely determine the audience's interests. This can also have positive effects: for example, Kiepenheuer & Witsch re-published Özdamar's texts *Das Leben ist eine Karawanserei, Die Brücke vom Goldenen Horn* and *Seltsame Sterne starren zur Erde* in one volume as *Sonne auf halbem Weg: Die Istanbul-Berlin-Trilogie* [*Sun Halfway: The Istanbul-Berlin Trilogy*] in 2006.[43] With this publication, Özdamar is now likely to be perceived beyond academia and a literary elite (she has won numerous prizes after all).[44] However, the trilogy-title is clearly designed for the market: it guides the reader into believing that Özdamar's protagonists will explore the *in-between* of migrants between Turkey and Germany, a position which the writer challenges.[45] That shows that the idea of separate cultures continues to determine the public's view on (post-) migrants, an attitude which is no longer suitable in a transcultural reality.

It follows that the question of the definition of the self in the light of the Other in a multicultural society is still widely relevant: the Other remains our main point of identification, and Islam is the quintessential Other in a post-9/11 Western world. Yet most of the writers discussed in this book make clear that — as Jamal Tuschick notices — 'Migration bleibt ein Dauerzustand' [migration remains a constant state].[46] They highlight the changing nature of Islam and its believers, its trans-European outlook, and thus keep challenging the West's perceptions of Islam, a religion which is visibly shaping the face of Europe more than ever.

Texten von Şenocak, Özdamar, Ağaoğlu und der Online Community vabee! (Göttingen: Universitätsverlag Göttingen, 2005), 28–33.

43 E. S. Özdamar, *Sonne auf halbem Weg: Die Istanbul-Berlin-Trilogie* (Cologne: Kiepenheuer & Witsch, 2006).

44 For example, Ingeborg Bachmann Prize (1991), Adelbert von Chamisso Prize (1999), Kleist Prize (2004).

45 Another example of a republication which meets a public post-9/11 interest in Islam is Kathleen Jamie's *Among Muslims: Meetings at the Frontiers of Pakistan* (London: Sort of Books, 2002 [2003 printing]). It was originally published as *The Golden Peak* (London: Virago, 1992). The new title reminds the reader of V. S. Naipaul's *Among the Believers*, thus promising an inside view into 'real' Muslim life, which, as we have seen, is not possible for most Western travel writers.

46 J. Tuschick, 'Nachwort von Jamal Tuschik: Träger von Zukunftsinformationen', in *Morgen Land: Neueste deutsche Literatur*, ed. J. Tuschick (Frankfurt a.M.: Fischer Taschenbuch Verlag, 2000), 290.

Bibliography

Aboulela, Leila, *The Translator*, new edn (Edinburgh: Polygon, 2005 [1999])

—, *Coloured Lights*, new edn (Edinburgh: Polygon, 2005 [2001])

—, *Minaret* (London: Bloomsbury, 2005)

Adelson, Leslie A., 'Against Between: A Manifesto', in *Zafer Şenocak*, ed. Tom Cheesman and Karin E. Yeşilada (Cardiff: University of Wales Press, 2003), 130–43

—, *The Turkish Turn in Contemporary German Literature: Toward a New Critical Grammar of Migration* (New York: Palgrave Macmillan, 2005)

Ahmad, Aijaz, *In Theory: Classes, Nations, Literatures* (London: Verso, 1994 [1992])

Ahmed, Leila, *Women and Gender in Islam: Historical Roots of a Modern Debate* (New Haven, CT: Yale University Press, 1992)

Ahrends, Maike, *Kaza Gecirmek: Having Accidents in Life-Identity Constructions Between Cultures: The Prose Texts by Aysel Özakin, Renan Demirkan, and Emine Sevgi Özdamar* (Ann Arbor, MI: UMI Dissertation Services, 2000) (= doctoral thesis, University of Michigan, 1999)

Akhtar, Shabbir, *Be Careful with Muhammad! The Salman Rushdie Affair* (London: Bellew, 1989)

Ali, Monica, *Brick Lane* (London: Black Swan, 2004 [2003])

Anderson, Benedict, *Imagined Communities: Reflections on the Origin and Spread of Nationalism*, rev. and extended edn (London: Verso, 1991 [1983])

Anthony, Michael, 'Sandra Street', in *Cricket in the Road* (London: Heinemann, 1973), 9–18

Ashcroft, Bill, and Pal Ahluwalia, *Edward Said: The Paradox of Identity* (London: Routledge, 1999)

Ashcroft, Bill, *et al.*, *The Empire Writes Back: Theory and Practice in Post-Colonial Literatures* (London: Routledge, 1989 [2001 printing])

Atasoy, Yildiz, *Turkey, Islamism and Democracy: Transition and Globalization in a Muslim State* (London: I. B.Tauris, 2005)

Ayata, Imran, *Hürriyet Love Express: Storys* (Cologne: Kiepenheuer & Witsch, 2005)

Ayşe, *Mich hat keiner gefragt: Zur Ehe gezwungen — eine Türkin in Deutschland erzählt*, ed. Renate Eder (Munich: Blanvalet, 2005)

Bachmann-Medick, Doris, 'Einleitung', in *Kultur als Text: Die anthropologische Wende in der Literaturwissenschaft*, ed. Doris Bachmann-Medick (Frankfurt a.M.: Fischer Taschenbuch Verlag, 1996), 7–64

—, 'Einleitung: Übersetzung als Repräsentation fremder Kulturen', in *Übersetzung als Repräsentation fremder Kulturen*, ed. Doris Bachmann-Medick (Berlin: Schmidt, 1997), 3–25

Badran, Margot, 'Islamic Feminism Revisited', *Al-Ahram Weekly Online*, no. 781, 9–15 February 2006, http://weekly.ahram.org.eg/2006/781/cu4.htm [accessed 28 June 2010] (30 para.)

Badran, Margot, and Miriam Cooke, 'Introduction', in *Opening the Gates: A Century of Arab Feminist Writing*, ed. Margot Badran and Miriam Cooke (London: Virago, 1990), xvii–xxxix

Barbieri Jr., William A., *Ethics of Citizenship: Immigration and Group Rights in Germany* (Durham, NC: Duke University Press, 1998)

Bassnett, Susan, 'Travel Writing and Gender', in *The Cambridge Companion to Travel Writing*, ed. Peter Hulme and Tim Youngs (Cambridge: Cambridge University Press, 2002), 225–41

Bauman, Zygmunt, 'From Pilgrim to Tourist — or a Short History of Identity', in *Questions of Cultural Identity*, ed. Stuart Hall and Paul du Gay (London: Sage, 1996), 18–36

Beck-Gernsheim, Elisabeth, *Wir und die Anderen* (Frankfurt a.M.: Suhrkamp, 2004)

Begemann, Christian, '"Kanakensprache": Schwellenphänomene in der deutschsprachigen Literatur ausländischer AutorInnen der Gegenwart', in *Schwellen: Germanistische Erkundungen einer Metapher*, ed. Nicholas Saul *et al.* (Würzburg: Königshausen & Neumann, 1999), 209–20

Benhabib, Seyla, *The Rights of Others: Aliens, Residents and Citizens* (Cambridge: Cambridge University Press, 2004)

Benjamin, Walter, 'Charles Baudelaire, Tableaux parisiens. Deutsche Übertragung mit einem Vorwort über die Aufgabe des Übersetzers', in *Gesammelte Schriften*, with the assistance of Theodor W. Adorno and Gershom Scholem, ed. Rolf Tiedemann and Hermann Schweppenhäuser (Frankfurt a.M.: Suhrkamp, 1972), IV.I.: *Gesammelte Schriften*, ed. Tillmann Rexroth, 7–63 (originally publ. in C. Baudelaire, *'Tableaux parisiens': Deutsche Übertragung mit einem Vorwort über die Aufgabe des Übersetzers, von Walter Benjamin* (Heidelberg: Weißbach, 1923))

Betts, Christopher J., 'Introduction', in Montesquieu, *Persian Letters*, trans. with an Introduction and Notes by Christopher J. Betts (London: Penguin, 1993 [2004(?) printing]), 17–33

Bhabha, Homi K., 'Postcolonial Criticism', in *Redrawing the Boundaries: The Transformation of English and American Literary Studies*, ed. Stephen Greenblatt and Giles Gunn (New York: Modern Language Association of America, 1992), 437–65

—, 'The Commitment to Theory', in *The Location of Culture* (London: Routledge, 1994), 19–39

—, 'The Other Question: Stereotype, Discrimination and the Discourse of Colonialism', in *The Location of Culture* (London: Routledge, 1994), 66–84

—, 'Of Mimicry and Man: The Ambivalence of Colonial Discourse', in *The Location of Culture* (London: Routledge, 1994), 85–92

—, 'Signs Taken for Wonders: Questions of Ambivalence and Authority Under a Tree Outside Delhi, May 1817', in *The Location of Culture* (London: Routledge, 1994), 102–22

—, 'DissemiNation: Time, Narrative and the Margins of the Modern Nation', in *The Location of Culture* (London: Routledge, 1994), 139–70

—, 'How Newness Enters the World: Postmodern Space, Postcolonial Times and the Trials of Cultural Translation', in *The Location of Culture* (London: Routledge, 1994), 212–35

Biller, Maxim, 'Die dritte Ethnie', in Fatih Akin, *Gegen die Wand: Das Buch zum Film: Drehbuch, Materialien, Interviews und Pressestimmen* (Cologne: Kiepenheuer & Witsch, 2004), 267–68 (originally publ. in *FAZ Sonntagszeitung*, 22 June 2003)

Bird, Stephanie, *Women Writers and National Identity: Bachmann, Duden, Özdamar* (Cambridge: Cambridge University Press, 2003)

Blahak, Boris, '"Du feine Rose meiner Gedanken ...": Orientalismen in der Darstellung von Liebe, Erotik und Sexualität als tiefere Ebene einer Hybridität in Emine Sevgi Özdamas *Mutter Zunge — Großvater Zunge*', *Wirkendes Wort*, 56.3 (December 2006), 455–74

Boa, Elizabeth, 'Sprachenverkehr: Hybrides Schreiben in Werken von Özdamar, Özakin und Demirkan', in *Interkulturelle Konfiguration: Zur deutschsprachigen Erzählliteratur von Autoren nichtdeutscher Herkunft*, ed. Mary Howard (Munich: Iudicium, 1997), 115–51

Bock, Christoph, 'Ortswechsel: Interview mit Michael Ebmeyer und Ilija Trojanow', *Parapluie*, no. 19: *Worte, Worte, Worte*, http://parapluie.de/archiv/worte/ortswechsel [accessed 28 June 2010] (53 para.)

Bonadei, Rossana, 'Theory into *écriture*: Travel Literature Encounters Touring Cultures', in *Cross-Cultural Travel: Papers from the Royal Irish Academy International Symposium on Literature and Travel, National University of Ireland, Galway, November 2002*, ed. Jane Couroy, Travel Writing Across Disciplines, Theory and Pedagogy, 7 (New York: Peter Lang, 2003), 417–28

Bouhdiba, Abdelwahab, *Sexuality in Islam*, trans. Alan Sheridan (London: Routledge & Kegan Paul, 1985; originally publ. as *La sexualité en Islam* (Paris: PUF, 1975))

Bourdieu, Pierre, *Outline of a Theory of Practice*, trans. Richard Nice, Cambridge Studies in Social and Cultural Anthropology, 16 (Cambridge: Cambridge University Press, 1998 [1977]; originally publ. as *Esquisse d'une théorie de la practique, précédé de trois études d'ethnologie kabyle* (Geneva: Librairie Droz, 1972)

Brahm Levey, Geoffrey, 'Secularism and Religion in a Multicultural Age', in *Secularism, Religion and Multicultural Citizenship*, ed. Geoffrey Brahm Levey and Tariq Modood (Cambridge: Cambridge University Press, 2009), 1–24

Brandt, Bettina, 'Collecting Childhood Memories of the Future: Arabic as Mediator Between Turkish and German in Emine Sevgi Özdamar's *Mutterzunge*', *Germanic Review*, 79.4 (Fall 2004), 294–315

Brennan, Timothy, *At Home in the World: Cosmopolitanism Now* (Cambridge, MA: Harvard University Press, 1997)

Brenner, Peter J., *Der Reisebericht: Die Entwicklung einer Gattung in der deutschen Literatur* (Frankfurt a.M.: Suhrkamp, 1989)

Brick Lane. Dir. Sarah Gavron. Sony Pictures Classics. 2007.

Brunner, Maria E., 'Die Türkei, ein Mutterland — Deutschland, ein Bitterland? Emine Sevgi Özdamars Buch "Das Leben ist eine Karawanserei"', *Info DaF*, 26.6 (December 1999), 556–65

Bundesministerium des Inneren, Deutsche Islam Konferenz, www.bmi.bund.de/cln_165/DE/Themen/PolitikGesellschaft/DtIslamKonferenz/dtislamkonferenz_node.html [accessed 28 June 2010]

Bunyan, John, *The Pilgrim's Progress*, Nelson's Royal Classics (Nashville: Nelson, 1999; originally publ. as *The Pilgrim's Progress from This World, to That Which Is to Come: Delivered Under the Similitude of a Dream*, 1678)

[Burckhard, Johann Ludwig], *Travels in Arabia: Comprehending an Account of Those Territories in Hedjaz Which the Mohammedan Regard as Sacred*, by the late John Lewis Burckhardt, published by the Authority of the Association for Promoting the Discovery of the Interior of Africa (London: Colburn, 1829; repr. in Publications of the Institute for the History of Arabic-Islamic Science, ed. Fuat Sezgin, The Islamic World in Foreign Travel Accounts, 43 (Institute for the History of Arabic-Islamic Science at the Johann Wolfgang Goethe University Frankfurt am Main, 1995))

Burton, Richard F., *A Secret Pilgrimage to Mecca and Medina*, intro. Tim Mackintosh-Smith (London: The Folio Society, 2004; originally publ. as *Personal Narrative of a Pilgrimage to El-Medinah and Meccah* (London: Longman, Brown, Green, and Longmans, 1855–56))

Buruma, Ian, and Avishai Margalit, *Occidentalism: A Short History of Anti-Westernism* (London: Atlantic Books, 2004)

Butler, Judith, *Gender Trouble: Feminism and the Subversion of Identity*, 10th anniversary edn (New York: Routledge, 1999 [1990])

—, *Bodies That Matter: On the Discursive Limits of 'Sex'* (New York: Routledge, 1993)

—, *Excitable Speech: A Politics of the Performative* (New York: Routledge, 1997)

—, 'Performative Acts and Gender Constitution: An Essay in Phenomenology and Feminist Theory', in *Writing on the Body: Female Embodiment and Feminist Theory*, ed. Katie Conboy *et al.* (New York: Columbia University Press, 1997), 401–17

Butor, Michel, 'Travel and Writing', trans. John Powers and K. Lisker, *Mosaic*, 8.1 (1974), 1–16 (repr. in *Temperamental Journeys: Essays on the Modern Literature of Travel*, ed. Michael Kowalewski (Athens: The University of Georgia Press, 1992), 53–70; originally publ. as *Le voyage et l'écriture, Romantisme*, no. 4 (1972), 4–19)

Butt, Nadia 'Negotiating Untranslatability and Islam in Leila Aboulela's *The Translator*', in *Transcultural Modernities: Narrating Africa in Europe*, ed. Elisabeth Bekers *et al.* (Amsterdam: Rodopi, 2009), 167–79

Campbell, Mary Baine, 'Travel Writing and its Theory', in *The Cambridge Companion to Travel Writing*, ed. Peter Hulme and Tim Youngs (Cambridge: Cambridge University Press, 2002), 261–78

Cerri, Chiara, review of Norbert Mecklenburg, *Das Mädchen aus der Fremde: Germanistik als interkulturelle Literaturwissenschaft* (München: Iudicium, 2008), *Zeitschrift für Interkulturellen Fremdsprachenunterricht*, 15.1 (April 2010), 125–28, http://zif.spz.tu-darmstadt.de/jg-15-1/docs/Mecklenburg.pdf [accessed 18 June 2011] (15 para.)

Chambers, Iain, *Migrancy, Culture, Identity* (London: Routledge, 1994)

Cheesman, Tom, 'Akçam — Zaimoğlu — "Kanak Attak": Turkish Lives and Letters in German', in *Emerging Writers*, ed. Frank Finlay and Stuart Taberner (= Special Number, *German Life and Letters*, 55.2 (April 2002)), 180–95

—, 'Talking *"Kanak"*: Zaimoğlu contra *Leitkultur*', in *Multicultural Germany: Art, Performance, and Media*, ed. Deniz Göktürk and Barbara Wolbert (= Special Issue, *New German Critique*, 92 (Spring/Summer 2004)), 82–99

—, 'Juggling Burdens of Representation: Black, Red, Gold and Turquoise', in *Crossing Boundaries*, ed. Jim Jordan (= Special Number, *German Life and Letters*, 59.4 (October 2006)), 472–87

—, *Novels of Turkish German Settlement: Cosmopolite Fictions* (Rochester, NY: Camden House, 2007)

—, unpublished paper 'Feridun Zaimoğlu on Religion', given at the conference 'Religion in Contemporary German Culture' (Swansea University, 9–11 July 2008)

Clarke, John, *et al.*, 'Subcultures, Cultures and Class: A Theoretical Overview', in *Resistance Through Rituals: Youth Subcultures in Post-War Britain*, ed. Stuart Hall and Tony Jefferson (London: Routledge, 1993 [2000 printing]; first publ. as *Working Papers in Cultural Studies*, 7/8 (Birmingham: Centre for Contemporary Cultural Studies, University of Birmingham, 1975)), 9–74

Clifford, James, *The Predicament of Culture: Twentieth-Century Ethnography, Literature, and Art* (Cambridge, MA: Harvard University Press, 1988)

—, *Routes: Travel and Translation in the Late Twentieth Century* (Cambridge, MA: Harvard University Press, 1997)

Colebrook, Claire, 'Nomadicism', in *The Deleuze Dictionary*, ed. Adrian Parr (Edinburgh: Edinburgh University Press, 2005), 180–83

Cook, Michael, *The Koran: A Very Short Introduction* (Oxford: Oxford University Press, 2000)

Cooke, Miriam, *Women Claim Islam: Creating Islamic Feminism Through Literature* (New York: Routledge, 2001)

Cooper, Brenda, *A New Generation of African Writers: Migration, Material Culture and Language* (Woodbridge: James Currey; Scottsville: University of KwaZulu-Natal Press, 2008)

Crapanzano, Vincent, 'Das Dilemma des Hermes: Die verschleierte Unterwanderung der ethnographischen Beschreibung', in *Kultur als Text: Die anthropologische Wende in der Literaturwissenschaft*, ed. Doris Bachmann-Medick (Frankfurt a.M.: Fischer Taschenbuch Verlag, 1996), 161–93

Cronin, Michael, 'The Cracked Looking Glass of Servants: Translation and Minority Languages in a Global Age', in *Translation and Minority*, ed. Lawrence Venuti (= Special Issue, *The Translator*, 4.2 (1998)), 145–62

—, *Across the Lines: Travel, Language, Translation* (Cork: Cork University Press, 2000)

Cuddon, J. A., *The Penguin Dictionary of Literary Terms and Literary Theory*, 3rd edn (London: Penguin, 1991 [1976])

Culler, Jonathan, 'Philosophy and Literature: The Fortunes of the Performative', *Poetics Today*, 21.3 (Fall 2000), 503–19

Davidson, Robyn, 'Introduction', in *The Picador Book of Journeys*, ed. Robyn Davidson (London: Picador, 2001), 1–7

Dayıoğlu-Yücel, Yasemin, *Von der Gastarbeit zur Identitätsarbeit: Integritätsverhandlungen in türkisch-deutschen Texten von Şenocak, Özdamar, Ağaoğlu und der Online-Community* vaybee! (Göttingen: Universitätsverlag Göttingen, 2005)

Defoe, Daniel, *The Life and Adventures of Robinson Crusoe*, ed., with an Introduction by Angus Ross, Penguin English Library (1965); repr. in Penguin Classics (London: Penguin, 1985; first publ. London: Taylor, 1719)

Deleuze, Gilles, and Félix Guattari, *A Thousand Plateaus: Capitalism and Schizophrenia*, trans. Brian Massumi (London: Continuum, 2004 [1987]; originally publ. as *Mille Plateaux*, II of *Capitalisme et Schizophrénie* (Paris: Minuit, 1980))

de Nerval, Gérard, *Voyage en Orient*, 2 vols, ed. Michel Jeanneret (Paris: Ganier-Flammarion, 1980; first publ. Paris: Carpentier, 1851)

Dirim, İnci, and Peter Auer, *Türkisch sprechen nicht nur die Türken: Über die Unschärfebeziehung zwischen Sprache und Ethnie in Deutschland*, Linguistik — Impulse und Tendenzen, 4 (Berlin: de Gruyter, 2004)

Egbene, Choga Regina, *Hinter goldenen Gittern: Ich wurde im Harem geboren*, 9th edn (Munich: Ullstein, 2005 [2001])

Eickelman, Dale F., and James Piscatori, 'Preface', in *Muslim Travellers: Pilgrimage, Migration, and the Religious Imagination*, ed. Dale F. Eickelman and James Piscatori (London: Routledge, 1990), xii–xxii

—, 'Social Theory in the Study of Muslim Societies', in *Muslim Travellers: Pilgrimage, Migration, and the Religious Imagination*, ed. Dale F. Eickelman and James Piscatori (London: Routledge, 1990), 3–25

Eissa, Saleh, 'Interview with Leila Aboulela', *iWitness*, July 2005, www.iwitness.co.uk/features/0705fe03.htm [accessed 4 July 2006] (24 para.), URL no longer available

El-Din, Mursi Saad, 'Plain Talk', *Al-Ahram Weekly Online*, no. 556, 18–24 October 2001, http://weekly.ahram.org.eg/2001/556/cu3.htm [accessed 28 June 2006] (10 para.)

Endress, Gerhard, *Einführung in die islamische Geschichte* (Munich: Beck, 1982)

Esposito, John L., *Islam: The Straight Path*, 3rd edn (New York: Oxford University Press, 1998 [1988])

—, *The Islamic Threat: Myth or Reality?*, 3rd edn (New York: Oxford University Press, 1999 [1992])

—, ed. in chief, *The Oxford Encyclopaedia of the Modern Islamic World*, 4 vols (New York: Oxford University Press, 1995)

—, 'Introduction: Women in Islam and Western Society', in *Islam, Gender, and Social Change*, ed. Yvonne Yazbeck Haddad and John L. Esposito (New York: Oxford University Press, 1998), ix–xxvii

—, *The Oxford Dictionary of Islam* (New York: Oxford University Press, 2004 [2003])

Fischer, Sabine, and Moray McGowan, 'From *Pappkoffer* to Pluralism: On the Development of Migrant Writing in the German Federal Republic', in *Turkish Culture in German Society Today*, ed. David Horrocks and Eva Kolinsky, Culture and Society in Germany, 1 (Providence, RI: Berghahn, 1996), 1–22

Flaubert, Gustave, *Lettres d'Orient*, Foreword Pierre Bergouioux, Collection 'de mémoire' (Bordeaux: L'Horizon chimérique, 1990; first publ. in *Correspondance*, I, Bibliothèque de la Pléïade (Paris: Gallimard, 1973))

Foucault, Michel, *The Will to Knowledge: The History of Sexuality, Volume 1*, trans. Robert Hurley (London: Penguin, 1998 [1978]; originally publ. as *La Volonté de savoir* (Paris: Gallimard, 1976))

Geaves, Ron, 'Who Defines Moderate Islam "Post"-September 11?', in *Islam and the West Post 9/11*, ed. Ron Geaves *et al.* (Aldershot: Ashgate, 2004), 62–74

Ghaussy, Sohelia, 'Das Vaterland verlassen: Nomadic Language and "Feminine Writing" in Emine Sevgi Özdamar's *Das Leben ist eine Karawanserei*', *German Quarterly*, 72.1 (Winter 1999), 1–16

Al Ghazāli, *The Revival of Religious Science*, A Translation of the Arabic Work *Ihyā 'ulūm al-dīn* by Bankey Behari, with a Foreword by Shree Humayun Kabir (Farnham: Sufi Publishing, 1972 [1964])

Ghazoul, Ferial J., 'Halal Fiction', *Al-Ahram Weekly Online*, no. 542, 12–18 July 2001, http://weekly.ahram.org.eg/2001/542/bo4.htm [accessed 28 June 2010] (13 para.)

Gilroy, Paul, *The Black Atlantic: Modernity and Double Consciousness* (Cambridge, MA: Harvard University Press, 1993)

Goethe, Johann Wolfgang von, *Sämtliche Werke nach Epochen seines Schaffens*, Münchner Ausgabe, ed. Karl Richter *et al.* (Munich: Hanser, 1998), XI.I.II: *West-östlicher Divan*, ed. Karl Richter with the assistance of Katharina Mommsen and Peter Ludwig

Göle, Nilüfer, *The Forbidden Modern: Civilization and Veiling*, Critical Perspectives on Women and Gender (Ann Arbor: The University of Michigan Press, 1996)

Gorra, Michael, *After Empire: Scott, Naipaul, Rushdie* (Chicago: The University of Chicago Press, 1997)

Göttsche, Dirk, 'Emine Sevgi Özdamars Erzählung *Der Hof im Spiegel*: Spielräume einer postkolonialen Lektüre deutsch-türkischer Literatur', in *Crossing Boundaries*, ed. Jim Jordan (= Special Number, *German Life and Letters*, 59.4 (October 2006)), 513–25

Güngör, Murat, and Hannes Loh, *Fear of a Kanak Planet: HipHop zwischen Weltkultur und Nazi-Rap* (Höfen: Hannibal, 2002)

Günter, Manuela, '"Wir sind bastarde, freund ...": Feridun Zaimoglus Kanak Sprak und die performative Struktur von Identität', *Sprache und Literatur in Wissenschaft und Unterricht*, 30.83 (1999), 15–28

Gupta, Suman, *V. S. Naipaul* (Plymouth: Northcote House in association with the British Council, 1999)

Hà, Kiên Nghi, *Ethnizität und Migration*, Einstiege, 9 (Münster: Westfälisches Dampfboot, 1999)

Habermas, Jürgen, 'Vorpolitische Grundlagen des demokratischen Rechtsstaates', in Jürgen Habermas and Joseph Ratzinger, *Dialektik der Säkularisierung: Über Vernunft und Religion* (Bundeszentrale für politische Bildung: Bonn, 2005/Herder: Freiburg im Breisgau, 2005), 15–37

—, 'Ein Bewußtsein von dem, was fehlt', in *Ein Bewußtsein von dem, was fehlt: Eine Diskussion mit Jürgen Habermas*, ed. Michael Reder and Josef Schmidt (Frankfurt a.M.: Suhrkamp, 2008), 26–36

Haines, Brigid, and Margaret Littler, 'Emine Sevgi Özdamar, "Mutter Zunge" and "Großvater Zunge" (1990)', *Contemporary Women's Writing in German: Changing the Subject* (Oxford: Oxford University Press, 2004), 118–39

Hall, Stuart, 'New Ethnicities', in *Black Film, British Cinema*, ed. Kobena Mercer, BFI/ICA Documents, 7 (London: Institute for Contemporary Arts, 1988), 27–31

—, 'Introduction: Who Needs "Identity"?', in *Questions of Cultural Identity*, ed. Stuart Hall and Paul du Gay (London: Sage, 1996), 1–17

—, 'What Is This "Black" in Black Popular Culture?', in *Stuart Hall: Critical Dialogues in Cultural Studies*, ed. David Morley and Kuan-Hsing Chen (London: Routledge, 1996), 465–75

—, *The Multicultural Question*, Pavis Papers in Social and Cultural Research, 4 (Milton Keynes: The Open University, 2001)

Hall, Stuart, and Tony Jefferson, eds, *Resistance Through Rituals: Youth Subcultures in Post-War Britain* (London: Routledge, 1993 [2000 printing]; first publ. as *Working Papers in Cultural Studies*, 7/8 (Birmingham: Centre for Contemporary Cultural Studies, University of Birmingham, 1975))

Helicke, James, 'Turks in Germany: Muslim Identity "Between" States', in *Muslim Minorities in the West: Visible and Invisible*, ed. Yvonne Yazbeck Haddad and Jane I. Smith (Walnut Creek, CL: AltaMira, 2002), 175–191

Herder, Johann Gottfried, *Ideen zur Philosophie der Geschichte der Menschheit*, in *Werke*, ed. Martin Bollacher *et al.* (Frankfurt a.M.: Deutscher Klassiker Verlag, 1989), VI, ed. Martin Bollacher, Bibliothek Deutscher Klassiker, 41

Hestermann, Sandra, 'The German-Turkish Diaspora and Multicultural German Identity: Hyphenated and Alternative Discourses of Identity in the Works of Zafer Şenocak and Feridun Zaimoğlu', in *Diaspora and Multiculturalism: Common Traditions and New Developments*, ed. Monika Fludernik, Crosscultures: Readings in Post/Colonial Literatures in English, 66 (Amsterdam: Rodopi, 2003), 329–73

Hinnenkamp, Volker, 'Türkisch Mann, Du? Sprachverhalten von Deutschen gegenüber Gastarbeitern', in *Mehrsprachigkeit in der Stadtregion*, ed. Karl Heinz Bausch, Jahrbuch des Landes NRW, Sprache der Gegenwart, 56 (Düsseldorf: Schwann, 1981), 171–93

Hlavin-Schulze, Karin, *'Man reist ja nicht, um anzukommen': Reisen als kulturelle Praxis* (Frankfurt a.M.: Campus, 1998)

Hodkinson, James, and Jeff Morrison, eds, *Encounters with Islam in German Literature and Culture* (Rochester, NY: Camden House, 2009)

Hofmann, Michael, *Interkulturelle Literaturwissenschaft: Eine Einführung* (Paderborn: Fink, 2006)

Holdenried, Michaela, unpublished paper '"Weltensammeln" — ein neues Hobby für Literaten und Literaturwissenschaft?', given at the XII. Congress of the International Association for Germanic Studies, 'Vielfalt und Einheit der Germanistik weltweit' (University of Warsaw, 30 July–7 August 2010)

Holland, Eugene, 'Nomadicism + Citizenship', in *The Deleuze Dictionary*, ed. Adrian Parr (Edinburgh: Edinburgh University Press, 2005), 183–84

Holland, Patrick, and Graham Huggan, *Tourists with Typewriters: Critical Reflections on Contemporary Travel Writing* (Ann Arbor: The University of Michigan Press, 1998)

Holt, Peter Malcolm, and M. W. Daly, *A History of the Sudan: From the Coming of Islam to the Present Day*, 5th edn (Harlow: Longman, 2000 [1961])

hooks, bell, *We Real Cool: Black Men and Masculinity* (New York: Routledge, 2004)

Horrocks, David, 'In Search of a Lost Past: A Reading of Emine Sevgi Özdamar's Novel *Das Leben ist eine Karawanserei, hat zwei Türen, aus einer kam ich rein, aus der anderen ging ich raus*', in *Turkish Culture in German Society Today*, ed. David Horrocks and Eva Kolinsky, Culture and Society in Germany, 1 (Providence, RI: Berghahn, 1996), 23–43

Horrocks, David, and Eva Kolinsky, 'Living and Writing in Germany: Emine Sevgi Özdamar in Conversation with David Horrocks and Eva Kolinsky', in *Turkish Culture in German Society Today*, ed. David Horrocks and Eva Kolinsky, Culture and Society in Germany, 1 (Providence, RI: Berghahn, 1996), 45–54

Huggan, Graham, *The Postcolonial Exotic: Marketing the Margins* (London: Routledge, 2001)

—, 'Derailing the "Trans"? Postcolonial Studies and the Negative Effects of Speed', in *Inter- und Transkulturelle Studien: Theoretische Grundlagen und interdisziplinäre Praxis*, ed. Heinz Antor (Universitätsverlag Winter: Heidelberg, 2006), 55–61

Hulme, Peter, 'Travelling to Write (1940–2000)', in *The Cambridge Companion to Travel Writing*, ed. Peter Hulme and Tim Youngs (Cambridge: Cambridge University Press, 2002), 87–101

Huntington, Samuel, *The Clash of Civilizations and the Remaking of the World Order* (London: Touchstone, 1998)

[Ibn Battutah], *The Travels of Ibn Battutah*, abr., intro. and annot. Tim Mackintosh-Smith (London: Picador, 2003 [2002])

[Ibn Dschubair (Ibn Jubayr, Muhammad ibn Ahmad)], *The Travels of Ibn Jubayr: Being the Chronicle of a Mediaeval Spanish Moor Concerning His Journey to the Egypt of Saladin, the Holy Cities of Arabia, Baghdad the City of the Caliphs, the Latin Kingdom of Jerusalem, and the Norman Kingdom of Sicily*, trans. R. J. C. Broadhurst, with an Introduction and Notes (London: Jonathan Cape, 1952)

'"Ich bin Teil der deutschen Literatur, so deutsch wie Kafka": Ist Fremd-Sein ein Problem, ein Thema oder ein Markt-Vorteil? Vier nicht ganz deutsche Autoren — Terézia Mora, Imran Ayata, Wladimir Kaminer und Navid Kermani — im Literaturen-Gespräch', *Literaturen*, 4/2005, 26–31

Jamie, Kathleen, *Among Muslims: Meetings at the Frontiers of Pakistan* (London: Sort of Books, 2002 [2003 printing]; originally publ. as *The Golden Peak* (London: Virago, 1992))

Jordan, Jim, 'Migrant Writing in Germany and the Politics of the Multicultural Society: Three Case Studies', in *Migrants in German-Speaking Countries: Aspects of Social and Cultural Experience*, ed. Jim Jordan and Peter Barker, Modern German Studies, 2 (London: CILT Publications, 2000), 97–113

—, 'More than a Metaphor: The Passing of the Two Worlds Paradigm in German-Language Diasporic Literature', in *Crossing Boundaries*, ed. Jim Jordan (= Special Number, *German Life and Letters*, 59.4 (October 2006)), 488–99

—, 'Identity, Irony and Denial: Navid Kermani's *Kurzmitteilung*', in *Aesthetics and Politics in Modern German Culture: Festschrift in Honour of Rhys W. Williams*, ed. Brigid Haines, Stephen Parker and Colin Riordan (Oxford: Peter Lang, 2010), 165–77

Kabbani, Rana, *Imperial Fictions: Europe's Myths of Orient*, rev. and expanded edn (London: Pandora, 1994 [1986])

Kaleta, Kenneth C., *Hanif Kureishi: Postcolonial Storyteller* (Austin: University of Texas Press, 1998)

Kanak Attack. Dir. Lars Becker. Concorde Filmverleih. 2000. [on DVD]

Kanak Attak, 'Kanak Attak und basta! Manifest gegen Mültikültüralizm, gegen demokratische und hybride Deutsche sowie konformistische Migranten', www.kanak-attak.de/ka/down/pdf/textos.pdf [accessed 28 June 2010] (originally published in *die tageszeitung* (28 January 1999))

Kandiyoti, Deniz, 'Contemporary Feminist Scholarship and Middle East Studies', in *Gendering the Middle East: Emerging Perspectives*, ed. Deniz Kandiyoti (London: I. B.Tauris, 1996), 1–27

Kaplan, Cora, 'Language and Gender' (1986), in *The Feminist Critique of Language: A Reader*, ed. Deborah Cameron, 2nd edn (London: Routledge, 1998 [1990]), 54–64

Karakasoglu, Yasemin, 'Turkish Cultural Orientations in Germany and the Role of Islam', in *Turkish Culture in German Society Today*, ed. David Horrocks and Eva Kolinsky (Providence, RI: Berghahn, 1996), 157–79

Kermani, Navid, *40 Leben* (Zurich: Ammann, 2004)

—, *Du sollst* (Zurich: Ammann, 2005)
—, *Kurzmitteilung: Roman* (Zurich: Ammann, 2007)
—, *Wer ist wir? Deutschland und seine Muslime* (Munich: Beck, 2009)
Khan, Mohammed Ayub, 'A Nobel for Islamophobia', *The Milli Gazette*, 2.22, www.milligazette.com/Archives/15112001/29.htm [accessed 28 June 2010] (10 para.)
King, Bruce, *V. S. Naipaul*, 2nd edn (Basingstoke: Palgrave Macmillan, 2003 [1993])
Kluge, Friedrich, *Etymologisches Wörterbuch der deutschen Sprache*, 22nd edn, with the assistance of Max Bürgisser and Bernd Gregor, fully rev. Elmar Seebold (Berlin: de Gruyter, 1989 [1883])
Kontje, Todd, *German Orientalisms* (Ann Arbor: The University of Michigan Press, 2004)
Konuk, Kader, 'Das Leben ist eine Karawanserei: Heim-at bei Emine Sevgi Özdamar', in *Kein Land in Sicht: Heimat — weiblich?*, ed. Gisela Ecker (Munich: Fink, 1997), 143–59
—, '"Identitätssuche ist ein [sic!] private archäologische Graberei": Emine Sevgi Özdamars inszeniertes Sprechen', in *AufBrüche: Kulturelle Produktionen von Migrantinnen, Schwarzen und jüdischen Frauen in Deutschland*, ed. Cathy S. Gelbin *et al.* (Königstein/ Taunus: Helmer, 1999), 60–74
—, *Identitäten im Prozeß: Literatur von Autorinnen aus und in der Türkei in deutscher, englischer und türkischer Sprache*, Literaturwissenschaft in der Blauen Eule, 28 (Essen: Verlag Die Blaue Eule, 2001) (= doctoral thesis, University of Paderborn, 1999)
Der Koran, trans. Max Henning, Introduction Ernst Werner and Kurt Rudolph, ed. Kurt Rudolph (Leipzig: Reclam, 1968)
The Koran, trans. J. M. Rodwell, Foreword and Introduction Alan Jones (London: Phoenix, 1994 [2004 printing]; first publ. London: Everyman, 1909)
Korte, Barbara, *English Travel Writing from Pilgrimages to Postcolonial Explorations*, trans. Catherine Matthias (Basingstoke: Macmillan Palgrave, 2000; originally publ. as *Der englische Reisebericht: Von der Pilgerfahrt bis zur Postmoderne* (Darmstadt: Wissenschaftliche Buchgesellschaft, 1996))
—, 'Exploring Without a Mission? Postcolonial Travel in a Global World', in *Colonies — Missions — Cultures in the English-Speaking World: General and Comparative Studies*, ed. Gerhard Stilz, ZAA Studies: Language, Literature, Culture, 12 (Tübingen: Stauffenburg, 2001), 383–95
Kristeva, Julia, *Desire in Language: A Semiotic Approach to Literature and Art*, ed. Leon S. Roudiez, trans. Thomas Gora *et al.* (New York:

Columbia University Press, 1980; originally publ. as *Σημειωτιχή: Recherches pur une sémanalyse* (Paris: Éditions du Seuil, 1969) and *Polylogue* (Paris: Éditions du Seuil, 1977)

Kureishi, Hanif, 'The Rainbow Sign' (1986), in *My Beautiful Laundrette and Other Writings* (London: Faber and Faber, 1996), 71–102

—, 'Bradford' (1986), in *My Beautiful Laundrette and Other Writings* (London: Faber and Faber, 1996), 121–44

—, 'The Road Exactly: Introduction to *My Son the Fanatic*' (1986), in *Dreaming and Scheming* (London: Faber and Faber, 2002), 215–21

—, *The Black Album* (London: Faber and Faber, 1996 [1995])

—, 'We're Not Jews', in *Love in a Blue Time* (London: Faber and Faber, 1997), 41–51

—, 'My Son the Fanatic', in *Love in a Blue Time* (London: Faber and Faber, 1997), 119–31

—, 'Sex and Secularity: Introduction to *Collected Screenplays One* (2002)', in *The Word and the Bomb* (London: Faber and Faber, 2005), 81–87

—, 'The Word and the Bomb', in *The Word and the Bomb* (London: Faber and Faber, 2005), 1–11

Kürsat-Ahlers, Elçin, 'The Turkish Minority in German Society', in *Turkish Culture in German Society Today*, ed. David Horrocks and Eva Kolinsky, Culture and Society in Germany, 1 (Providence, RI: Berghahn, 1996), 113–35

Lacan, Jacques, *Écrits* (Paris: Éditions du Seuil, 1966)

Lahiri, Jumpa, 'My Two Lives', *Newsweek*, 6 March 2006, www.newsweek.com/2006/03/05/my-two-lives.html [accessed 26 July 2010] (7 para.)

Lea, Richard, and Paul Lewis, 'Local Protests over Brick Lane Film', *Guardian*, 17 July 2006, www.guardian.co.uk/books/2006/jul/17/film.uk [accessed 28 June 2010] (14 para.)

Leaman, Oliver, *Islamic Aesthetics: An Introduction*, The New Edinburgh Islamic Surveys (Edinburgh: Edinburgh University Press, 2004)

Lessing, Gotthold Ephraim, *Nathan der Weise: Ein dramatisches Gedicht, in fünf Aufzügen*, in *Werke und Briefe in zwölf Bänden*, ed. Wilfried Barner *et al.* (Frankfurt a.M.: Deutscher Klassiker Verlag, 1993), IX: *Werke 1778–1780*, ed. Klaus Bohnen and Arno Schilson, Bibliothek Deutscher Klassiker, 94, 483–666

Lévinas, Emanuel, *Time and the Other*, trans. Richard A. Cohen (Pittsburg: Duquesne University Press, 1987; lectures originally publ. in *Le Choix — Le Monde — L'Existence*, ed. Jean Wahl

(Grenoble-Paris: Arthaud, 1947), 125–96, then separately with a new Preface (Montpellier: Fata Morgana, 1979))

—, 'Time and the Other', trans. Richard A. Cohen, in *The Levinas Reader*, ed. Seán Hand (Oxford: Blackwell, 1989 [1999 printing]), 37–58 (lectures originally publ. in *Le Choix — Le Monde — L'Existence*, ed. Jean Wahl (Grenoble-Paris: Arthaud, 1947), 125–96, then separately with a new Preface (Montpellier: Fata Morgana, 1979))

Levy, Judith, *V. S. Naipaul: Displacement and Autobiography* (New York: Garland, 1995)

Lewis, Geoffrey, *The Turkish Language Reform: A Catastrophic Success*, 2nd edn (Oxford: Oxford University Press, 2002 [1999])

Lewis, Philip, *Islamic Britain: Religion, Politics and Identity Among British Muslims: Bradford in the 1990s* (London: I. B.Tauris, 1994)

Littler, Margaret, 'Diasporic Identity in Emine Sevgi Özdamar's *MutterZunge*', in *Recasting German Identity: Culture, Politics, and Literature in the Berlin Republic*, ed. Stuart Taberner and Frank Finlay (Rochester, NY: Camden House, 2002), 219–34

—, 'Intimacies Both Sacred and Profane: Islam in the Work of Emine Sevgi Özdamar, Zafer Şenocak, and Feridun Zaimoğlu', in *Encounters with Islam in German Literature and Culture*, ed. James Hodkinson and Jeff Morrison (Rochester, NY: Camden House, 2009), 221–35

—, 'Profane und religiöse Intensitäten: Die islamische Kultur im Werk von Emine Sevgi Özdamar und Feridun Zaimoğlu', in *Von der nationalen zur internationalen Literatur: Transkulturelle deutschsprachige Literatur und Kultur im Zeitalter globaler Migration*, ed. Helmut Schmitz, Amsterdamer Beiträger zur neueren Germanistik, 69/2009 (Amsterdam: Rodopi, 2009), 143–54

Mackintosh-Smith, Tim, 'Foreword', in *The Travels of Ibn Battutah*, abr., intro. and annot. Tim Mackintosh-Smith (London: Picador, 2003 [2002]), vii–xviii

MacNeil, Kevin, and Alec Finley, eds, *Wish I Was Here: A Scottish Multicultural Anthology*, Pocketbooks, 5 (Edinburgh: Pocketbooks 2000)

Malak, Amin, *Muslim Narratives and the Discourse of English* (Albany: State University of New York Press, 2005)

Malcolm X, *The Autobiography of Malcolm X*, with the assistance of Alex Haley. With an introduction by Paul Gilroy (London: Penguin by arrangement with Hutchinson, 2001 [1965])

Malkani, Gautam, *Londonstani* (London: Fourth Estate, 2006)

Mani, B. Venkat, *Cosmopolitical Claims: Turkish-German Literatures from Nadolny to Pamuk* (Iowa City: University of Iowa Press, 2007)

Matthes, Frauke, unpublished interview with Ilija Trojanow conducted prior to his reading at the Goethe Institute Glasgow, 14 November 2006 (abbreviated version publ. as 'Die Fremde muss wie ein Stein sein', *Kreuzer*, 1/2007, 57)

—, 'Of *Kanaken* and *Gottes Krieger*: Religion and Sexuality among Feridun Zaimoğlu's Young Muslim Men', in *Edinburgh German Yearbook*, 2: *Masculinities in German Culture*, ed. Sarah Colvin and Peter Davies (Rochester, NY: Camden House, 2008), 250–61

—, '"Authentic" Muslim Voices? Feridun Zaimoğlu's *Schwarze Jungfrauen*', in *Religion and Identity in Germany Today: Doubters, Believers, Seekers in Literature and Film*, ed. Julian Preece *et al.* Leeds-Swansea Colloquia on Contemporary German Literature, 2 (Oxford and Berne: Peter Lang, 2010), 199–210

—, 'Islam in the West: Perceptions and Self-Perceptions of Muslims in Navid Kermani's *Kurzmitteilung*', *German Life and Letters*, 64.2 (April 2011), 305–16

Mayer, Ruth, and Mark Terkessidis, 'Retuschierte Bilder: Multikulturalismus, Populärkultur und Cultural Studies: Eine Einführung', in *Globalkolorit: Multikulturalismus und Populärkultur*, ed. Ruth Mayer and Mark Terkessidis (St. Andrä/Wörden: Hannibal, 1998), 7–23

McGowan, Moray, 'Brücken und Brücken-Köpfe: Wandlungen einer Metapher in der türkisch-deutschen Literatur', in *Die andere deutsche Literatur: Istanbuler Vorträge*, ed. Manfred Durzak and Nilüfer Kuruyazıcı with the assistance of Canan Şenöz Ayata (Würzburg: Königshausen & Neumann, 2004), 31–40

—, 'Turkish-German Fiction since the mid 1990s', in *Contemporary German Fiction: Writing in the Berlin Republic*, ed. Stuart Taberner (Cambridge: Cambridge University Press, 2007), 196–214

McLeod, John, *Beginning Postcolonialism* (Manchester: Manchester University Press, 2000)

Mecklenburg, Norbert, 'Eingrenzung, Ausgrenzung, Grenzüberschreitung: Grundprobleme deutscher Literatur von Minderheiten', in *Die andere deutsche Literatur: Istanbuler Vorträge*, ed. Manfred Durzak and Nilüfer Kuruyazıcı with the assistance of Canan Şenöz Ayata (Würzburg: Königshausen & Neumann, 2004), 23–30

—, *Das Mädchen aus der Fremde: Germanistik als interkulturelle Literaturwissenschaft* (Munich: Iudicium, 2008)

Melman, Billie, 'The Middle East/Arabia: "The Cradle of Islam"', in *The Cambridge Companion to Travel Writing*, ed. Peter Hulme and Tim Youngs (Cambridge: Cambridge University Press, 2002), 105–21

Mennel, Barbara, 'Bruce Lee in Kreuzberg and Scarface in Altona: Transnational Auteurism and Ghettocentrism in Thomas Arslan's *Brothers and Sisters* and Fatih Akin's *Short Sharp Shock*', in *Postwall Cinema*, ed. Eric Rentschler (= Special Issue, *New German Critique*, no. 87 (Fall 2002)), 133–56

Mernissi, Fatima, *Beyond the Veil: Male-Female Dynamics in Muslim Society*, rev. edn (Cambridge, MA: Saqi Books, 2003 [1975])

Metcalf, Barbara D., 'The Pilgrimage Remembered: South Asian Accounts of the *hajj*', in *Muslim Travellers: Pilgrimage, Migration, and the Religious Imagination*, ed. Dale F. Eickelman and James Piscatori (London: Routledge, 1990), 85–107

Milz, Sabine, 'Ethnicity and/or Nationality Writing in Contemporary Canada and Germany: A Comparative Study of Marlene Nourbese Philip's and Emine Sevgi Özdamar's Writing of Hybridity and its Public and Critical Reception', *Zeitschrift für Anglistik und Amerikanistik*, 48.3 (2000), 254–68

Modood, Tariq, *Multiculturalism: A Civic Idea* (Cambridge: Polity, 2007)

Moghadam, Valentine M., ed., *Gender and National Identity: Women and Politics in Muslim Societies* (London: Publ. for the United Nations University World Institute for Development Research by Zed, 1994)

Moghissi, Haideh, *Feminism and Islamic Fundamentalism: The Limits of Postmodern Analysis* (London: Zed, 1999), 65–66

Montesquieu, Charles de Secondat, Baron de, *Persian Letters*, trans. with an Introduction and Notes by Christopher J. Betts (London: Penguin, 1993 [2004(?) printing]; originally publ. as *Lettres Persanes* (Amsterdam: PAGE Brunel, 1721))

Moore-Gilbert, Bart, *Hanif Kureishi* (Manchester: Manchester University Press, 2001)

Moss, Laura, 'The Politics of Everyday Hybridity: Zadie Smith's *White Teeth*', *Wasafiri*, 39 (Summer 2003), 11–17

Müller, Regula, '"Ich war Mädchen, war ich Sultanin': Weitgeöffnete Augen betrachten türkische Frauengeschichte(n): Zum Karawanserei-Roman von Emine Sevgi Özdamar', in *Denn du tanzt auf einem Seil: Positionen deutschsprachiger MigrantInnenliteratur*, ed. Sabine Fischer and Moray McGowan, Stauffenburg discussion, 2 (Tübingen: Stauffenburg, 1997), 133–49

Mustafa, Fawzia, *V. S. Naipaul* (Cambridge: Cambridge University Press, 1995)

My Son the Fanatic. Dir. Udayan Prasad. Miramax Films. 1997. [on DVD]

Naipaul, V. S., 'Jasmine' (1964), in *Literary Occasions: Essays*, intro. and ed. Pankaj Mishra (London: Picador, 2003), 45–52

—, *The Mimic Men: A Novel* (London: Picador, 2002 [1967])

—, *Among the Believers: An Islamic Journey* (London: Picador, 2003 [1981])

—, *The Enigma of Arrival: A Novel in Five Sections* (London: Picador, 2002 [1987])

—, 'Our Universal Civilization' (1992), in *The Writer and the World: Essays*, ed. Pankaj Mishra (London: Picador, 2003 [2002]), 503–17

—, *Beyond Belief: Islamic Excursions Among the Converted Peoples* (London: Abacus, 1999 [1998] [2002 printing])

—, 'Reading and Writing, a Personal Account' (1998), in *Literary Occasions: Essays*, intro. and ed. Pankaj Mishra (London: Picador, 2003), 3–31

—, 'Two Worlds (The Nobel Lecture)' (7 December 2001), in *Literary Occasions: Essays*, intro. and ed. Pankaj Mishra (London: Picador, 2003), 181–95

Nash, Geoffrey, 'Re-siting Religion and Creating Feminised Space in the Fiction of Ahdaf Soueif and Leila Aboulela', *Wasafiri*, 35 (Spring 2002), 28–31

Natambu, Kofi, *The Life and Work of Malcolm X* (Indianapolis: Alpha, 2002)

Ngũgĩ wa Thiong'o, *A Grain of Wheat* (London: Heinemann, 1967)

Nielsen, Jørgen S., *Muslims in Western Europe*, 2nd edn, Islamic Surveys (Edinburgh: Edinburgh University Press, 1995 [1992])

Nixon, Rob, *London Calling: V. S. Naipaul, Postcolonial Mandarin* (New York: Oxford University Press, 1992)

Nünning, Ansgar, ed., *Metzler Lexikon Literatur- und Kulturtheorie: Ansätze — Personen — Grundbegriffe*, 2nd, rev. and expanded edn (Stuttgart: Metzler, 2001)

Obendiek, Eduard, *Der lange Schatten des babylonischen Turmes: Das Fremde und der Fremde in der Literatur* (Göttingen: Vandenhoeck & Ruprecht, 2000)

Okara, Gabriel, *The Voice* (London: Heinemann, 1970 [1964])

Olearius, Adam, *Moskowitische und persische Reise: Die Holsteinische Gesandtschaft beim Schah 1633–39* (Schleswig 1647), ed. Detlef Haberland, Alte abenteuerliche Reiseberichte (Stuttgart: Edition Erdmann in Thienemann, 1986)

Ortiz, Fernando, *Cuban Counterpoint: Tobacco and Sugar*, trans. Harriet de Onís, intro. Bronislaw Malinowski (New York: Alfred A. Knopf, 1947)

Oxford English Dictionary Online, www.oed.com

Özdamar, Emine Sevgi, *MutterZunge: Erzählungen*, 2nd edn (Cologne: Kiepenheuer & Witsch, 2002 [1990])
—, *Mother Tongue*, trans. Craig Thomas, Passport Books, 3 (Toronto: Coach House Press, 1994)
—, *Das Leben ist eine Karawanserei hat zwei Türen aus einer kam ich rein aus der anderen ging ich raus: Roman*, 5th edn (Cologne: Kiepenheuer & Witsch, 2003 [1992])
—, *Life Is a Caravanserai Has Two Doors I Came In One I Went Out the Other*, trans. Luise von Flotow (London: Middlesex University Press, 2000)
—, *Die Brücke vom Goldenen Horn: Roman* (Cologne: Kiepenheuer & Witsch, 2002 [1998])
—, *The Bridge of the Golden Horn*, trans. Martin Chalmers (London: Serpent's Tail, 2007)
—, 'Fahrrad auf dem Eis', in *Der Hof im Spiegel* (Cologne: Kiepenheuer & Witsch, 2001), 77–112
—, 'Die neuen Friedhöfe in Deutschland', in *Der Hof im Spiegel* (Cologne: Kiepenheuer & Witsch, 2001), 117–24
—, *Seltsame Sterne starren zur Erde: Wedding — Pankow 1976/77* (Cologne: Kiepenheuer & Witsch, 2004 [2003])
—, *Sonne auf halbem Weg: Die Istanbul-Berlin-Trilogie* (Cologne: Kiepenheuer & Witsch, 2006)
Özdoğan, Selim, *Die Tochter des Schmieds: Roman* (Berlin: Aufbau, 2005)
Pau Rubiés, Joan, 'Travel Writing and Ethnography', in *The Cambridge Companion to Travel Writing*, ed. Peter Hulme and Tim Youngs (Cambridge: Cambridge University Press, 2002), 242–60
Pfaff, Carol W., '"Kanaken in Alemannistan": Feridun Zaimoglu's Representation of Migrant Language', in *Sprachgrenzen überspringen: Sprachliche Hybridität und polykulturelles Selbstverständnis*, ed. Volker Hinnenkamp and Katharina Meng, Studien zur deutschen Sprache: Forschungen des Instituts für deutsche Sprache, 32 (Tübingen: Narr, 2005), 195–225
Pollock, Sheldon *et al.*, 'Cosmopolitanisms', in *Cosmopolitanism*, ed. Carol A. Breckenridge *et al.* (Durham, NC: Duke University Press, 2002), 1–14
Porter, Dennis, *Haunted Journeys: Desire and Transgression in European Travel Writing* (Princeton: Princeton University Press, 1991)
—, '*Orientalism* and its Problems', in *Colonial Discourse and Post-colonial Theory: A Reader*, ed. Patrick Williams and Laura Chrisman (New York: Columbia University Press, 1993), 150–61 (originally publ. in *The Politics of Theory*, ed. Francis Barker *et al.*, Proceedings

of the Essex Sociology of Literature Conference, University of Colchester, 1983, 179–93)

Powell, Rachel, and John Clarke, 'A Note on Marginality', in *Resistance Through Rituals: Youth Subcultures in Post-War Britain*, ed. Stuart Hall and Tony Jefferson (London: Routledge, 1993 [2000 printing]; first publ. as *Working Papers in Cultural Studies*, 7/8 (Birmingham: Centre for Contemporary Cultural Studies, University of Birmingham, 1975)), 223–29

Pratt, Mary Louise, *Imperial Eyes: Travel Writing and Transculturation* (London: Routledge, 1994)

Preece, Julian, 'Faking the Hadj? Richard Burton Slips between Lines in Ilija Trojanow's *Der Weltensammler*', in *Religion and Identity in Germany Today: Doubters, Believers, Seekers in Literature and Film*, ed. Julian Preece *et al.*, Leeds-Swansea Colloquia on Contemporary German Literature, 2 (Oxford and Berne: Peter Lang, 2010), 211–25

Quinet, Edgar, *Le Génie des religions* (Paris: [?], 1842)

Raban, Jonathan, *Arabia Through the Looking Glass* (London: Fontana/Collins, 1980 [1979])

Ranasinha, Ruvani, *Hanif Kureishi* (Tavistock: Northcote House in association with the British Council, 2002)

Reder, Michael, 'Wie weit können Glaube und Vernunft unterschieden werden?', in *Ein Bewußtsein von dem, was fehlt: Eine Diskussion mit Jürgen Habermas*, ed. Michael Reder and Josef Schmidt (Frankfurt a.M.: Suhrkamp, 2008), 51–68

Reder, Michael, and Joseph Schmidt SJ, 'Habermas und die Religion', in *Ein Bewußtsein von dem, was fehlt: Eine Diskussion mit Jürgen Habermas*, ed. Michael Reder and Josef Schmidt (Frankfurt a.M.: Suhrkamp, 2008), 9–25

Robbins, Bruce, *Secular Vocations: Intellectuals, Protestantism, Culture* (New York: Verso, 1993)

Robinson, Douglas, *Translation and Empire: Postcolonial Theories Explained*, Translation Theories Explained, 4 (Manchester: St Jerome, 1997)

Roy, Kate, 'German-Islamic Literary Interperceptions in Works by Emily Ruete and Emine Sevgi Özdamar', in *Encounters with Islam in German Literature and Culture*, ed. James Hodkinson and Jeff Morrison (Rochester, NY: Camden House, 2009), 166–80

Rushdie, Salman, 'Imaginary Homelands' (1982), in *Imaginary Homelands: Essays and Criticism 1981–91* (London: Granta in association with Penguin, 1991 [1992 printing]), 9–21

—, *The Satanic Verses* (London: Vintage, 1998 [1988])

Rutherford, Jonathan, 'The Third Space: Interview with Homi Bhabha', in *Identity: Community, Culture, Difference*, ed. Jonathan Rutherford (London: Lawrence & Wishart, 1990), 207–21

Ruthven, Malise, *Islam: A Very Short Introduction* (Oxford: Oxford University Press, 2000 [1997])

Saadi, Suhayl, *The Burning Mirror* (Edinburgh: Polygon, 2000 [2003 printing])

—, *Psychoraag* (Edinburgh: CHROMA, 2005 [2004])

—, 'Being Scottish', http://sarmed.netfirms.com/suhayl/NEW/articles_essays/being_scottish/index.htm [accessed 28 June 2010] (5 para.)

—, 'Psychoraag: An Interview', with Nick Mitchell, www.spikemagazine.com?0406-suhayl-saadi-psychoraag-interview.php [accessed 28 June 2010] (43 para.)

—, 'A Taste of Gangsta Sikh: *Londonstani*, by Gautam Malkani', *Independent*, 21 April 2006, 22, www.independent.co.uk/arts-entertainment/books/reviews/londonstani-by-gautam-malkani-474920.html [accessed 28 June 2010] (12 para.)

Said, Edward W., *Orientalism: Western Conceptions of the Orient*, repr. with a new Afterword (London: Penguin, 1995 [1978])

—, *Covering Islam: How the Media and the Experts Determine How We See the Rest of the World*, fully rev. edn with a new Introduction (London: Vintage, 1997 [1981])

—, 'Orientalism Reconsidered', *Cultural Critique*, 1 (Autumn 1985), 89–107

—, 'Third World Intellectuals and Metropolitan Culture', *Raritan*, 9.3 (1990), 27–50

—, 'An Intellectual Catastrophe', *Al-Ahram Weekly Online*, no. 389, 6–12 August 1998, http://weekly.ahram.org.eg/1998/389/cu1.htm [accessed 28 June 2010] (9 para.)

Sardar, Ziauddin, *Desperately Seeking Paradise: Journeys of a Sceptical Muslim* (London: Granta, 2004 [2005 printing])

Sardar, Ziauddin, and Merryl Wyn Davies, *Distorted Imagination: Lessons from the Rushdie Affair* (London: Grey Seal, 1990)

Sayyid, S., 'Contemporary Politics of Secularism', in *Secularism, Religion and Multicultural Citizenship*, ed. Geoffrey Brahm Levey and Tariq Modood (Cambridge: Cambridge University Press, 2009), 186–99

Schäffter, Ortfried, 'Modi des Fremderlebens', in *Das Fremde: Erfahrungsmöglichkeiten zwischen Faszination und Bedrohung*, ed. Ortfried Schäffter (Opladen: Westdeutscher Verlag, 1991), 11–28

Schami, Rafik, *Die dunkle Seite der Liebe: Roman* (Munich: Deutscher Taschenbuchverlag, 2006 [2004])

—, *The Dark Side of Love*, trans. Anthea Bell (London: Arabia, 2009)

Scherpe, Klaus R., and Alexander Honold, 'Auf dem Papier sind Indianer weiß, im Ritual die Weißen farbig: Fremdheitsforschung in der Literaturwissenschaft', in *Humboldt-Spektrum*, 4 (1995), 28–34

Schlegel, Friedrich, *Über die Sprache und Weisheit der Indier: Ein Beitrag zur Begründung der Altertumskunde von Friedrich Schlegel: Nebst metrischen Uebersetzungen indischer Gedichte* (Heidelberg: Mohr und Zimmer, 1808; repr. in *History of Linguistics: 18th and 19th Century German Linguistics*, 8 vols, with a new Introduction by Chris Hutton (London: Routledge and Thoemmes, 1995))

Schlösser, Hermann, 'Reiseliteratur als Literatur der Reisenden', in *Reiseformen des Geschriebenen: Selbsterfahrung und Weltdarstellung in Reisebüchern Wolfgang Koeppens, Rolf Dieter Brinkmanns und Hubert Fichtes*, Literatur und Leben: Neue Folge, 34 (Wien: Böhlau, 1987)

Schmidt, Gary, 'Feridun Zaimoglu's Performance of Gender and Authorship', in *German Literature in a New Century: Trends, Traditions, Transitions, Transformations*, ed. Katharina Gerstenberger and Patricia Herminghouse (New York: Berghahn, 2008), 196–213

Schmitz, Helmut, 'Einleitung: Von der nationalen zur internationalen Literatur', in *Von der nationalen zur internationalen Literatur: Transkulturelle deutschsprachige Literatur und Kultur im Zeitalter globaler Migration*, ed. Helmut Schmitz, Amsterdamer Beiträger zur neueren Germanistik, 69/2009 (Amsterdam: Rodopi, 2009), 7–15

Schwarzer, Alice, 'Ludin — die Machtprobe: Die Kopftuch-Entscheidung des Verfassungsgerichtes ist für uns alle von großer Bedeutung', Editorial, *Emma*, 31.4 (July/August 2003), 3

Şen, Faruk, 'Der Islam in Europa', in *Der Islam: Eine Einführung durch Experten*. Christoph Burgmer spricht mit Reinhard Schulze, Baber Johansen, Yann Richard, Gudrun Krämer, Annemarie Schimmel, Faruk Şen und Gernot Rotter (Frankfurt a.M.: Suhrkamp, 1998 [1996]), 82–96

Şenocak, Zafer, 'Spielräume für Mehrdeutigkeit I: Paradigmen für ein Gespräch mit den Muslimen', *Das Land hinter den Buchstaben: Deutschland und der Islam im Umbruch* (Munich: Babel Verlag Tulay, 2006), 45–47

—, 'Glaube und Krise', in *Das Land hinter den Buchstaben: Deutschland und der Islam im Umbruch* (Munich: Babel Verlag Tulay, 2006), 91–93

—, 'Authentische Türkinnen: Der Streit zwischen Feridun Zaimoglu und Emine Sevgi Özdamar zeigt, wie sehr die so genannte

Migrantenliteratur in der biographischen Falle sitzt. Sie spielt das Spiel der Typisierung mit', *Die Tageszeitung*, 10/11 June 2006, 13

Sethi, Anita, 'Keep the Faith: Award Winning Novelist Leila Aboulela Tells Anita Sethi Why Her Religious Identity Is More Important Than Her Nationality', *Observer*, 5 June 2005, www.guardian.co.uk/books/2005/jun/05/fiction.features2/print [accessed 28 June 2010] (14 para.)

Seyhan, Azade, 'From Minor Literature, Across Border Culture, to Hyphenated Criticism', in *Reading the Shape of the World: Toward an International Cultural Studies*, ed. Henry Schwarz and Richard Dienst, Politics and Culture, 4 (Oxford: Westview Press, 1996), 15–29

—, 'Lost in Translation: Re-Membering the Mother Tongue in Emine Sevgi Özdamar's *Das Leben ist eine Karawanserei*', *German Quarterly*, 69.4 (Fall 1996), 414–26

—, 'Scheherazade's Daughters: The Thousand and One Tales of Turkish-German Women Writers', in *Writing New Identities: Gender, Nation, and Immigration in Contemporary Europe*, ed. Gisela Brinker-Gabler and Sidonie Smith (Minneapolis: University of Minnesota Press, 1997), 230–48

—, 'Geographies of Memory: Protocols of Writing in the Borderlands', in *Multiculturalism in Transit: A German-American Exchange*, ed. Klaus J. Millich and Jeffrey M. Peck, International Political Currents, 3 (New York: Berghahn, 1998), 193–212

—, *Writing Outside the Nation*, Translation, Transnation (Princeton: Princeton University Press, 2001)

Shafi, Monika, 'Constructions of Islam: Select Voices from Germany and the Netherlands', in *Religion and Identity in Germany Today: Doubters, Believers, Seekers in Literature and Film*, ed. Julian Preece *et al.*, Leeds-Swansea Colloquia on Contemporary German Literature, 2 (Oxford and Berne: Peter Lang, 2010), 163–81

Shankland, David, *Islam and Society in Turkey* (Huntington: Eothen, 1999)

Skiba, Dirk, 'Ethnolektale und literalisierte Hybridität in Feridun Zaimoglu's Kanak Sprak', in *Migrationsliteratur: Schreibweisen einer interkulturellen Moderne*, ed. Klaus Schenk *et al.* (Tübingen: Francke, 2004), 183–304

Sommer, Roy, *Fictions of Migration: Ein Beitrag zur Theorie und Gattungsgeschichte des zeitgenössischen interkulturellen Romans in Großbritannien*, ELK (Studien zur Literatur- und Kulturwissenschaft) / ELCH (Studies in English and Cultural

History), 1 (Trier: Wissenschaftlicher Verlag Trier, 2001) (= doctoral thesis, Justus Liebig University, Gießen, 2000)

Spender, Dale, *Man Made Language*, 2nd edn (London: Pandora, 1990 [1980])

Spivak, Gayatri Chakravorty, 'The Rani of Simur: An Essay in Reading the Archives', in *History and Theory*, 24.3 (1985), 247–72 (repr. in *Europe and its Others*, I: *Proceedings of the Essex Conference on the Sociology of Literature 1984, University of Essex*, ed. Francis Barker *et al.* (Colchester: University of Essex, 1985), 128–51)

—, 'Can the Subaltern Speak?', in *Marxism and the Interpretation of Culture*, ed. Cary Nelson and Lawrence Grossberg (Basingstoke: Macmillan Education, 1988), 271–313

—, 'Theory in the Margin: Coetzee's Foe Reading Defoe's *Crusoe/ Roxana*, *English in Africa*, 17.2 (1990), 1–23

—, 'The Politics of Translation', in *Destabilizing Theory: Contemporary Feminist Debates*, ed. Michèle Barrett and Anne Phillips (Cambridge: Polity, 1992), 177–200

—, *Death of a Discipline*, The Wellek Library Lectures in Critical Theory (New York: Columbia University Press, 2003)

Sprung, Christoph S., 'Aspekte der Heterogenität des Islam in Indien', *Islam in Südasien*, Themenschwerpunkt des Südasien-Informationsnetz e.V.: *suedasion.info*, ed. Nadja-Christina Schneider *et al.* (2006), www.suedasien.info/analysen/1611 [accessed 28 June 2010] (17 para.)

Stein, Mark, *Black British Literature: Novels of Transformation* (Columbus: The Ohio State University Press, 2004)

Strasheim, Lorraine A., 'We're all Ethnics: "Hyphenated" Americans, "Professional" Ethnics, and Ethnics "By Attraction"', *The Modern Language Journal*, 59.5/6 (1975), 240–49

Tan, Dursun, and Hans-Peter Waldhoff, 'Turkish Everyday Culture in Germany and its Prospects', in *Turkish Culture in German Society Today*, ed. David Horrocks and Eva Kolinsky (Providence, RI: Berghahn, 1996), 137–56

Taylor, Charles, 'Foreword: What is Secularism?', in *Secularism, Religion and Multicultural Citizenship*, ed. Geoffrey Brahm Levey and Tariq Modood (Cambridge: Cambridge University Press, 2009), xi–xxii

Tibi, Basam, *Islam Between Culture and Politics*, 2nd edn (Basingstoke: Palgrave Macmillan in association with The Weatherhead Center for International Affairs, Harvard University, 2005 [2001])

Todorov, Tzvetan, *Die Eroberung Amerikas: Das Problem des Anderen* (Frankfurt a.M.: Suhrkamp, 1985; originally publ. as *Conquête de l'Amérique* (Paris: Éditions du Seuil, 1982))

Tohidi, Nayereh, 'The Issues at Hand', in *Women in Muslim Societies: Diversity Within Unity*, ed. Herbert Bodman and Nayereh Tohidi (Boulder, CO: Rienner, 1998), 277–94

Trojanow, Ilija, *Zu den heiligen Quellen des Islam: Als Pilger nach Mekka und Medina* (Munich: Malik, 2004)

—, *Mumbai to Mecca*, trans. Rebecca Morrison (London: Haus Publishing, 2007)

—, *Der Weltensammler* (Munich: Hanser, 2006)

—, (Trojanow, Iliya) *The Collector of Worlds*, trans. William Hobson (London: Faber and Faber, 2008)

—, *Nomade auf vier Kontinenten: Auf den Spuren von Sir Richard Francis Burton* (Frankfurt a.M.: Eichborn, 2007)

Tuschick, Jamal, 'Nachwort von Jamal Tuschick: Träger von Zukunftsinformationen', in *Morgen Land: Neueste deutsche Literatur*, ed. Jamal Tuschick (Frankfurt a.M.: Fischer Taschenbuch Verlag, 2000), 283–91

Uerlings, Herbert, *'Ich bin von niedriger Rasse': (Post-)Kolonialismus und Geschlechterdifferenz in deutscher Literatur* (Cologne: Böhlau, 2006)

Venn, Couze, *Occidentalism: Modernity and Subjectivity* (London: Sage, 2000)

Vertovec, Stephen, *Hindu Trinidad: Religion, Ethnicity and Socio-economic Change* (London: Macmillan Caribbean, 1992)

—, *The Hindu Diaspora: Comparative Patterns* (London: Routledge, 2000)

Waris Maqsood, Ruqaiyyah, *Islam*, new edn (London: Hodder Education, 2003 [1994])

Weiss, Hilde, ed., *Leben in zwei Welten: Zur sozialen Integration ausländischer Jugendlicher der zweiten Generation* (Wiesbaden: VS Verlag für Sozialwissenschaften, 2007)

Weiss, Timothy, *On the Margins: The Art of Exile in V. S. Naipaul* (Amherst: The University of Massachusetts Press, 1992)

Welsch, Wolfgang, 'Transculturality: The Puzzling Form of Cultures Today', in *Spaces of Culture: City — Nation — World*, ed. Mike Featherstone and Scott Lash (London: Sage, 1999), 194–213

—, 'Transkulturalität: Zwischen Globalisierung und Partikularisierung', *Jahrbuch DaF*, 26 (2000), 327–51

Wesche, Marjorie Bingham, 'Input and Interaction in Second Language Acquisition', in *Input and Interaction in Language*

Acquisition, ed. Clare Galloway and Brian J. Richards (Cambridge: Cambridge University Press, 1994), 219–49

Wierlacher, Alois, *Das Fremde und das Eigene: Prolegomena zu einer interkulturellen Germanistik*, Publikationen der Gesellschaft für Interkulturelle Germanistik, 1 (Munich: Iudicium, 1985)

Wierschke, Annette, *Schreiben als Selbstbehauptung: Kulturkonflikt und Identität in den Werken von Aysel Özakin, Alev Tekinay und Emine Sevgi Özdamar; mit Interviews* (Frankfurt a.M.: IKO, 1994) (= doctoral thesis, University of Minnesota, 1994)

—, 'Auf den Schnittstellen kultureller Grenzen tanzend: Aysel Özakin und Emine Sevgi Özdamar', in *Denn du tanzt auf einem Seil: Positionen deutschsprachiger MigrantInnenliteratur*, ed. Sabine Fischer and Morey McGowan, Stauffenburg discussion, 2 (Tübingen: Stauffenburg, 1997), 179–194

Williams, John Alden, ed., *The Word of Islam* (London: Thames and Hudson, 1994)

Wilpert, Gero von, *Sachwörterbuch der Literatur*, 7th, improved and expanded edn (Stuttgart: Kröner, 1989 [1995])

Wolf, Michaela, 'Culture as Translation — and Beyond: Ethnographic Models of Representation in Translation Studies', in *Crosscultural Transgressions: Research Models in Translation Studies II: Historical and Ideological Issues*, ed. Theo Hermans (Manchester: St Jerome, 2002), 180–92

Yeğenoğlu, Meyda, *Colonial Fantasies: Towards a Feminist Reading of Orientalism* (Cambridge: Cambridge University Press, 1998)

Yeşilada, Karin, '"Die geschundene Suleika": Das Eigenbild der Türkin in der deutschsprachigen Literatur türkischer Autorinnen', in *Interkulturelle Konfiguration: Zur deutschsprachigen Erzählliteratur von Autoren nichtdeutscher Herkunft*, ed. Mary Howard (Munich: Iudicium, 1997), 95–114

—, 'Dialogues with Islam in the Writing of (Turkish-)German Intellectuals: A Historical Turn?', in *Encounters with Islam in German Literature and Culture*, ed. James Hodkinson and Jeff Morrison (Rochester, NY: Camden House, 2009), 181–203

Yildiz, Yasemin, 'Critically "*Kanak*": A Reimagining of German Culture', in *Globalization and the Future of German*, ed. Andreas Gardt and Bernd Hüppauf (Berlin: Mouton de Gruyter, 2004), 319–40

—, 'Turkish Girls, Allah's Daughters, and the Contemporary German Subject: Itinerary of a Figure', *German Life and Letters*, 62.4 (2009), 465–81

Young, Robert, *White Mythologies: Writing History and the West* (London: Routledge, 1990)

Zaimoğlu, Feridun, *Kanak Sprak: 24 Mißtöne vom Rande der Gesellschaft*, 6th edn (Hamburg: Rotbuch, 2004 [1995])

—, 'sicarim süppkültürünüze, züppeler! Ich scheiße auf eure Subkultur, ihr Schmöcke!', in *Mainstream der Minderheiten: Pop in der Kontrollgesellschaft*, ed. Tom Holert and Mark Terkessidis (Berlin: Edition ID-Archiv, 1996), 86–95

—, *Abschaum: Die wahre Geschichte von Ertan Ongun*, 5th edn (Hamburg: Rotbuch, 2003 [1997])

—, 'KümmelContra', in *Kursbuch Jugendkultur: Stile, Szenen und Identitäten vor der Jahrtausendwende*, ed. SPoKK (Arbeitsgruppe für Symbolische Politik, Kultur und Kommunikation) (Mannheim: Bollmann, 1997), 174–81

—, *Koppstoff: Kanaka Sprak vom Rande der Gesellschaft*, 3rd edn (Hamburg: Rotbuch, 2000 [1998])

—, 'Gastarbeiterliteratur: Ali macht Männchen', in *Globalkolorit: Multikulturalismus und Populärkultur*, ed. Ruth Mayer and Mark Terkessidis (St Ändra-Wördern: Hannibal, 1998), 85–97

—, 'Eure Coolness ist Gigaout: Eine Gespräch mit Jutta Winkelmann', in *Kanaksta: Von deutschen und anderen Ausländern*, ed. Joachim Lottmann (Berlin: Quadriga, 1999), 23–32

—, *Liebesmale, scharlachrot: Roman* (Cologne: Kiepenheuer & Witsch, 2002 [2000])

—, 'Gottes Krieger', in *Zwölf Gramm Glück: Erzählungen*, 2nd edn (Cologne: Kiepenheuer & Witsch, 2006 [2004]), 122–56

—, *Leyla: Roman*, 2nd edn (Cologne: Kiepenheuer & Witsch, 2006)

—, 'Bitte Bodenhaftung!', *ZEIT-online*, 4/2006, podcast, www.zeit.de/online/2006/41/Buchmesse-Zaimoglu [accessed 28 June 2010]

—, '"Die Polemik vergiftet das soziale Klima": Gespräch mit dem Regisseur Neco Celik und dem Schriftsteller Feridun Zaimoglu über ihr Stück "Schwarze Jungfrauen"', *Islamische Zeitung*, 6 April 2006, www.islamische-zeitung.de/?id=7106 [accessed 28 June 2010] (25 para.)

—, 'Es gibt eine Ethno-Avantgarde' (interview with Vera Gaserow), *Frankfurter Rundschau*, 2 May 2007, www.fr-online.de/_inc/_globals/print.php?sid=3c2e2cb255acc9acf215774a0cal.html, URL no longer available (21 para.)

—, *Liebesbrand: Roman* (Cologne: Kiepenheuer & Witsch, 2008)

—, 'Gespräch zu *Schwarze Jungfrauen*' on NDR Kultur, 2 April 2008, www.ndrkultur.de/media/gespraech196.html, URL no longer available

—, reading of *Liebesbrand* and discussion at Swansea University, 26 June 2008, www.swan.ac.uk/german/Video/#Zaimoglu [accessed 28 June 2010]

—, *Hinterland: Roman* (Cologne: Kiepenheuer & Witsch, 2009)

Zaimoğlu, Feridun, *et al.*, '"Was deutsch ist, bestimmen wir": Dokumentation der Talkshow 'III nach neun' (N3) mit Feridun Zaimoglu, Heide Simonis, Wolf Biermann, Norbert Blüm und Harald Junke', *Blätter des Informationszentrums 3, Welt* (*iz3w*) (February-March 2000; first publ. as 'Fear of a Kanak Planet: Heide Simonis Meets Feridun Zaimoglu', *Karoshi*, 4 (1998)), 38–41

Zaimoğlu, Feridun, and Günter Senkel, *Schwarze Jungfrauen*, Stückabdruck, *Theater Heute*, 5 (2006), 46–55

Zentrum für Literaturforschung, Berlin, Research Focus: 'Figurationen des Märtyrers in nahöstlicher und europäischer Literatur', www.zfl.gwz-berlin.de/forschung/europaeische-kulturgeschichte/maertyrer/ [accessed 28 June 2010]

Index

www.ingramcontent.com/pod-product-compliance
Lightning Source LLC
LaVergne TN
LVHW012052300826
846742LV00017B/58
* 9 7 8 0 8 5 4 5 7 2 3 1 1 *